SOMATIC STATES

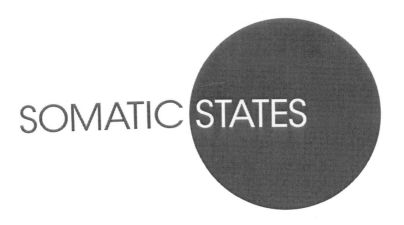

SOMATIC STATES

On Cartography, Geobodies, Bodily Integrity

Franck Billé

DUKE UNIVERSITY PRESS

Durham and London   2025

© 2025 DUKE UNIVERSITY PRESS
All rights reserved
Printed in the United States of America on acid-free paper ∞
Project Editor: Michael Trudeau
Designed by David Rainey
Typeset in Georgia by Westchester Publishing Services

Library of Congress Cataloging-in-Publication Data
Names: Billé, Franck, author.
Title: Somatic states : on cartography, geobodies, bodily
integrity / Franck Billé.
Description: Durham : Duke University Press, 2025. |
Includes bibliographical references and index.
Identifiers: LCCN 2024041565 (print)
LCCN 2024041566 (ebook)
ISBN 9781478031727 (paperback)
ISBN 9781478028499 (hardcover)
ISBN 9781478060703 (ebook)
Subjects: LCSH: Political geography. | Cartography—Political
aspects. | Geopolitics. | Nation-state—History. Classification:
LCC JC319 .B526 2025 (print) | LCC JC319 (ebook) |
DDC 320.1/2—DC23/ENG/20241216
LC record available at https://lccn.loc.gov/2024041565
LC ebook record available at https://lccn.loc.gov/2024041566

Cover art: Michael Joseph, *Freddie*, New Orleans, Louisiana,
2017. From the series "Lost and Found: A Portrait of American
Wanderlust." Courtesy of the artist.

For Valerio and the kids

Contents

Acknowledgments

The idea of phantom territories that haunts the book grew out of a casual remark dropped by a Russian colleague in 2012 at a workshop about the Russia-China-Mongolia border. Speaking of the territories Russia had lost in its recent history, Viktor Dyatlov used the term *phantom pains*. The vividness of the metaphor immediately struck me. I wrote it down. Over the next few days, then weeks, the analogy kept circling in my head. These early reflections eventually percolated into an article, published in *Environment and Planning D* in 2014, which mobilized the metaphor in the context of the Sino-Russian relationship. For planting the initial seed, I am ever grateful to Viktor.

Northeast Asia, specifically the Russia-China border, was the original ethnographic locus of the book as well as the site of a postdoctoral project at the University of Cambridge (2012–15)—a project that led to a joint monograph with my colleague Carrie Humphrey (*On the Edge*, 2021). While this region still looms large in *Somatic States*, feedback and comments received at conferences in Cambridge, Berkeley, Seoul, and Tokyo, and at panels at the AAA and AAG meetings, quickly convinced me that the argument warranted a more global and sustained treatment. I am thankful to audiences at these events for drawing my attention to similar deployments of corporealized narratives elsewhere in the world.

From what was initially envisioned as a side project, destined to be sandwiched between worthier writing endeavors, *Somatic States* eventually grew into the main event—a ten-year-long book project that accompanied me in a transatlantic move and saw me become the dad to two amazing kids and one wonderful dog. This book was also a companion in a bit of an academic identity crisis, from anthropology to geography back to anthropology by way of cultural studies, and the final acceptance that the book (and me) would have to sit somewhere between the three. Although several other writing projects ended up intercalating themselves in the last decade, *Somatic States* was the closest to my heart. The "phantom book," as friends and colleagues referred to it, was my baby, a labor of love, one I never tired of. Occasionally I would get sidetracked, but a text or email from a friend (Thank you Adam Levy and Evangeline McGlynn!)—sending me a geobody they had spotted in a book, on a car sticker, or as a tattoo—would fan my creative flames again. At other times, a kind, unexpected email would land in my inbox, assuaging self-doubts (Thank you Alexei Yurchak and Caren Kaplan!) and get me, unknowingly, back into writing mode.

I am delighted *Somatic States* found a home at Duke, a press I have long admired for its vision, politics, and beautifully designed books. Elizabeth Ault was a dream editor through the entire process, always responding immediately to any question I might have, and displaying endless patience as I navigated the pandemic-inflected challenges of parenthood and as weeks turned into months and months into years. I am grateful to the entire Duke production team, as well as my editor Andrew Ascherl.

During my time at Cambridge, where this book first began germinating, I was fortunate to receive encouragements and suggestions from many friends and colleagues. I am grateful to Henryk Alff, Doreen Bernáth, Ted Boyle, Sharyn Graham Davies, J. J. Fong, Sarah Green, Paula Haas, Shozo Hakozaki, Martin Hofmann, Carrie Humphrey, Agnieszka Joniak-Lüthi, Laurent Legrain, Christos Lynteris, Nayanika Mathur, Libby Peachey, Ivan Peshkov, Steve Pile, Ed Pulford, Natalia Ryzhova, Tatiana Safonova, István Sántha, Jasnea Sarma, Jonas Tinius, Milan Vrućinić, and Umut Yıldırım for sharing their thoughts and knowledge about other regions of the world. In the later part of the writing process, while at UC Berkeley, I received further intellectual fuel and emotional support from friends and colleagues Alexander Akin, David Ambaras, Arjun Appadurai, Laurence Broers, Rebecca Bryant, Shane Carter, Chris Cristóbal Chan, Jason Cons, Alexandra Dalferro, Maria José de Abreu, Klaus Dodds, Elizabeth Dunn, Ryan Gourley, Bruce Grant, Stéphane Gros, Reece Jones, Sanjyot Mehendale, Lisa Min, Aihwa Ong, Sumathi Ramaswamy, Angel Ryono, Steven Seegel, James Sidaway, Gerard Toal, Jason Weidemann, and Kären Wigen.

Somatic States is dedicated to my family—to my parents and sister, and to the three little ones, Milo, Luna, and Max, who replay, in human/nonhuman variation, age-old dynamics of sibling affection, competition, and rivalry. It is also, and primarily, dedicated to my husband, Valerio, without whom this book would never have seen the light of day. Book writing is a long and arduous task, as most authors note in their acknowledgments. Book writing is also a task accomplished through privilege, one that requires financial and temporal resources. *Somatic States* was completed only because I was lucky to have an understanding spouse who frequently took on more than his fair share, providing me with ample time to think and write.

Introduction

We don't have a country if we don't have borders.

—Donald J. Trump, 2016 political campaign ad

For most of human history, the border was a peripheral thing, a dusty land of criminality and relegation, a haven for tax evasion and non-conformity. A forgotten, far-flung place. Today, it is the center of the political world.

—Matthew Longo, *The Politics of Borders*

CARTOGRAPHIC ANXIETIES

On April 22, 2015, Indian viewers of Al Jazeera's English TV channel were suddenly confronted with a blank screen showing the message: "As instructed by the Ministry of Information and Broadcasting, this channel will not be available from 00.01 hours on 22nd April till 00.01 hours on 27th April 2015." The five-day suspension had been imposed on the channel as a penalty for displaying a wrong map of India in some of its broadcasts in 2013 and 2014. The Surveyor General of India, to whom the matter was referred, concluded that a portion of the Indian territory of Jammu and Kashmir had not been shown as a part of Indian territory and that the channel had also failed to include Lakshadweep and the Andaman Islands on some of its maps.[1]

This robust reaction from India concerning the mapping of its territory was in fact not the first.[2] In 2014 the Indian government had already filed a complaint against Google Maps for an alleged wrong depiction of India's international boundaries. A couple of years later, in what was claimed to amount to a criminal offense, Twitter was accused of disrespecting New Delhi's sovereignty after showing Indian-ruled Ladakh as part of China. Against a backdrop of social media sites showing Jammu and Kashmir and Arunachal Pradesh as part of Pakistan and China, respectively, a measure was envisaged by the Indian government to punish violators with a hefty fine as well as with imprisonment for a period of up to seven years.[3]

Nor is India the only state enforcing strict policing over the production of maps. In 2007, China passed a law forbidding unauthorized foreigners from mapping any part of the country.[4] In addition, all maps produced in China must receive approval from the national Administration of Surveying, Mapping, and Geoinformation before publication, and must include the so-called U-shaped line that encompasses all of its territorial claims in the South China Sea.[5] Many other states—such as Russia, discussed extensively in this book—have a similar relationship to maps and routinely place limits on access and reproduction. At most borders, photography is strictly prohibited.

These forms of cartographic insistence are at the core of *Somatic States*. They speak, on the one hand, to a modern vision of maps as true reflection of, and occasionally precedence over, political geography and, on the other, to an undue focus on edges and corners of the state. Cartographic anxieties are of course not the exclusive domain of India, China, or Russia. But that these massive entities, ranking among the largest in the world, would feel threatened by the loss of a mountain peak, a river island, or another seemingly minute fragment of territory speaks volumes about the place of territory with respect to political sovereignty. As George Perec described evocatively, "People have fought for tiny fragments of space, portions of hills, a few meters of seaside, rocky peaks, the corner of a street. For millions of men, death came from a slight difference of level between two points located sometimes less than a hundred meters apart."[6]

This state of affairs feels familiar, yet such concerns about edges and borders would have been meaningless until a couple of centuries ago. As I develop in more detail in chapter 1, before the modern understanding of territorial sovereignty became hegemonic worldwide, the medieval world was hierarchical and localized. Sovereign power was radial—organized around alliances, networks of patronage, and fealty ties—and frequently coexisted and overlapped with a number of religious and imperial entities. By contrast, the modern state is theorized as bounded and homogeneously operative, thus placing inordinate emphasis on borders and outlines. Its primary analogy is that of the container:

a fixed, ahistorical unit of sovereign space, containing a given society in dichotomous contrast to the outside.[7] As a result, the equation between territory and state power has become emotionally loaded and the logic of the inherent value of territorial control deeply internalized, thus making the control of a forbidding and minuscule piece of land seem worth the bloodshed, economic costs, and political repercussions to both domestic publics and elites.[8]

If the territorial equation of political sovereignty only emerged, piecemeal and partially, after the treaties of Westphalia were signed in 1648, the preoccupation with distant corners and outlying territorial fragments is even more recent. The Siachen Glacier, for instance, embroiling India and Pakistan in a bitter conflict during which over two thousand soldiers have died, had been left unmapped during the 1949 Karachi and 1972 Simla border agreements, on the assumption that there would be no dispute over such a cold and barren region. The Liancourt Rocks (better known by their Korean name of Dokdo or their Japanese name of Takeshima), a group of ninety islets and reefs lying between the Korean peninsula and the Japanese archipelago, are an important point of contention between the two countries. In South Korea, the salience of these islets is unprecedented, and there are dozens, if not hundreds, of South Korean organizations engaged in Dokdo-related activism.[9] Featured on countless types of material, the islets are one of the first historic sites a foreign visitor to South Korea will notice.[10] As Alexander Bukh writes, education about their history and environment has become an integral part of the mandatory school curriculum, and numerous public and private institutions have Dokdo-dedicated corners, maps, and pamphlets that explain Korea's rightful ownership over the islets.[11] In a recent survey in Japan, 93 percent of respondents said they knew about the territorial issue, 59 percent stated that they were interested in it, and 78 percent "knew" that Takeshima was "Japan's inherent territory."[12] By contrast, a 1966 poll indicated that only 9 percent were interested in the Northern Territories, and 55 percent had no knowledge regarding the historical justifications for Japan's claims.[13] So low, in fact, ranked the disputed islets in Japanese and Korean consciousness a few decades ago that in a 1960s bilateral normalization treaty, negotiators even considered blowing them up as a solution to the dispute.[14]

GEOGRAPHIC IMAGINARIES

Somatic States asks why borders and outlines have come to take on such symbolic significance, in ways that are often economically and politically detrimental, especially given the current context of an increasingly staggered and delocalized border management. A number of scholars have drawn attention to this disconnect between a proliferation of border walls, on the one hand, and a concurrent intensification of transnational processes and neoliberal forms of globalization, on the other. In *Walled States*, Wendy Brown suggests border walls have come to matter as symbols of control precisely in the face of an erosion of nation-state sovereignty.[15]

That border walls function essentially as symbols has been amply demonstrated. The strident calls for "big and beautiful" border walls have been central to populist narratives of taking back control in the United States and elsewhere, even if these are largely empty promises. In the United States the border wall is largely ineffective, given that the majority of illegal migrants enter the country legally and overstay their visas. If the construction of a border wall, costing millions of dollars, suggests a strong political will to stem the flow of immigration, the fact that there are no controls in place to monitor lapsed visas and virtually no financial deterrents for employers of illegal immigrants directly undermines political narratives outwardly tough on immigration. Further, most immigrants to the United States, including refugees, do not enter at the US-Mexico border and come from countries other than Central America, yet the southern border looms large as a political, economic, and cultural fault line. Donald Trump's "beautiful wall" resonates with voters because it is easy to visualize and very much in line with a geopolitical imagination that codes Mexico as a source of danger.[16]

Where Brown's argument is less convincing is in her claim that we are witnessing an erosion of nation-state sovereignty. Of course, the publication of her book precedes many events that have upended assumptions held about the state and the evolution of the international order, such as the Brexit vote, the further proliferation of border walls, or the election of a new crop of populist leaders preaching protectionism and national enclosure. These political developments speak to the enduring, overwhelming place of the state (and more precisely of the nation-state, unpacked below) in the political imaginary. The state, Thomas Blom Hansen and Finn Stepputat already asserted at the turn of the century, "institutionalized in the international state system after 1945," remains "the globally most powerful idea of political order in the twentieth century" and is "pivotal in our very imagination of what a society is."[17] Contrary to suggestions that global linkages have weakened its position, the state remains the dominant vector of political power in the world.[18] Indeed, as John Agnew has argued, the two logics of state territoriality and global finances are not necessarily in opposition.[19] Russia's war on Ukraine, waged through both traditional forms of warfare and new technologies such as fake news, cyberattacks, and electronic terraforming, demonstrates that the logics of spatial expansionism and territorial domination have not been displaced.[20] Assertions that we are moving toward an erosion of the state bespeak "an almost unbelievable naivety."[21] Far from being an "etiolated entity," the state retains control over "much of what exists, politically, economically, juridically, and territorially as well as biologically, environmentally, and . . . conceptually."[22]

Deeply embedded in institutions, the state is "universally taken for granted as the natural unit of analysis in geopolitics and political life."[23] It has co-opted our spatial imaginations, in ways that we accept uncritically.[24] As Martin Lewis and Kären Wigen have argued, our thinking about space is framed by what they term a *metageography* that organizes "studies of history, sociology, anthropology, economics, political science, or even natural history." Categories such as continents and states guide our "basic conceptions of the natural world" to the extent that we talk of African wildlife, for instance, "as if it constituted a distinct assemblage of animals" and of states, no matter how internally divided they might be, as distinct and comparable units of analysis.[25] This framing of political and cultural space dominates the thinking of diplomats, journalists, politicians, and military strategists, but also informs "the highest levels of academic discourse."[26] It structures research questions, observations, and results in academic disciplines, thereby reinforcing further the reification of the state as a clearly delineated entity.[27] This "methodological statism," embedded in cultural studies and transnational migration studies, renders largely invisible those phenomena that take place outside of the statist imaginary, such as conflicts between states and insurgent groups.[28]

The vast and growing field of border studies has sought to shed a light on local conceptions of space in state interstices and emphasize the realities of cross-border exchange in social, familial, and commercial exchanges. Anthropology in particular has been attentive to giving voice to migrants, to the excluded, and to the displaced. While recognizing the crucial ethical significance of this endeavor, it is important to bear in mind that the vast majority of the world population lives within the borders of the state in which they were born and that this shapes their worldviews and attachments.[29] On one of my field sites, in the Russian border town of Blagoveshchensk, though only a stone's throw from China's economic powerhouse, locals routinely describe themselves as living in a remote location, on the edge of the polity. Moscow, thousands of miles away, remains for them the ultimate reference point.[30] Even in the case of the comparatively porous US-Canada border, the presence of the border has a structural effect, and two distant Canadian provinces will trade more with each other than with US states bordering them.[31] Borders may be human-made and comparatively recent, but the spatial imaginary they project shapes nonetheless a sense of distance and proximity as well as a sense of self.

Intersecting with the work of scholars such as Timothy Mitchell, Rebecca Bryant, Yael Navaro, Sumathi Ramaswamy, and others, *Somatic States* is concerned with these state imaginaries. As I discuss in the book, the strident calls for taller and more secure border walls are symptomatic of a broader insistence on demarcations and territorial integrity. In the Russian Far East, for residents of closed towns and border exclusion zones, it can feel like being utterly cut off from the world insofar as visits from outsiders are restricted and regulated, making it impossible to open a business, for example. But being a resident in a restricted zone nonetheless confers special status from which to derive pride: membership in a special entity in an otherwise homogeneous national space and a proactive role to play in the protection of the sacredness of boundaries.[32] Similarly, on the US-Mexico border in South Texas, polls carried out prior to the construction of the border wall showed a majority of US residents were in favor of it, in spite of the infrastructural issues this would cause.[33] For these two communities as well as for many others discussed in the book, striving toward an isomorphic relation between the physical and the cartographic feels crucial.

State imaginaries are in this sense anything but abstract. As Timothy Mitchell has persuasively argued, the state may be a common ideological and cultural construct, but the institutions and practices that cohere around it will have nonetheless strong structural effects. In particular, the political and social practices of border management (such as barbed-wire fencing, passports, immigration laws, inspections, currency control, etc.) help manufacture the nation-state—the idea that a distinct human community, or nation, shares the same territory as the state—as "an almost transcendental entity," as a structure that contains and gives order and meaning to people's lives.[34] State practices also have an incremental effect. In spite of their initially arbitrary location—the outcome of historical circumstances—borders eventually come to acquire a material quality. Political borders are as a result some of the few human-made processes visible from space, with agricultural activity and animal herding practices accruing incrementally into stark distinctions on the landscape. China's deforested and densely populated regions thus contrast with Russia's and Kazakhstan's uninhabited and underused lands, and Guatemala's intense deforestation practices compared to Belize's show the two countries in completely different colors, while part of the Egyptian-Israeli desert appears as two different shades of yellow as a result of trampling by people and their cattle on the Egyptian side.[35]

I argue in part I of the book that the imaginary of the state as a discrete, bounded entity with a unique outline has emerged out of two dramatic developments. The first one, detailed in chapter 1, is the evolution of cartographic practices that led to the central positioning of the map as support of the European national project and as core spatial metaphor denoting organization of knowledge. The second sea change, analyzed in chapter 2 and retraced briefly in the next section below, occurred through the corporeal deployment of sovereignty, with a shift from the body of the sovereign to that of the citizen.

The activity of mapping has frequently been described as an enduring human instinct, but as Matthew Edney reminds us, maps as we understand them today only developed after around 1800. In fact, the words *cartography* and *cartographer* did not exist until then, demonstrating that cartography is not a universal and transcultural endeavor.[36] It is also important, he argues, to dissociate the terms *mapping* and *cartography*—the former denoting what people do, and the latter what people think they do—lest we confuse "personal, cognitive acts with social, semiotic acts."[37] As I retrace in chapter 1, the history of cartography emerged out of a particular context of nationalism, namely the need of European governments to know and control their territory, but it was also an indirect product of the Scientific Revolution with its emphasis on quantification and measurement. Thus it was out of a specific convergence and coproduction of social, historical, intellectual, and political developments that maps gained such prominence and became hegemonic. This convergence helps account for the fact that while the "mapping impulse" was primarily European and helped disseminate a "model of territorial statehood and state-centered political economy from Western Europe into the rest of the world," modern maps also arose independently elsewhere, notably in East Asia.[38]

Further, that modern cartographic practices emerged in Europe and propagated throughout the rest of the world largely through empire and colonization should not lead to the assumption that cartography and the West are two coextensive fields. While Westerners certainly saw their own cartographic practices as superior to the seemingly "non-geometrical maps of colonized peoples," marking the latter as "innately irrational and therefore properly subject to Western rule," I highlight in the course of the book the multiple ways in which Western practices continue to be informed by premodern views.[39] If medieval European maps included religious symbolism such as the presence of heaven and hell, or were organized as a representation of the body of Christ, the scientific maps produced in the Renaissance retained much nonscientific symbolism. As I explore in chapter 2, they also remained heavily suffused with body imagery, replacing the body of Christ with that of the sovereign, before gradually morphing again toward an equation of national territory and the body of the citizen.

Modern cartographic practices, both in Europe and elsewhere, led to new visuals of political geography. No longer polycentric and comparatively fluid, the state gradually solidified into its contemporary bounded form, its frontiers hardening into borders. These clearer demarcations were prompted by the need of rulers to gain a fuller knowledge of their territory and were greatly aided by surveying endeavors that facilitated the emergence of homogenization of territorial authority. The most comprehensive of these efforts, by far, was Great Britain's Ordnance Survey County Series, begun in the 1840s, which mapped the counties of Great Britain at both six-inch and twenty-five-inch scales with accompanying acreage and land use information.

Compounded by the eighteenth-century fascination with atlases, these surveys helped citizens visualize the country to which they belonged and familiarize them with a particular state outline. While it took comparatively longer for people living in borderlands to identify with a notional state, the visual force of the state's contour eventually took hold.[40] This logomap, in Benedict Anderson's felicitous phrasing, ultimately became a pure sign. Instantly recognizable, everywhere visible, and infinitely reproducible, the logomap penetrated deep into the popular imagination, forming a powerful emblem—including "for the anticolonial nationalisms being born."[41] Testament to the prominence of these visuals, the world's first jigsaw puzzle, designed by cartographer John Spilsbury in 1766, was a puzzle called Europe Divided into Its Kingdoms.

I argue in this book that the logomap has become the primary visual support for the idea of the nation-state, well ahead of the census and the museum, which Anderson saw as the other two primary components of a grammar of nationhood.[42] Given the increasing complexity of political and economic entanglements on a global scale, the logomap might strike us as indexical of a moribund worldview. Yet, if certainly anachronistic in its imaginary, I argue in this book that it is timely in its impact precisely because of its simplicity. In fact, the logomap remains ubiquitous, both for emerging states that need reiteration of the outline for international recognition and domestic instruction, and for old states whose contours have grown icon-like.[43] It functions in this sense, Madeleine Reeves writes, as a symbol analogous to the flag, the coat of arms, or the effigy of the president: "to be viewed and committed to memory rather than carried or used."[44]

Reeves contrasts the logomap with maps used for navigation, which, especially in the post-Soviet context in which she works, are "rare and may be regarded with suspicion."[45] This suspicion extends well beyond the former Soviet Union and other authoritarian contexts. US law stipulates, for instance, that Google show certain parts of Israel/Palestine at low resolution, while many other areas of the world are deliberately censored.[46] While these restrictions are largely motivated by security reasons, the symbolism of the map is such that it is perceived to exist at a higher level of reality. The map does not simply denote a state's sovereignty, *it is that sovereignty*.[47] It is similar in this sense to the national flag whose desecration might be subject to criminal charges, fines, and/or imprisonment.[48] A map, and particularly a logomap, also holds the power to summon alternative sovereignties. Just as brandishing the flag of an unrecognized entity, a breakaway province, or a colonized country can be perceived as an offense against the integrity of a state, the use of an alternative logomap might be viewed as political and territorial separatism.[49] As the national map stands in for the sacred nation, Timothy Brook writes, "more real in some ways than the nation itself, a regime anxious about its legitimacy cannot afford to let it out of its sight."[50]

The symbolism previously contained in the body of the sovereign has now been displaced and sublimated into the body of the nation through its graphic representation. If earlier the body of the monarch was treated as a fetish, with a physical attack constituting the highest possible treason, the loss of territory, through marriage of descendants for instance, was not perceived as a threat to sovereign power. Today, by contrast, the shift of a boundary or the loss of an inch of territory places a state's entire legitimacy at risk.[51] The logomap thus represents nothing less than a state's physical integrity, reverberating the earlier symbolism contained in the body of the sovereign. More than just a logo, then, it operates as a fetish. The statement of the US clothing company Gap, responding to the outcry that followed the design of a map of China on one of their T-shirts that left out Taiwan, makes this manifest. In its apology, the company stated that the product had been "recalled from the Chinese market and *completely destroyed*."[52] Its removal was not sufficient—its mere physical existence was deemed a threat that required its obliteration. Upending philosopher Alfred Korzybski's famous statement that "the map is not the territory," I argue in chapter 1 that the map has in fact become the territory itself.[53]

CORPOREAL GEOGRAPHIES

If the contemporary focus on edges and remote corners has become hegemonic (I return to the question of hegemony and to its limitations in the next section), another ubiquitous component of cartographic anxieties is its strong corporealization. From military attacks conceptualized as rape, to territorial loss described as mutilation and dismemberment, and to narratives mobilizing corporeal terms such as strangulation, illness, death, and various others, chapter 2 analyzes the metaphoric constellations that tie the state and the body together.[54] Building on the foregoing discussion about the transformation of political space from a centrifugal, hierarchical, and labile spatial formation to one that is territorially bounded and homogeneously distributed, chapter 2 traces the shift of an imaginary of the nation-state initially equated with the body of the sovereign to a state outline and body of the citizen having become metaphorically coextensive. If anthropomorphic and zoomorphic maps, popular in the nineteenth century, emerged at a time when it was crucial to stage the nation-state as a natural and organic entity, I argue that modern representations have become more sophisticated, yet organic metaphors continue to undergird the concept of nation-state. In parallel with sedimented corporeal analogies such as "head of state" or "organs of the state," new somatic metaphors continually emerge in lexical coinages, in line with new understandings and conceptualizations of the body, such as "national DNA," for instance, which has gained much currency in the last two decades—with significant repercussions for understandings of nativeness and belonging.[55] Mark Neocleous also provides a slew of examples of headlines published in the space of a few months in 2018 and 2019 where the concept of "nervous breakdown" was applied to Brexit Britain, Spain, China, Russia, Australia, and Ireland, among others.[56] This suggests that, while organic narratives might strike us as quaint if not dangerous in their association with racism, the body continues to act as a potent source of analogies to think of the state, notably to discuss territorial loss and unshapely or fragmented territory. In the second part of *Somatic States*, I explore in particular the concepts of phantom pains, territorial prosthetics, and the idea of the monstrous body as points at which imaginaries of the state and imaginaries of the body fruitfully intersect. Exploring these conceptual overlaps helps lay bare the myriad assumptions we continue to hold about both the state and the body, and opens up potential spaces for reconceptualization.

Leveraging ethnographic cases from both within and beyond the Euro-American region, I show that the mobilization of somatic analogies, in places as diverse as Thailand, India, or Mongolia, has turned the potent melding of corporeality and nationhood into a truly global narrative. Many of these similarities in the corporealization of political space find their origins in the history of European colonization, which provided a political grammar of sovereignty. To be recognized as a sovereign state, it was essential for post-colonial and non-Western states to be perceived as commensurably modern. This required adopting and projecting an organic view of the state bounded by unambiguous borders and administered up to its territorial limits—a trajectory traced very nicely by Thongchai Winichakul in the context of Thailand.[57] Unavoidably, hegemonic nationalist discourse expressed in corporeal metaphors has overridden, and alloyed with, a rich tapestry of indigenous conceptualizations of place and sovereignty. Corporeal deployments thus all have different lexical lineages and cultural reverberations. Accounts from Tibet, India, and China show, for instance, a frequent overlay of deities and other celestial bodies onto the land through a host of bodily metaphors, allegories, and similes that are unique to each place. The example of the nation shaped as a mother goddess that Sumathi Ramaswamy discusses in her work is thus specific to India yet taps into a body/territory analogy that makes it immediately recognizable to individuals from other cultural contexts.[58]

I contend in chapter 2 that the ease and rapidity with which this global shift occurred suggests that an interpretation narrowly focused on colonialism or formal education is inadequate and that there is something else at play. George Lakoff and other cognitive linguists have argued that metaphors are largely preconceptual and precultural, and that they are not found in random assemblages but come prepackaged in larger metaphoric constellations founded on experiential gestalts. Metaphors thus rely on family resemblances, and on a semantic grid that is both systematic and coherent.[59] It is of course critical to bear in mind that metaphors are contextual pieces of discourse and therefore not always decoded in the same way. Metaphors come embedded in particular historical and cultural narratives, are uttered by individuals with specific positions of power and authority, and their evocative power thus ultimately depends on geopolitical, social, and economic contexts.

Nonetheless, without losing sight of the danger of overextending the value of metaphors, which can certainly flatten and obfuscate differences, I make the case that these globalized metaphoric narratives share sufficient overlaps to be analyzed as a single phenomenon. An important reason for doing so is because metaphors are much more than ornamental rhetorical devices and serve an indispensable communicative function.[60] Individuals make sense of the world in figurative terms such as metaphors and metonymies because these underlie the way we think, reason, and imagine, and are also the "main mechanism through which we comprehend abstract concepts and perform abstract reasoning."[61]

Importantly, metaphors are not simply descriptive or interpretive but also generative devices in that they shape societal understandings and have political effects. The choice of one metaphor over another can have dramatic impacts and repercussions. Metaphors can also obscure and sanitize, as in the context of battle and occupation analogized as urgent medical interventions.[62] Once established and sedimented, metaphors become invisible and thereby gain additional potency. These metaphors become "sticky," and it then becomes extremely difficult to think of those concepts otherwise.[63] *Somatic States* argues that the metaphor of the state as an organic and bounded entity constitutes such a case.

Laura Kurgan writes that maps are like "extensions" of ourselves, as omnipresent as utilities such as electricity, water, gas, telephone, or television. What she has in mind is that maps have become infrastructural, like other forms of media.[64] But her statement also gestures toward a corporeal entanglement of people and maps. As I unpack in chapter 2 and then flesh out through the rest of the book, the numerous metaphors and discursive parallels used to speak of the state are likely to have emerged out of a corporeal experience. Cognitive linguists and anthropologists have persuasively argued that the concepts of top, bottom, left, right, inside, and outside are first learned in terms of the body and then extended to the wider environment.[65] Measurement terms in the English language take the body as primary model—again, an ostensibly universal trait—using hands and feet, or the yard (the length from the nose to the fingers at the end of an outstretched arm) to apprehend the environment. The world of tools, Susan Stewart remarked, is similarly "a world of handles, arms, blades, and legs."[66]

The synecdochic relationship between the margins of the human body and the boundaries of the social that Mary Douglas famously theorized has led to a situation whereby body and state are imagined to be commensurable if not wholly isomorphic.[67] At the core of this isomorphism is the organic coding of the logomap as geobody—a concept Winichakul coined in his analysis of Thailand's transformation into a modern nation-state and which rapidly established itself as a valuable paradigm to trace the affective presence of the state in a host of contexts outside of its original deployment.[68] Conceptualized as an organic entity, the state-as-geobody taps into the cognitive undercarriage that embeds individuals in their environment, thereby facilitating a view of the logomap as a natural extension of the individual's body.

As various scholars have noted, there is of course nothing intrinsically organic or corporeal about the logomap, whose existence is recent and the notion of which would have been meaningless before the emergence of the modern cartographic imagination.[69] In fact, eighteenth- and nineteenth-century political imagery employed human and animal images to emphasize the naturalness of the cartographic state, suggesting that the linkage needed to be made explicitly.[70] As I detail in chapter 2, such visual practices were commonly used for a host of nascent states in Europe as well as in India, Turkey, the United States, and elsewhere, and they continue to be employed in postsocialist states like Azerbaijan, Armenia, and the former Yugoslavia.[71]

These visuals have proven crucial to foster and nurture state-bound attachments. Intertwined in organic metaphors and symbols such as national fauna and flora, the arbitrary and historically contingent boundaries of the state have become naturalized, hinting at a teleological destiny. In fusing together the territorial state and the people—indeed confusing one for the other, with *nation* and *state* often used interchangeably—organic metaphors have also helped birth the myth of the nation-state.[72] The notion that the two are coextensive, although this is rarely if ever the case, has proven very potent in bolstering the spatialization of the modern state as container. In addition, the figure of the logomap made possible an "affective identification with a bounded, defined political community."[73] As Benedict Anderson and others have emphasized, nationalism may be operationalized around an imagined community, but this does not make it an abstract concept. On the contrary, it is experienced as vividly present, a viscerally felt reality.[74]

While nationalism's very potency has been useful to elites and purposely promoted by them, there are dangers inherent to viewing it simply as a narrative foisted upon a hapless populace as a tool of control and domination. Alexander Bukh points out that appeals to certain ideals and norms by those he terms "national identity entrepreneurs" may simply be rhetorical resources concealing other mundane interests, and this rings true for many in the new crop of populist leaders who have emerged globally in the last decade or so.[75] Nevertheless, the top-down approach this suggests is partial and thus not particularly helpful. Scholars of nationalism have shown that the national state in which we are born leaves a strong imprint on all its citizens, the majority of whom "will retain a quiet loyalty" to their respective nation.[76] This includes, as noted above, individuals framing political and academic discourse, such as military strategists, diplomats, and academics.[77] Placing them outside of, and largely immune to, nationalist discourse is thus quite misleading.

Somatic States argues that a potentially manipulative behavior in fact takes nothing away from the very visceral way in which the message is received. Examples abound of popular sentiments, once roused, exceeding government policies in terms of territorial ambition and revanchism.[78] The case of Russia's current war on Ukraine is in this sense quite telling. Vladimir Putin's goals may have been geopolitical in nature, prompted by access to the Black Sea, natural resources, territorial expansion, and a longing to emerge from the humiliation of post-Soviet collapse, but the affect-laden official narrative—reconstituting the Russian nation, correcting border errors, and rescuing fellow Russians—has clearly reverberated very powerfully for his constituents. The war on Ukraine was "emotionally comprehensible" in ways that an attack on another lost Soviet territory, like the much larger Kazakhstan, would not have been. Ukraine's history is deeply enmeshed with Russia's, the two nations, along with Belarus, claiming the Kyivan Rus' Kingdom (882–1240) as their cultural ancestor. In consequence, despite gaining its independence thirty years ago, Ukraine has never felt quite foreign to most Russians. More crucially, Ukraine is also part of many Russians' personal geographies—the birthplace of family members and, in the case of Crimea in particular, a "beloved vacation spot that held happy memories" for generations of Russians.[79]

Ukraine evokes what I call territorial phantom pains—an enduring affective resonance for a loss that remains incompletely mourned. Lost territories are no longer included within the national body, and this new spatial configuration is made unequivocal through visual reiterations of a new logomap. However, as part of a previous national incarnation, they remain subject to sudden reactivation, as was indeed seen with Ukraine, taking much of the world by surprise. The ease with which Vladimir Putin was able to awaken this dormant affect is here again testament to the potency of a corporealized view of national territory. The reintegration of Ukraine into Russia's mutilated geobody, without which Russia was merely a stump (*obrubok*) of its former Soviet self, was clearly perceived to be worth the risks of international criticisms, economic sanctions, and potential military retaliation. These events may also presage flare-ups elsewhere in the region as phantoms reactivate, including in contexts where governments are attempting to rein in popular imaginaries around territorial loss.[80] In the specific case of Ukraine, it seems likely that the military decisions of Putin himself were to a large extent the outcome of affective calculations, notably his strong belief that Russia had been wronged and that the collapse of the Soviet Union had been nothing less than a historical catastrophe. This demonstrates once again the capacity of imaginaries to shape the political world in ways that span the entire political spectrum, encompassing both political actors and their putative audiences.

Anthropologists Mateusz Laszczkowski and Madeleine Reeves have argued that studies of the state need to remain attentive to visceral, prelinguistic, unsettled moments of intensity. *Unsettled* does not mean unmoored or free-floating. Indeed, they clarify that this attention to affect "does not necessarily entail a displacement of considerations of history or of power and inequality."[81] Affect ultimately filters through a historical, social, and cultural context. Thus, Emma Hutchison notes, if it constitutes a "visceral force that influences political thinking in a diffuse yet analytically inaccessible way," affect traces intensities that defy or escape deliberate reflection.[82] As such, its contours are often difficult to anticipate or predict. The loss of one region may lead to a huge public outcry, while the loss of another may have little to no impact.[83]

HEGEMONY AND MYTHS

Somatic States is a global study of corporealized affective attachment to the state, particularly to its logomap. In presenting a ubiquitous and immediately recognizable narrative, the book might appear to tread familiar ground un-necessarily. However, in giving voice to a feeling that is "often articulated but rarely diagnosed," *Somatic States* seeks to defamiliarize a "commonsense understanding" of the state as well as to probe the origins and aptness of this "geopolitical analogy and its applications."[84] In the course of its narra-tive arc, the book questions the sticky metaphors that inform the body-state isomorphic relation, teases out the gender and racial assumptions smuggled in representations common to political geography, deconstructs the cultural notion of the body as a discrete unit, and finally offers suggestions for alter-native forms of belonging.

Telling a story on a global scale also poses issues of cultural translatability. In particular, arguing that a given conceptualization of the state transcends cultural boundaries to become hegemonic can contribute to muting hetero-geneity and can flatten multivocality. Cross-cultural comparisons are always a perilous exercise, warns anthropologist Léopold Lambert in the preface of his own study of a globalized French colonial system. Cross-cultural analyses silence specificities linked to contexts, peoples, histories, and struggles, and can percolate into simplistic conclusions.[85] Maps, and especially logomaps, also obfuscate forms of social organization that do not align with nonna-tional categories such as religious affiliations and racial, ethnic, and linguistic categories.

In fact, alternative forms of social, cultural, racial, and political organization continue to coexist with the boundedness of the modern state. Religious communities such as Islam, Buddhism, or Judaism exist in ways that are both tied to particular geographies and exist across diasporic space.[86] Buryat Buddhism, Anya Bernstein writes, complicates understandings of sovereignty, for instance, in sitting astride religious and political realms, with links to Mongolian and Tibetan Buddhism beyond the borders of the modern Russian state yet also able to proclaim the Russian president an emanation of a Buddhist goddess.[87]

Analyses of sovereignty by North American indigenous scholars similarly add an important layer to the story woven in this book. In *Mohawk Interruptus*, Audra Simpson draws attention to many forms of resistance deployed against the settler states of Canada and the United States, ranging from refusals of social assistance and medical coverage to rejections of national passports.[88] While her analysis does not necessarily contradict the core argument of *Somatic States* in that the Kahnawà:ke Mohawk modes of resistance she describes aim to carve spaces of sovereignty within the existing international state system (Haudenosaunee passports indeed requiring the discretionary recognition of formally established states), various attempts are certainly made by indigenous groups to reconceptualize sovereign space in radically different ways.[89] Rather than map space "as homogenous, bounded, and temporally linear," some Native women thus view space "not as bounded by geopolitics, but storied, continuous, and developing."[90] The collective contribution made by this literature is that, clearly, not everyone is equally seduced by the map.[91]

Perhaps even more problematic than these forceful inclusions are the violent exclusions exacted upon certain groups. Arguing for a radical reconceptualization of Black geography, eschewing the "dangerous fictions like citizenships, states, and maps, and all the restrictions they entail," William Anderson reminds us that Black people have always been "*residents in* but not *citizens of* the United States," ultimately stateless within the borders of empires, states, and nations.[92] This exclusion, unresolvable via "assimilation, inclusion, or civil or human rights," makes it ultimately impossible to establish alternative forms of territorial organization outside the established order, leading to the "destruction of Black communities that make even the slightest move toward becoming autonomous, semi-autonomous, or even self-sufficient."[93] African Americans (and other minority groups elsewhere) are thus largely confined to what Hortense Spillers aptly termed a vestibular position in reference to the slave "who is of the plantation household but not fully in it"—a situation Imani Perry encapsulates as "monstrous," in ways in fact analogous to my own deployment of the term in chapter 5.[94]

As I retrace in chapters 1 and 2, the contemporary model of territorial sovereignty was never a teleological given. Numerous other forms of spatial organization existed prior to the emergence and consolidation of the post-Westphalian model, such as empires, city-state systems, and clan societies. In an analysis of nomadic and imperial formations that have historically existed seemingly outside national boundaries, sociologist William Brenner argues that the international system tends to reinforce similarities among the system's constituents in both structure and behavior.[95] In order to survive and preserve their autonomy, former nomadic and imperial states have imitated successful practices and as a result have ended up becoming very similar to modern nation-states. For "entities that arrive late to the contest for power, in part due to previous conditions of domination," innovation can prove key to survival.[96] However, here again, innovation does not necessarily equate with a lack of engagement. In the case of Al Qaeda, what we see is a synthesis of religious zealotry and modern ideology and technology. While the pan-Islamist organization may be opposed to the international system, it is nonetheless very much part of it, having emerged from the defeat of the Arab world by Israel in 1967 and the trauma of "being initiated into an international system in which they were not full participants."[97]

Similarly, borderlands populations, with cultural and familial ties woven across the border, complicate the idealized view of the state as a discrete container. I argue however that such examples supplement rather than displace the imaginary of the bounded state, and that these communities exist across, rather than outside, the boundaries of modern states. Hybrid rather than radically Other, these hyphenated identities in fact reinforce the notion of boundedness insofar as hybridity presupposes the stable identities of discrete subjects.[98]

Here the argument made by Anna Tsing can be helpful in reconciling the seemingly divergent forces toward hegemony and local variation. As she convincingly argued, "universal" does not necessarily designate homogeneity. The typical focus anthropology places on local notions and exceptionality, while contributing to weaving a rich tapestry of human experience, also "disengages/uncouples them from the cultural flows of which they are part."[99] The challenge of cultural analysis, instead, is to work against "the assumption of the autonomous self-generation of culture" and to attend to cultural friction by addressing "both the spreading interconnections and the locatedness of culture."[100]

It seems incontestable in any event that radically different forms of spatial organization, such as nomadic empires, or James Scott's deployment of the concept of Zomia, are proving increasingly difficult to accommodate within a modern political imaginary narrowly articulated around a state system of bounded containers.[101] The vanishingly small number of exceptions to this global modern view speaks to the power exerted by European models—a model predicated on an evolution toward commensurability, or at least mutual intelligibility, "in their structures and in the rationalities governing their actions."[102]

Inherently, this commensurability is tied to a presumptive audience. As political theorist Jens Bartelson insightfully remarked, the benchmark of a state's success in projecting its claims of legitimate sovereignty ultimately depends on its claims of "being recognized as such by other similar entities."[103] By way of example, as a member of the European Union, Spain was proactive in adopting restrictive EU policing guidelines and in setting up border controls in order to help prove "not only to the rest of the EU but to itself" that it truly "belonged."[104]

The hegemonic force toward commensurability, and the need to adhere to particular forms of sovereignty, are felt especially keenly by de facto states. The work of Rebecca Bryant on the Turkish Republic of Northern Cyprus illustrates how de facto states, "subject to international condemnation and hemmed in by embargoes and isolations," are states "in practice." The TRNC, like other de facto states, possesses the necessary institutions of governance to hold elections, control their borders, issue identification documents, and provide health care and social security. In effect, a de facto state looks and acts like a state, requiring only recognition from other states to become de jure.[105] These "states" (the quotation marks indexing the gap between real and fake) resemble a drag performance—"a parodic displacement that calls attention to the made-up nature of *any* state."[106] Bryant's discussion of the state as drag recalls here Elizabeth Dunn's conceptualization of the refugee camp "always just on the cusp of becoming a real village like all the others," a place that is "almost nearly something, an asymptote, something that never really comes together or never really reaches the point it curves towards."[107]

The de facto state, the camp, the postcolonial, the enclave, the microstate, and a host of other entities approaching the Westphalian model show us something fundamental about the fictive nature of the state. Indeed, the closer one looks at the deployment of territorial sovereignty on the ground, the more exceptions appear to be the norm.[108] There does not seem to be, as

Bryant and Reeves have pointed out, any state that is "not touched by some form of sovereign exceptionality."[109] The gap between the idea of the state—confidently enmapped as a discrete, bounded, and homogenous entity—and the realities of the state—uneven, leaky, topological—has given rise to numerous coinages in the attempt to better theorize the contemporary nature of the state. Sovereignty has been described, in turn, as partial, overlapping, graduated, flexible, unbundled, aleatory, paternal, attenuated, spectral, variegated—to use some of the conceptual tools proposed by political anthropologists and international relations scholars.

In her analysis of social phenomena multiplying beyond the territory of the state (yet remaining spatially anchored to that state), Anne-Laure Amilhat Szary has suggested that these forms of extraterritoriality be interpreted not as aterritorial but as more-than-territorial.[110] While this approach is helpful in its incorporation of spaces beyond the terrestrial, this persistent framing through exceptionality implicitly reinscribes the Westphalian model as the norm.[111] And yet the trouble with sovereignty is not simply post-Westphalian, but pre-Westphalian, and Westphalian as well.[112] It is thus not simply that tumultuous times and distant realms create unmanageable complexity. As Laura Benton writes, political space everywhere generates irregularities.[113]

If Westphalian territorial sovereignty is a myth, an illusion, an organized hypocrisy, as a number of historians and theorists have convincingly argued, continued attempts to find fault with this system seem misdirected.[114] One of the points I make in this book is that the emerging forms of extraterritoriality we are witnessing are less a symptom of weakening or exceptionality than integral spaces of articulation enabling the very functioning of a system. Rather than exceptions, then, special economic zones, corridors, export processing zones, and offshore spaces function instead as instruments designed to work within the agreed system without having to challenge its core tenets.[115] As Jens Bartelson suggests, the principal ideological function of the concept of sovereignty may therefore not be "to legitimize particular claims to political authority, but rather to legitimize the international system within which those claims can be understood as meaningful."[116]

A longing for sovereign power—an "object of desire and collective aspiration"—thus "continues to haunt contemporary politics."[117] This particular point on the aspirational nature of territorial sovereignty is crucial. In dispelling the myth that political maps represent a reality that exists in the West, it challenges the entrenched assumption that the de facto state, the postcolonial, and the microstate imitate, but can only approximate, those political standards. My argument about the hegemonic imaginary of the state as discrete and bounded does not place therefore the postcolonial world as mere consumer of modernity, as Parha Chatterjee protested, but as cocreator—as indeed demonstrated by examples I provide in the book from outside the Global North.[118]

It also challenges, as mentioned earlier, the resistant notion that this imaginary of the nation-state primarily constitutes a tool of subjection wielded by elites and governments. I fully agree with Rebecca Bryant and Mete Hatay and others who insist that, contrary to a "strand of anthropological and sociological literature focused on resistance to the state," more attention should be given to the seductiveness of the state as an idea, and to the ways in which average individuals expect certain standards and structures from the state and voice criticisms when they are absent.[119] After all, if the state is first and foremost a performance—the very fact of "acting like a state [bringing] the state into existence"—this performance is one coconstituted by both states and their citizens.[120]

Finally, the emphasis on territorial sovereignty as aspiration draws attention to the state's lack of internal cohesiveness. As a collection of institutions, organizations, stakeholders, agencies, and other state, parastate, and nonstate actors—many of whom are in competition with one another—the state is inherently multiple and as such pulls in different directions.[121] It is in part on account of these gaps and misalignments that the logomap, further reinforced by a host of somatic metaphors and analogies, derives its force. A powerful reiterative visual representation, it projects an imaginary of totality and integrity, a pictorial confirmation of a state that is bound, discrete, and exists in a dichotomous relation of inside/outside to other states.

As such, the logomap is indexical of that state imaginary. Through its cartographic solidity and its simplicity, it gives coherence to the state's amorphous nature and labile anatomy, particularly at a moment of increasing complexity. It neatly conceals the messy realities and blurry edges as well as the true footprint of (post?)imperial states such as Great Britain and France, and of territorial hegemons like the United States, as I discuss in chapter 5. Importantly, it also obfuscates the misalignment between state and nation, reinforcing the "convergence of analogies between nature and nationalism" whereby society is imagined to be coterminous with the boundaries of the state.[122] This convergence, placing undue emphasis on the role of state borders, finds itself reinforced in a feedback loop through the very visuality of a logomap portraying nothing but borders. This intimate entanglement, retraced in chapters 1 and 2, is what the second part of *Somatic States* proposes to unravel.

SOMATIC STATES

The title of this book, *Somatic States*, plays on the two significations of *state*. Its primary meaning gestures toward an imaginary of the state as an organic entity—not in a Ratzelian, biological sense, but in one that coheres through a constellation of metaphors shaping current understandings of borders and territoriality. It speaks to the visceral attachment to the state, how territorial loss for instance is analogized as mutilation through hegemonic linguistic coding. But the title also plays with the other meaning of the term *state*—as an impermanent mode of being, a condition of inherent spatial lability, and lack of temporal fixity. *Somatic States* denotes the tension, in other words, between the apparent weightiness and solidity of the political state and its actual impermanence.[123]

Somatic States also points to a political imaginary that is eminently corporeal. The second part of the book takes as its jumping-off point the metaphor of phantom pains, routinely used by my interlocutors in Russia (and which resonates more broadly on some intuitive level, as the work of various border scholars suggests).[124] Of course, in its focus on the body/state enmeshment, *Somatic States* unavoidably offers a partial account of the contemporary political imaginary and as such does not make claims of exhaustiveness. There are many other ways of thinking of the state in ways that are not primarily corporeal.[125] I do argue nonetheless that the ubiquity and range of corporeal deployments in political narratives on a global scale make it an important and worthwhile tool of analysis. Taking somatic metaphors in earnest—not as casual offhand remarks but as the somatized by-product of political narratives framed through organic analogies—chapters 3 through 5 further excavate their historical, sociocultural, linguistic, and cognitive entanglements. In doing so, I commandeer a wide range of cultural texts, including literature on neurobiology, in order not only to explore the full range of metaphoric resonances between the body and the political state, but also to shed light on the cobuilding of both representational models.[126]

Indeed, the notion of the somatic state relies on the assumption of the body as unitary, integral, and autonomous. But as Celia Lury reminds us in the opening paragraph of *Prosthetic Culture*, building upon Marilyn Strathern's work in Melanesia, this ideal construct of the person is both locally and culturally specific.[127] Thus the paradox I unpack in this book is that the body metaphor gives weight (or body) to the abstract concept of the state, yet is itself a construct that gains weight through its various deployments. The notion of immunity, for instance, is originally based in a sociopolitical discourse, not a biological one. It is riddled, W. J. T. Mitchell argues, "with images drawn from the sociopolitical sphere—of invaders and defenders, hosts and parasites, natives and aliens, and of borders and identities that must be maintained." The body and the political, he writes, thus exist as a "bipolar image" whose effect is to "produce a situation in which there is *no literal meaning*, nothing but the resonances between two images, one biomedical, the other political."[128]

My exploration of the political ideals of integrity, contiguity, and homogeneity in chapters 3, 4, and 5 pulls at various threads in the fabric that weaves state and body together. By the time we reach the coda, this connective tissue has become frayed: state and body have lost the apparent solidity that helped sustain one another and are revealed for the myths that they are.

The conceptual trajectory of part II focuses specifically on misalignments of various kinds. These chapters speak to what lies beyond the bounds of the somatopolitical framework neatly laid out in part I—the lost, the unrepresentable, the unsaid, the repressed, the monstrous—in other words, the underside of a logomap projecting ideals of simplicity and visual clarity. In chapter 3, I focus on the question of territorial loss. I explore what happens when a breach opens between the geographical extent of the nation and the mental map held by its inhabitants. I argue that lost territories, no longer included within the national body, remain nonetheless part of a previous national incarnation and elicit an affective force resembling phantom pains. Through this lens I also unpack the geopolitical notions of buffer and backyard and introduce the idea of prosthetic territory—a phantasmatic extension of the national self where dreams and aspirations are mobilized, deployed, and reanimated. Intangible and unpredictable in their affective potential (unlike the spatially static imaginary of the palimpsest), these supplementary spectral layers hover invisibly and threateningly over the map.[129] The war waged by Russia on Ukraine provides here a vivid example of how a settled border hitherto free of disputes remains nonetheless suffused with affect and can see its territorial phantoms become reactivated through political expediency and erupt into violent territorial deflagration.

The fantasy of singularity, contiguousness, and organic integrity projected by the geobody has placed undue emphasis on the borders of the state, turning them into fetishized sites. As I develop in chapter 4, the denial of the nation-state's deeply fragmentary nature has led to cartographic anxieties nestled in boundaries, edges, and remote corners. The fetishization of the border thus indexes a political will seeking to guarantee sovereignty and legitimacy, but it also sustains the continued fantasy of the state as singular. Mobilizing the metaphor of skin, I argue that skin and border both occupy a key position with respect to the individual and the nation insofar as they project, as containers, an image of coherence and cohesiveness. Tightly enmeshed in political and popular somatic metaphors, skin/border indexes the unresolvable gap between, on the one hand, the topographic inscription of unambiguous boundary lines and, on the other, the concealed topological realities of networks and flows that maintain the illusion of political boundaries. What this hints at is that the nation's visual emphasis on containment and hermeticity is actually sustained by a phantasmatic, abjected double.

I turn in the final chapter to this uncanny doppelgänger. Chapter 5 opens with an examination of territorial entities that depart from idealized geographical norms such as colonial dominions, enclaves, archipelagoes, and other atomized and fractured national spaces where the skin of the nation has been stretched beyond breaking point. These monstrous geographies, sprawling, uncontainable, and irreconcilably extraneous to the logomap, speak to the central argument of the chapter, namely that the visual clarity of the logomap emerges through the suppression of similarities and entanglements. The visually unambiguous logomap is thus accompanied by the shadowy figure of the monster, threatening to disrupt the idealized portrayal of the nation-state as autonomous and independent. I specifically marshal in this chapter the figure of conjoined twins, who powerfully dispel the fantasy of bodily unicity and open up paths to bring back and integrate monstrous bodies hitherto relegated to the hinterland of political national discourse: queer, Black, female, and disabled bodies. The chapter builds here on corporeal aspects drawn earlier in chapter 2, specifically on the symbolic use of able-bodied, heterosexual, fertile female bodies as tropes for the wholesomeness of the nation, and its protection by patriotic males.[130]

If it is addressed explicitly in chapter 5, the figure of the monster lurks in fact throughout the book. A crucial point made in *Somatic States* is that the sea monsters and monstrous races who previously roamed around the edges of medieval maps have not disappeared. They tend today to be mapped onto real-world ethnic groups—suggesting a survival of pernicious stereotypes—as well as onto bodies that deviate from the usual vector of somatic analogies: bodies that are cisgender, heteronormative, and, in a first-world context, white.

My aim in giving the monster center stage is twofold. First, importantly, it is to ensure that a multiplicity of voices continues to shape cultural and geopolitical narratives, particularly those voices that have long been silenced.

Alexander Weheliye points out that European thinkers have generally been given carte blanche to transpose theories and concepts to a variety of spatiotemporal contexts because they do not speak from an explicitly racialized viewpoint. By contrast, "nonwhite scholars who have written about racial slavery, colonialism, indigenous genocide" frequently find themselves "relegated to ethnographic locality within mainstream discourses." One often finds the presumption that the Western theoretical apparatus precedes, and is "uncontaminated by and prior to reductive or essentialist political identities."[131] Thinking through monsters here helps us develop a recognition of Otherness, thereby enabling an ethical understanding of difference.[132] But it is also to suggest alternative ways of envisaging political geography. *Somatic States* suggests that the use of corporeal analogies to apprehend the state is unlikely to melt away. Indeed, the use of new bodily metaphors that continually emerge with the increase of biological knowledge and subsequent scientific conceptual shifts shows that the body-state cognitive interface is extremely resilient and adaptable.

I suggest that the work on new materialisms by philosophers such as Karen Barad or Jane Bennett can be instructive for political geography. The recognition of widespread cross-species entanglements means that symbiogenesis is gradually replacing the earlier cruder model of neo-Darwinian evolutionary theory. To be entangled, Barad writes, "is not simply to be intertwined with another . . . but to lack an independent, self-contained existence."[133] Jane Bennett's notion of vibrant matter has also been helpful in highlighting the complex enmeshments of nonhuman material with the human, showing how "human agency is always an assemblage of microbes, animals, plants, metals, chemicals, word-sounds."[134]

In addition to rendering the container model obsolete, I argue that a body existing and thriving across species, scales, and life-forms constitutes a better model for the neoliberal landscape as well as for military geographies. As I discuss in the book's brief coda, the changing scale and speed of warfare is motivating military strategists to reconceptualize spatial models beyond the limiting imaginaries that have so far prevailed in political geography. Ushering a complete rupture in the body/state isomorphic relation discussed in *Somatic States*, new organizational models based on other biological architectures are privileging alternative kinds of bodies, eliciting new corporeal metaphors—this time avian and entomological rather than human. The model of the swarm in particular, giving precedence to autonomy, emergence, and distributed functioning, defies the fiction of the body as organic, natural, and unitary insofar as it continually finds itself on the verge of materialization and dissolution.[135] Yet, through its fractured and dispersive nature, the swarm reflects a psychoanalytical view of the body as "always and already fragmented" (chapter 3), thereby dispelling the fiction of the body as discrete and singular.[136] Embracing such fragmented and dispersive models—of a corporeality otherwise—may thus help reconfigure metaphors of the neoliberal state in line with its actual spatiality and modes of operation, no longer resorting to qualifiers or exceptions, and jettisoning once and for all the Westphalian myth.

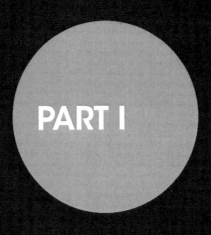

PART I

CARTOGRAPHIC REVOLUTIONS

The map is the perfect symbol of the state. If your grand duchy or tribal area seems tired, run-down, and frayed at the edges, simply take a sheet of paper, plot some cities, roads and physical features, draw a heavy, distinct boundary around as much territory as you dare claim, colour it in, add a name—perhaps reinforced with the impressive prefix of "Republic of"—and presto: you are now the leader of a new sovereign, autonomous country. Should anyone doubt it, merely point to the map. Not only is your new state on paper, it's on a map, so it must be real.

—Mark Monmonier, *How to Lie with Maps*

MAPPING WORLDS

The Human Genome Project formally launched in October 1990 amid great publicity. This pioneering project, the first large, coordinated effort in the history of biological research, aimed to discover all the estimated 20,000–25,000 human genes and make them accessible for further biological study. Heralded as revolutionary, it was set to forever transform our relation to the body, health, and evolution. With technological advances finally permitting us to better understand human evolution, there emerged a clear "sense of creating a new order in biology, a revolution in which computers and automation are joined with advanced technologies in molecular biology to speed the process of DNA analysis."[1]

From the very launch of the project, the metaphor of the map loomed large. In fact, "mapping the human genome" was such a recurrent expression

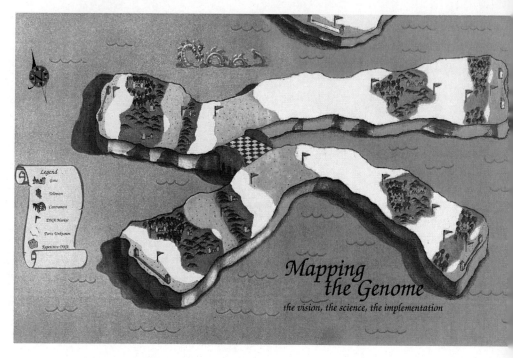

Mapping the Genome
the vision, the science, the implementation

1.1. Baltimore et al., "Mapping the Genome," 68–69.

that it rapidly turned into a set phrase, and *map* became the verb commonly associated with this particular scientific enterprise. An article published by *Los Alamos Science* in the first years of the project was thus called, unsurprisingly, "Mapping the Genome." Addressed primarily to the scientific community, it summarized the goals, potentialities, and limitations of the project in ways that were unambiguously spatial: "Like sixteenth-century maps of the new world, present maps of the human genome contain few landmarks and many parts unknown. And like the explorers of the new world, the genome explorers are pushing forward into vast uncharted territory in the face of great uncertainties—both political and technological."[2]

The cover of the article itself resembled a medieval map (figure 1.1). An island in the shape of a chromosome portrayed the territory to be mapped and was dotted with icons representing chromosomal constituents such as telomeres and centromeres. Like a medieval map, it was surrounded by sea monsters.[3] And, like a medieval map, it included terrae incognitae, blank spots awaiting discovery and labeling.

If this particular article was overtly and purposefully metaphoric, employing spatial terms such as *landmarks, explorers,* or *vast uncharted territories,* it was less unusual in its linkage of maps to scientific discoveries. Since the emergence of political cartography in the sixteenth century, the term *map* has been durably melded to scientific pursuits and discoveries. Thus the visualization afforded by mapmaking was productively extended to nonspatial experiences and phenomena.[4] Mapping has proved a pervasive and powerful metaphor for organization and classification, leading to the mapping of virtually everything, from knowledge practices to population growth and human relations.[5] "Maps locate," writes Laura Kurgan. "They show us where we are and thereby contribute to a "sense of security and self-possession." The solidity and certainty of the phrase *You are here* is thus at the core of "that identity-reinforcing—and maybe even identity-constitutive—function of maps."[6]

This metaphoric fusion of cartography and scientific development is in many ways unsurprising given their closely interwoven history. As David Turnbull has argued, the development of cartography, viewed as a progressive, cumulative, objective, and accurate representation of geographical reality, is assumed to be synonymous with the growth of science and mapping.[7] While cartographers no longer subscribe to the view that maps constitute an objective mirror of geographic and social realities, what we are witnessing is nonetheless an increased synergy between science and mapping, a veritable "spatialization of knowledge," with spatial tropes suffusing every scientific domain.[8] Cartographic metaphors run to the very heart of Western thought: not only have maps shaped identities and spaces, but "the cartographic imagination has influenced the very structure and content of language and thought itself."[9] If cartographic equivalences rarely strike us as metaphors, this is largely due to the ubiquitous presence of maps and the central role they are increasingly playing in our lives. The advent of Google Maps and geographic information system (GIS) technology has had a wholly transformative effect on social, economic, and political realms. Maps are such an integral part of how we apprehend the world that it is difficult to imagine life without them. They have effectively become second nature.

Yet map reading is far from intuitive, and the skills necessary to interpret maps have to be formally acquired.[10] As Denis Wood reminds us, the predominance of maps is in fact very recent—almost all of them having been made in the last hundred years, and the vast majority in the past few decades.[11] That rulers of vast territories, from Genghis Khan to Charlemagne, from Egyptian pharaohs to Roman emperors, reigned without maps strikes us as simply unimaginable today.[12]

The absence of maps prior to around 1500 does not mean that pictorial depictions of human environments did not exist before that time. But such depictions rarely qualify as maps as we understand them today. As Matthew Edney points out, an important distinction exists between mapping and cartography.[13] The latter, he argues, is a very specific product of European history, "permeated by many of the myths that Westerners tell themselves about their rationality and superiority." In an attempt to be more inclusive and recognize cultural forms of mapping that have been routinely excluded from histories of cartography, a number of scholars have suggested more capacious and inclusive definitions. For David Turnbull, maps are a "knowledge space within which certain kinds of understandings and of knowing subjects, material objects and their relations in space and time are authorised and legitimated."[14] Similarly, in their monumental *History of Cartography*, J. B. Harley and David Woodward define maps as "graphic representations that facilitate a spatial understanding of things, concepts, conditions, processes, or events in the human world"—a seemingly vague definition that allows the inclusion of the so-called stick charts of the Marshallese.[15] But the consensus remains that, given the historical contingency of the emergence of cartography, speaking of premodern maps, let alone prehistoric maps, is still highly problematic. Denis Wood insists that there were no maps before 1500 and that to refer to older sketches as "maps" is to apply a conceptual filter created by modern mapmaking. He defines maps exclusively as "more or less permanent, more or less graphic artifacts that support the descriptive function in human discourse that links territory to other things, advancing in this way the interests of those making (or controlling the making) of the maps."[16]

This is of course especially true of political maps insofar as they explicitly and purposefully seek to convince and persuade; but all maps, even the most seemingly benign, are similarly embedded in social and political practices. Primarily because of their selectivity of content, but also through the signs and styles of representation they employ, maps articulate and structure an object in ways that are neither impartial nor objective. Inherently biased, the duplicity of maps lies at the very heart of cartographic representation: "as images of the world, maps are never neutral or value-free or ever completely scientific."[17] A well-known example is the Mercator projection (figure 1.2). Gerard Mercator, a sixteenth-century cartographer, created several world maps that had a profound and lasting impact in geography. He was not the only active mapmaker at the time, but because his maps were scientific—insofar as they relied on mathematics and did not include religious

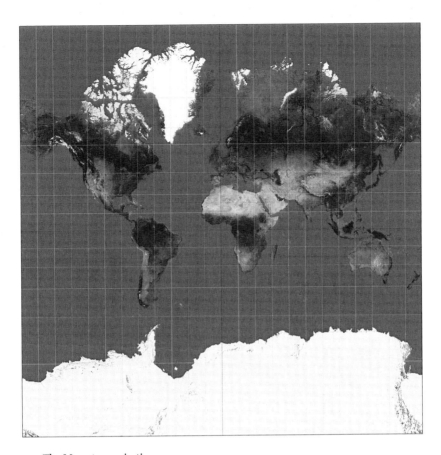

1.2. The Mercator projection.

motifs—his representations remained standard for several centuries. Yet the projection was problematic in several respects. If it provided true compass readings along straight lines, particularly for east-west voyages parallel to the equator, the meridians did not narrow at the poles, which resulted in increasing distortion as one moved away from equator. A plain example of this misrepresentation can be seen with Greenland, depicted at the same size as Africa despite being fourteen times smaller.

Mercator's map was prepared as a guide for navigation, not as a true representation of the world. As polar navigation was barely possible at the time, the projection distorts the Arctic region in favor of a true-to-scale temperate zone. Similarly, if the map places Europe at the center, thereby cutting off at least one-third of the earth's surface and shrinking Africa, it was primarily because the southern hemisphere remained largely unexplored. Regardless

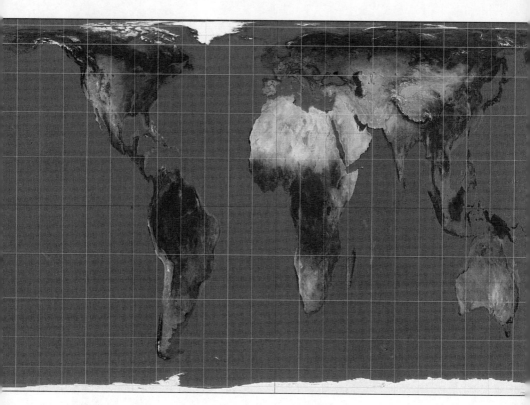

1.3. The Gall-Peters projection.

of intent, the legacy of Mercator's projection has been dramatic on generations of students throughout the world who have internalized Mercator's proportions and regularly grossly overestimate Europe's size in comparison with other continents, particularly Africa.[18] These structural, and frequently unintentional, consequences are an important point I revisit in chapter 5.

Seeking to redress the cartographic inequalities embedded in Mercator's projection, German historian Arno Peters published in the early 1970s a different map focusing on "fidelity of area." His map was almost identical to one created by Reverend James Gall in 1885, though Peters has denied knowledge of Gall's work. The Gall-Peters projection (figure 1.3) uses the same scale throughout but is problematic in other ways, notably because of its extensive north-south shape elongation near the equator and its lack of improvement over Mercator's projection with regard to polar regions.[19] Peters was strongly criticized by cartographers who saw his map as a publicity stunt and were angered by his uninformed, dismissive remarks concerning cartography.[20]

Despite its shaky scientific basis, the Gall-Peters projection was rapidly adopted by a number of organizations including the World Council of Churches and the Lutheran Church of America as well as by various United Nations bodies. Because of the way it seemed to champion the colonized and the oppressed, the Gall-Peters projection was seen as a more egalitarian representation of the world. Yet, as Mark Monmonier sarcastically remarks, a cartogram where each country is scaled according to number of inhabitants may have been a better choice to contrast the demographic importance of China, India, and Indonesia with the less substantial populations of Canada, Russia, or the United States. Despite its egalitarian claims, the Gall-Peters projection in fact gives prominence to Africa and Latin America whose population densities are much lower than Asia's.[21]

If all maps are inherently biased, national political maps—the maps foregrounded in this book—are a particular kind of rhetorical device, intimately melded to the emergence of the nation-state and print capitalism.[22] While the cartographic impulse cannot be reduced to the nationalist project, the modern map would probably not exist without it. In fact, as David Buisseret pointed out, whereas in 1400 very few people except navigators used maps, by 1600 maps had become indispensable to a wide range of professions.[23] The sudden proliferation of maps at a crucial historical juncture prompted Denis Wood to assert that maps do not originate in "some primal instinct 'to communicate a sense of place, some sense of *here* in relation to *there*,' but in the needs of nascent states to take on form and organize their many interests."[24]

While his point is certainly convincing, it may be a little reductive to see the emergence of cartography purely as an instrument of political objectives. Maps undeniably help states run more efficiently and more uniformly, as they enable citizens to take possession, visually and conceptually, of their nation.[25] But if cartography became an ideal vehicle for the nascent nation-state, it was also because mapping practices were embedded within a larger movement, namely the Scientific Revolution, with its emphasis on quantification and measurement. Just as the geographical features of the natural world were being measured ever more accurately, the human body was similarly being delineated, and the art world was also witnessing the emergence of realist paintings that would later encourage a profusion of utilitarian topographical views.[26] It is therefore likely that maps gained such prominence out of a specific convergence, and coproduction, of social, historical, and political developments, not merely as state-imposed narratives. This appears to be substantiated by the fact that modern maps arose independently elsewhere in the world under similar stimuli, notably in Japan and China.[27]

CARTOGRAPHIC REVOLUTIONS

Cartographic terms such as *map, chart,* and *cartography* are primarily derived from the materials that originally supported them; in Latin, *mappa* designated cloth, while *carta* referred to paper or parchment. The lack of specific terminology no doubt reflects a certain imprecise beginning of these practices.[28] In fact, before they acquired a scientific standing and morphed into the political and national discourse, maps were not a discrete category, and until the Renaissance no formal distinction was made between "painting" and "map."[29] Indeed maps and paintings were often created by the same individuals, including artists such as Leonardo da Vinci. A similar cultural continuity is seen in the case of China, where the standard term for *map, tu* (圖), can also be translated as *picture, diagram,* or *chart* depending on the context.[30] If contemporary Chinese does make a distinction between these different genres, Chinese culture has traditionally shown a unique synthesis of painting, calligraphy, and poetry.[31]

The term *revolution* in this section's title is not hyperbolic. From the medieval era to the beginning of the twentieth century, what was witnessed was nothing less than a fundamental transformation, a "cultural earthquake" in the very concept of political space.[32] As Richard Helgerson argued in a germinal study, maps—along with other discursive practices such as poems, law books, and narratives of overseas exploration—were at the core of the emergence of England as a nation. Indeed, it was only with the emergence of cartographic practices that an inchoate nation-state could be imagined.[33] They enabled monarchs to imagine their realm in a coherent whole, ushering in a new era of what J. B. Harvey famously called "map-mindedness," ultimately making it possible later for citizens to identify with their nation-state and its territory. This epistemological fracture accompanied the age of nationalism and witnessed the formation of a new kind of subjectivity. The many kinds of polities that had existed previously—empires, dynastic states, city-states, nomadic or religious communities—were by and large no longer viable models.[34]

John Agnew makes the important point that much of this border-making work was the result of the global spread of a model of territorial statehood and state-centered political economy originating in Western Europe.[35] He asserts that European cultural hegemony has "written the script" for the growth and consolidation of a global nation-state system and that a nation could no longer be imagined without firm boundary lines.[36] The emergence of the science of cartography, which I briefly retrace below, was of course not exclusive to Europe, but it was there that the "mapping impulse" was especially strong.[37] These developments were to lay the groundwork for the most radical and lasting transformations to take place, initially in Europe and its colonies, and later the rest of the world.[38] I argue in this book that contemporary understandings of national sovereign space and cartography have now become largely homogeneous around the world. More importantly, concepts such as the logomap tend to be enmeshed in bodily metaphors, and tend to be emotionally loaded—suggesting that there are aspects of territorial sovereignty that are shared across space and time, as I discuss further in chapter 2.

Of course, the history of political cartography is complex and cannot be neatly subsumed within the European experience. Claims to universality can also be deeply problematic. No two nationalisms are exactly the same—indeed, my own discussion of Russia and China in later chapters goes a long way to illuminate these productive differences. But it is undeniable that Western forms of cartography have imparted an imprimatur on the rest of the world. The vast compendium of historical accounts from many parts of the world substantiates John Agnew's position that international borders, worldwide, are "the direct result of the imposition and subsequent breakup of European empires outside of Europe into statelike units," and, more broadly, "the result of the spread of a model of territorial statehood and state-centered political economy from Western Europe into the rest of the world."[39] Agnew further insists that an emphasis on the existence of local alternatives works to downplay the degree to which the model of the nation-state has become hegemonic and the ways in which state practices and symbols, regardless of their specificities, have been imported from a European-based model.[40] While his argument is compelling, this does not mean that these Western cartographic practices were transmitted into a void.[41] The work of Zayde Antrim, rightly critical of Eurocentric histories of cartography, has demonstrated that early mapping practices in the Middle East were in fact complex and profoundly connective: "Maps tended to stress mobility, overlap or contiguity between the places they depicted and to serve as links to meaningful spaces or pasts." Colonial encounters with Europeans later constrained this cartographic and spatial thinking, making it harder to envision alternative possibilities.[42] The work of historians Thongchai Winichakul or Sumathi Ramaswamy, discussed in more depth later, similarly shows that in Thailand and India, respectively, locally and culturally specific modes of spatial representation eventually came to align with Western models in order to gain recognition and commensurability.[43] A further example is China, where the first national surveys carried out during the Qing dynasty were not simply a copy of Western practices but emerged through similar political ambitions.[44] Historians Nianshen Song, Laura Hostetler, and Valerie Kivelson have shown, for instance, that maps helped China and Russia gain awareness of the physical extent—and respective limits—of their territory, thus mutually reinforcing the reality of the state for both countries.[45] In the case of Qing China, it was specifically to counter Russian expansionism that the emperor emphasized the importance of creditable maps, creating a highly accurate imperial atlas that incorporated Chinese as well as Inner Asian territories.[46]

The cartographic revolution has thus been highly palimpsestic and multifaceted, the adoption of maps often supplementing local understandings of space, sovereignty, and belonging.[47] At the same time, these transformations often emerged dialogically, and Western and non-Western populations often shared spatial and cartographic notions despite divergent mapping practices and histories. Challenging a tenacious belief that European colonizers and Native Americans shared little in terms of perceptions of space and geography, Nancy Shoemaker writes that Native Americans could in fact draw maps comprehensible to Europeans just as they could read their maps and recognize and correct errors.[48] If their own maps featured specific cartographic devices that had to be explained to Europeans, such as circles to indicate nations and lines to indicate paths of alliance and trade, there was a sufficiently strong bedrock of shared ideas that made mutual comprehension possible.[49] As further examples discussed in chapter 2 will suggest, premodern non-Western cartography similarly echoes, in locally specific ways, many of the characteristics of early European maps.

The inclusion of non-Western examples in the history of cartography is important insofar as it shows variation and diversity. But the attendant danger is to picture them as departures from an archetype located in the West. European maps, both premodern and contemporary, are also not coextensive with the Westphalian ideal. In a groundbreaking study of the relation of law and geography in European empires, Laura Benton has shown the ubiquity of "irregularly shaped corridors and enclaves" with ambiguous and shifting relations to European imperial sovereignty—suggesting that a more faithful representation of imperial power would include colors of varying intensity to better portray "the changing and locally differentiated qualities of rule within geographic zones."[50] Jordan Branch also notes that new ideas of jurisdictionally defined authority found themselves layered on top of previous ones, which were not displaced, thus accounting for the gradual and incomplete process of territorialization.[51] Along similar lines, I argue in the final chapter of this book that the Westphalian model has provided a powerful narrative but has not replaced established practices and concepts, including in Europe and the United States where a panoply of hyphenated qualifiers has been coined by social science and political scholars to account for forms of sovereignty that deviate from the archetype, such as gaps, breaches, and exceptions. A core argument made in the book is that the Westphalian model is aspirational and that organicist metaphors have buttressed it in order to convey a sense of physicality and stability. The irony, as I discuss in chapter 3 through the lens of phantom limbs and prosthetics, and in chapter 5 on monsters and entanglements, is that the body itself is culturally constructed. Yet, despite their limitations, the two components of the body-territory doublet mutually reinforce and reify one another.

Another challenge to the generally accepted history of cartography is the place of the treaties signed at Münster and Osnabrück in 1648 (also known as the Peace of Westphalia). In his work, Jordan Branch has shown that they barely contained "any change in the deep grammar of political authority" and that it is only in the post-Napoleonic reconstruction of European politics that the alignment of political rule on territoriality as defined by the modern state system was fully consolidated.[52] Therefore, he further argues, if maps from the early modern period depict bounded and homogeneous territorial entities, this should not be read as representations of a political reality.[53] It is much later, in the nineteenth century, that maps finally reflected reality on the ground, but only "because cartography itself had shaped those practices by changing actors' ideas about the legitimate form of authority."[54] In a study about the French-German borderlands, Catherine Dunlop similarly notes that European views of territory changed quite late, in the last part of the eighteenth century, as they were becoming increasingly interconnected with the idea of the nation.[55] But very much against the grain of most histories of cartography, she argues that popular engagement in, and democratization of, cartography led to modes of viewing and interpreting European land becoming increasingly malleable and heterogeneous.[56] This important work by historians and international relations scholars highlights the gradual nature of the transformation of political space toward the forms of cartography we are accustomed to. It also allows for the understanding that this process is multifaceted and remains incomplete, as I develop in chapter 5.

My use of the term *Westphalian* in this book should thus be assumed to be accompanied by an asterisk to denote this gradual and piecemeal evolution. It remains nonetheless a useful milestone for the sea change witnessed in the realm of modern political cartography. Indeed, in spite of these important caveats, the maps that existed in Europe (and elsewhere) up until the fifteenth century differ dramatically from modern maps. The medieval *mappamundi*, or "map of the world," for instance, is one that tends to strike modern viewers as exceedingly odd and barely recognizable as a map. Incomplete and not to scale, the *mappamundi* depicted strangely shaped countries and continents and also frequently featured monsters and beasts, just like the chromosome island at the beginning of this chapter.[57] It was not the only type of map in existence in medieval Europe, and it existed in parallel with local topographical maps, portolan charts, and celestial maps—each type belonging to a relatively independent tradition of mapmaking.[58] The *mappamundi* was alone, however, in its inclusion of a symbolic conception of the world as well as in its bodily representations of political space—two particular aspects that helped shape, very differently, the maps that came after it.[59]

Typically shaped as a circle (O) split into three parts by an inner T corresponding to the Mediterranean, the Nile, and the Don, the medieval "T-O" map divided the world into the three continents inherited from the classical tradition—Asia, Europe, and Africa—with Jerusalem at the center.[60] Despite its inclusion of religious motifs such as the Garden of Eden, or the landing of Noah's Ark—and indeed the body of Christ overlaid upon the cruciform shape of the map[61]—the T-O map was not simply a vehicle of religious instruction. It is likely the medieval *mappaemundi* fulfilled several functions and that they were "statements of philosophical, political, religious, encyclopedic and conceptual concerns" and functioned as minor encyclopedias of medieval knowledge.[62] Their placement at such sites as the Parliament in the case of the famous Hereford map would suggest that they were partly of a political nature.[63] Medieval maps were thus "historical aggregations or cumulative inventories of events," compiled from a variety of sources.[64] The Hereford map, for instance, represented "an asynchronous geography ranging from the fourth-century Roman Empire to contemporary thirteenth-century England."[65]

Mappaemundi were thus essentially tools of orientation in both physical and social space, like in fact all maps, including modern ones.[66] Indeed, even with a new emphasis on scientific practices through the use of abstract, geometric, and homogeneous space, maps produced in the Renaissance and later continued to be symbolic and metaphorical as well. As I explore in more depth in chapter 2, they also remained heavily saturated with bodily imagery, even as geography moved toward greater specificity and mathematical accuracy.[67] The body of the sovereign, initially equated with the land, instead gradually gave way to the body of the citizen, thereby laying the ground for more corporealized metaphors to gain ground.[68] Of course, the cartographic revolution I briefly sketch below takes as its focus the evolution of the relationship between territory and the body—the core argument of the book—but this revolution was considerably more complex. The emergence of modern maps was also prompted, in part, by a rationalization of the countryside and its economic potential—what Charles Maier terms the "cadastral century"— as well as by a "quantum leap in technology."[69]

It was also greatly aided by key texts, including those of the ancient Greeks. When Ptolemy's *Geographia* was rediscovered and began circulating in Europe at the beginning of the fifteenth century, its influence on Western cartography was dramatic, especially as it coincided with the beginning of the great European overseas geographical discoveries of the Renaissance.[70] Whereas medieval maps might have been described as impressionistic, the aim of Renaissance artists and scientists was now to be mathematically accurate and achieve an objective representation of the world.[71] This transformation, which led to Renaissance principles of linear perspective, and eventually pictorial realism, constituted no less than a revolution in the European way of seeing the world.

The *Atlas of the Counties of England and Wales*, published in 1579, marks a turning point for British—as well as for European, and later global— mapmaking. These maps, created by British cartographer Christopher Saxton, were so innovative in their indication of relief and settlements that they became the gold standard for many subsequent generations of cartographers. If these maps were useful primarily for property owners, they were also an expression of royal power. It was in fact precisely for these reasons that the first detailed survey of England and Wales was commissioned by the queen's government.[72] Through their prominent display of royal and imperial arms on every sheet, the maps proclaimed "royal sovereignty over the kingdom as a whole and over each of its provinces."[73] This literal stamping of royal power onto the map is perhaps nowhere clearer than with Elizabeth I's *Ditchley Portrait*, painted circa 1592, where the queen stands on a map of England, her feet on Oxfordshire (figure 1.4).

If maps had initially been used as illustrations appended to texts, needs for cartographic representation were gaining ground. As a result, images such as the *Ditchley Portrait* were felt to be increasingly inadequate insofar as the body of the queen concealed what the users of the maps were eager to see. Later maps and atlases reflect this enthusiasm for cartography, and symbols of the state become literally marginalized: information regarding sovereignty or royal patronage is gradually relegated to the margins of the map in the form of royal arms and cartouches, "merely decorative, and thus ultimately dispensable."[74]

1.4. Marcus Gheeraerts the Younger, *Queen Elizabeth I ("The Ditchley Portrait")* (ca. 1592).

In later maps, such as *The Theatre of the Empire of Great Britaine,* by British cartographer John Speed and published in 1610/11, the royal arms are further reduced in scale. They are also accompanied by a whole slew of features such as plans of cities, monuments, notable buildings, and local heroes.

This subtle but fundamental change was cogently analyzed by Richard Helgerson. He shows that the gradual exclusion of royal insignia was nothing

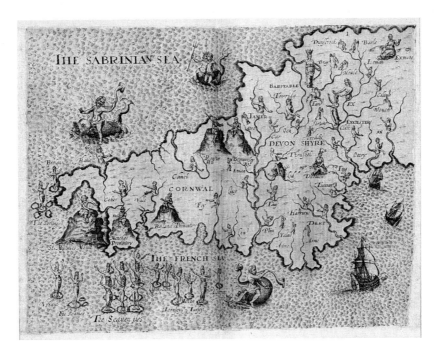

1.5. Michael Drayton, *Poly-Olbion Map* (1612).

less than an ideological transformation, shifting emphasis away from royal power onto the land itself, and eventually into the hands of the people.[75] This shift is especially visible with the publication, in 1612, of Michael Drayton's *Poly-Olbion* maps, where coats of arms are conspicuously absent, and where prominence is instead given to natural and manmade landmarks such as streams, hills, and towns (figure 1.5). That the monarch was now the land is made unambiguously evident by the figure on the frontispiece—an allegorical personification of Great Britain, a goddess-like woman draped in a map.[76]

The ideological effect of these cartographic representations, produced at a time when accurate maps were still very much a novel and unfamiliar experience, was especially potent:

The attractive force of this new enterprise could not be ignored. Its products provoked an almost sensual response, aroused an undeniable passion—a passion that could draw a man from what otherwise would have remained his deepest allegiance. Among those touched by the new cartographic and chorographic representations, "natural affection" for one's country . . . was pushing all other affection to the side. Affection for the monarch that had been so powerful an element in Elizabeth's success was being marginalized, just as the signs of royal authority were marginalized on maps and frontispieces.[77]

This affective response was greatly facilitated by the emergence of what Benedict Anderson refers to as print capitalism, the printing revolution allowing, for the first time, thousands and perhaps tens of thousands of people throughout Europe to have access to maps. A society-wide fascination with maps—and with atlases in particular—led to full-scale chorographic, that is, textual, descriptions of the land and people of Britain. The interest of these chorographers also shifted, with a focus on genealogy replacing concerns with place names and etymology. Chorography slowly evolved from a practice revolving around royal records to a "topographically ordered set of real-estate and family chronicles."[78] Unsurprisingly, therefore, by the end of the sixteenth century chorography had become a dangerously political activity, Britannia and the British monarch now occupying separate and mutually hostile camps.[79]

The proliferation of atlases in eighteenth-century England was more than a simple fad. Atlases had direct political reverberations insofar as they portrayed a very different kind of space. According to map historian Brian Harley, they in fact led to an epistemological break in their influence of various aspects of group consciousness.[80] This is especially visible in the way in which atlases became increasingly sensitive to political territoriality, with the introduction of boundary lines differentiating territorial units by style, boldness, or color.[81] That these techniques were routinely employed by the second half of the eighteenth century is testament to the enduring transformation in spatial consciousness that had been witnessed in the space of three hundred years or so. Now attuned to the geopolitical imagination, British subjects—as well as most Europeans—could visualize the country to which they belonged only with the aid of a map.[82] However, as Tom Conley rightly insists, it is crucial to remain attentive to the multifaceted production of imaginary space, nation, and selfhood. If the emergence of the nation-state (and its attendant epistemological break) would have been unthinkable without the existence of the census and the national map, the sudden emergence of cartography was also greatly facilitated by the "new importance afforded to the emerging *self* and to the self's relation to the idea of national space."[83] In other words, what occurred was not a simple causal reaction but a more complex crossing and distillation of discrete historical forces, including colonial expansion, European maritime empires, and territorial extension and consolidation.[84]

It was also, as Jordan Branch rightfully points out, "an unintended by-product of the visual language of maps": as the modern concept of territoriality became hegemonic, jigsaw-like political maps became the standard way of depicting the world.[85] It was therefore also a recursive process. Changes in mapping technology prompted the view that actors held of political space, which in turn created more demand for mapping "in terms of both the kind of maps being produced . . . and the cartographic technologies pursued."[86] This multiplicity of factors accounts for the coeval fascination with maps in other parts of the world, notably China and Japan, in ways that are not wholly tied to Western influences or imagined as mere slavish reproduction. The creation of many atlases produced in the late Qing era thus used both Western and indigenous quantitative methods. Qing cartographers saw no division between *scientific* and *unscientific*: different maps had different purposes for different audiences and were hybridized as necessary.[87]

One of the most drastic changes in spatial conceptualizations—and one at the core of this book's concerns—was a specific shift of sovereignty from radial to homogenous. In medieval Europe—and indeed much of the world—premodern states were defined by centers. The ruler's power would decrease with distance and sovereignties fade imperceptibly into one another. Borders were porous and indistinct, and remote communities at the frontiers of polities were not infrequently subject to multiple sovereignties. Because there might be pockets of individuals "scattered across noncontiguous spaces who might be under the jurisdiction of multiple princes or vassals at the same time"—themselves potentially beholden to two or more others—"medieval borders cannot be defined as fixed geographical lines, or even zones."[88] As a result, rulers frequently paid more attention to the manpower they could summon than to sovereignty over land that had no value in the absence of labor.[89] Thus even in formal agreements such as peace treaties, territory was described as lists of places rather than as bound, linearly divided spaces.[90]

In contemporary political geography, by contrast, rule is understood as the precedence of space, and state sovereignty is conceptualized as "fully, flatly, and evenly operative over each square centimeter of a legally demarcated territory."[91] As historian of cartography David Woodward argues, the "medieval center/periphery frame of mind, in which places in the world were accorded widely different levels of importance" gradually gave way to a more abstract notion whereby "space could be referenced to a geometrical net of lines of longitude and latitude and could thus everywhere be accorded the same importance."[92]

The homogenization of territorial authority (and its attendant elimination of nonterritorial forms of organization) has been heavily reliant on the linearization of political boundaries as well as on a novel concern for borders. While previously identities in borderlands had been polycentric and comparatively fluid, they increasingly became nationally defined. Thus from a people-based understanding, what was witnessed was a territorialization of the state, that is, a decline in relationship-inflected views of the nation and a progressive isomorphic identification between the state's physical and political reach. By the beginning of the twentieth century, frontiers—in the sense of liminal zones of transition from one state to another—had given way to clearly demarcated borders.

This shift was so dramatic that spaces that elude national maps have mostly disappeared from our intellectual life and, conversely, uninhabitable corners of the state frequently become suffused with affect, as discussed in more depth in later chapters. As David Ludden notes, the cartographic imagination has had such a defining influence that space now makes sense only within national maps. Since 1950, when national boundaries covered the globe, "all histories of all peoples have come to appear inside national maps, in a cookie-cutter world of national geography, the most comprehensive organization of spatial experience in human history."[93] Yet, as I develop in later chapters, and particularly in chapters 3 and 5, spaces and territories that lack cartographic representation survive in spectral form and return in unexpected ways.

The force of the Western hegemonic model is also visible insofar as the modern concept of the nation-state relies on a homogenous territory where every citizen participates fully and equally in the national project. This teleological vision projected a gradual filling-in of all blank spaces—the very concept of blank space a by-product of cartography's gratricular network of latitudes and longitudes. Unlike medieval *mappaemundi*, which had a clearly defined center (usually Jerusalem), modern cartography could be centered anywhere. With every square of the territory now functionally and symbolically equivalent to all others, the intimate knowledge of all space in the far reaches of the polity and the securing of the borders became critical to the state's success and survival. That the United States launched a survey of the entire country immediately following independence is indeed testament to the core significance of mapping for the national project. As Rachel Hewitt writes, there is something very powerful in the image of a complete map of a nation.[94] Unsurprisingly, as this book in fact argues, it is precisely in its completeness that the power of the map has resided.

THE LOGOMAP

The origins of what Benedict Anderson has famously referred to as the "logo-map" were innocent enough. To make maps more legible, and particularly to highlight their colonial possessions, imperial states began to color their colonies on maps with an imperial dye. Part of the motivation was also commercial, as the addition of color was an easy way for mapmakers to make their product more attractive.[95] As a direct result, representations of national maps became increasingly common, with each state and colony now appearing like a piece of a jigsaw puzzle: "Each 'piece' could be wholly detached from its geographic context. In its final form all explanatory glosses could be summarily removed: lines of longitude and latitude, place names, signs for rivers, seas, and mountains, neighbors."[96] Regardless of the original political or commercial motivations, this color-coding, ubiquitous on wall maps and atlases, accentuated further the linear boundaries demarcating state territories across the earth's surface. The filling in of each national territory turned each "piece" into a discrete, autonomous entity, dividing one sovereignty from the next, and "implying that its interior is a homogeneous space, traversed evenly by state sovereignty."[97]

This portrayal of the political world could not be more different from the maps preceding the advent of the age of nationalism. A wonderfully visual comparison by Ernest Gellner makes this explicit: "The first map resembles a painting by Kokoschka. The riot of diverse points of color is such that no clear pattern can be discerned in any detail. . . . Look now instead at the ethnographic and political map of an area of the modern world. It resembles not Kokoschka, but, say, Modigliani. There is very little shading; neat flat surfaces are clearly separated from each other, it is generally plain where one begins and another ends, and there is little if any ambiguity or overlap."[98] This representation of the nation as a discrete and internally homogenous entity also greatly facilitated the socialization of individuals into citizens. Maps, and particularly political maps, hold strong symbolic power. As logos bestowing a physical shape on the nation, they are constitutive of the very being of modern subjects.[99] Indeed, as I discuss in chapter 2 and continue exploring in the subsequent chapters, the national contour has become a graphic representation of the national subject.

A nation requires firm boundaries to be recognizable as such. It exists by virtue of this recognition, and its incarnation requires commensurability with that of others in order to be recognizable. In addition to having a flag, an anthem, and a currency, possessing well-defined borders constitutes an essential constituent of this national toolkit.[100] The precise locations of these boundaries may be disputed by neighbors, but these differences of opinion do not appear on national maps. On maps created for domestic (and sometimes international) use, there are no question marks, no blank spaces, no territorial overlaps, no terrae incognitae. To be recognized as a nation among nations, to gain commensurability, it is imperative that the national contour appear incontestable and timeless.[101]

That the national outline has now become central to the nation's emergence and continued existence is evident through its iconic and quasi-totemic use. A common example is weather maps, typically isolating countries from their geographical context.[102] In the case of France, writes Christian Jacob, the national territory is "entirely sectioned off by a continuous line that confuses borderlines and coastlines."[103] Unsurprisingly, when asked to draw the French map from memory, children in elementary school sometimes draw it as an island surrounded by yellow beaches and a blue sea.[104] In fact, the island shares substantial metaphoric resonance with the logomap, conjuring a "power of miniaturization for the real, the imagined, or the armchair traveler."[105] Not only do island maps occupy a privileged place in the typology of fictive maps, as Christian Jacob has noted, but in earlier centuries it was customary to depict any new space as islands.[106] Even places like England and Scotland, known to occupy a continuous landmass, were sometimes represented, particularly on portolan charts, as two different islands. This division was due, argues Philip Steinberg, to a strong association of "islandness" with territorial unity.[107] In fact, he asserts, the very "mapping of islands, as organic socio-physical units within oceans of movement, inadvertently established a grammar for the imagining and mapping of the territorial state that was to emerge in later years."[108]

Detached from its geographic context and turned into a logomap, the national contour is routinely employed as a powerful emblem of the nation-state. Benedict Anderson places the logomap on a par with the census and the museum as a critical practice at the root of the emergence of the nation. I argue however that symbolically the logomap is far stronger.[109] Unlike the museum and the census, which lack a visual presence, the logomap is ubiquitous. In fact, as Anderson himself notes, this logomap, instantly recognizable and everywhere visible, has penetrated deep into the popular imagination. His choice of the term *logo* is especially apt: with the advent of print capitalism, the nation's shape has become "available for transfer to posters, official seals, letterheads, magazine and textbook covers, tablecloths, and hotel walls."[110] In fact, used as a commercial logo, the national shape functions as a branding device, as shorthand for the nation itself.[111] Fully coextensive, the logomap and the actual territory have become undistinguishable, and occasionally, the signifier-map even comes to precede its signified-territory. As a metasign, Winichakul cogently argues, the logomap becomes a sign in itself, no longer tied to the territoriality of that nation. Dissociated from its signified, it can carry independent meanings and values.[112] It can also act as ersatz—displacing and condensing affect.

This enmeshing of map and territory has been a fertile terrain for scholars and writers. In a much-quoted short story, Jorge Luis Borges describes a fictitious empire where the art of cartography has become so elaborate that a map of the country is created at a 1:1 scale.[113] But too unwieldy to be used as a map, it is later abandoned to the inclemency of the weather, gradually disintegrating, tattered pieces remaining here and there in the empire's deserts. This story was certainly inspired by Lewis Carroll's *Sylvie and Bruno Concluded*, where a character mentions the existence of a map at a scale of a mile to the mile. Though perfectly accurate, it was never used: "the farmers objected: they said it would cover the whole country, and shut out the sunlight! So we now use the country itself, as its own map, and I assure you it does nearly as well."[114]

A tongue-in-cheek analysis of Borges's 1:1 map was also developed by Umberto Eco in a short text where he points out core paradoxes inherent to the existence of such a map. To function as a map, Eco posits, the map needs to be opaque, but its very opacity will effect a separation between the territory and the sun, thereby altering the ecological balance and driving a wedge between the object and its representation. Similarly, if the land's inhabitants must also be represented on the map, this would constitute another paradox, since the empire's subjects would now be living on the map rather than on the territory. More importantly for our present concerns, Eco insists that the map must be a semiotic instrument, capable of standing for the empire, especially in the event the empire may not be otherwise discernible.[115]

These several versions of the story imagine a map that is coextensive with the land and which, as a result of this very coextensiveness, loses all utility. The humor of these pastiches resides in that the utility of the map is found in its symbolism rather than through faithful reproduction. "The map is not the territory," goes philosopher Alfred Korzybski's famous quote.[116] Likewise, in *The Sovereign Map*, Christian Jacob argues that an essential difference exists between the map and real space, "a difference indelibly marked by a deficit and an excess, the map being both something less and something more than real space."[117] As an image that is analogical rather than mimetic, the map is the product of an "abstraction that interprets the landscape and makes it intelligible by translating the profusion of what can be observed into a dynamic order of contiguities and relationships."[118]

While this can be understood in the immediate sense that "maps are not mirrors," that they are slippery and duplicitous as J. B. Harley has written, the actual line of separation between the signifier (map) and the signified (territory) is considerably far more difficult to trace.[119]

This misalignment between reality and representation was potently illustrated graphically in René Magritte's work, notably his *Trahison des images* (1928), depicting a pipe captioned with the text "Ceci n'est pas une pipe" (This is not a pipe). One of his most famous paintings, it was the first of a series of prints seeking to challenge the coextensiveness assumed to exist between the signifier and the signified. But perhaps a more apt illustration of these concerns is his later painting, *Les deux mystères* (1966), where the 1928 painting *La Trahison des images* is reproduced, standing on an easel, and is accompanied by a second pipe outside of the painting (figure 1.6). The second pipe may (but may not) be the model of the *Trahison* painting. Similar in shape though not in color, the pipe outside the painting appears disembodied and almost theoretical. By contrast, the pipe within the painting is represented in a more realistic way. More accurate and figurative, it also looks more real. In addition, unlike the second pipe, which lacks coordinates, the pipe in the painting is "wedged solidly in a space of visible reference points."[120] The force of this painting seems to be the potent way in which it severs the link between the model and the reproduction, effectively destabilizing both. To which pipe does the statement "Ceci n'est pas une pipe" now refer—the pipe in the painting or the floating, disembodied model?

Returning to Borges's short story, we see that there as well, the signifier and the signified are barely distinguishable. Vestiges of the map have survived in the desert and are "inhabited by animals and beggars." Like shed skin, these cartographic shreds have become organically part of the territory itself, inhabitable land supplementing the model they sought to symbolize. A realm of animals and beggars, two marginal figures "lodged in its ruined interstices . . . between the map and real space, in the interval of the representation," these map-lands now differ from the territory only hierarchically, not by their nature.[121] In fact, by superposing itself onto existing territory, not only has the map become land itself, but it has replaced the territory. The representation has become the model. The image has become more real than the real.[122]

This assimilation of the image to the real—and the consequent emergence of the hyperreal—is discussed at length by Jean Baudrillard in *Simulacres et simulation*. Baudrillard breaks down this transformation into several stages.

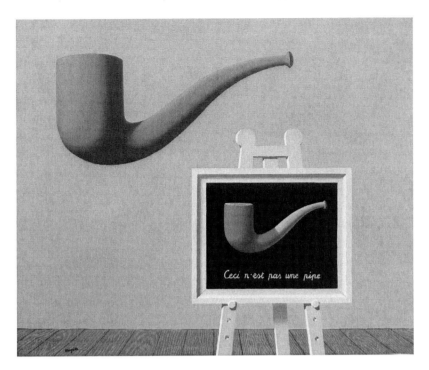

1.6. René Magritte, *Les deux mystères* (1966).

From the reflection of a true reality (*réalité profonde*), the image begins to mask and distort that reality. Later it masks the very absence of reality and, finally, it comes to stand as a pure simulacrum, without a connection to any reality whatsoever.[123] Revisiting Borges's story, Baudrillard argues that the territory no longer precedes the map nor survives it. It is the real, and not the map, whose vestiges subsist here and there in the desert. It is the territory itself whose shreds are slowly rotting across the map.[124]

Following Geoff King, I would contest the claim that an initial stage ever existed when the map was the representation of a "true reality"—or indeed that the territory ever anticipated the map.[125] Maps have played a key role in colonizing new territories by portraying, ahead of actual exploration, entire continents as blank spaces or, alternatively, as places inhabited by monsters or fantastical creatures.[126] Nonetheless, Baudrillard's portrayal "à la Dorian Gray" of a territory slowly decaying across the map makes for a powerful image. This analogy was developed in yet another version of the tale, employed here as a political allegory. In this instance, the map was created as a present for Joseph Stalin's seventieth birthday and was unrolled at night on December 21, 1949, by Internal Ministry soldiers: "Some suggest that due to certain natural causes and the negligence of the keepers, the map gradually deteriorated and that today only fading fragments of it can be seen in distant parts of the state. . . . Others believe, on the contrary, that the map, which was made of Stalitex® (light, firm plastic) has survived but that it was the country that deteriorated and began to decay. The gigantic map exists and underneath it, the remnants of the state keep decaying like the body of a fossilized creature."[127] In this particular version of the story, the map takes precedence over the actual territory and conceals the reality it purports to represent. The map has fared well, whereas the land below is slowly decaying. This is plainly a satire of Soviet realities where official statistics and five-year plans typically depicted ideal conditions that failed to match people's experiences. This story also echoes descriptions of contemporary Russia, notably in the writings of political strategist Alexander Dugin, who has analogized post-Soviet Russia as a moribund simulacrum.[128] It is also reflected in the prose of Ukrainian writer and poet Yuri Andrukhovych, who wrote that the Soviet Union, "having been denied its external face," survives in spectral form in people's brains at the subcortical level.[129]

I have devoted considerable space to these multiple versions of Borges's short story because they all speak to the contradictions inherent to cartography, not only to the aspiration of reproducing objectively a reality "out there," but also to the unexpected ways in which the maps can simulate, conceal, anticipate, replace, and stand in for the territory they represent. Deeply embedded in practices of knowledge and power, the map has also become, as I noted earlier, second nature. Thus whereas Magritte insisted that the figurative representation was merely an ensemble of lines, not the object itself, the map in fact takes precedence over the realities of the territory. The map, in effect, has become the territory itself (figure 1.7).[130]

As I will be developing below as well as through the next chapters, it is precisely through this symbolic equivalence that the map gains its force. Marc Monmonier's quote at the beginning of this chapter illuminates this unambiguously. It is through the existence of the map that the object gains reality. In fact, as Geoff King notes, the lines traced on the map occasionally come to acquire an existence on the ground as well. Thus the Four Corners Monument celebrates the geographical point where four states—Utah, Colorado, Arizona, and New Mexico—intersect at right angles; a site of no particular significance on the ground but a "place of mathematical perfection on the map of the United States."[131]

1.7. "Ceci est la France."

THE POWER OF (LOGO)MAPS

Over the last decades historians and cartographers have increasingly drawn attention in their work to the inherent power of maps. Although the core concern of this book is not how maps are wielded but how they have become "constitutive of the very being of modern subjects," a brief overview of the social, political, and cultural reverberations of cartography's discursive realm is nonetheless useful.[132] In this book I seek to go beyond a top-down approach and draw attention to popular affective engagement with maps, and particularly logomaps, and the ways in which this affect is experienced and described as visceral. However it would be disingenuous to excise the potent, and very real, affective molding imparted by the state. I have in mind in particular the discursive isomorphism between the territory and the male, cisgender, heterosexual, and normative body of the citizen—representations that are powerful and that routinely silence and suppress other bodies, as Judith Butler has discussed in the forms of communal grieving experienced following 9/11.[133]

As I develop in subsequent chapters and particularly in chapter 5, cartographic representations matter. Noncontiguous fragments, including fetishized and disputed ones such as Russia's Kuril Islands, frequently fall out of political maps.[134] In fact, if the power of cartography can be deliberately harnessed for propaganda purposes, it can also have more benign origins, such as being prompted by particular design choices, with accidental and unintentional consequences that can nonetheless have broad and long-lasting repercussions. A fitting example is the Mercator projection discussed earlier, where a purely pragmatic enlargement of the Northern Hemisphere's landmass unwittingly gave undue emphasis to that region, to the detriment of tropical zones. In the same way, the standard practice of northward orientation bestows symbolic and cognitive precedence on the Northern Hemisphere.[135] The reversal of this cartographic tradition, as in the south-up version of the Hobo-Dyer equal-area projection map (figure 1.8) potently illustrates the symbolic values embedded in orientation. In this alternative map, Australia is given visual precedence, while Russia, the United States, and particularly Europe are flattened into insignificance, relegated to the margins.[136] Richard Francaviglia has noted that logomaps can be reversed horizontally without any adverse effect.[137] By contrast, turn them upside down, and they are no longer recognizable. In this sense, logomaps are perceived in a similar way to faces—an important point developed further in chapter 2.

The power visually inherent to maps is also deliberately harnessed by various actors not limited to governments. In an influential article Judith Tyner famously coined the phrase "persuasive cartography" to refer to the willful manipulation of cartographic elements through distortion, selection, symbolization, and typography in order to attain particular goals.[138] These practices, she argued, often associated with wartime propaganda, are also routinely employed by advertisers to sell their products, and even theologians to illustrate certain beliefs.[139] It is commonplace for map publishers themselves to engage in such practices in order to protect their intellectual copyrights, in the event a competitor should attempt to copy their maps.[140] Thus even well-respected maps, such as the London A to Z street map, contains so-called trap streets, small, fictitious cul-de-sacs and alleyways that exist only on the map. As they are out of the way, these phantom additions are rarely noticed by the public and generally remain inconsequential.[141] But in some rare cases cartographic falsification may have far-reaching effects. For example, at the time of Australia's gold rush, it was through a deliberately misleading map that Melbourne supplanted Geelong as state capital. As the

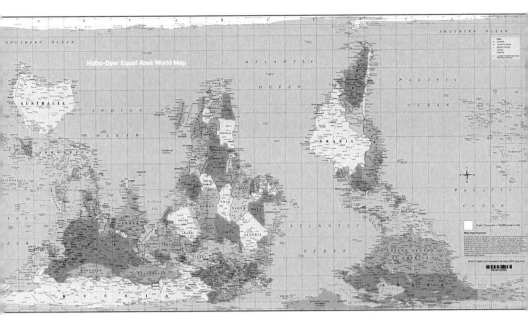

1.8. Hobo-Dyer equal-area projection map.

map portrayed Melbourne as the town closest to the Ballarat gold fields, it grew much faster as a result.[142]

Tyner's concept of persuasive cartography is germane to the notion of "magic geography" introduced by Hans Speir, who as early as 1941 had already pointed out the numerous techniques by which mapmakers could influence their publics.[143] They could, for instance, exaggerate a sense of threat through a clever exploitation of symbols, choice of color, thickness of boundaries, or use of arrows. These techniques were routinely used during the Cold War by both the United States and the Soviet Union—the former through the Mercator projection inflating Soviet territory and portraying it as a looming menace, the latter through color, suggesting encirclement. The Soviet Union was particularly wont to "cartographic creativity," going in fact to great lengths to distort its maps.[144] Coastlines were altered, and latitudes and longitudes were frequently represented incorrectly, while the position of rivers, railroad hubs, and bridges was slightly altered.[145]

Mapping has also commonly been used as a powerful device to make territorial claims. The serious and occasionally devastating consequences of cartographic aggression—a term referring to the inclusion on a map of a territory under the control of a neighboring country—are testament to the symbolic force exerted by maps. China's new official passport, issued in late 2012, bears a watermark map that has set off diplomatic disputes with several of its neighbors. The map portrays the island of Taiwan as well as territories claimed by India, Vietnam, and the Philippines as within China's territory. This new map led to a flurry of diplomatic protests: Vietnam and the Philippines refused to stamp the new travel document, while India decided to stamp its own version of the map on visas issued to Chinese citizens.[146] Such incidents are by no means isolated.[147] Cartographic claims through official maps and postage stamps have routinely led to political storms or to open warfare.[148] Given the volatile emotions attached to the logomap, third parties have to be particularly attentive to these issues in their own cartographies. Kashmir, disputed by India, Pakistan, and China, is a case in point, and in the maps they produce of Kashmir, mapmakers such as Google or Apple need to exercise extreme caution in their labeling and placement of boundary lines lest this be interpreted as giving support to one claim over another. The color of the disputed region must also appropriately contrast with that of the surrounding countries, to ensure it does not show as part of any country's logomap.

The potency of cartographic aggression is perhaps best exemplified by the appropriation of vast territories in the New World in the seventeenth and eighteenth centuries. As European colonial powers penetrated deeper and deeper inland, physical occupation of land was paralleled by cartographic representations. Maps frequently anticipated empire insofar as they were used in colonial promotion, and lands were claimed on paper before they were effectively occupied.[149] Early maps were thus replete with blank spaces that fired intellectual curiosity and appeared wide open for conquest.[150] The term *terrae incognitae*, Christian Jacob writes, inscribed on hypothetical continents and the innermost recesses of landmasses, was "a way of foretelling future knowledge, of submitting this space to a particular temporality, that of the perfectibility of knowledge and the linear and continuous progress of discovery."[151]

Evocations of plenty were visually conveyed through the use of illustrative margins and cartouches depicting riches such as gold, tobacco, and sugarcane as well as through the recurrent use of the symbol of the cornucopia.[152] Cartographic representations also showed these lands swept clean of their inhabitants, thus portraying this enormous wealth as ready for the taking and turning the map's blank spaces into potentially white spaces.[153] As Brian Harley argued, wilderness was tamed on paper even before it had been encountered, and maps often ran ahead of the settled frontier, preceding the ax and the plow.[154] Effectively, the Americas were not discovered but invented, and cartography was an essential ingredient of this discursive construction.[155]

Mapping was not only useful to take possession of distant lands. It also played a significant role in "internal colonialism." Cartographic portrayals of the nation as a discrete and "evenly operative" entity directly led to a hardening of borders as well as to the absorption, displacement, and extermination of frontier populations.[156] As the rigidness of the nation's borders on the map required similar cultural and ethnic discontinuities on the ground, much effort has typically been expended by nascent nations to transform their frontiers into fixed, natural borders (see chapter 2).[157] For instance, Benjamin Fortna's studies of late nineteenth-century Turkey persuasively show how a shift in cartographic representations of the Ottoman Empire rapidly led to a geopolitical reframing.[158] Whereas older maps had consistently portrayed the Ottoman domains as marginal lands on the fringes of Europe, Asia, and Africa, school maps produced in the mid-1890s depicted, for the first time, the Ottoman Empire in its entirety.[159] The empire now "appeared as a single, large and coherent territory, forming an arc which encompassed all of the land surrounding the eastern Mediterranean and beyond."[160] Implying territorial solidity and permanence as well as coherence of religious and cultural identities, this graphic visualization of the empire in the form of a logomap greatly facilitated the emergence of Turkish nationalism.[161]

In her fascinating work on Indian cartography, Sumathi Ramaswamy retraces through national representations the emergence of "map-mindedness" in India. As she illustrates, Indians in both the colonial and postcolonial period "succumbed to the lure of cartography," echoing the contemporaneous developments seen in Thailand, China, Turkey, and elsewhere.[162] While she recognizes that modern patriotism requires important technology of persuasion and that, undeniably, the map of the national territory is an especially compelling one, Ramaswamy poses a fundamental question, which in fact underlies the core concerns of this book, namely, "How does the scientific map with its representation of 'India' as abstract, empty and dead social space foster the sentiment of belonging and possession which is so crucial to the imagined community of the nation? How is it possible for the citizen-subject who obviously stands abstracted from the nation-space, viewing it from a point *outside*, to come to see this space as his 'homeland,' *inside* which he belongs. . . . How can the citizen-subject feel moved enough to give up his life for a map?"[163]

Ramaswamy argues that the logomap constitutes a profoundly unhomely representation of the nation, "emptied of quotidian meanings and local attachments and, most consequentially, voided of prior sentiments of longing and belonging."[164] Her assessment thus closely echoes J. B. Harley's analysis of the logomap as a "socially empty space" and his more general point that maps tend to privilege space over place.[165] For Ramaswamy, this very lack explains the emergence of what she refers to as "barefoot cartography," that is, late nineteenth- and early twentieth-century practices that contrasted with the instruments of surveillance, measurement, and inscription of modern cartography. These alternative practices supplemented, and frequently disrupted, state cartography with anthropomorphic, devotional, and maternal images and typically portrayed the national logomap as a woman, often as a mother or goddess.[166] These images, which circulated in the form of cartoons, newspaper mastheads, posters, and calendars, were for the average Indian citizen the first encounter with a cartographic representation of the nation.[167] Ramaswamy argues that these practices lastingly invested the national contour with patriotic affect, even as they were often transgressive and paid "scant regard to national borders and boundaries" and occasionally subversively undid or dissolved them.[168] Unlike the rational and abstract, bounded entity confined to a fixed graticular grid on the earth's surface, these barefoot cartographies were able to harness emotions and evoke imaginaries as well as a sense of enchantment.[169]

Ramaswamy's argument is intriguing, and the abstract, void ("disembodied") logomap would indeed seem to be a poor support of national affect. Yet investment in the national shape endures despite the modern logomap having largely displaced earlier barefoot cartographic practices.[170] That Indian attachments to the national borders remain as strong as ever would in fact suggest that the logomap can, and indeed does, act as an apt vector of patriotic sentiments. This hypothesis appears to be supported by ethnographic data from other cultural regions where earlier anthropomorphic maps, in Europe, Thailand, and elsewhere (see chapter 2), have also been supplanted by the abstract logomap without incurring any significant loss of affective investment. Indeed, as I develop in chapter 2, if the Indian case presents certain cultural and historical specificities, the early juxtaposition of political maps and corporeal imagery is not unique to India. The national map and the body have in fact a long history of intimate cohabitation.

The abstract logomap may have replaced the barefoot cartography Ramaswamy discusses in her work, but its poetic properties (which Jacob describes as its oneiric and mythic implications) have endured. The very emptiness of the logomap makes it a perfect container, a "privileged space of projection for the viewer's desires, aspirations, and affective and cultural memories."[171] Further, as I discuss in chapter 2, the somatic connection that helped channel national affect subsists in other, more subtle, metaphoric ways. No longer crudely portraying nation-states in anthropomorphic or zoomorphic form, we continue to refer to territorial loss as mutilation, or speak of national DNA. The monsters lurking around islands and continents also survive in the unholy shapes of some of the world's logomaps, as I discuss in the next chapter, as well as in the unrepresentable spaces beyond (but still pertaining to) the nation, which I foreground in the final chapter.

2

THE GODDESS, THE BOOT, AND THE SQUARE

At midday they arrived within sight of their destination. The land had
been flat, but now the whole area rose to a towering peak on the
horizon.... It stood up from the ground, bulging and bristling, its walls
veined by blue streaks. So vast, so steep, so mighty that it seemed a
new world rising out of the old; a world of its own; beautiful and men-
acing. A vast erection of the earth....
"Do you like it?" asked Pill, with an inflection that denoted contempt.
"Yes," Gombold said. "Don't you?" ...
"I thought it'd be bigger. It's not what I expected."

—Joe Orton, *From Head to Toe*

Following the breakup of the Soviet Union in 1989, former Soviet republics
suddenly appeared on world maps as independent nations, complete with
international boundaries and individual logomaps. One of the most unusual
of these new political entities was perhaps Turkmenistan. Unlike its neighbors that showed eagerness to open up to the world and become recognized
independent states, Turkmenistan became inward-looking and increasingly
autarchic. Under the leadership of Saparmurat Niyazov, in power from 1990
to 2006, the country rapidly turned into a surreal political entity worthy of
Orwell. Several monumental buildings were erected in honor of the leader,
with one of them in particular—a gilded statue of the president-for-life that
rotated with the movement of the sun—dominating the Turkmen capital
Ashgabat.

Eager to bolster his hold on power, Niyazov began to refer to himself as Turkmenbashi (Türkmenbaşy in Turkmen), that is, "head of all Turkmen," and proceeded to rename countless places throughout Turkmenistan after himself. By the time of his death in 2006, at least ten towns, a river, a mountain, a bay in the Caspian Sea, and even a star in the Ursa Major constellation had been renamed Turkmenbashi. In cities and urban settings, various squares, parks, streets, and other public places carried his name, as did countless buildings and institutions—airports, schools, museums, banks, and stadiums—as well as artistic ensembles, agricultural cooperatives, and factories.[1] Along with his name, his face became virtually omnipresent, adorning all banknotes, basic foodstuffs, and vodka, and a golden outline of his profile was stamped on the top right-hand corner of every TV channel. Through lexical and pictorial means, Niyazov effectively signaled his intention to achieve semantic equivalence with the Turkmen territory. Blurring the boundaries between himself and Turkmenistan's geographic materiality, he even sought to extend this isomorphic quality to a temporal level, renaming the month of January after himself.

Niyazov's project, absurd as it might appear, was in fact a typical, if extreme, deployment of authoritarian regimes. If Niyazov tried to stamp his physical imprint on the face of the capital, he was not the first ruler to try to do so. During World War II, Mussolini had a building erected in the shape of an M in Latina, a city he founded in the Pontine Marshes, in the south of Rome. Mussolini's intention was to extend construction to spell out his whole name across the city—an ambition he ultimately failed to see through. One also recalls the central somatic role played by Mao's and Lenin's bodies in the context of their embalming.[2] Closer to us, we might also think of Donald J. Trump, who throughout his presidency installed his own body at the core of political debates and revealed, through raw/unpresidential practices, something fundamental about the state.[3] The Trump presidency has been largely interpreted as "un-American"—a blip in the history of the United States—but this compartmentalization in fact reproduces "a long European tradition of projecting the most extreme forms of political despotism and otherness onto non-Western societies and imagining beyond the edges of the European universe oddly passive or irrational peoples who mysteriously accept intolerable regimes."[4] In fact, as Natalie Koch points out, there is a long American tradition of "personality cults."[5] The United States are clearly not immune to "Stan-the-absurd" political scripts.[6]

Indeed, fascist projects might strike us as dystopian and narcissistic, but they speak to the well-established link between the state and the sovereign body. As Ariella Azoulay writes, the figure of the sovereign making their mark on political space is familiar to us since antiquity, and evidence of this dimension of sovereign power survives, including in contemporary democratic contexts, in the right to build monuments and effect changes in the built-up space. She notes that in contemporary France, for instance, the *fait du prince* refers to the right of the president to erect monuments without official tender or civil agreement: "The sovereign is entitled to this privilege as long as he makes measured, controlled use of it. The monument is supposed to glorify the president through the pleasure and benefit he bestows on all citizens."[7]

In a groundbreaking book, Eric Santner argues the complex symbolic structures and dynamics of sovereignty did not "simply disappear from the space of polities once the body of the king [was] no longer available as the primary incarnation of the principle and functions of sovereignty." Instead, they migrated to a new location, assuming "a turbulent and disorienting semiotic density previously concentrated in the 'strange material and physical presence' of the king."[8] A central problem, writes Santner, is then to "learn how to track the vicissitudes of these *royal remains* in their now-dispersed and ostensibly secularized, disenchanted locations."[9]

This particular concern is at the very core of this chapter. I briefly sketched in chapter 1 the important sea change that saw the body of the sovereign gradually replace that of Christ on maps, imparting a secular orientation to the linkage between body and territory. In turn, Ernst Kantorowicz's magisterial study *The King's Two Bodies* has been critical in tracing the gradual shift whereby the notion of the body of Christ came to mold the contours of the secular state and its institutions—even though a "whiff of incense" has continued to permeate secular entities.[10] Kantorowicz demonstrates in particular how kingship remained endowed with the sublime aura of the ecclesiastical realm and how the practices of juridical speech became the new locus of performative magic.[11] Of particular significance to this chapter's argument and to the overall concern of the book is how corporeal analogies, despite this shift, also remained central to (equally evolving) notions of territorial sovereignty. Later still, democratization processes marked another shift, this time away from the body of the king to the body of the citizen, yet without a notable loss of the articulatory link between body and territory.[12] This somatic undercarriage, this book argues, helps account for the ways in which attachment to the state's territory, particularly loss of territory or the impermeability of borders, is routinely described in corporeal language and experienced so viscerally. My central argument in this chapter is that the concept of body has been routinely employed as a support of political affect, providing a tangible material presence to the state.[13] But as the next chapters progressively make clear, the body itself is an imaginary anatomy insofar as it is also culturally constructed.[14] What we have then, ironically, is an imaginary propped up by another imaginary.[15]

The conceptual enmeshment of the body and the political is of course not a particularly novel argument. A sizable literature already traces the corporeal metaphors smuggled into the political from the bodily register and vice versa. Emily Martin's work on how military metaphors have shaped an imaginary of disease, or Ed Cohen's study on the legal/medical interface of the concept of immunity have been especially generative.[16] But what is especially fascinating about these entanglements is how both concepts are transformed in the process.[17] Mark Neocleous notes that the concept of immunity, for instance, despite being "transported into the world of biology," did not lose "its foothold in the legal and political world" and that the biological notion of immunity ended up being "reinterpreted in all sorts of political ways."[18]

The corporeal undercarriage that endures in the evolution of political theory—from Christ (or other religious figure) to the monarch to the citizen— is shifting and labile. Old metaphors give way to new metaphors, reflecting dominant cultural understandings of the body and personhood. The seemingly self-evident imagery to think of the body and disease in military terms, for instance, is in fact quite recent and did not become central until the second half of the nineteenth century. Previously the dominant metaphor in European views of medicine articulated around the notion of an imbalance between humors (blood, phlegm, black bile, and yellow bile)—offering a more holistic view of the body.[19] As the concept of the body becomes increasingly frayed in the arc of the book's narrative, I will suggest in the last chapter that the recent work of philosophers on more-than-human entanglements and symbiotic assemblages might offer a more productive set of metaphors to think of territorial sovereignty and political geography.

But what emerges clearly in this chapter is that the metaphoric link between body and territory is resilient and is not confined to a particular place or time.[20] Histories of cartography have understandably focused largely on the European experience since it provided a particular model to much of the rest of the world, in part via imperialism and colonialism. In order to gain recognition and commensurability, non-European states (and postcolonial states in particular) had to redefine their traditional notions of territoriality in line with Western views. As Thongchai Winichakul shows in his important book *Siam Mapped*, premodern Thai geography placed little to no importance on borders and boundaries—indeed, like premodern European geographies—since sovereignty and a bounded territory were not cotermi-nous.[21] It is only after the second half of the nineteenth century, as Thailand became involved in territorial disputes with European powers, that the idea of a bounded territorial entity with inviolable borders became dominant.

The image on the cover of *Siam Mapped*, depicting a human-shaped Viet-nam attempting to devour the body of Thailand, could only gain its visual potency once the concept of a bounded sovereign space had emerged and sta-bilized. To be viscerally understood as an impending threat, it also required an organic melding of state and people in the form of the concept of the nation-state, as I unpack later in this chapter. The term *geobody*, coined by Thongchai Winichakul to convey the organic undercarriage of the logomap, gave expression to a set of implicit but largely unreflected-on assumptions about the nature of the modern state and territorial sovereignty. Instantly comprehensible and seamlessly translatable across cultural contexts, the idea of a geobody quickly became a useful tool to track the emergence and further the analysis of modern statehood and territorial sovereignty in a wide range of environments.[22]

As I argue in this chapter, the evolution of visual representations in the context of Thailand echoed transformations elsewhere, as the work of schol-ars has shown for Turkey, Mongolia, India, Palestine, and other places. My aim in providing this wide range of examples is primarily to emphasize the ease and rapidity with which this global shift occurred—suggesting that an interpretation narrowly focused on colonialism, or indeed on formal educa-tion, is not sufficient.

Accounts from Tibet, India, China, and elsewhere thus show frequent overlays of deities and other celestial bodies on the land through a host of bodily metaphors, allegories, and similes. The traditional recounting of the introduction of Buddhism from India into Tibet, for instance, is narrated in a clearly anthropomorphic manner. According to tradition, the demoness Srin-mo, ruling over Tibet, was particularly resistant to the new faith and had to be subdued. The territory of Tibet was conceived as formed by the vast supine body of the demoness, making the two coextensive and indistin-guishable. The king, feeling that the demoness was resisting Buddhism and was waving her arms and legs, decided to place edifices on her land-body in order to pin her down and physically immobilize her: "The buildings on her shoulders and hips will suppress the four main sectors. . . . Those on her knees and elbows will control the four borders . . . those on her hands and feet, the four further borders. . . . Thus is articulated an elaborate scheme of thirteen Buddhist temples, with the Jo-khang poised on her heart, and with three concentric squares encompassing the Tibetan map: the center, the inner realm, the borders, and the borders beyond."[23] A similar topographic delineation of the anatomy of a divine being was also involved in the context of Beijing. Yamantāka, one of the most formidable creations of Tantric imagination, was believed to be reflected in the Chinese capital's city plan. Numerous correspondences and analogies were read between Beijing's architecture and the god's body, such as the rectangular plan of the city reflecting Yamantāka's rectangular face, or the numerous streets and lanes radiating from the Forbidden City like so many arms and legs.[24]

Mary Douglas has convincingly argued that the margins of the human body and the boundaries of the social exist in a synecdochic relationship, and indeed research from many parts of the world bears out the premise that the ordering of space takes the body as primary model.[25] Like many other languages, English shows a consistent overlap between parts of the body and the landscape. Terms such as *body of water, river mouth, face of the earth*, or even *foot* to designate the base of a mountain are so deeply sedimented in language that the original metaphors are no longer seen as such. A similar process appears to be at work in non-European cultures as well, where it can even be more extensive.[26]

These discursive parallels, cognitive linguists and anthropologists have persuasively argued, are likely to have emerged out of a corporeal experience. The concepts of top, bottom, left, right, inside, and outside are thus first learned in terms of the body and then extended to the wider environment.[27] With few exceptions, emotional states such as happiness or sadness are mapped as up or down in ways that transcend cultural differences.[28] This does not mean of course that these bodily orientations are all mapped in the same way, and we see in fact much cultural variation across both time and space.[29] While many conceptual metaphors appear to be near-universal, metaphorical linguistic expressions vary cross-culturally since people do not use their cognitive capacities in the same way from culture to culture.[30] Cross-linguistic and cross-cultural surveys of the concept of a body politic thus reveal competing analogies showing variation both between cultural environments and between individuals in a given linguistic and national context.[31] Yet what emerges from these surveys is a widely shared assumption that body and state (or land, or nation) are commensurable if not wholly isomorphic, suggesting deeply embedded practices of corporeal mapping of space.

I argue in this chapter that this cognitive undercarriage helps account for the ease with which political ideas formed in a European context became naturalized in a range of environments, how notions like the geobody were integrated so smoothly culturally, and how territorial loss came to be experienced so viscerally. Linguistic metaphors impart a certain orientation, an interpretive grid to make sense of the world, with the body constituting a crucial and universal resource of metaphoric vehicles. Employing corporeal metaphors in such an extensive and wide-ranging manner creates associative patterns between the state and clusters of organic features that dialogically reinforce one another in ways that extend well beyond formal instruction.

I unpack later in this chapter the complex ways in which continual use of a metaphor tends to give what was originally a mere analogy the appearance of being literally true.[32] The central argument I make in this book is that political space is suffused with organic metaphors to such a degree that the state ends up being perceived as quasi-organic. I discuss below the continued relevance of sedimented and lexicalized metaphors such as *head of state* or *nerve center* and how new metaphors and analogies coined around modern views of the body continue to emerge—suggesting their usage remains relevant. I show that this organicity is then further reinforced through the notion of the nation-state, which fuses together the political and the corporeal through an array of organic accoutrements such as national fauna and flora. Given shape through the contours of the state—its geobody—the nation-state is thus more than a mere logo. Its reiterative usage endows it with a kin-like aura, molding it into the reflective familiar embodiment of the citizens themselves.

SOMATOPOLITICS

In the late nineteenth and early twentieth centuries, Europe witnessed a sudden explosion of anthropomorphic and zoomorphic maps (see figures 2.1–2.3). These political maps sought to represent the geopolitical situation of the time through caricatures of national characters. These representations were mostly human, but occasionally also animal, particularly to emphasize a threat. The *Serio-Comic War Map for the Year 1877* (figure 2.3), which became known as the Octopus Map, shows Russia as a large octopus, its tentacles "stretching out in all directions, grasping at the most accessible parts of Europe."[33] The other characters in the map are caricatures of their respective nations: Turkey is a swarthy gun-toting pirate, Holland a gentle land of windmills, and Italy is depicted as child playing with a toy in the shape of the pope, while Spain sleeps, her back to the rest of Europe.[34]

Once very popular, by the end of World War II these maps had completely disappeared from the European cultural landscape. Today they often strike

2.1. Paul-Joseph Hadol, *Carte drôlatique d'Europe pour 1870* (1870).

2.2. C. Schmidt, *Das heutige Europa* (1887).

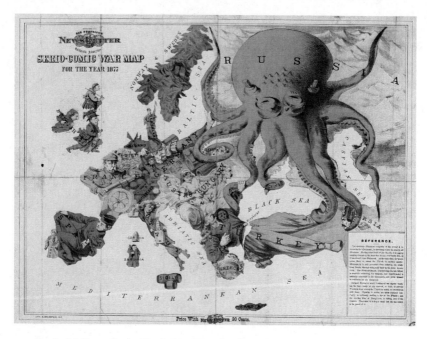

2.3. Frederick Rose, *Serio-Comic War Map for the Year 1877*.

us as somewhat grotesque and crude—their particular brand of humor no
longer making them useful vectors of political messages. As historian Antoine de Baecque notes, the ontological vehemence of metaphors is firmly
linked to a particular historical moment.[35] And so, in the same way that
the theomorphic model of the medieval T-O maps eventually gave way to
anthropomorphic and zoomorphic maps, they lost their cultural relevance
and mostly faded away.

It is perhaps no accident that the efflorescence of anthropomorphic maps
corresponded closely with a period of political instability in Europe. From
the mid-nineteenth to the beginning of the twentieth century, European
international borders were in constant flux. Europe saw the collapse of the
Austro-Hungarian Empire (1918) and the Ottoman Empire (1922) and the
disappearance of Prussia (1932) as well as the waxing and waning of Poland.
Faced with such instability, anthropomorphic and zoomorphic maps were
crucial to reassure viewers about the timeless and intrinsically natural quality of their nations.[36] The final settling of European borders eventually made
such maps redundant, and the constant graphic reiteration of the logomap
in corporeal form much less crucial.[37]

2.4. Kent Barton, editorial cartoon, *Miami Herald*, September 4, 1983.

A less common occurrence of the logomap in animate form does not imply, however, that the conceptual link between body and nation has been weakened, let alone severed. In fact this corporeal imagery often reemerges in times of crisis or to drive home a particular political point. As tension peaked between the United States and the Soviet Union in the 1980s, for instance, the Russian bearmotif suddenly became dominant once again in the American media. When the USSR shot down a Korean passenger plane in 1983, for instance, the *Miami Herald* depicted the Soviets as a ferocious bear crushing a plane in its jaws (figure 2.4). The 2022 attack on Ukraine similarly saw the reappearance of the bear as visual index of political threat—one particularly powerful example being the depiction of a giant bear stepping on a Ukrainian Lego brick (figure 2.5). Mobilizing the cultural association of Russia with a bear and the all-too-recognizable routine trauma of parents stepping on kids' toys, this image very quickly turned into an Internet meme.

The representation of Russia as a bear can be traced back to European travel writings that, as early as the sixteenth century, propagated the notion that bears roamed Russian streets. The metaphor of the bear was used extensively in political cartoons from the nineteenth century, and especially during the

2.5. Paweł Jońca, editorial cartoon of a giant Russian bear stepping on a Ukrainian Lego brick.

Cold War, as a symbol of cruelty and bloodthirstiness.[38] On the occasion of the 1980 Moscow Olympic Games, Russia embraced this totemic animal but reframed it as a symbol of strength and bravery. The choice of a mascot in the form of a teddy bear named Misha was clearly intended to counter the image of Russia as a big and brutal beast.[39] The brute force of the Russian bear remains very present, however, as Vladimir Putin made abundantly clear in a very zoomorphic manner when, a few months before the attack on Ukraine, he threatened to knock the teeth out of anyone trying to bite parts of Russia away.[40]

In a similar attempt to soften its image for the 2008 Olympics, China toyed with the idea of replacing its national animal, the dragon. Although 90 percent of the 100,000 polled respondents voted to keep the dragon as the national symbol, the Olympics committee eventually selected five less controversial mascots, the so-called five friendlies (*fuwa*): the fish, the panda, the Tibetan antelope, the swallow, and the flame.[41] Over the past decades, the symbol of the panda especially has increasingly been associated with China's nation-state even though, unlike the dragon, the giant panda is not an animal of prominent ancient symbolic importance and "does not conjure up metaphorical meanings."[42] But with its cute and nonthreatening face, it has proven an invaluable diplomatic tool.

The dragon remains, however, central as a symbol of China, particularly in political analyses where the country is described as an actor in geopolitical struggles. Headlines such as "Racing the Elephant against the Dragon" (*The Economist*, February 2015), "The Eagle and the Dragon" (*The Economist*, November 2021), or *The Bear Watches the Dragon* (a 2003 book by Alexander Lukin) are testament to this practice of using animals indexically. The visual immediacy of such animal representations relies of course on cultural assumptions such as the organicity of nation-states and the notion that a group of people living on a given territory share innate and immutable traits with a particular animal, as I unpack further in the following section. The zoomorphic maps discussed above were created largely for propaganda purposes and are thus generally exogenous in origin, with derogatory associations, but animals can also have symbolic meanings and emphasize national characteristics. In Korea there is, for instance, a strong tradition, dating back to the Japanese annexation of Korea, to portray the country cartographically as a tiger in order to emphasize qualities of strength and courage.[43]

Another zoomorphic element that has shown strong resilience is the figure of the octopus. Appearing for the first time in the 1877 map shown in figure 2.3, in the midst of the Russo-Turkish War, this potent visualization in fact launched a trend of cartographic cephalopods. Perhaps speaking to "humanity's primeval fears [and] evoking a terrifying and mysterious creature from the depths," the figure of the octopus has been used extensively to portray countries or entities hungry for power and seeking to increase their influence.[44] It was used in various contexts, including as a critique of the British and French colonial empires, and as a way to convey a sense of threat from an advancing Soviet Union in the 1980s (figure 2.6). It has recently become prominent again as I am writing this book, as Russia is waging war on Ukraine. Originally published in 2008 at the time of the Russo-Georgian War, a graphic showing Putin as an octopus with tentacles on former Soviet republics remains timely (figure 2.7).[45]

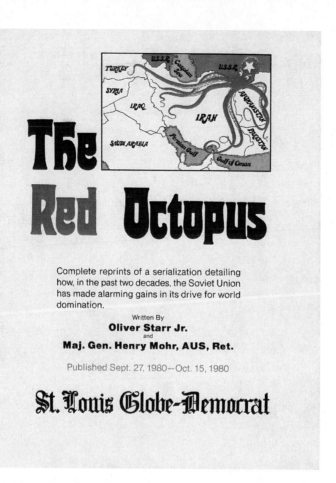

The Red Octopus

Complete reprints of a serialization detailing how, in the past two decades, the Soviet Union has made alarming gains in its drive for world domination.

Written By
Oliver Starr Jr.
and
Maj. Gen. Henry Mohr, AUS, Ret.

Published Sept. 27, 1980—Oct. 15, 1980

𝔖t. 𝔏ouis 𝔊lobe-𝔇emocrat

2.6. The Soviet Union as a red octopus (*St. Louis Globe-Democrat*, pamphlet, 1980).

I wrote earlier that the anthropomorphic and zoomorphic maps of the late nineteenth and early twentieth centuries strike us today as simplistic and crude in their portrayals of state outlines in organic form. The need to emphasize this organicity may no longer be seen as crucial—at least, as I mentioned earlier, in contexts where state borders are perceived as lastingly stable—but the disappearance of these maps does not index the obsolescence of the model, merely the depth to which it has become embedded and internalized. Similarly, I would argue that a dismissal of metaphors like *head of state*, *organs of the state*, or *nerve center* as linguistic fossils without any contemporary relevance is a little hasty. Analytical studies of metaphors by linguists and cognitive psychologists have demonstrated that unreflected and

2.7. Petr Polák, Putin as octopus.

linguistically entrenched associations tend to be especially powerful in naturalizing views of the world.[46] That somatic analogies continue to emerge in
lexical coinages that resonate with a modern understanding of the body show
in fact that the body remains a powerful source of analogies to conceptualize
the political.[47] I am thinking in particular of the metaphor of *national DNA*,
which I first heard used by Cindy McCain during the American presidential
campaign of 2008, and which has since gained considerable currency.[48] Other
bodily metaphors with a definitive modern slant include *bypass*, *syndrome*,
or *virus*.[49] Far from inert, then, sedimented and fossilized metaphors cohabit
with other corporeal associations within a broader constellation of organic
similes and metaphors of the state. This deep and extensive enmeshment of
the political and the corporeal, what I refer to here as somatopolitics, is clearly
indebted to European political ruminations on the notion of the body politic.

The concept of body politic was popularized through many texts in the
Middle Ages and later, such as John of Salisbury's *Policraticus* (c. 1159), Thomas
Aquinas's *On Kingship* and *Summary of Theology* (c. 1266–73), Shakespeare's
Coriolanus (c. 1605), and Hobbes's *Leviathan* (1651) but harkens back to a
much earlier period, to the writings of Plutarch and to Aesop's tale "The Belly
and the Members." It also shares more than a passing resemblance to stories
and myths found in other parts of the world, as I discuss below.

Aesop's tale describes a community functioning organically as a single
body and in which a one-to-one correspondence exists between political

constituents and bodily organs. The belly of the fable represents the monarch, requiring food while the other organs toil relentlessly. As the hands and feet denounce the belly for doing nothing and refuse to give it any more food, the whole body starts to waste away. The fable thus clearly argues for the preservation of the existing order and underscores the established and definite role of each organ. Importantly, it also proposes a corporeal analogy to the workings of the state, one that has become dominant, pervasive, and extremely resilient in political discourse. Aesop's fable in fact served as a template for political texts in the following centuries.

Published around 1159, John of Salisbury's *Policraticus* proved especially crucial in the modern evolution of the concept insofar as it was the first treatise of political philosophy in the Middle Ages. In this particular narrative, the prince represents the head of the body, while the other members of the body all stand for parts of the political apparatus: the senate as heart, the soldiers and officials as the hands, and workers as the feet. Widely read during the Middle Ages, *Policraticus* provided inspiration for numerous subsequent works in all kinds of literary genres, from drama, poems, and essays to philosophical treatises, sermons, and political pamphlets.[50] The somatic correlation appears to have gained particular prominence in the sixteenth century in discussions of issues of economics, government, and religion.[51] These works sought to delineate, through organic corporeal analogies, the responsibilities of rulers and their relationship to their subjects. Later writings codified this relationship more precisely, typically with the king as head—or soul in the case of Hobbes's *Leviathan*—and the populace as the body. Varying from one political regime to another, analogies were then extended, with the legal system assimilated to the body's nerves for instance, the military to its arms, and so on.[52] In Tudor and Stuart England, some writers also drew further correspondences between bodily organs and types of citizens, such as, for instance, the tongue with lawyers, commoners, Catholics, unruly women, and witches.[53]

The cartographic transformation described in chapter 1 from royal space to a space organized around the citizens can also be traced here through the body politic analogy. The medieval view of the Christian Church as a body headed by Christ gave way to the idea of the feudal society as a body with Christ's representative (the pope, emperor, or king) as its head. Later, the understanding of the king as possessing both a sacred and a physical body (his body politic and body natural) shifted to the idea of the state itself as body politic, and eventually the nation, that is, its citizens as a whole, taking on that role.[54]

Antoine de Baecque, who traced the shift away from the body of the monarch in revolutionary France, describes how revolutionaries drew a discursive wedge between the two bodies of the king—the political body, on the one hand, and the physical, mortal body, on the other.[55] He shows in particular how rumors of the king's impotence were used by revolutionaries to suggest a fundamental moral and political weakness of the regime. While popular satires on the topic had first appeared in the late 1770s, they gained particular force following the fall of the Bastille. Pamphlets were widely circulated, depicting the king as a limp penis, suggesting that the king's mortal body was unable to match his dynastic responsibilities. But if the defeat of the body of the king represented a major caesura in French political representation, given that procreation was a primary function in a hereditary monarchy, the corporeal metaphor of the body politic did not lose any of its force. It simply transitioned from one regime to another.[56] Indeed, the national conversation that took place on the subject of Trump's penis in 2018 could not make this more explicit.[57]

As Claude Gandelman points out, this equivalence between territory and the king's body was so well established in the sixteenth and seventeenth centuries that it was common to designate the monarch by the name of the country he or she ruled. Thus in Shakespeare's plays *Henry IV* or *Henry V*, the English king is referred to as "England."[58] The stability of the simile has allowed for numerous literary explorations, and authors have staged in various ways and for various purposes imaginary landscapes inspired by the human body. One may recall here the mythical lands peopled by giants in Jonathan Swift's *Gulliver's Travels*, Dante's Inferno representing the body of Satan, or the corporeal universe of modern playwright Joe Orton's *Head to Toe* in the epigraph for this chapter. Particularly relevant for the present argument is Rabelais's use of the simile for satirical motives when he turned the king into a grotesque anthropomorphic geography. His tale *Les horribles et épouvantables faits et prouesses du très renommé Pantagruel Roi des Dipsodes* (1532) depicts the body of glutton and debonair giant Pantagruel as a fantastical landscape, his teeth described as large rocks and his ears as vast forests.[59] As I develop further in chapter 5, Pantagruel's huge and grotesque body, sprawling and uncontained, makes a particularly apt metaphor for a contemporary state obsessed with entry points and orifices.[60] The figure of the giant, whose fragmented body is sprawled across the landscape, is a common theme in a range of cultural texts that posit identity and place as mutually constitutive.[61]

The idea of the body politic has now largely fallen into disuse—at least in its crude original form. Writing in 1971, David Hale argued that the analogy has essentially become a dead metaphor, used only as shorthand for the state, with no further meanings implied or accepted.[62] This assessment feels, however, a little hasty in the current context of populist and right-wing politics. The state may no longer be conceptualized as an organic entity on the model of a human body, but nationalist discourse continues to be framed in terms taken from the corporeal register—this in spite of the cartographic revolution and attendant ascendency of rational mathematical space. The idea of a body politic has largely lost its appeal for social and political discourse, Mark Neocleous writes, for two reasons that are mutually at odds. On the one hand, it feels premodern "and therefore either redundant or irrelevant for the liberal democratic age"; on the other hand, its association with fascist regimes "has rendered it politically suspect."[63] It is thus positioned contradictorily as both ineffective and excessively effective.

One of the most influential attempts to theorize states as living organisms that grow, decay, and die was by German geographer Friedrich Ratzel. Originally trained in the natural sciences, as was indeed typical of German geographers at the time, Ratzel attempted to formulate a synthesis of previous state doctrines inspired, among others, by new insights into zoology and biology as well as by a rapidly growing anthropological and ethnographic literature.[64] Strongly influenced by Darwinism, he came to develop the concept of lebensraum, or living space, arguing that a state's territory was relative to its population size and metabolic needs, and that stronger states naturally expanded to the detriment of weaker ones. Such views were consonant with Germany's nascent nation-state project and thus provided a scientific basis for the argument that Germany needed colonies to make room for its rapidly growing population.[65]

Ratzel's concept of lebensraum was elaborated and further theorized by Swedish political scientist and geographer Rudolf Kjellén, who sought to elucidate in particular the reasons why a given people (*ethnos*) constituted, in Ratzel's terminology, an "aggregated organism." Kjellén rejected genealogical and linguistic reasons given that nations are racially heterogeneous and that language can change over time. In *The State as a Living Organism*, he argued instead for a biological understanding of the nation—an entity that would straddle the geographical, physical, and cultural realms and constitute a "macroanthropos."[66]

Ratzel's and Kjellén's writings have been largely discredited through their association with Nazi ideology, but given their strong imprint on the discipline of political geography, their ideas have proven both resilient and culturally adaptative.[67] The Russian political movement of Eurasianism, originally developed in the 1920s by Russian émigrés and later expounded by historian Lev Gumilev (1912–92), represents, for instance, a more recent attempt at creating a synthesis between geography, history, and the natural sciences. Gumilev defined the *ethnos* as a biophysical reality constituting both a population and a natural phenomenon.[68] In his view, ethnic groups are part of the "biosphere," with particular ethnicities "attached to their areas in the same way animals [are] attached to their habitats."[69] Gumilev's writings on ethnogenesis are well known in the former Soviet cultural sphere, where contemporary conceptualizations of ethnicity and territorial belonging are closely aligned with his thoughts. In Mongolia, for instance, ethnic authenticity is predicated on linkages between individuals, land, local foods, and sustained residence in addition to genetic lineage.[70] Mongols and their country exist in a relationship of corporeal isomorphism that is readily recognizable in a host of cultural settings, including contemporary European and North American contexts.[71]

This isomorphism does not mean that the state is believed to be an actual living entity, even if it often comes discursively close.[72] There is, for instance, a well-established tendency to speak of countries as organisms that are born, grow, thrive, decline, and die. Similarly, terms such as *birth, youth, vigor, decadence, blood,* and *death* commonly refer to the origin, rise, and fall of political nations and empires, cultures and civilizations.[73] As I discuss in more depth in the following chapters, territorial loss is routinely expressed through terms such as dismemberment, maiming, or mutilation; political encirclement is compared to being strangled; and economic or political difficulties are described as illness.[74] It is also common to speak of bringing a nation to its knees, or for nations to struggle to breathe freely, or even to be born and to die.

In a germinal text, Ernest Gellner has also drawn attention to how the nation-state is commonly imagined as a transhistorical entity in spite of its relatively recent emergence. This paradox is generally justified through the claim that the nation was always there; it was merely asleep.[75] Gellner has argued that this very potent imagery has cloaked the nation-state in a veil of naturalness, thereby "transcending the ephemeral beings and generations in which it is transiently incarnated."[76] Intriguingly, the organic undercarriage of this analogy (being asleep) has elicited little scholarly attention, possibly because the somatic metaphor is so pervasive as to have become virtually invisible.

The ostensible naturalness of the state and its boundaries is such that it has become extremely difficult to escape its gravitational pull. Three decades ago John Agnew warned us against viewing the state as a container on account of three related assumptions—that states are fixed units of sovereign space, that there exists a domestic/foreign polarity, and that states are conceptualized as containers of societies.[77] Along similar lines, David Ludden points out in a later piece that this view has also colonized the academy and that scholars have come to work inside that experience. As a result, and I return to this important point in chapter 5, "spaces that elude national maps have mostly disappeared from our intellectual life"—mapping practices having expunged "dissonance from our geographical imagination by invisibly burying disorderly spaces under neat graphics of national order."[78]

The core argument I make in this book is that this seemingly ineluctable force is sustained, on the one hand, by the ubiquitous presence of logomaps and, on the other, by a fusion of the political with the somatic. As such, the logomap is not an abstract representation. It is instead enveloped in an intricate web of corporeal metaphors that have morphed it into a mirror image of the citizen. I discuss later in this chapter the significance of shapes, particularly how some outlines have proven specially powerful on account of their recognizability and iconicity. But regardless of form, constellations of somatic metaphors require a broader framework to latch onto and be articulated around. That framework is the modern concept of the nation-state—the fusion of the principle of territorial sovereignty with that of a sovereignty organized around a specific national community. Without this foundation, as I point out earlier in this chapter, corporeal representations of the state would be simply meaningless.

As the understanding of the state shifted, as it came to be imagined as a discrete, bound area on a map; and as the earlier focus on royalty and elites was replaced by one on national peoples, the assumption of an isomorphic relation between space and society gradually became dominant.[79] As a consequence, if the nation—a somewhat "amorphous, border-transgressive phenomenon"—contrasts with the bounded, uniform state, the two terms are often used interchangeably in practice.[80] As states became nation-states, the corporeal associations shifted from the body of the sovereign to that of the population as a whole, implying a high degree of cultural homogeneity and, as fleshed out in chapter 5, silencing female, queer, and Black and brown bodies in the process.

THE SUTURED NATION-STATE

One of the first examples of political maps depicting countries in human or animal form was the so-called *Leo Belgicus* (figure 2.8), introduced in 1583 by an Austrian cartographer. It proved to be a powerful and lasting image, in no small part because Belgium, just like the Netherlands, was then a part of the Spanish Empire and did not exist at the time as an independent state.[81] Literally a map that roared, *Leo Belgicus* depicted a singular corporeal image of a country yet to emerge as a political entity.[82] Harnessing the metaphoric force of an organic body in the form of an animal, the lion evoked the teleological destiny of the Belgian nation as well as underscoring the naturalness of its borders.

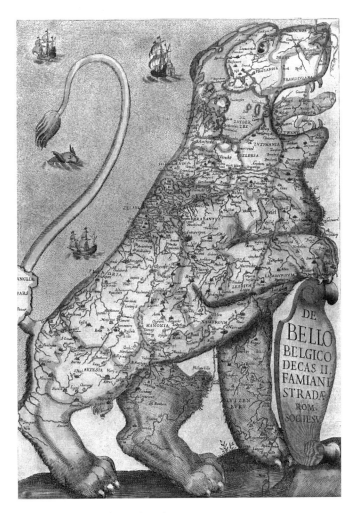

2.8. Stradæ, *Leo Belgicus* (1647).

A similar strategy was adopted by Finland in the nineteenth century, then a grand duchy in the Russian Empire, with the symbol of the Finnish Maiden (Suomineito) devised to represent national independence. Both personification of the state and anthropomorphic representation of the national borders, the Suomineito was depicted as a young woman, facing west with her right hand raised (figure 2.9). Less benign versions of the image showed Suomineito being attacked by Russia in the form of an eagle, or even an octopus, as discussed earlier.[83] The Finnish Maiden proved very potent as the country sought independence, remaining in fact a strong symbol of Finland's identity

2.9. Olavi Vepsäläinen, *Suomineito, the "Finnish Maiden"* (1948).

to this day, with the identification of its northwestern extremity still commonly referred to as Käsivarsi (the Arm).[84] Literally prying herself loose from Russia's embrace, Suomineito offered a powerful anthropomorphic vision of the country's right to self-determination as well as an emphasis on its natural borders.

Geographer John Prescott once quipped that there is no recorded case of a state wishing to withdraw to natural boundaries, since natural boundaries are always the limits to which a state seeks to expand.[85] Linked to the emergence of nationalism in Europe, the notion of natural boundaries enjoyed much success in eighteenth-century France and later in nineteenth-century Germany. It paralleled the shift discussed earlier whereby the understanding of national territory gradually shifted from a radial, royal, and hereditary space to an evenly operative and egalitarian space. The isomorphism between political space and geography had emerged much earlier and was even found on maps drawn in antiquity, but it acquired particular significance with the rise of the nation-state.[86] Conceptualizing national territory as a spatial container bound by natural borders helped foster a "teleological and paradoxically ahistorical vision that naturalized politics by appealing to spatial myths of homogeneity and geometric destiny."[87] Reference could be made to geography and natural laws, that is, to an authority higher than history's arbitrary and chance events.[88] Just as cartography had ensured that "states appear as facts of nature, as real enduring things," mountain ranges, rivers, and deserts could offer tangibility to the tenuous social line dividing one group from another.[89]

The notion of natural boundaries also allowed for anticipatory readings, with boundaries seen as preceding the nation. Predestined and God-given, natural features could be used as geographic anchors, requiring conquest to ensure the nation would grow into its intended shape—an idea that remains very much current with maritime and Arctic claims (see chapter 5). The visual force of this political idea ensured its popularity among philosophers such as Herder, who saw geographical features as natural dividers of peoples, customs, languages, and empires; or Rousseau, who argued for the interdependent and mutually sustaining nature of a territory and its inhabitants. If, unlike Herder, Rousseau did not envisage borders to be prescriptively imposed by geography, he nonetheless suggested nations had an ideal size that was, somehow, the work of nature.[90] These views whereby an idealized model of the nation exists, and to which actual nations need to be reconciled, has shown great resilience. Thus the idea remains that many African states are unnatural entities because their borders are straight and cut across at right angles instead of being squiggly lines following sinuously along natural features and separating ethnic groups in a more organic way. If many, if not all, contemporary African borders are the unfortunate legacy of a colonial enterprise that saw the continent carved up and quartered by foreign powers, there is in fact nothing inherently natural about a border, be it straight or squiggly.[91]

The distinction between natural and artificial borders is no longer a particularly useful one for analytical purposes, given that a consensus acknowledges all borders to be intrinsically artificial. In fact, geographical features rarely

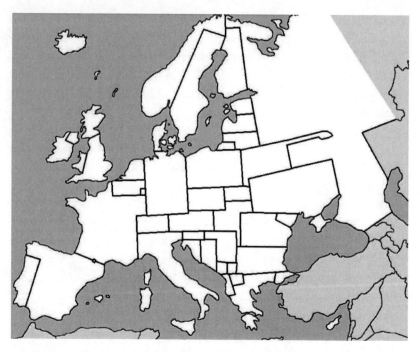

2.10. Colonized Europe (@TerribleMaps on X/Twitter, February 21, 2022).

make boundaries more secure or durable. Rivers see their courses shift over time, creating overlapping claims of sovereignty or, more rarely, pockets of unclaimed land (see chapter 5), while mountain peaks are subject to changes due to climate change and the melting of glaciers (see chapter 4).[92] Borders also sit athwart ecosystems—itself a problematic concept—slicing across land-based and marine habitats, some of them extending thousands of miles, and intersecting with numerous corridors of movement, such as the spawning grounds of salmon, the migratory routes of birds, or the flight paths of commercial airline jets.[93]

Problematic as it may be, the concept of natural borders continues to shape understandings of space. The enduring conviction that political boundaries should ideally follow natural features is complemented by efforts to make this a reality. Political entities are first demarcated along topographical identifiers such as mountains, rivers, or lakes. These political lines are then reaffirmed and accrue through different forms of land use, deforestation, or the digging of trenches, and political demarcation is increased further by ecological zones such as nature reserves.[94] These changes are in part incidental to political and

2.11. International Boundary Commission, "A visible line between friendly neighbors."

economic policies as well as to agricultural practices, levels of urbanization, and income levels, but they are also often intentional as there is a clear political drive to etch the abstract line drawn on maps into the physical environment.[95]

A good example is the so-called Vista, also called informally the Slash. A twenty-foot-wide deforestation zone, the Vista marks a physical rupture in the landscape over the entire length of the world's longest border (5,525 miles), between the United States and Canada (figure 2.11). A two-state project with an allocated annual budget of US$1,400,000, the corridor is deforested for the sole purpose of making sure that the "average person . . . knows they are on the border." In order to "make the boundary visible and unmistakable," the Vista, managed by the International Boundary Commission, extends ten feet on either side of the line through dense forests, over mountain ranges, across wetlands and highlands as well as across some of the most rugged terrain in North America.[96]

The Vista is a potent illustration of the political ambition to replicate a cartographic reality on the ground and to naturalize it. Here again, the territorial ideal of separation and discreteness is confidently inscribed at the surface, in a way that silences the multiple economic and cultural entanglements between the two countries. The fact that it is deployed, at a substantial annual cost, on one of the world's least contentious borders also testifies to the enduring enmeshment of the natural and the political, and the aspiration that the two should be coextensive.

The naturalizing language in which discussions of ecosystems or national entities are couched is both pervasive and extensive. It presents the nation as a discrete entity, bound and unique, yet commensurable with others. Insofar as each nation is furnished with a particular set of symbolic material—mineral and organic—from which it draws historic and cultural meaning, it operates in quasi-autonomous mode, as a universe onto itself. A nation-state is not merely equipped with a unique flag, currency, and hymn, it also has its own organic trappings: its national animal, flower, tree. These symbols are not required for a state to be recognized as such or to be fully operative, but they confer additional force to the national project insofar as they appeal to essentialisms and nature. A national symbol is usually, though not always, an indigenous animal, and preferably one that is awe-inspiring.[97] The bald eagle, chosen in 1782 by the United States as a national emblem, evokes for example the animal's inherent qualities of majesty, strength, and longevity as symbols of the great American spirit.

The lion, Britain's animal emblem, similarly projects qualities such as strength, bravery, and dignity. The imagery associated with the lion is potent, and the animal is in fact the symbol of a large number of nations, many of them in Europe, like Armenia, Belgium, and Bulgaria. The idea of the lion as the king of the animal world may have originated with *Physiologus*, an early Christian book about animal symbolism. Written in Greek in the second century CE, it was translated into many European and Middle Eastern languages and proved an influential cultural—and transnational—narrative of animal symbolism for centuries. More recently, the English bulldog has also been employed as shorthand for England. Evoking the animal's qualities of courage and tenaciousness, it has been widely used since the early nineteenth century but gained greater currency during World War II, as a symbol for Winston Churchill's defiance of Nazi Germany. Unlike the lion, associated with monarchical power, the bulldog had a more earthy and relatable quality, and indeed proved a popular symbol of patriotism and bravery for the "common man."

The symbolic linkage between animality and place facilitated the formation and stabilization of the nation-state but long preceded its emergence. The totemic role of animals features in numerous mythical narratives about the foundation of cities, as in the case of Rome for instance, where according to legend the city's founders, the twins Romulus and Remus, were suckled by a she-wolf. Such foundational myths centered around animals frequently harnessed the force of predators such as wolves or tigers. Sometimes the protection offered by an animal related to its capacity to nurture, as in Norse mythology, when the primeval cow Auðumbla fed the first human being, the giant Ymir, with four streams of milk running from her udders.

If the use of animal imagery as national symbols is a clear legacy of these early associations, the relation is no longer one of protection or nurturance but of direct equivalence, where the characteristics of the animal are seen to reflect a national essence or spirit. In nineteenth-century Britain, Harriet Ritvo writes, British naturalists saw natural environments as culturally and politically loaded. They believed variation to be reflective of overall differences between nations and routinely assessed animals that they considered their fellow Britons as superior to alien beasts.[98] Nature also followed the flag in the eyes of their nonspecialist compatriots, and Ritvo gives the example of white cattle, described as "ancient Britons," and believed to be "representative of the historical dignity, nobility, and ethnic isolation of their country."[99]

As the work of Juliet Fall has shown, contemporary views have not shifted as radically as one might think, and it remains common to imagine plants or animals as imbued with diverse national characteristics.[100] Describing the reintroduction of lammergeyers, a type of vulture, in a natural reserve located on the mountains between France and Italy, Fall shows that fauna continue to be conceptualized in terms of national belonging: "One bird was released each year, in alternate countries. French managers repeatedly noted that the 'French' birds, bearing French names, inevitably went to live in Italy. . . . For the French managers, this implied that the neighbours had 'stolen' the French birds; for the Italians this meant that the birds preferred to live in Italy because 'nature was more natural' there."[101]

Laws governing the acquisition of citizenship are complex and vary from state to state, but two fundamental pillars are the two concepts of *jus sanguinis* (citizenship by descent) and *jus soli* (citizenship by birth in the country's territory). Legally, the two systems are frequently seen as contrasting with each other—the former indexing an ethnic or racial interpretation of national belonging; the latter a civic one. Culturally, they are often interlinked and complementary.[102] Even in countries with a civic system like the United States, metaphors of blood, genetics, and nativeness are commonly embedded in considerations of identity. I discussed earlier how new corporeal metaphors such as *national DNA* are regularly being coined, just as others become outdated and obsolete. Contemporary American identities, encompassing a whole range of "hyphenated Americans" yet leaving the implicit English baseline category unacknowledged and unmarked, highlight the uneasy cohabitation of the civic system with understandings of indigeneity and nativeness.

In the United States, as elsewhere, migrants and individuals of mixed racial heritage are routinely met with assumptions that their national origin or racial ancestry has a direct relevance for who they are. In turn, these assumptions are commonly framed through corporeal metaphors. Mediterranean "blood" is seen as being indicative of "passion" or "fieriness," German ancestry is intrinsically equivalent to being methodical and organized, while Asian origins—at least in the United States—will make you a bad driver but will give you a competitive advantage in math.[103] Such assumptions about national essences are also regularly churned out by national media, in school textbooks and lessons, and in everyday conversations. National stereotypes are particularly evident in sport competitions, where supporters speak of matches through a military language of attacks, victories, and defeats.[104] Similarly, playing styles have commonly been interpreted as expressions of national identity: "the regimented Germans, the dramatic Italians, the stylish Spanish, the technical English, the sensuous Brazilians, the artful French, the athletic Africans."[105] In cultural texts, stereotypes are both common and stable. British people, like the bulldog, are portrayed as proud, brave, and tenacious; Americans are as free, strong, and powerful as the bald eagle; while Russians, as discussed earlier in this chapter, remain bearlike: big and strong, but also wild and occasionally clumsy.

Through such practices of banal (and often benign) nationalism, the equivalence between *state* and *citizen* gets further reinforced.[106] Paralleling the momentous cultural shift whereby the understanding of political territory turned into a homogenous and evenly operative space, the discourse of natural borders, fused with the idea that the citizens of a given state share characteristics encoded at a fundamental, quasi-biological level, has given shape to a very powerful model. The logomap thus represents far more than a simple exercise in branding.[107] It also serves a more primal need, whereby it depicts the nation as something coming close to a biological entity, a natural habitat for the modern political subject.

SHAPING THE NATION-STATE

The emergence of the logomap as we understand it today is intimately tied to the rise of the nation-state, where the logomap was used in a concerted effort to facilitate education and elicit patriotic sentiments. Anthropomorphic and zoomorphic shapes were useful to drive home the political claim that the nation's borders were both timeless and natural, particularly when they were under attack or more likely to fluctuate. Some of the animals that later became symbols of nation-states emerged originally as zoomorphic shapes. The eagle that represents the United States is such an example. In the nineteenth century, geographer Joseph Churchman published a map of the United States overlaid with the drawing of a bird (figure 2.12). As he explained, he was "looking at a wall map of the US when the dim light in the room cast its shadow in such a way as to suggest the shape of an eagle. He was ready to dismiss it when he realised that such an image might increase the 'facility with which [geography] lessons may be impressed and retained upon the youthful memory.'"[108] Later, with the extension of the borders to Texas and the West Coast, this cartographic bird no longer matched the shape of the country, but the eagle remained a powerful and ubiquitous national symbol.

As noted in chapter 1, the emergence of the modern nation-state in India was accompanied by a proliferation of anthropomorphic maps that typically portrayed the national logomap as a woman, often as a mother or goddess. Sumathi Ramaswamy recounts an episode when poet and nationalist Aurobindo, pointing at a wall map of India, asked: "Do you see this map? It is not a map, but the portrait of Bharat-mata [Mother India]: its cities and mountains, rivers and jungles form her physical body. All her children are her nerves, large and small."[109] As in the case of Finland, the figure of a female body was overlaid upon the political map of the country to harness patriotic sentiments and naturalize borders. The connection between landscape and female bodies has been comprehensively analyzed by feminist scholars.[110] This conventional association can, as in the example above, convey a sense of the land as a maternal support, but it can also, especially through its specific correlation between geographical features and bodily organs, tend toward the pornographic.[111] Such instances of "gynocartography" thus represent an unambiguous masculinist discourse—through a "complex transcoding between women and nature"—as well as a colonialist endeavor.[112]

In the vast majority of the contexts evoked in this book, the bodies of women have been routinely mobilized as national icons, as surfaces upon which narratives could be written.[113] A critical consequence of this imaginary of the nation-as-female is that it has not allowed women to become active participants. Even when they were energized by nationalism, women have found themselves chiefly relegated to the role of "patriarchally sculpted symbols."[114] In colonial liberation struggles, including contemporary settings, the "woman question" has thus often been slated for "after the revolution."[115] If this has helped foster fantasies of sovereign rescue by patriotic males, it has also elided the pain suffered by men.[116] In the context of contemporary Afghanistan, Jennifer Fluri and Rachel Lehr write, Afghan men have been largely absent from representations

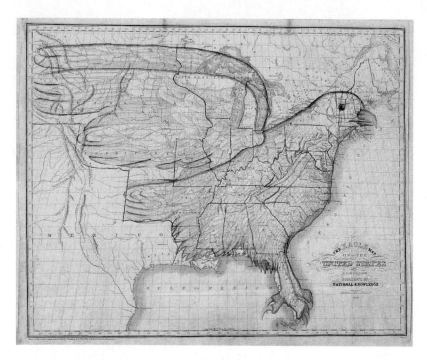

2.12. Isaac W. Moore, after a drawing by Joseph Churchman, the original American Eagle, engraving (1833).

of suffering, even if they have been five times more likely than women to be the victims of corporeal punishment, including amputations, flogging, and executions. It proved far more politically expedient for Western nations to depict Afghan men as abusive patriarchs and Afghan women as victims.[117]

The primary ambition of the maternal imagery conveyed by Indian barefoot cartography was, like other anthropomorphic and zoomorphic maps elsewhere, to naturalize the borders of the state and imprint the national logomap on its citizens. Interestingly, some of these maps did not fully delineate the borders. As Ramaswamy notes, in a number of such bodyscapes, the body of Mother India suggestively curved toward West and East Pakistan, partly covering these regions with a piece of clothing.[118] Insofar as these representations left considerable space to interpretation—and possibly expansion—these pictorial representations differ from most anthropomorphic maps, where the objective is to portray the nation-state as a bounded entity, with fixed and authoritative borders. But they do, like anthropomorphic maps, demonstrate the intricate melding of cartographic practices and state ambitions as well as the symbolic force exerted by visual representations of geobodies.

The rise of the nation-state is frequently accompanied by several competing symbols until one eventually becomes predominant. As one particular symbol gains metaphoric dominance, the link between the nation (the metaphrand) and the corporeal image (the metaphier) becomes naturalized through hegemonic and reiterative pictorial practices. In the case of France, as the monarchic symbol lost much of its valence, it was replaced by the figure of Marianne, a powerful woman storming the barricades, and thus a complete reversal of the iconographic model.[119] At first, the symbol was multivalent and unstable: the figure of Marianne represented ideas of youthfulness and revolution but also encompassed multiple characters: "a stern but benign figure of justice and liberty; a nurturing matriarch for all citizens; or an irresponsible whore (squandering the state's finances on worthless people and projects)."[120]

Later, the symbol of Marianne came to be supplemented by the hexagon. The symbolic use of this perfect geometric shape was closely linked to the emergence of France as one of the first fully territorialized states of Europe. Jordan Branch writes that the seventeenth-century notion of frontier rationalization was initially driven by practical military needs and that it was not until much later that the idea of rationalization focused on eliminating overlaps and enclaves and demarcating linear boundaries.[121] The recasting of France as a hexagonal entity, as a space no longer monarchic and bodily but one founded on equality and rationality, was symbolically powerful.[122] Imbuing geometry with meaning, it gave France a different kind of natural borders as well as a potent symbolism that continues to exert its force.

In *Cartophilia*, Tatiana Dunlop notes that the practice of superimposing a hexagonal outline over the relief map of France became commonplace in French geography texts throughout the Third Republic. "The hexagonal form created a public perception of France's authentic national shape as preordained and almost God given in its mathematical perfection, giving the French a strategy for arguing against the ethnic and linguistic justifications for national borders that other Europeans had embraced."[123] Early on, an alternative octagonal shape was also used, but the hexagon prevailed since one of its six points was Strasbourg, thus confirming the natural inclusion within France of Alsace-Lorraine, long disputed with Germany.[124]

This perfect shape, as I unpack in more depth in chapter 5, does not of course correspond to the actual political boundaries of France, whose national territory extends in fact well beyond the metropolitan area. In addition to noncontiguous but fully fledged *départements* such as Corsica, Martinique, or French Guyana, various overseas dependencies (*départements et régions d'outre-mer et territoires d'outre-mer*, or DOM-TOM) such as New Caledonia or the Kerguelen Islands, are also part of political France. Yet *l'Hexagone*, commonly used in French as shorthand for *France*, is a powerful logomap and one that remains "piously revered."[125] Its regular outline, balanced in terms of weight and neatly circumscribable within a Vitruvian circle—itself the perfect model of the nation-state—makes it a prototypical logomap.[126] Like the state of Texas, it is in fact frequently used as a geographical unit of measure—such and such country being x times the size of Texas or France.

The ubiquity of the French and Texan logomaps, used on countless types of material support, suggests that their effectiveness has more to do with the kind of shape they are than with their explicit symbolism. Indeed, while a state's symbol may be that of a beautiful woman (as in the case of Finland and India) or a powerful and noble animal, in many cases the national logomap is far less glamorous. Denmark's similarity to an old man's face, or Italy's famous iconic boot, would not seem to be intrinsically capable of eliciting patriotic sentiments on the same level as a lion or eagle, yet their symbolic force does not appear to be in any way diminished. It would appear, therefore, that the fundamental feature is the organicity imparted by the shape, rather than the shape itself.[127]

This appears in fact to be confirmed by the very weak power elicited by political entities with overly regular lines. As mentioned earlier, many African states feel unnatural because of their overly orthogonal shapes. Similarly, American states such as Colorado or Wyoming lack the branding dynamism of California or Texas in that they do not have a strong graphic identity and are not immediately recognizable (figure 2.13). While the hexagonal symbol of France is also a regular shape, the country's actual borders of course are not. The hexagon represents here an abstraction, an idealized shape overlaid upon France's actual borders. Should France's borders actually be a hexagon, its power might find itself considerably weakened. In addition, the hexagon presents the advantage of coming close to a perfect shape, whereas the rectangle and the square feel abstract, unnatural, without personality.

In a book-length study on the shape of Texas, Richard Francaviglia analyzed the widespread usage of the Texan cartogram—a term he favors over *map* given that its form is "less important for its geographic content than for its associative or evocative value."[128] Found on hundreds of formats such as license plates, food product advertisements, billboards, and clothes, no other state outline has been used quite as aggressively or effectively, and none is more readily recognizable.[129] The logoization of the Texas map is due, in part, to its ubiquitous presence, but it is likely also attributable to its inherent shape: roughly cruciform or star-shaped, it is about as wide as it is tall.

2.13. Sidney Harris, *Colorado or Wyoming?* (1992). Courtesy of ScienceCartoons Plus.com.

The Lone Star shape thus perfectly fits in a circle, which greatly facilitates its use as a logo.[130] Texas, like France, constitutes a prototypical example of the logomap rubric in the same way that "robins are judged to be more representative of the category 'bird' than are chickens, penguins, and ostriches."[131] As birds that do not fly, the latter violate some of the principles by which we categorize them as birds and are therefore grudgingly admitted.[132] Unlike elongated shapes such as Chile's, or dispersive ones such as archipelagoes (discussed in chapter 5), the Texan outline is also far more malleable. Its unique shape, with its wavy or irregular natural borders on its eastern perimeter, its western rectangular borders, and most particularly its northwestern panhandle, makes it truly distinctive and instantly recognizable as well as an ideal support of affective investment.

Francaviglia's interlocutors frequently associated Texas's logo with specific shapes, such as a boot, a cowboy hat, or a saddle—all core symbols of Texan culture.[133] In line with the masculine cowboy image projected by the state, a few also saw the panhandle as a phallic shape. Such corporeal associations are not unusual given the extensive linkages between the body and the state.

The Florida peninsula thus resembles a bodily extremity dangling into the Atlantic Ocean, an appendage particularly at risk of attack. The United States has in fact a well-established morphology, with the East as front and the West as back, the Northeast as the intellectual head, and the South as the vulnerable underbelly.[134] This is not an isolated case. Russia possesses a similar geopolitical orientation, with its face toward Europe and its back to Asia. This spatial imaginary has repercussions for border management policies (the border with China is traditionally more heavily militarized than the one with Europe; see chapter 4) as well as for geopolitical configurations, since orientations translate into corporealized associations—coding Ukraine as Russia's soft underbelly.

There also seems to be something universal about the intrinsic value of shapes. Experiments on infants have demonstrated that people do not attach sounds to shapes arbitrarily and that some sound–shape mappings precede language learning. These cognitive predispositions may in fact aid with language learning by "establishing a basis for matching labels to referents and narrowing the hypothesis space for young infants."[135] In a well-known 1929 experiment, test subjects were shown two shapes and asked which one was called *takete* and which *maluma* (see figure 2.14). The strong preference to pair the jagged shape with *takete* and the rounded shape with *maluma* suggests that the human brain attaches abstract meanings to shapes and sounds in a consistent manner.[136]

The visual potency of the logomap may also be further strengthened by pareidolia, the recognized tendency for humans to anthropomorphize shapes they encounter. From seeing a face in a house to finding Jesus in a burrito, the cognitive predisposition to recognize faces, including in inanimate things, greatly facilitates the affective investment in the logomap. Maps and faces share further similarities, notably the fact that they must be seen from a specific angle in order to be recognized.[137] It is fine to flip them horizontally—Francaviglia provides various examples of reversed Texas maps—but turn them upside down and they are no longer recognizable.[138] The uncanniness of the south-up version of the Hobo-Dyer equal-area projection map discussed in chapter 1 thus lies primarily in that the iconic world map becomes barely identifiable.

As Francaviglia notes with respect to the Texas cartogram, "associative meanings are deeply personal and have their limitations. If anything, the map of Texas means many things to many people as a literal symbol. It is the *ambiguity* of the shape of Texas that ensures its symbolic use."[139] Thus the force of the Italian boot as an affective metaphor is found in the gap

Takete   # Maluma

2.14. Takete or Maluma?

between the imagined shape and the actual borders. It works because the shape is a familiar outline, because it evokes a familiar object. If the country's borders were the actual outline of the object, it would lose all of its symbolic power. It is because the logomap can be read in different ways, because it is not overly and unambiguously defined that it can become vehicular of affective transfer. Thus even the simplest silhouette map can serve as repository for nationalist narratives and become an associative device capable of triggering memories and activating passions.[140]

An important point I want to make in this book is that if patriotic sentiments must be shaped in specific ways to neatly map onto the national contour, they are not entirely subsumable to these state practices. And whereas populist narratives have the capacity to inflame territorial passions, they are far less powerful in containing them. Two examples taken from eastern Europe can illustrate this contrast. Hungary lost two-thirds of its former territory through the Treaty of Trianon (June 4, 1920) that saw the distribution of formerly Hungarian territory to four bordering states: Austria, Romania, Czechoslovakia, and Yugoslavia. Hungary's political discourse has been heavily shaped as a result of the treaty and remains heavily suffused with metaphors of amputation and truncation.[141] These narratives have been used openly by various political factions, to much success. By contrast, Polish political discourse has attempted to rein in popular imaginaries around territorial loss. Arguing that making peace with the loss of the Eastern Borderlands was crucial to ensure good neighborly relations and future peace, Polish governments since World War II have continually reaffirmed the new borders of the state and sought to silence dissenting voices.[142] And yet, after seventy years, there are intimations that irredentism continues to simmer under the surface and that it would not take much for those phantoms to awake again.[143]

Seemingly unimaginable in contemporary Europe, Russia's wars on Ukraine—first in 2014 with the occupation of Crimea, and then again in 2022 over the entire Ukrainian territory—have demonstrated that geopolitical imaginaries organized around metaphors of bodily loss remain extremely potent. As I discuss further in chapter 3, in spite of the risks of military retaliation, economic sanctions, and international criticisms, Russia was prepared to go to war in order to recompose what it considered a mutilated geobody.[144] Part of the implicit rationale, Elizabeth Dunn notes, was a longing to emerge from the humiliation of post-Soviet collapse, regain a place on the world stage, and reestablish a Russian "sphere of influence" on the territory of its historical empire.[145] But a more pressing yearning was to reintegrate Ukraine into the original cradle of Russian civilization, without which Russia was merely a stump (*obrubok*) of its former Soviet incarnation.[146]

Gaston Bachelard has argued that the house in which an individual lives is experienced as an extended body, as a larger self. One's first house in particular, familiar through tactile sensations and repeated gestures, gets inscribed physically in the individual's body.[147] Bachelard's exploration of the psychological significance of different parts of the house, notably the contrast between the cellar and the attic, also evokes the resident's mental topography. Thus the cellar as buried darkness and fearsome realm of the unconscious stands in opposition to the rationality of the attic. Bachelard's poetic evocations of one's house as a larger self recall processes of incorporation into an individual's body image of tools such as glasses, canes, or vehicles. As the attachments people form with place are central to self-identity and as, even at the most innocuous level of self-definition, people define themselves primarily in terms of their nationality, it is but a small step to make to argue the nation-state constitutes a larger embodiment of what Étienne Balibar has called the *homo nationalis*.[148]

As I discuss at length in chapter 3, recent research in neurobiology has established that these forms of bodily incorporation are spontaneous and commonplace. This extensibility suggests a greater corporeal plasticity than was previously assumed and undermines in fact the idea of a fixed, autonomous body. The breach between the visually unambiguous and bounded logomap, on the one hand, and the actual malleability of the body, on the other, opens up possibilities of spatial explorations relevant to territorial sovereignty and border management. It allows me to introduce three concepts in particular—territorial phantom pains, territorial prosthetics, and cartographic monsters—coalescing though a cognitive scaffolding that relies on meta-phoric constellations tying the citizen to the outline of their nation-state.

METAPHORIC WORK

In 2005, the California-based giant Google released Google Earth, a new geo-graphical information program offering access to detailed online maps and images at a planetary scale. For the first time, it was now possible to travel virtually and instantly to any place in the world, to zoom down on any locale, and to view any city or village. Overwhelmingly, users excitedly searched for the place they knew best: their own home.[149]

Jacques Lacan called the "mirror stage" that early phase in an infant's life when a sense of individual identity is first gained through the reflection pro-vided by others. It is only when that image is reflected back to the subject, he argued, that the self is constituted. I suggest that the process whereby an indi-vidual becomes constituted as a national subject is similar, and just as the sub-ject learns to recognize her body in the mirror, the citizen learns to recognize herself in the map. This mirroring process plays out in various ways through both personal choices and social practices, ranging from tattoos to formal education and religious rites.[150] Thus in Texas, Francaviglia writes, "students learn from an early age that they carry a map of Texas with them at all times—their right hand. The thumb is West Texas, the upwardly extended index finger is the Panhandle, and the three remaining fingers form East Texas."[151] In the context of Israel, Yair Wallach notes, the fact that Israelis can draw the shape of the country with their eyes closed is cause for celebration. Automatically inscribed in bodily gestures, the nation's geobody has been fully internalized.[152]

Formal instruction and socialization are clearly paramount in corporeal-izing national and state outlines. In Russia, schoolchildren learn to concep-tualize their country as an organic entity that is part of them—"its success is their success," notes Gerard Toal.[153] But these processes also take place in communities beyond the context of state instruction.[154] Interestingly, social and religious instruction on territorial boundaries existed well before the advent of the modern nation-state. Every February 23, Thomas Nail writes, "Romans celebrated the 'Terminalia'—for the Roman god Terminus, the god of borders—by marching around in a large group to sanctify the regional boundary markers. . . . Practiced by medieval Europeans, the Christian ritual of 'beating of bounds' descended from the Roman Terminalia. Priests would march a crowd of young boys around (the perambulation, to walk around) with green birch or willow boughs to literally beat the parish borders so that the young boys would carry on the knowledge of the borders."[155] This entanglement between the physical and the national body, between the literal and the metaphorical, can be illuminated further through Vivian Sobchack's discussion on the nature of the relation between the body and cinematic representation. She convincingly argues that the cinematic experience creates a synesthetic enjoyment fusing a "real" sensual experience and an "as-if" real sensual experience with a precise phenomenological structure.[156] Body and language thus do not simply oppose or reflect each other. Rather, she argues, "they more radically *in-form* each other in a fundamentally nonhierarchical and reversible relationship that, in certain circumstances, manifests itself as a vacillating, ambivalent, often ambiguously undifferentiated, and thus 'unnameable' or 'undecidable' experience."[157]

Neuroscience research corroborates that the sense of self is primarily a bodily sense of self, and that it emerges out of the fusion or convergence of multisensory inputs. Visual feedback in particular has been shown to play a crucial role in the relation between Self and Other and was demonstrated to productively augment tactile sensations in a process not unlike synesthesia.[158] This suggests that our sense of reality emerges out of an enmeshing of the metaphorical and the literal, and that the two fields frequently bleed into each other.

The literal against which the metaphorical is defined is, itself, not unproblematic. Plato may have decried metaphorical language as a form of sophistry manipulating and twisting arguments through poetic, but ultimately misleading, analogies, but contemporary linguists and theorists agree that metaphors are at the core of language. Rather than seeing metaphoric language as deviant from the literal, it is in fact more productive to see both as interlinked and complementary. In fact, *literal* and *metaphorical* are largely idealized categories. According to Paul Ricœur, it is only with the emergence of a classificatory logic seeking to distinguish between the two that a "specific and narrowed notion of metaphor came into use."[159] Many linguistic usages that are seen as literal are previous metaphors that have become deeply sedimented in language. The common usage of the verb *to see* with the meaning "to know," "to understand" is such a case. It is not generally thought of as a metaphor, yet historical evidence suggests that words in Indo-European languages meaning "to see" have regularly acquired the meaning "to know" at various times and places.[160]

If these so-called dead metaphors have lost their metaphoric quality through continual use, their ubiquity suggests they satisfy some semantic need.[161] As philosopher John Searle asserts, certain metaphorical associations are so deeply sedimented in our "mode of sensibility" that we assume the existence of an underlying similarity. Thus, if *passage of time* is recognized as a metaphor, we rarely reflect on the implicit similarity drawn between time and space that carries the metaphor.[162]

The invisibility of this metaphoric undercarriage largely rests on the fact that the "relation between the sentence meaning and the metaphorical utterance meaning is systematic rather than random or ad hoc."[163] The sentence "Sally is a block of ice" will thus easily be understood to mean that Sally is a cold, unfeeling, or unresponsive individual, while the utterance "Sally is a prime number between seventeen and twenty-three" is also likely to be seen as a metaphor, but the meaning will not be interpreted so readily. The comparison of Sally with a block of ice requires little explanation, since the relation between cold things and unemotional people is embedded within a specific set of perceptions, sensibilities, and linguistic practices.[164] The implicit analogy that enables metaphoric constructions is thus itself a metaphor.

Far from being an ornamental rhetorical device then, metaphoric language reflects our very cognitive processes. If people conceptualize their experiences in figurative terms such as metaphor, metonymy, irony, or oxymoron, it is because these principles underlie the way we think, reason, and imagine.[165] Metaphoric entailments (the relationship binding two sentences whereby the truth of one requires the truth of the other) rely on family resemblances along a semantic grid that is both systematic and coherent. Thus the implicit equivalence between coldness and lack of emotionality appears not to be confined to English speakers but to be operational across several different cultures.[166]

This view of metaphors relies primarily on a cognitive—and therefore largely preconceptual and precultural—analytical frame, an approach spearheaded by linguist George Lakoff. In his book *Women, Fire, and Dangerous Things*, Lakoff contends that an analysis of language's metaphoric undercarriage reveals that metaphors are not found in random assemblages but that they come organized within larger metaphoric constellations founded on experiential gestalts. While metaphors seem to show incredible range, this creativity is not infinitely malleable, Lakoff argues. They are found, instead, within a larger superset that is internally coherent. The generative core metaphor for anger, for example, is that of a heated fluid in a container.[167] Expressions such as "you make my blood boil," "he was filled with anger," or "she was brimming with rage" thus all gravitate around that central idea and find their origin in the physiological response associated with anger:

namely body heat, increased internal pressure (blood pressure, muscular pressure), and agitation.[168] By providing the initial grid or prism, these embodied experiences thus place constraints on our apprehension of our social and cultural life.[169]

This line of argument is both convincing and seductive, yet does not quite account for the vast cultural variation witnessed worldwide. If the metaphor associating lack of emotion with coldness appears to be shared widely across cultures, many metaphors and similes fail to translate so seamlessly into other cultural contexts. A comparative exploration of conceptualizations of the body across cultures and languages shows that not all cultures locate the seat of the mind in the same place, for instance. It is associated primarily with the heart in China and other East Asian cultures, with the abdomen in Southeast Asia or Polynesia, while European and North African cultures conceptualize a dualism between the brain (as the seat of the intellect) and the heart (as the seat of emotions).[170]

What this suggests is that metaphors are not necessarily universal and that metaphorical conceptualizations are sensitive to cultural influences.[171] Even emotions generally considered universal, such as anger, for example, may in fact be mapped quite differently in other cultures, as Catherine Lutz's research on Ifaluk, a small Micronesian atoll of four islands, has shown.[172] The existence of metaphoric constellations does not therefore imply that they are in any way predictive. In his later work, Lakoff is in fact careful to point out that they are radial categories, that is, clusters of contiguous conceptual metaphors that have central models as well as variations on those models.[173]

Even within a single society or community, different metaphors occasionally jostle against one another and do not always cohere under a single cognitive superset. This is especially true in the case of new technologies, or political or social change, such as the emergence of the nation-state. Corporeal metaphors can be useful and familiar interpretative tropes, "a terminological prosthesis ready to fill the symbolic vacuum."[174] But not all metaphors are equally valuable or captivating, and the effectiveness of a metaphor largely depends on shared social conventions, on other family resemblances already in place, and more importantly, on the authoritativeness of its user.[175] Cultural exchange can also lead to transformations of metaphoric structures and bring greater homogeneity. Thus if the bulk of idioms, compounds, and idiomatic sayings in Chinese point at the heart as the seat of the mind, recent coinages suggest that Western concepts are making inroads.[176] These changes have crucial repercussions given that metaphors are not merely descriptive or interpretive, but generative insofar as they shape understanding. Metaphors are not merely constructions or images removed from social reality; they engender and enact social and political effects.[177] An experiment carried out by psychologists P. H. Thibodeau and L. Boroditsky with a group of students demonstrated, for instance, the importance of linguistic framing and the impact of competing metaphors. When the issue of crime was compared to a virus, the solutions offered by the students included social reforms and prevention measures. By contrast, when the analogy of a beast was employed, responses gravitated around capture and incarceration.[178]

As I discussed earlier in this chapter, the emergence of nationalism and the dominant conceptualization of nations as organic, bound entities has had a significant impact on subjectivities well beyond its original Euro-American context. In India, Thailand, Turkey, and elsewhere, the various autochthonous notions of place and sovereignty have rapidly given way to a monochrome discourse. As I showed, this hegemonic narrative has been, and continues to be, suffused with corporeal analogies. If cognitive anthropologist Pascal Boyer is correct, and cultural differences are really variations along a single, universal "intuitive ontology," then this metaphoric undercarriage is in fact likely to have been key to its success.[179]

Socialization as *homo nationalis* may have equipped us with a similar set of conceptual tools to grasp the concept of nation, to the extent that somatic analogies seem natural and therefore unproblematic and invisible, but the nation-state remains an abstract spatial model that could in fact be grasped in entirely different ways. I mentioned earlier the recent coinage of *national DNA*. While this metaphor is another somatic variation on the nation-body equivalence, it nonetheless opens a different corporeal horizon, no longer presenting an image of the nation as a totalizing body, but a less hierarchical, a delocalized, perhaps even deterritorialized, vision. The fact that this metaphor originated in the United States, a country with a cultural framework based on civic identity, is perhaps not coincidental.

If hegemonic nationalist discourse couched in corporeal metaphors has overridden a rich and varied tapestry of indigenous conceptualizations of place and sovereignty, it is nonetheless critical to bear in mind that metaphors are contextual pieces of discourse and therefore not always decoded in exactly the same way.[180] Metaphors come embedded in particular narratives, are uttered by individuals positioned in a certain way relative to power and authority, and also gain and lose evocative power depending on geopolitical, social, and economic contexts. These differences can go a long way to explain why territorial loss, for instance, does not necessarily produce phantom pains and can in some contexts lead to unproblematic spatial reconfigurations.

Finally, the hegemonic dominance of the Western model does not necessarily mean that previous cultural understandings have been completely supplanted.[181] In fact, the opposition between *Western* and *Other* is somewhat fallacious as it presupposes both fields to be internally homogenous and coherent. As Le Breton convincingly argues, in Europe itself modern biomedical knowledge coexists with older, sedimented lay understandings of the body. Though the biomedical tradition may be the official representation of the human body, it nonetheless remains an esoteric knowledge not fully grasped by nonspecialists, as suggested by the routine appeal to ancient or superstitious practices still witnessed today.[182] A similar point has also been made by Pascal Boyer, who argues that scientific concepts often challenge or displace intuitive expectations. "Cultural transmission requires dedicated institutions with specialized personnel and systematic training extending over many years . . . but scholarly concepts never quite dislodge intuitive expectations despite systematic and prolonged tuition."[183] As a result, the ethnographic texture presented throughout this book—and the Manchurian case of chapter 3 in particular—is found at a critical juncture between global and local narratives: each case hewing closely a discourse having originated elsewhere; each one also a unique precipitate of particular histories and traditions.

PART II

3

TERRITORIAL PHANTOM PAINS

A man sets out to draw the world. As the years go by, he peoples a
space with images of provinces, kingdoms, mountains, bays, ships,
islands, fishes, rooms, instruments, stars, horses, and individuals. A short
time before he dies, he discovers that the patient labyrinth of lines
traces the lineaments of his own face.

—Jorge Luis Borges, "Epílogo"

NEW AND OLD INCARNATIONS

In 1927, as he walked around Moscow, the German philosopher and critic
Walter Benjamin remarked on the ubiquitous presence of maps: "Russia is
beginning to take on shape for the man on the street. . . . On the street in the
snow lie maps of the SSR, piled up there by street vendors who offer them for
sale. . . . The map is almost as close to becoming the center of a new Russian
icon cult as is Lenin's portrait."[1] That this emphasis on visual representations
of the country took place just as the Soviet Union was consolidating its power
is not coincidental. As the country firmed up its grip on various parts of the
former Tsarist empire—notably with the full incorporation of Central Asia as
part of the national entity—such visualizations were becoming all the more
crucial. The formation of the notion of the Soviet Man (*sovetskii chelovek*)

could be comprehensible only when anchored to a cartographic representation and an iconic logomap.[2]

Sixty years later, in the late 1980s and early 1990s, the situation appeared to be subject to almost exact replication. As Emma Widdis noted, "At metro stations and in street kiosks, maps were once again a product of choice, piled up on makeshift tables for the consumer's perusal. As the Soviet Union collapsed in 1991, so there were new atlases of the new Russian Federation, and of the CIS (Commonwealth of Independent States). As Moscow's streets were renamed, shaking off their Soviet heritage, so new maps of the city itself were needed. Russia once again, and in a quite different context, was 'taking shape for the man of the people.'"[3] Suddenly Russians had to come to terms with a much reduced, seemingly mutilated territory and grow accustomed to a new national logomap. The loss of Central Asia—and Kazakhstan in particular—though less traumatic than the loss of Ukraine, made the familiar outline of the Soviet Union completely unrecognizable. Eviscerated of its geographical underbelly, Russia was now an elongated shape, with more republics threatening to break away, including potential enclaves such as Tatarstan, and large parts of Siberia like Yakutia. The cultural and political dominance of Russia over the other republics of the union throughout the Soviet period had meant that *Russia* and *Soviet Union* had often been coextensive and indistinguishable.[4] As a result, the breakup of the Soviet Union proved especially destabilizing for Russia. Like the Russian doll in figure 3.1, many Russians saw their country literally emptied of substance.

While reminiscing about the collapse of the Soviet regime in the early 1990s, Natalia, an economic sociologist and a good friend then based in Blagoveshchensk, in the Russian Far East, confided that she had found the territorial dislocation of the Soviet Union extremely distressing:

> I felt Russia had suddenly become so small! . . . Looking at the new state map I saw how big Kazakhstan was, and wondered how Russia would ever be able to go on with half of the country missing. The biggest losses were Kazakhstan but also Ukraine and Belarus. It was like the country had been mutilated. The loss of Ukraine and Belarus was particularly odd to local people because that's where most [in the Russian Far East] are originally from. My grandmother is from a town between Russia and Ukraine and she wondered, "would she need a visa to go there now?"

Along with the sudden and unfamiliar presence of new political entities such as Kazakhstan, Kyrgyzstan, or Turkmenistan, Russians also had to reconcile themselves with the loss of lands long associated with Russian history and

3.1. "We are declaring our independence." Samandariin Tsogtbayar, *Uchirtai Ineed*, Ulaanbaatar (2001).

culture. The loss of Ukraine, the birthplace of Kyivan Rus' and fount of modern Russian culture, was especially painful. Despite facing grave political and economic sanctions and the possibility of military retaliation, the reintegration of Crimea into Russia's mutilated geobody was clearly a risk worth taking and one that was largely supported by Russian popular opinion. As Gerard Toal writes, Crimea held "powerful affective appeal to ordinary Russians both as a storied sacred place in Russian history and as a beloved vacation spot that held happy memories for many people."[5]

The Crimean peninsula was also home to strategic Russian military bases, and unquestionably the 2014 invasion was geopolitically motivated—as was the war on the rest of Ukraine in 2022. A number of op-eds have made the argument that the West was in part responsible for these invasions because of a reckless enlargement of both NATO and the European Union, causing Russia to feel increasingly encircled.[6] While I find such explanations deeply problematic insofar as they posit Ukraine and other post-Soviet countries as mere pawns rather than autonomous entities with their own aspirations, the prospect that Ukraine might be permanently removed from its geobody was certainly a very real trigger for Russia. Ukraine (like Belarus) is affectively and symbolically important for Russia and complementary to its own identity. Reintegrating Ukraine into the original cradle of Russian civilization— whether through a merging into a single political entity or through the installation of a regime friendly to Moscow—was perceived as crucial to re-compose a nation that had become a mere "stump" of its former self.[7] Expansion of NATO and the European Union to Ukraine was thus experienced by Russia as an attack on its own body, not that of a neighbor—in other words, not encirclement but outright mutilation.[8]

In that sense, the loss of other former Soviet regions such as the Baltic states, the Caucasus, or Central Asia did not have the same cultural and affective resonance even though their independence dramatically impacted Russia's geobody. Kazakhstan in particular, with a footprint of 1,052,100 square miles, made up roughly an eighth of the Soviet total (8,649,500 square miles). No longer within the nation, acknowledged as such and generally not the subject of territorial claims or revanchist discourse, they have not quite become foreign either. On an emotional level, these new states and regions remain attached to the national body—a liminal quality perceptible in the post-Soviet neologism of "near abroad" (*blizhnee zarubezh'e*) to refer to the republics that emerged following the dissolution of the Soviet Union. As I discuss further in chapter 5, in its acknowledgment of a "new arrangement of sovereignty and an old familiarity," the concept of "near abroad" finds echoes in familiar political categories such as "backyard" that blur the line between domestic and international.[9]

In its broad range of spatialized cultural memories and political claims, the former Soviet Union provides many illustrations for the kinds of phantoms discussed in this book. Some of these phantomic spaces, like Ukraine, are potent and unresolved, and can erupt into violent warfare; others merely add a layer of complexity to the unambiguous cartographic representations of the post-Soviet space and index unresolved trauma of the twentieth century's political violence. Unsurprisingly, central and eastern Europe is a region generally rife with phantoms. A 2020 Pew Research survey asked a number of Europeans whether they agreed that "there are parts of neighboring countries that really belong to us." A majority of Hungarians (67 percent), Greeks (60 percent), Bulgarians (58 percent), Turks (58 percent), and Russians (53 percent) agreed that there were.[10] In Poland, Prime Minister Jaroslaw Kaczynski even argued in 2007 that his reform plan would take the number of Poles killed in World War II into account in order to increase the country's voting influence in a reworked EU treaty.[11] Thus even when de jure and de facto borders coincide, something frequently survives beyond state sovereignties. Previous national incarnations, extending beyond the official logomap, act as affective vectors not easily circumscribable by state narratives. The geobody has changed but a surplus, an excess, survives after revisualization of the territory. Sometimes the phantom fades away, and the affective contour remolds around the new geobody; at other times the old geobody may become reactivated or survive in other forms.[12]

In the case of India's bodyscapes, discussed in chapter 2, where the country's shape was anthropomorphized as a goddess, Ramaswamy writes that the floating vestments of the goddess, potentially encompassing parts of the surrounding nations, "mark the eruption of the poetic, the religious and the gendered imaginations of and about the nation."[13] The affective contours traced by the veil of the goddess make for an excellent illustration of the potency of other outlines surviving in spectral form and hinting at alternative possibilities. A powerful visual of the phantomic force elicited by logomaps is also the one described by anthropologist Umut Yıldırım. In 2007, the Turkish courts accused the mayor of the town of Diyarbakır of political and territorial separatism following the construction of a recreational swimming pool allegedly built in the shape of Kurdistan. Yet paradoxically, since the court did not accept the existence of such a territory, it did not recognize the map of Kurdistan, making it very difficult to render a judgment.[14] In effect, the outline of Kurdistan hovered ominously over that of Turkey, lacking jurisdictional power yet saturated with affective force.

Often, these affective geographies also stir up sentiments of melancholy and nostalgia.[15] The evocative force of past logomaps can be stronger than contemporary representations, especially when older incarnations are suffused with power and glory. These past incarnations are sometimes harnessed by state-driven nationalist discourse to elicit and foster patriotic sentiments—such as the Italian or Mongolian use of maps depicting the maximum extent of their respective former empires—but they can also run counter to state narratives. When popular sentiments collide with state ambitions, claiming, for instance, more territory than their governments are prepared to do, political elites are forced to play a two-level game of negotiations between both the other nation and their own constituents.[16]

These interferences potentially lead to the fracturing and destabilization of state discourse, cultivating particular forms of nostalgia and mourning in the resulting interstices. These nostalgic longings are often resistant to counterdiscourse insofar as the loss of nostalgia, as Marilyn Ivy has compellingly argued, can be more unwelcome than the original loss itself.[17] Unsurprisingly, as elucidated further in chapter 4, lost territories frequently become invested with fetishistic affect, condensing in remote and seemingly unimportant corners and edges the very totality of the nation. As anthropologist Sarah Green has noted with respect to the Balkans, border politics do not always follow a Euclidian geometry. Borders can, and often do, operate as fractals: "breaking fractals down into parts simply gives you more parts and more wholes; however small you break it up, each part is still a complete replication of the whole."[18]

Nostalgia, Susan Stewart contends, is in fact always ideological: "The past it seeks has never existed except as narrative, and hence, always absent, that past continually threatens to reproduce itself as a felt lack. Hostile to history and its invisible origins, and yet longing for an impossibly pure context of lived experience at a place of origin, nostalgia wears a distinctly utopian face, a face that turns toward a future-past, a past which has only ideological reality."[19] Nostalgia may be hinging on utopian future-pasts, and never-to-be-realized futures, but physical traces of earlier presences nonetheless also weigh heavily in these narratives. As discussed in chapter 2, all borders are unnatural, recent, and historically contingent. They are therefore intrinsically palimpsestic, and new layers of sovereignty are only as powerful as their continued efficacy to suppress foreign pasts. Tinged with ghostly afterimages, territories lying astride competing sovereignties—but often extending in fact to the entire polity—need to be brought within discursive range through processes of co-opting, rewriting, or erasure. Architectural palimpsests, as well as cultural, historical, and etymological ones, thus form a cultural substratum always liable to resurface and break through the apparent cultural homogeneity put forth by nationalist narratives.[20]

This hyperspectral imagery resonates with Sarah Green's notion of tidemarks—those elusive yet powerful and evocative traces of past incarnations that stubbornly refuse to fade away. Green defines tidemarks as "traces of movement, which can be repetitive or suddenly change, may generate long-term effects or disappear the next day, but nevertheless continue to mark, or make, a difference that makes a difference."[21]

Like sea levels shifting with the waxing and waning of the moon, political boundaries are prone to fluctuation—in some cases they have occasionally expanded to encompass vast areas, at other times retracted to a core nucleus. This process was especially dramatic in the European corridor between Poland and Russia, which over the last three hundred years alternatively found itself under Russian, German, Polish, and Ukrainian control.[22] Other borderlands, found on the margins of imperial entities, have also been the theater of political fluctuations. Manchuria, described by Owen Lattimore as one of the "pivots of Asia," in the borderlands of Russia and China, is such a case.[23] In what follows, I take Manchuria, a somewhat problematic term, to encompass not only the three Chinese provinces of Heilongjiang, Jilin, and Liaoning (usually referred to as *dongbei* or "northeast" in Chinese), but also the Russian regions of Primorsky Krai and parts of Khabarovsk Krai, Birobidzhan, and the Amur Oblast.

Manchuria is found at the crossroads of various empires and the subject of historical claims by their successor states, principally Russia and China, but the region is also crucial to a number of other groups, such as the Koreans and Japanese.[24] For Koreans, Manchuria carries great symbolic weight, as it is the ancestral home of the Koguryŏ Kingdom (37 BCE–668 CE) and associated with national foundation myths.[25] Cradle of Korean civilization, southern Manchuria is also the site of the sacred Paektu mountain, worshiped by both Koreans and Manchus as the place of their ancestral origin.[26] In addition to these ancient and mythical ties, Korean national affect also seeps northward, in the shadow of the traumatic experience of World War II, when vast population transfers occurred, with millions encouraged (or compelled) by Japan to relocate from the southern peninsula to Manchuria with the view to colonize and develop the region.[27] As these population transfers occurred largely from the southern half of the peninsula, resettlement of these displaced masses led to the emergence of a spectral Korean peninsula, literally flipped over on itself and overlaid upon southern Manchuria.[28] For Koreans, Manchuria is more than a territory simply abutting their country: steeped in both positive and negative affect, the region features prominently in Korean narratives of both cultural authenticity and loss.[29] As Nianshen Song summarizes, Manchuria represented for Koreans a "visionary homeland that bore all the past glories of an imagined community that had fallen into crisis; it was a spiritual ballast for a stateless nation."[30]

For the Japanese, Manchuria has been just as crucial to their country's modern history. With the creation of the "puppet state" of Manchukuo (1932–45), Japan hoped to secure a foothold on the mainland with the further goal of controlling the rest of the Asian continent.[31] Japanese involvement in Manchuria led to countless human and personal tragedies. In addition to the numerous Chinese and Korean casualties, around 1.5 million Japanese perished in Manchuria—the highest death toll, in fact, of Japanese civilians in World War II.[32] After the war, 1.2 million Japanese civilians were repatriated, but many were left behind.[33]

But if the Japanese psyche associates Manchuria with war, loss, and suffering, Manchuria is for Japan also a place that had been imbued with much hope and anticipation and imagined as a place where utopia, or "a new heaven on earth" (*shintenchi*) could be built.[34] As Prasenjit Duara wrote, "Idealists and visionaries of every hue saw there a frontier of boundless possibilities that were unlikely to be found in any other part of the Japanese

Empire."[35] It was presented to the Japanese as vast, virgin lands where the nation could be reinvented and renewed.[36]

These wartime Japanese narratives in fact closely echoed Russian (and Soviet) discourse about the region. In the middle of the nineteenth century, the nation's attention was redirected toward northeast Asia, focusing specifically on the Amur River. Suddenly, geographer Mark Bassin writes, "an obscure region which had not only been a virtual *terra incognita* for the Russians but moreover did not even figure as a part of their imperial dominions was able to attract the interest of the entire society, excite widespread enthusiasm, and even nourish the dreams of the country's most outstanding social and political visionaries."[37] In fact, the very lack of knowledge about this region made it possible to imbue it with a rich "kaleidoscope of meanings and significations."[38] It constituted an empty signifier that could become the vector for the political and social preoccupations of the moment.

The Amur region, and later the Primor'e and Chinese Manchuria, became in fact a blank canvas onto which a renewed and revitalized Russian future could be projected. Parallels with the New World and America were rife, with Russian writer and activist Kropotkin comparing the Amur River to the Mississippi, and Murav'ev equating the town of Nikolaevsk with San Francisco. The discovery of gold and other riches, and the subsequent mushrooming of settlements such as the so-called Zheltuga Republic, greatly facilitated these associations.[39] Later, the founding of Harbin—a node of Russian culture deep in Chinese Manchuria—was invested with similar significance, as a later section of this chapter shows.

Manchuria has also been symbolically central to the Chinese nation, with many contemporary Chinese cultural associations directly inherited from the Manchu, after whom the region is known, at least outside China.[40] The Amur River, which later came to delineate the international border between Russia and China, was especially crucial to both: for Russians it was the only access to the Pacific Ocean; for the Manchu it was a sacred river integral to their mythology. As the Russians consolidated their presence in the region, they gradually began encroaching upon Manchu territory. The treaties of Nerchinsk (1689) and Beijing (1860) were the outcome of the dramatic encounter between two culturally different groups, and the seed of much lasting hostility. If neither Russia nor China is currently making territorial claims to parts of Manchuria no longer under its control, the region remains, for both of them, as well as for Japan and Korea, a place suffused with affect and steeped in narratives of modernity, progress, and loss (see figure 3.2).

The formation of the Chinese state has often been described as a process of gradual expansion outward, slowly incorporating lands on its margins in

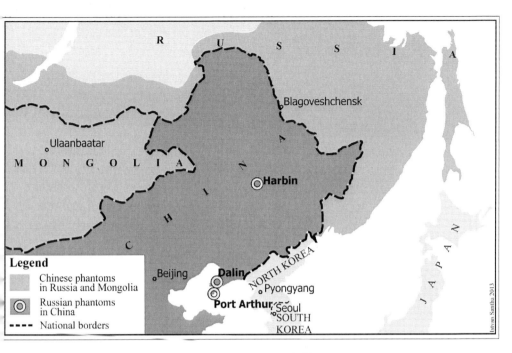

3.2. István Sántha, phantom territories in Russia and China.

a process of Sinicization or "cooking" of surrounding barbarian groups.[41] From a cultural center located in the North China Plain, China is perceived to exist "at the center of an ever-widening series of concentric borderlands."[42] Current Chinese cartographic practices similarly convey a somewhat elastic sense of China. As William Callahan has noted, official Chinese maps are often imaginative and aspirational, and they inscribe territories not under state control but that could (or should) be part of China's sovereign territory.[43] Maps of the PRC thus include Taiwan as a province of China, along with the territory of Kashmir and numerous islands disputed by Japan, Korea, the Philippines, and other southern neighbors. In the same way, until very recently Republic of China (ROC) maps included Outer Mongolia as well as Tuva and other regions included within the territory of the Qing Empire. These numerous, overlapping, and inconsistent cartographic footprints elicit both confusion and anxiety in China's neighbors and lead to an image of China viewed as imperialistic and land hungry.

From a Chinese perspective, lost territories formerly included within the national boundaries qualify as phantoms insofar as they are closely associated with traumatic events and with what is called the Century of National

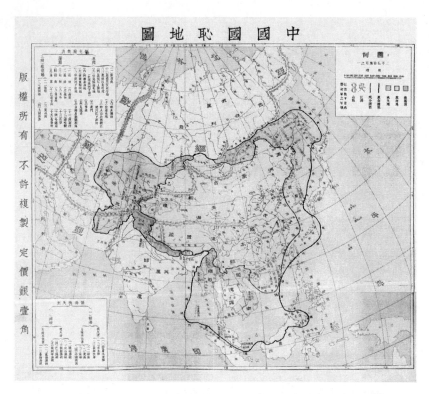

3.3. Map of China's national humiliation, reprint (中國百年國恥地圖, 再版) Shanghai: Zhonghua Shuju (上海中華書局), 1927. Chinese University of Hong Kong. Courtesy of William A. Callahan, https://sensiblepolitics.net.

Humiliation (*bainian guochi* 百年国耻), the period of foreign intervention and imperialism by Western powers and Japan in China between 1839 and 1949 (figure 3.3). This is made graphically evident in maps of national humiliation, which often mark in red ink the treaty ports, massacres, and other wounds inflicted upon China during that time.[44] Even if these lost regions are not all officially claimed by China, they retain a strong metaphoric force. Some of these territories may be little more than tiny specks of land, yet they condense much pride and national affect, and are often invested with a significance that extends well beyond their geopolitical value or the material resources that they hold (see chapter 4).

A fascinating aspect of the Sino-Russian border in Manchuria is that the layered structure of China's cultural space is mirrored across the international boundary. While Chinese space has traditionally been conceptualized as a series of concentric circles around a Chinese core, Russian sovereign space is similarly striated by several layers of protection and buffer zones marking the limits of the polity. But unlike Chinese political space that extends outward beyond a cultural core, Russian political space is inward-looking. The Russian state border is thus supplemented by further lines of defense, and virtually the whole length of Russia's border with China is insulated by two additional kinds of demarcation: a no-man's land (*dublirovanie pogranichnoi polosy*) that frequently includes plowed-out strips and which, at some points along the border, may extend to widths of several miles; and a zone of fortification (*ukreplennye rayony*), which typically includes obstructions and/or minefields. In addition, at several points one also finds what historian Prescott has called "relict boundaries," that is, ancient lines of demarcation that have been abandoned but continue to endure through differences in the landscape.[45]

The Great Wall is perhaps the most visible and emblematic of such relict boundary lines, but it is not the only one. The cultural front between China and her northern neighbors is in fact replete with supplementary boundary markers. Chingis Khan's Northern Wall (Severny Val Chingis-Khana), for instance, a 340-mile-long demarcation line built during the Jin dynasty (1115–1234), was the first and unsuccessful attempt by Jurchen rulers to protect themselves from Tatar and Mongolian tribes.[46] Some of these older lines of defense have now grown faint and barely perceptible, but their effects tend to be long lasting. At sites that marked the divide between Eastern and Western Europe, for instance, lines of fracture are still apparent on the ground.[47] A palimpsest of overlapping political realms, borderland environments are frequently dotted with ruins—of castles, churches, and fortifications.[48] At times, differing practices of land use also lead to drastic differences in the physical landscape and ecology. These various historical lines are, I suggest, a fitting illustration for Sarah Green's notion of tidemarks, that temporal oscillation of lines of sovereignty over space.

The geographical space found at the juncture of sovereignties is perhaps best envisaged as constituted of interstices, ridges, whorls, and folds, forming a complex entanglement of social, cultural, and personal histories. Like two skins pressing on each other—I return to this particular aspect in chapter 4— the contact surface between two bodily/national entities is an interface of zones of varying sensitivity and affective intensity. Enmeshed rather than merely touching, the inherently palimpsestic nature of borders speaks to the multilayered social realities that must be tamed, reconciled, co-opted, and frequently erased by national narratives.

This intricate folding of space was expertly staged in *The City and the City*, a fantasy fiction novel by British author China Miéville, in which he describes twin cities that occupy the same physical space and where the populations of both are made to "unsee" all evidence of the other. Some of the buildings, streets, and squares are found exclusively in one city, while other parts of the cities are "crosshatched"—shared between the two. In these overlapping areas, interaction between the two cities' residents is consistently avoided: pedestrians, cars, dogs, and other "foreign obstacles" from the other city must be circumvented without explicit acknowledgment. Miéville's coinage of terms such as "unseeing" and "polite stoic unsensing" is an apt illustration of the social, racial, and economic stratification of real cities, and the invisibility of poverty and the homeless.[49] It recalls the treatment of refugees, relegated to the margins of both their own societies and the international order.[50] It also speaks to the power exerted by national imaginaries that seek to channel loyalties and affect in racial and gendered ways.[51] That this process can never be completed and therefore requires continual reinscription is hinted at by Miéville with respect to trash: "Only rubbish is an exception, when it is old enough. Lying across crosshatched pavement . . . it starts as a protub, but . . . when it coagulates with other rubbish, including rubbish from the other city, it's just rubbish, and it drifts across borders, like fog, rain and smoke."[52] In this, his reading is consonant with the work of anthropologist Yael Navaro-Yashin, whose book on material remainders in the aftermath of war, displacement, and expropriation foregrounds the ghostly materiality of postconflict environments. Specters, she argues, are not mere figments of the imagination. Lingering in the form of nonhuman tangible objects, ghosts "challenge the agencies geared to phantasmatically transform a territory," thereby exerting a force against the grain of what she calls the "make-believe"—the space, territory, administration and modes of governance, and material practices that are concurrently mobilized in the quotidian work of a national state.[53] Unsurprisingly, ruins and debris are commonly located at peripheries and in borderlands, in liminal spaces associated with the limits of the self and the abject.[54]

Just as material remnants of human presence are found in the wake of colliding geobodies, social and cultural flotsam also include place names—sometimes in fact the sole surviving trace of past presences. In the Americas, vestigial names with obscure etymologies bear witness to displaced communities and forgotten indigenous cartographies—"haunting reminders of lingering trouble," in the words of Avery Gordon.[55] Regions that have witnessed lengthy and extensive colonization are commonly dominated by names resonant of migrants' original homes, and in these new cultural cartographies autochthonous names generally constitute a barely visible palimpsest. In the Russian Far East (RFE), geography is similarly inlaid with ethnonyms evoking native homelands thousands of miles to the west. The names of the largest cities—Vladivostok (Ruler of the East), Khabarovsk (named after Russian explorer Yerofey Khabarov), and Blagoveshchensk (Annunciation)— boldly assert Russian military, cultural, and religious dominance over the region. Yet these names never entirely replaced the Chinese names given to the settlements established prior to the arrival of Russian settlers. In Chinese official documents these cities are now known by their Russian names, that is, Fuladiwosituoke, Habaluofisike, and Bulageweishensike, but these transliterations have not displaced former names, and older Chinese names often resurface in informal conversations.[56] As I finalize this book, China's Ministry of Natural Resources published new rules to be implemented on all toponymy maps, stipulating that the transliterated names of these towns should be followed by their Chinese equivalents in brackets. According to the Chinese authorities, this was merely meant to bring uniformity across Chinese maps.[57] However, surprised by the timing of these rules, against the backdrop of strengthening ties with Moscow, foreign media have been quick to interpret the decision as a symptom of incipient irredentism.

Indeed, for local Russians, these Chinese alternative names elicit much anger and anxiety. They are commonly interpreted as territorial claims and perceived as typical of Chinese geopolitical aims. By contrast, Manchu names are problematic neither for Russians nor for Chinese, insofar as the Manchu have virtually vanished and do not constitute a political threat.[58] Their physical absence renders them innocuous and subject to reinvention. In the same way that dinosaurs represent "ideal animals for the nostalgia industry because nobody remembers them," the phantomic presence of the Manchu can be evoked in various guises and for various objectives.[59] In China, despite their official presence, the Manchu are, in practice, a category eviscerated of any cultural or political content. For Russians they are categorized as extinct and therefore no more threatening than Roman ruins might be for contemporary Europe. As echoes of a defunct geobody, Manchu ethnonyms and historical presence do not impinge on Russia's footprint or claims to the region.

For Russia, Chinese historical presence understandably constitutes much more of a threat, and Russian narratives have been especially keen to disentangle Chinese involvement from regional history. In Blagoveshchensk's museum, the history of the region prior to the arrival of Russian settlers describes at length the Manchu, Evenki, and other ethnic groups but makes no mention of the Chinese. Another glaring absence is the tragic events of June 1900, when five thousand Chinese men, women, and children lost their lives at the hands of the Russians. Fearing that the Boxer Rebellion would incite the eight thousand local Chinese residents to form a fifth column, local authorities decided to deport the Chinese community in its entirety, driving them out of the city at bayonet point and forcing them to swim across the river.[60]

For Russians, Manchuria also differs from other regions lying beyond national borders in that it is enlivened with national affect. Despite not being part of the nation's geobody, Manchuria is nonetheless intimately tied to it, and "animated," in the sense evoked by both Brian Massumi and Sianne Ngai.[61] Chinese Manchuria has long exerted a powerful phantomic force for local Russians. It was the theater of crucial historical battles, particularly at the time of the Russo-Japanese War (1904–5), when ninety thousand Russian soldiers lost their lives at the battle of Mukden (February–March 1905). "On the Hills of Manchuria" ("Na sopkah Manchzhurii"), a song to the memory of the fallen soldiers, was composed the following year, to become one of Russia's most famous and popular melodies.

The accommodation in Russian cultural narratives of the phantoms of the Chinese dead, by contrast, is far more problematic. Over the last decade, a number of Russian scholars have written about the traumatic events of 1900, but this unearthing of long-forgotten events was not particularly welcome. As historian Viktor Dyatlov writes, his initial writings on the topic elicited criticisms among Russian audiences who have contested his accounts, or thought it might be preferable not to reminisce about such negative aspects of Russian history.[62] Unlike the Russian soldiers fallen in Manchuria, Chinese ghosts cannot be commemorated, remembered, or grieved.[63] Yet the repressed do return in unanticipated and indirect ways, through Chinese commemorative practices from which Russians are excluded.[64]

A museum in the Chinese town of Aihui, forty miles south of Blagoveshchensk, is dedicated to the events of 1900. A modern structure, surrounded by a park with memorial stones bearing the names of the Sixty-Four Villages East of the River, it houses numerous photographs of old Blagoveshchensk as well as a multimedia diorama recounting the fateful events of June 1900.[65] The museum is open to all visitors except Russians. To them, the museum remains shrouded in mystery, rumored to include terrible photographs as well as anti-Russian narratives. Yearly commemoration of the event is also said to take place on June 2, when residents of the neighboring city of Heihe allegedly deposit into the river little paper boats containing a candle, one for each departed soul.[66]

In *Spectres de Marx*, Jacques Derrida asks, "*What* is a ghost? What is the *effectivity* or the *presence* of a specter, that is, of what seems to remain as ineffective, virtual, insubstantial as a simulacrum?"[67] Narratives about Chinese ghosts lingering on Russian territory suggest here much more than unresolved national guilt.[68] Sustained by the remembrance and commemoration practices of the Chinese across the border, these ghosts also condense larger issues of territorial legitimacy and integrity. Just like a ghost haunting a house claims continued ownership beyond death, the phantomic presence of the Chinese victims hovering over Russia evokes the shadow of an older Chinese geobody extending deep into Russian territory. One may also interpret Chinese predatory practices in the RFE as a deployment of these phantoms. The Chinese hunger for Siberian ginseng, bear paws, tiger bones, or sea cucumbers bolsters Russian anxieties of a vampiric neighbor sucking out vital resources from the region.

In a later text, Derrida notes that "we are structured by the phantasmic, and in particular that we have a phantasmic relation to the other."[69] In the context of Russia, and in particular the Far East region, the defunct yet still potent Qing geobody continues to mold and frame Russian understanding of space. In her own work on northern Cyprus, Navaro-Yashin is careful to disentangle phantomic space from the phantasmatic—the former referring concretely to the presence of material objects and perceived by the Turkish-Cypriot inhabitants as connected to the former Greek-Cypriot residents, and the latter an affective presence belonging to the register of the imaginary, in a Lacanian sense.[70] I would argue, however, that the two are not always so easily distinguishable, and that it is perhaps in this very overlap that phantoms gain most sway and potency.

Resonant spaces have tangible and material effects and, in the case of the Russian Far East, this has percolated into a proliferation of monuments and statues seeking to imprint the region in a lasting manner. However, this continual marking of space, this very insistence on enforcing political legitimacy and cultural hegemony, unwittingly powers this phantomic force. Phantoms return in a different guise as an uneasy sense of menace, threatening to surface and submerge the region. These anxieties are often coded in racial terms, through the trope of the "Yellow Peril" for example, but can also find expression as narratives of purity and protection, equating Chinese presence with depleted flora and fauna.[71]

At the same time as Russia insists on the absence of folded space as far as the RFE is concerned, several places throughout Chinese Manchuria remain invested with affect and a ghostly Russian presence. The most important of such nodes is Harbin, a city originally founded by Russians at the turn of the twentieth century, as the Chinese Eastern Railway (or Kitaisko-Vostochnaya Zheleznaya Doroga) was being built. A Russian-owned enterprise that linked Chita to Vladivostok, the Chinese Eastern Railway brought a large contingent of Russians to the region and led to the founding of Harbin, a Russian city within Chinese territory.

For several decades, the city of Harbin remained very Russian, spatially and culturally organized around the Saint Sophia Cathedral, one of the largest Christian churches in Asia. Harbin grew significantly after the Bolshevik Revolution, to eventually become the largest center of Russian population outside the state of Russia. The streets of Harbin were lined with European-style buildings, and the city was known as the Paris of the East on account of its European presence and rich cultural life.[72] But in the 1930s, following Japanese occupation of Manchuria, most Russians left the city, some for the Soviet Union, others for other cities in China and eventually abroad. By the early 1960s, only a handful of Russians still remained, most of them elderly.

In the course of my research in Blagoveshchensk, whenever I spoke with local residents about Harbin, the city was unfailingly described to me as Russian. Irrespective of the age of the interviewee, the impression generally conveyed was that Harbin had somehow remained part of the Russian cultural topography. Harbin is the nearest sizeable Chinese city for Blagoveshchensk residents, and this is one of the reasons why it is an important destination for tourism and education, but the appeal is also due to its perceived Russianness. The sentiments expressed by Irina, a PhD student, echo what a number of other respondents also felt: "I've been to Harbin. I liked it. It's a Russian city, and the Chinese in Harbin have good attitudes towards Russians. Quite a few Chinese there can speak Russian. Some of them have Russian ancestors. There are also Russian schools, a Russian church, and many buildings left from the time Russians lived there. Many Russians also study there. There is a shop called Churin. It used to be a big Russian shop. It's still there but it's a Chinese trade center now."

However, accounts of personal experiences of the city often differed from these descriptions. More often than not, those Harbin residents who spoke Russian were in fact interpreters or tour guides, so with the majority of Harbin residents, Russian visitors had to speak English or Chinese. Interestingly, Chinese residents of Harbin do not share these perceptions of cultural hybridity. For Zhang Min, a young Chinese woman from Harbin studying in Blagoveshchensk, Harbin is not particularly Russian. She conceded that some of the architecture is Russian and that the local beer is also quite similar to Russian beer. But neither she nor her family ever thought of Harbin in those terms. In fact, Harbin is in many ways a quintessentially Chinese city. It is known in China as the city with the purest unaccented Mandarin, and its residents are keen to stress that "a disproportionate number of China's television and radio announcers hail from this northernmost city."[73] Yet for Russians it remains a space that feels somehow familiar, with a ghostly Russian past that continues to endure.

If the original Russian buildings still found in Harbin constitute only a tiny fraction of the modern city, their central location gives them an undeniable prominence. Many of these buildings, like the Churin department store, have retained only their skeletal structure and have taken on a new Chinese life. These "urban palimpsests," evoke for many Russians a sense of nostalgia about a bright future that never came to fruition.

Indeed, the sense of loss that pervades accounts of Russian Harbin is not simply tied to a past era when Russia was playing an important role in Asia, it also mourns the loss of a promise of a golden future.[74] For Russians, Manchuria was a place where they could stage their own Europeanness and showcase technological advances. By building a railway line that would link European Russia to several sea ports in China, Russians were hoping to achieve equality with Europeans.[75] The very founding of Harbin was symbolically just as potent. The emphasis on the cosmopolitanism of the city and the recurrent comparisons with Paris were not casual. They constituted a claim that Russia was just as capable as the rest of Europe to take on the role of colonial ruler. As Dostoyevsky famously wrote, "In Europe we were hangers-on and slaves, but in Asia we shall be the masters. In Europe we were Tatars, but in Asia we too are Europeans."[76]

Just like the Russian buildings left standing in Harbin, the railway line remains the primary and underlying communication structure. Akin to a skeleton, its presence highlights the crucial role of infrastructure in the conceptualization of phantoms. Indeed, Russian phantoms are in fact articulated along these older links. While the spatiality of the Chinese phantoms is imagined as seeping outward somewhat homogenously, Russian phantoms are nodular, disconnected spots of Russian presence along the Chinese Eastern Railway line: Harbin, Dalian, Port Arthur. And whereas Chinese phantom territories are extensive, imagined to stretch across lands rich in ginseng, tigers, bears, and other resources, Russian phantoms are localized, some of them deep within China, like Dalian. And unlike the Chinese phantom territories, Russian phantom space is inherently fractured and discontinuous.

PHANTOM PAINS

The collapse of the Qing Empire in the early twentieth century signaled the end of China's dynastic succession and the advent of a republic. It also marked the loss of Outer Mongolia, which broke away in 1921 to become an independent political entity, and geopolitical dislocation was accentuated further by Japanese military intervention in Manchuria in the first part of the twentieth century. Upon the establishment of the People's Republic, China fully recognized Mongolia's independence in 1949 and formally renounced all claims to Siberia. Yet in the popular imagination these territories remain tied historically and culturally to the body of the Chinese nation. This loss regularly finds expression in informal conversation and occasionally in more formal settings as well. Thus, in the 1980s, the following story circulated in Chinese classrooms: "Japan, with its silkworm-like shape, ate away [Outer] Mongolia during the Second World War. Before the war, the geographic shape of China had looked like a type of leaf silkworms eat. After the war, the geographic shape of China resembled a cockerel which meant that it would 'conquer' Japan like a cockerel that eats any type of worms for lunch."[77] This amusing story, with its use of zoomorphic imagery, resonates with narratives of territorial loss heard in other ethnographic contexts and described in chapter 2. Metaphors of territorial loss are often far grislier. John Borneman, in his study of Berlin's reunification, described, for instance, the newly reassembled German capital as "suturing together its halved corpse composed of mangled limbs and appendages so out of place, so absurdly placed, as to mimic Picasso's wildest fantasies of dismembered bodies."[78]

I argued in chapter 2 that these similes are not simply expressive turns of phrase but that they reveal a conceptual overlap between national map and body map as well as the extent to which individuals (insofar as they have been successfully socialized as national subjects) come to perceive the national geocontour as an extension of their own body. Given this close parallel, the experience of territorial loss can elicit affect that discursively resembles the phenomenon known as phantom limbs. These eerie sensations are stubborn ghosts of limbs lost years or even decades before but not forgotten by the brain. Enduring through the mental map held in the brain's circuitry, these sensations continue to be perceived long after the disappearance of their sensory stimuli. Well known in popular culture, the concept of phantom pain has proven a potent metaphor for issues of unresolved territorial loss. Animated through the broader conceptual enmeshment of *body* and *state*, the phantom metaphor is one that immediately and intuitively makes sense and that, unsurprisingly, has been used by a number of border scholars and critical theorists, though often left untheorized.[79] However, as I show in this chapter, a deeper dive into the medical history of the term and the neurology literature helps tease out the mechanics behind this intuitive resonance, thus bringing to the surface the many assumptions smuggled into the body-state interface.

The phantom limb phenomenon was first medically observed as early as 1545 by French surgeon Ambroise Paré, who was a battlefield surgeon and one of the fathers of modern surgery. But it would be another three hundred years before a medical article was published on this unusual phenomenon, by American physician Weir Mitchell, though anonymously as he feared being ridiculed by his colleagues. Written as a fictional short story and published in 1866 in the *Atlantic Monthly*, "The Case of George Dedlow" recounts the experience of a wounded Civil War captain who loses his two arms and later both legs to amputation. Reduced to a head and a torso, Dedlow is the subject of vivid phantom pains in his missing limbs.

The story is believed to have been inspired by the many wounded soldiers Mitchell treated in the course of the Civil War. Although this was the first time the phenomenon was discussed seriously, phantom pains had been and remain relatively common, affecting 60 to 80 percent of individuals experiencing amputation.[80] Phantom pains usually affect arms and legs, but they are not limited to limbs. Phantoms have been noted after the loss of breasts, the nose, the larynx, and the rectum. Phantom ulcer pains have been reported following gastrectomies, while phantom penises have experienced phantom erections and even phantom orgasms.[81] Postamputation pain appears to be closely tied to the level of discomfort prior to amputation, which has in fact encouraged physicians to reduce pain levels prior to amputation in order to avoid the emergence of phantom limb pain. The limb may be missing, but the pain is very real—and all the more difficult to alleviate because the limb is missing. Not taken sufficiently seriously, the reality of phantom pains is too often devalued through its discursive use in the domains of aesthetics, culture, and philosophy.[82] As Mark Bishop writes, paraphrasing the comment of an attendee at a conference on phantom pains held at Goldsmiths College, London, "Phantom limbs don't instill a pleasant reminiscence of a mystical past but a simple, fucking excruciating, aching present."[83] The disconnect between the absence of a limb and the experience of pain may sound somewhat counterintuitive. Yet somatic sensations such as stinging, smarting, tickling, or itching do not have external equivalents: they are generated by structures in the brain. As Ronald Melzack points out, the body does not learn to feel these "qualities of experience"; our brains are built to produce them.[84] In fact, on account of the tingling or pins and needles experienced by an amputee, the phantom frequently develops "an overwhelming presence in the patient's awareness" and may be experienced as more "real" than the real limb.[85]

Often a phantom leg or arm will be experienced as a normal limb, moving in perfect coordination with the other limbs. But, over time, the limb tends to assume a pathological character, "becoming intrusive, 'paralyzed,' deformed, or excruciatingly painful—phantom fingers may dig into a phantom palm with an unspeakable, unstoppable intensity."[86] Melzack reports a case in which the phantom arm was experienced as extending straight out at the shoulder and at a right angle to the body.[87] The phantom was experienced so vividly that the patient turned sideways to walk through doorways so that the phantom arm would not hit the wall. Also very common is the telescoping phenomenon, where the phantom gradually shrinks and the arm becomes progressively shorter, the patient eventually left with just a phantom hand dangling from the stump.[88] As I discuss in more depth in chapter 4, this phenomenon is linked to cortical magnification and to the fact that the hand is overrepresented in the somatosensory cortex.

Until comparatively recently, surgeons were not sure how to treat the problem, let alone whether to take it seriously. To alleviate the pain, a second and sometimes third amputation was at times performed, thus making the stump shorter and shorter but failing to make the problem go away. In the 1990s, neurologist Vilayanur Ramachandran and his research team devised a new technique called "mirror visual feedback" to help alleviate the pain of phantom limbs. They constructed a "virtual reality box," made of a lidless cardboard box with a mirror placed vertically in the middle. The front of the box has two holes in it, through which the patient inserts both the real, physical hand and the phantom hand. The patient then positions the physical hand so that the mirror reflection appears to be superimposed on the felt position of the phantom hand.[89] As the patient moves the physical hand, her brain is tricked into seeing the missing limb move, thereby making it possible for her to unclench it from painful positions and eliminate the pain.

Mirror therapy appears to have met with considerable success, but only when the optical illusion is maintained. This is not altogether surprising: visual feedback has been shown to play a crucial role in the relation between Self and Other. Vision was demonstrated, for instance, to productively augment tactile sensations, and a number of scientific experiments have shown the highly synesthetic nature of body image formation. In one such experiment, known as the Pinocchio illusion, the subject sits blindfolded at a table, her arm flexed at the elbow, holding the tip of her own nose. When vibration is applied to the biceps, the subject feels that her arm becomes extended, but she is still aware of holding her nose. Confronted with this paradox, the brain concludes that the nose is now thirty centimeters long.[90] The mirror therapy devised by Ramachandran works precisely on such corrective corporeal feedback mechanisms. As Nicola Diamond argues, this play with mirrors is "a direct intervention into the visual imaginary . . . with the purpose to create misrecognition to reinforce the body image as an enacted schema."[91]

The current medical consensus is that phantom sensations are due to a discrepancy between the actual physical body and the body map held in the brain. For a long time it was believed that mental representations accrued and gained strength with time, and that prolonged sensory input was required for the formation of a cortical representation of the limb. This thesis appeared to be supported by research showing that younger amputees, whose mental map had not yet been fully integrated, experienced these sensations to a much lesser extent.[92] More recent research suggests that the occurrence of phantom limb pain is more complex, involves both somatic and psychological factors, and is also tied to the ways and speed with which the limb is lost. The phenomenon does not occur, for example, in patients who lose their limb progressively due to diseases such as leprosy. This would appear to confirm the hypothesis that the patient can gradually learn to register and assimilate the corporeal changes through visual feedback.[93]

However, the phenomenon is also reported by individuals who were born without that limb and who could therefore neither remember a previous bodily formation nor have experienced conflict in terms of visual feedback. In a more unusual case, a phantom limb formed postamputation in a patient who was born with a phocomelic hand—a rare congenital condition involving a malformation of the limbs. Following amputation due to an accident, she "sprouted a phantom hand that contained five digits, including a phantom thumb and index finger that had been absent since her birth."[94]

These examples would seem to suggest the existence of a bodily image that is hardwired in the brain rather than a surviving echo of a prior incarnation. As mentioned previously, vividness of the phenomenon appears to be linked to the levels of pain experienced prior to the loss, but more recent research also suggests the phenomenon is closely tied to personality types and coping styles. Thus, those with rigid personalities or the tendency to catastrophize have been shown to experience phantom limbs more than individuals who were "active copers."[95]

Psychoanalysts and cultural theorists tend to be in agreement with neuroscientists in that they view the emergence of a phantom limb as a coping strategy constructed by the unconscious to deal with sudden and overwhelming bodily transformations. For Ramachandran, phantom limbs are far from irrational. They constitute an emergency defense mechanism, on a par with strategies such as denial, projection, or repression.[96] For Elizabeth Grosz, the phantom limb specifically represents the "reassertion of the limb's presence" in an "attempt to preserve the subject's narcissistic sense of bodily wholeness."[97] Her argument is strongly Lacanian insofar as it sees the individual's sense of self tied to the mirror stage and therefore both visual and strongly corporeal.[98] For Grosz, bodily integrity is in fact at the core of human self-perception. Citing Paul Schilder, she argues that, unlike animals such as the dog or the wasp, who will readily gnaw off a broken limb that hampers their movement, humans appear to privilege corporeal wholeness above all else—thus demonstrating the culturally constructed nature of the body.[99]

A number of psychoanalysts and anthropologists have been uneasy with such universal claims and have contended that the presence and vividness of phantom limbs may not be the same in all cultures. Psychoanalyst Nicola Diamond asserts that phantom limbs, in that they signify an "unacceptable loss that resists integration into a new body schema," are tied to a particular culture's emphasis on body-self integrity. She posits that the "distressful symptoms of the phantom" are "inseparable from cultures . . . embedded in the egoistic conviction in a body-self" and asks whether "less self-obsessed and individualist cultures"—which I understand here as shorthand for Euro-America—experience phantom limbs in such a traumatic way.[100] While this insight is thought-provoking, the research carried out by Lindsey French on amputees at the Thai-Cambodia border would appear to support the idea that bodily integrity does extend beyond cultural variability. To a degree, French's findings do resonate with Diamond's critique of universality. She insists, for instance, that even the most apparently subjective and personal experiences such as the experience of one's own body are shaped by, and embedded in, the relations of power and domination in which the body is involved and that the loss of a limb does not therefore translate seamlessly between different cultural contexts.[101] At the same time, the sense of devaluation her informants express extends well beyond physical injury, social disability, or even the loss of the body as an economic resource.[102] Some of her interviewees report feeling less of a person compared to preamputation, reduced in their physical but also mental capacities. Her interviewees' cultural understandings of the body differ drastically from Euro-American conceptualizations in that they are deeply embedded in a Theravada Buddhist hierarchy of merit and virtue, and tied to the concepts of karma and reincarnation, but they nonetheless posit bodily integrity as deeply enmeshed in notions of the body and the self. The significance of bodily integrity also appears to be closely tied to ideals of masculinity, as the work of Jennifer Terry and Salih Can Açıksöz shows in the context of loss of limb among military men in the contemporary United States and Turkey, respectively.[103] In her research on amputations in Victorian England, Erin

O'Connor similarly traces a connection between loss of limb and feminization. Phantom limbs in particular were perceived as "neurological disorders that gave the fragmented male body . . . a distinctly feminine side."[104]

The centrality of bodily integrity resonates here strongly with my earlier argument about the importance of lost territories in the imagination of the nation-state. The corporeal discourse in which territorial loss is woven is surprisingly consistent, even in contexts as disparate as Russia, India, or South America. The point I want to make here is that territorial loss is discussed— and largely experienced—as a mutilation, as a loss that is affective and visceral, not cartographic, abstract, and disembodied.[105]

Of course, the struggle to come to terms with a new logomap cannot be assumed to be uniform across time and place, nor indeed to be experienced in the same way by all individuals in a given nation-state. Just as individuals show variation in their response to the loss of a limb, some nation-states will integrate a new national outline comparatively quickly, while for others the former logomap will continue to dominate self-representations and imaginations for decades or longer.[106] I suggest, and will discuss at length in chapter 4, that these national differences echo the variety of responses shown by individuals following the loss of a limb. In addition to security, economic, and geopolitical concerns, differences are also tied to the ways in which the loss has occurred, the perception of trauma, and the affective and fetishistic investment in the wound. It is crucial to bear in mind that the state is not one but multiple, constituted of diverse parts and actors. Consequently, as Elizabeth Dunn phrases it very nicely, "The building of a new state . . . unspools over time and in unpredictable ways."[107]

History is replete with examples of politicians making demagogic and self-serving usage of corporeal analogies to garner support. A pertinent illustration is Putin's political move to reintegrate Crimea into Russia's fold. The cartographic redrawing of borders that saw the loss of this small but crucial peninsula following the dissolution of the Soviet Union was experienced as a trauma by many Russians. Symbolically equivalent to what would represent the slicing off of Florida for the United States, the loss of Crimea has been couched in a language of male pride and castration.[108] Outside Russia, these narratives have often been described as a discursive strategy to gain a larger foothold in the Black Sea and to its subsoil oil reserves. While this may well be the case, the fact that such discursive strategies are so effective in harnessing political support substantiates my premise that national territory is suffused with deep emotional attachment. The reconquest of Crimea in 2014 has in fact greatly elevated Putin's standing, possibly above all other Russian leaders since Stalin, despite the suffering economic sanctions have caused to the majority of Russians. For many, the reintegration of Crimea represents nothing less than the reconstitution of a politically weakened and physically mangled country, a political endeavor worthy of great sacrifices.

Corporeal metaphors may seem hackneyed and facile, but they remain nonetheless highly potent and ubiquitous, and they index the depth of emotional investment in the logomap. In cultural contexts as different as India and Ireland, the surgical metaphors of operation, dissection, amputation, dismemberment, and vivisection have thus been some of the most common metaphors to discuss partition.[109] In his discussion of "cartographic anxieties," Sankaran Krishna recounts his shock when he was first confronted with an outline of India with the "crown of India (Kashmir) . . . lopped off."[110] And despite being later confronted with "various portions of India being gashed by lines of control, ceasefire lines, McMahon lines," he confesses that the "pristine image of an India suspended in space" remains indelibly inscribed in his mind.[111] The loss of that original logomap, so intimately tied to an individual's socialization as member of a political and cultural community, is unsurprisingly often akin to mourning. The rumor that Salman Rushdie always carries with him a small block of silver engraved with a map of a united, unpartitioned India makes for a beautiful and poignant illustration of this strong and resilient attachment.[112] Previous logomaps, such as those of unpartitioned India, undivided Yugoslavia, or unbroken Soviet Union, evoke aspirations of unity, progress, and social harmony that are no longer extant but have not been entirely abandoned. In the context of postsocialist Russia, as Alexander Etkind writes, the work of mourning remains incomplete and unsuccessful, the loss lastingly incorporated into the subject.[113] Past border outlines also retain an explosive power liable to "tear apart the present," all the more potent because their lifespans—longer than those of humans—"elicit, evoke, or emit possible alternative futures."[114]

PARTITIONS

Given the symbolic import of territorial/bodily integrity, the specter of dislocation is one that frequently proves terrifying. Anthropologist Madeleine Reeves recounts the shock and dismay of Kyrgyz audiences upon hearing Russian political commentators debate the merits of dividing their country into two, a familiar story that has been heard elsewhere countless times.[115] But if territorial redrawing can be a traumatic prospect—indeed one that is routinely precluded through military dissuasion—it can also be actively sought. The secession desires of minority groups, from Xinjiang to Tibet, Catalonia to Scotland, is a familiar narrative reminding us that territorial integrity is but one side of the story. As Arie Dubnov and Laura Robson show, the idea of territorial partition as an answer to ethnic, national, and sectarian conflict is in fact no more than a hundred years old, having emerged as "a consequence of a particular alignment of global interests" and "disguising continuities and even expansions" of French and British imperial power.[116] Partition, whose earliest and most prominent cases include Ireland, India, and Palestine, has undeniable colonial roots and is intimately entangled in the institutionalization of imperial privilege.[117]

Cultural and linguistic homogeneity often takes precedence over concerns of territorial magnitude at the potential cost of human lives and much suffering. Indeed, if territorial scission can occur through diplomatic means—as in the case of Czechoslovakia's smooth dissolution into two independent countries in 1993—more often than not it is a highly traumatic event involving rapes, killings, the displacement of vast populations, and the infliction of physical destruction. India's partition saw the displacement of around fifteen million people and caused tremendous violence, with between one and two million killed, 75,000 women and girls raped, and millions of refugees left impoverished.[118]

Yet even the most traumatic fractures are productive to the extent that they generate new lines, new maps, and new border regimes, fashion new identities, and reconfigure memories and histories.[119] As Benedict Anderson has famously argued, group categories such as *nation* involve not only internal homogeneity but also the casting out of what is alien and different: no nationalist, no matter how messianic, would ever dream of claiming the whole world.[120] To become a nation-state is thus not only a matter of gaining additional territory; it is also to relinquish, to pose barriers, to refuse enclosure of territory—in other words, a dual process of inclusion and exclusion.

Political scientist Sankaran Krishna has argued that India's partition was a "creation by amputation."[121] His reading can be productively augmented here by a further theorization of the etymological link between the terms *partition* and *parturition*. The process whereby India and Pakistan were wrenched apart from each other was akin to a birth insofar as it constituted a process of individuation.[122] Both nations did, and in fact still largely do, define themselves in contrast to each other. It is through expulsion, through casting out of the abject, that identity is formed, and it is therefore hardly surprising that the founding acts of nation-states are nearly always bloody and violent.[123] While the violence of partition was inflicted by both sides at unparalleled scale, causing an estimated one million deaths and the rape, abduction, and forcible impregnation of 75,000 women, much violence was also brought upon Hindus and Muslims by their own community in the form of honor killings to prevent women from being forcibly converted or becoming reproductive vessels for the Other.[124]

The mechanics whereby nations seek to limit themselves have not been accorded the same attention as desires for territorial extension. And yet expansion can be seen as just as threatening in that it constitutes a dilution of national or supranational identity. This has been especially visible with the enlargement of the European Union following the collapse of the Soviet Union, from twelve states in 1990 to twenty-seven as of 2023, with half a dozen potential candidates still on the waiting list. Initially empowering for the EU as it encroached on the former Soviet satellites, the seemingly endless enlargement quickly provoked much political and cultural anxiety in that it blurred Europe's borders and appeared to empty of substance the very geopolitical, cultural, and racial framework on which it operated.

I cited in chapter 2 John Prescott's assertion that "there is no recorded case of a state wishing to withdraw to natural boundaries," a statement implying that it is always in a state's interest to expand its borders further.[125] History tells us this is not entirely true. Despite strong lobbies by the Philippines at the turn of the twentieth century to become the United States' fifty-first state, for instance, Washington opposed these propositions, feeling that the integration of such a large community (eight million in 1900, i.e., 10 percent of the population of the United States) would be unworkable and would shift what "Americanness" was imagined to be, both in cultural and racial terms.[126] Similarly, the rapid eastward advance of the Russian Empire in the sixteenth and seventeenth centuries proceeded apace once the Urals were crossed: unhindered by any natural barriers, Russia's expansion only stopped when it reached the Altai mountains and the Pacific Ocean, and when it encountered the great powers of Japan, China, and the British and Ottoman Empires. The rapid ingestion of such a vast expanse provoked ambivalent responses. On the one hand, it elicited national pride and placed Russia on a par with other colonizing powers such as Britain or France, but on the other hand, it was also perceived as a dilution of Russianness. "Was Russia's new acquisition on the Manchurian frontier, with its monsoon climate and subtropical vegetation, really Russia after all?" asks geographer Mark Bassin.[127] The ingurgitation of Alaska was similarly interpreted by many contemporary Russians as territorially unmanageable and a dangerous dilution of Russianness. What this brought to light, Bassin adds, was "a particularly vulnerable aspect of

Russia's view of itself as a nation, namely the fact that there was no clear and commonly accepted notion of exactly, or even approximately, what its geographical contours were."[128] Russia differed in this sense from other colonial enterprises such as the British and the French, whose colonies were territorially discontinuous. For Russia, every advance shifted its own borders, morphing the country into an ever more powerful, but also increasingly Asiatic, polity.

From the perspective of a nation-state's center of gravity, an outlying territory that differs dramatically from the majority in ethnic or cultural terms, or is underperforming from an economic perspective, may be perceived as counterproductive to national interests and as a dead weight best jettisoned. Unlike cases of secession, where an outlying province or minority region desires to break away from a dominant majority, the perspective is reversed and it is here the center—or a region that perceives itself as such—that seeks a redrawing of the boundaries. Here, the underperforming region is perceived as poorly integrated in the state's self-image, not an organic part of the whole and lying outside the nation's true geobody.

If the loss of part of a territory produces an affective force reminiscent of phantom pains, the desire to cut off part of the territory under one's sovereign control indexes a similar disconnect between an imagined geobody and current geopolitical realities. The analogy between territorial loss and phantom pains that I am mining here in order to tease out the conceptual overlap between somatic and political symptoms can in fact be productively extended to other body integrity identity disorders. Somatoparaphrenia is a disorder whereby a patient denies ownership of one of his limbs, and which in rare cases may lead to apotemnophilia, a strong desire for the amputation of a healthy limb.[129] These two disorders are closely related to the phenomenon of phantom limbs insofar as they indicate the presence of a conflict between, on the one hand, the body map held in the patient's brain and, on the other, the proprioceptive and visual feedback from that particular limb.[130] Although rare, cases of apotemnophilia are sufficiently prevalent to have been the focus of both medical and legal studies. It is estimated that several thousand individuals worldwide "wish to get rid of a normal healthy limb," but the phenomenon is still poorly understood.[131] When it is reported in the media, apotemnophilia tends to be derided or equated with madness.[132] Both the public and physicians are divided on the issue—should it be treated as cosmetic surgery, or is it a symptom of a psychiatric disorder requiring treatment?[133] Current research suggests that these individuals are "typically rational, non-psychotic and non-delusional" and that desires of apotemnophilia are both specific and resistant to therapy.[134] Characteristically, these individuals strongly feel that the limb—it may be a leg or an arm—is extraneous and should be removed for their bodies to become complete and coherent, to "return them to what they truly are and should be."[135] They are also very specific as to where they feel their bodies should end, typically designating the exact point where amputation should be carried out, a location remaining fixed and constant over the years, here again suggesting the existence of a rigid and unchanging bodily map.

If apotemnophilia sounds like a very alien phenomenon, a number of scholars have drawn attention to the actual prevalence of body modifications to comply with various social and cultural norms. Surgical amputations in children born with perfectly healthy but superfluous limbs or digits in order to adhere to a "normative model of embodiment" is not qualitatively different.[136] Taking this further, one may also draw parallels with the excision of healthy tissue in the case of male circumcision or indeed with procedures such as liposuction.[137] In all these cases, the desired method and the ultimate goal are the same: the pursuit of pure identity.[138]

Political analogies for such disorders have occasionally been drawn, such as a Forbes article discussing somatoparaphrenia in the context of the European Union.[139] Arguably rare on account of their political, economic, and administrative repercussions, such geopolitical redrawings tend to be advocated by splinter political groups rather than central governments. One such group is the Italian right-wing party Lega Nord, a faction of which has relentlessly advocated amputation of boot-shaped Italy above the knee. With Milan and the northernmost regions the country's economic powerhouse, a sizable share of the region's inhabitants feel secession from the rest of Italy would be preferable. The rationale is thus partly economic—believing that the redrawn country would perform more efficiently without the culturally rich but economically weak south—but it is also one of image, sense of belonging, and desire for recognition. The proper geobody, for these Italian nationalists, is that of Padania, a compact central European state bordering France, Switzerland, and Austria, and which excludes the remainder of the Italian boot dangling into the Mediterranean.

While I am being somewhat facetious here, I would nonetheless suggest that body integrity identity disorders constitute useful categories to think with insofar as such misalignments and gaps can shed important light on the workings of modern nationalism, where an equivalence is implicitly made between the body of the nation and the individual bodies of its citizens. The phantoms discussed in this chapter evoke principally romanticized pasts and nostalgic longings, a mourning for a formerly complete self that is now mangled and incomplete. But phantoms can also be about never-quite-finalized separations, about a spectral image that persistently endures, a somewhat larger doppelgänger that refuses to fade away. A case in point is the so-called phantom fat of the anorexic—the self-image that survives despite visual feedback. Even after attaining her desired weight, the anorexic continues to see herself as overweight, the phantom of her formerly obese self driving her to shed even more weight.[140]

I highlighted in this section the crucial significance of secession and partition for processes of individuation and the emergence of a nation-state. Occasionally, "partitions also produce 'schizophrenic' entities claiming to be the true embodiment of the nation, and seeking reunification in their image."[141] Illustrations of this phenomenon are, for instance, Taiwan, which sees itself as the true repository of a Chineseness culturally and politically contaminated by the communist government, or the Korean peninsula— or Germany during the Cold War period—dissected into two antagonistic halves. Related to this is what I call "prosthetic territories," that is, cities, sites, and terrains that constitute extensions of the national self and where national dreams and aspirations are mobilized, deployed, and (re)animated. Not claimed as integral parts of the nation-state, these outlying fragments supplement the national self, extending it further and reaching beyond the limits of the logomap.

PROSTHETICS

I described earlier how the city of Harbin—present-day capital of the Chinese province of Heilongjiang—remains for many Russians a Russian space. Similarly, the whole region of Manchuria, while never integrated into Russia's political space, continues to hold a special place in its cultural imaginary. For Russians at the turn of the twentieth century, Manchuria was described as Russia's "entry ticket" (*vkhodnoi bilet*) into Europe, a step toward full membership in the European family of nations.[142] Descriptions of Harbin as a Paris of the East were, as I mentioned previously, a reflection of the city's rich cultural life and international flavor, but they also constituted a claim to parity with Europe. Cultural imaginations also extended far beyond assertions of equality. Manchuria, and to some extent Siberia and the rest of the Russian Far East, was a "repository of unspoiled national qualities that could regenerate or even replace Russia west of the Urals."[143] It was potentially a freer and more democratic place—where "Jews could be Russians"—ultimately a place of (re)discovery of Russianness itself.[144]

Located outside of Russia, Manchuria was nonetheless connected to it through modern railway technology, specifically the Chinese Eastern Railway along which was founded the city of Harbin. Russia's connection to Manchuria was one of aspiration and anticipation, narrated through a discourse of modernity and technology. If late and postsocialist Russian writing about Harbin tends to be characterized by nostalgic memoirs of a bygone era, its appeal is in fact a romanticism of past futures, of unrealized potential. As Svetlana Boym has shown, nostalgia and modernity are often coeval.[145] Nostalgia is not literal but lateral in the sense that nostalgic reconstructions are based on mimicry, with the past remade in the image of the present or a desired future.[146]

Other phantomic places are more firmly associated with the past, with the foundational myths of the nation. Ukraine is such a place for Russia—a separate nation-state yet not quite foreign either. Culturally and linguistically close to Russia, Ukraine—and particularly its capital Kyiv—is in fact the birthplace of modern Russia, with Kyivan Rus' (882–1240), a loose federation of East Slavic tribes, claimed as cultural ancestor.[147] As mentioned previously, the breakup of the Soviet Union, which saw Ukraine become an independent entity, elicited strong phantom pains for Russia. That these phantoms suddenly became reactivated—culminating with the recent reintegration of Crimea into the Russian geobody—shows the strong affective potentiality linked to phantasmatic territories and their capacity in harnessing and (re)animating past incarnations.[148] Phantoms may not always lead to irredentist aspirations. What they index is the problematic hyphen of the nation-state, that uncomfortable gap between the political entity delineated by the state and the imagined, fractured, and leaky space of the nation.

The phantomic phenomenon I call "prosthetic territories" is therefore not placed in direct equivalence to colonialism or irredentism.[149] Phantoms can, and indeed do, occasionally flare up into border disputes or turn into imperialist ventures, but they are qualitatively different. Ultimately, prosthetic territories relate not to possession but to extension, and the cultural claims they make tend to be expressed in a language of affinity and augmentation.[150] This is especially visible in the way Chinese state media and bloggers increasingly refer to China's "lost territories" with ethnonyms that imply a prolongation of the country's territory. Thus the ninety thousand square kilometers in Arunachal Pradesh is referred to as South Tibet.[151] Similarly, some Chinese nationalists have begun referring to China's lost territories in Manchuria (what are now the Russian regions of Primorsky Krai and parts of Khabarovsk Krai,

Birobidzhan, and the Amur Oblast) as Outer Manchuria (Wai Dongbei). While this name has not yet gained wide acceptance, it is clearly constructed on the same model as Outer Mongolia (Wai Menggu), thus suggesting that this vast territory was previously an integral part of China, on a par with Mongolia. The *outer* element (*wai*) denotes here a territory presently beyond the border but inherently linked to China, echoing an unspoken *inner* (*nei*), bringing the two parts in dialogue and hinting at a primordial unity. These lexical aspects are an apt illustration of the spectral afterimages discussed here in that they seek to culturally appropriate territories not included within the polity but which continue to exert an affective force in nationalist narratives.

The Chinese case may be unusual in its lexical usage,[152] but the extension of a state beyond its borders is common political practice. All states—at least those that are not landlocked—have maritime borders that extend miles outward. Coasts are lined by territorial waters (a ribbon of twelve nautical miles) and by a further twelve nautical miles labeled "contiguous zone" and finally by a two-hundred-nautical-mile-wide exclusive economic zone (EEZ)—a sea zone over which a state has special rights regarding the exploration and use of marine resources, including energy production from water and wind. However, the extraction of resources located in the EEZ, that is, beyond territorial waters, necessitates the installation of fixed investments and therefore a strong territorial regime to guarantee their security. As a result, EEZs are now increasingly constructed as "extensions of state territory amenable to development."[153] Like territorial waters, airspace is similarly subject to striations and delineations. In addition to the vertical zone making up national airspace, further areas and zones may also exist where flying activities are either restricted or subject to complete prohibition.

The logomap—this iconic and iconographic representation of the nation-state's borders as both organic and ageless—is thus not a true representation of the political entity. Visually hyperdefined and fetishized, the logomap is supplemented by a further layer that cannot be represented in maps, all the more so as it is in fact a three-dimensional volume, extending outward to sea, as well as skyward.[154] The always-more-than-itself phantomic space of the nation-state extends also, of course, into neighboring countries. The claims that Russia's incursion into Crimea was precipitated by the EU's and NATO's expansion into Russia's backyard illustrate the tension between the logomap and the unrepresentable space that surrounds it. The analogy of the backyard (not quite the house but nonetheless a space subject to sovereignty) and the politics of contiguousness and tactility that it indexes are crucial aspects to which I return in the next two chapters. Importantly, the assumption that the nation-state is lined with a zone that is both Other and an extension of personal space is one that gives further weight to somatopolitical metaphors.

Indeed, just like the nation-state, the body is extensible and does not end at the skin, and this characteristic may in fact account for the potency of the discursive parallels between *body* and *nation*. The body may look discrete, singular, and bounded, but it can in fact shrink and grow, and can incorporate objects that the body is in contact with: clothes, glasses, a stick. It can also incorporate much larger objects, such as a vehicle, which then becomes a "body shell" for the subject: "Its perils and breakdowns, chasing another car or trying to fit into a small parking spot, are all experienced in the body image of the driver."[155] Any object that participates in the conscious movement of the body is integrated into the model of ourselves and becomes part of these schemata.[156] This incorporation is in fact central to skill and virtuosity.[157] Without this mental process, we would be unable to use a cane, utensil, or instrument: "The surgeon would be unable to operate without the scalpel and medical implements being incorporated into the surgeon's body image. The writer would be unable to type, the musician unable to perform, without the word processor or musical instrument becoming part of the body image. It is only insofar as the object ceases to remain an object and becomes a medium, a vehicle for impressions and expression, that it can be used as an instrument or tool."[158]

The absorption of foreign objects into the body map of an individual is in fact surprisingly easy.[159] With the right type of sensory simulation, the mind can be tricked, effortlessly and in a matter of seconds, into incorporating a table as an extension of the hand, for instance, or into making an individual feel her nose is three feet long, as discussed above. Cultural theorist Vivian Sobchack, who has written about her own experience of wearing a prosthesis following amputation of her leg, describes it as an ambiguous event encompassing both a reduction of her body's boundaries but also a "surprising radical *expansion*."[160] She writes that her phantom was in fact less a "nostalgic *longing* than an anticipatory *lengthening* toward the ground."[161]

I described earlier the phenomenon of telescoped phantoms, whereby the overrepresented parts of the limb (hand, foot) survive longer in the body map. Sobchack describes how her former foot continued to feel prominent and clearly defined, and that two of her phantom toes felt numb just as they had before the surgery. By contrast, she experienced little of the rest of the leg, apart from "a certain ill-defined verticality."[162] As her phantom leg gradually "telescoped," she was left with "a certain auratic area" around her residual limb, a "no-man's land separating two different perceptions of [her] body that would admit no trespass."[163] It is only when she started walking with a prosthetic that the phantom elongated to fully occupy again the space between the stump and the ground.[164]

This experience is consonant with the results of neuroscientific research that have shown that, in giving weight to a phantom, the use of a prosthesis can be restorative as well as transformative.[165] This, in turn, suggests that body image is both dynamic and plastic, that it is continually remodeled and updated, and that it can reorganize itself in line with the contingencies of experience. That brain maps change, at times with astonishing rapidity, demonstrates that the presumption that circuitry is hardwired and inflexible is inaccurate: highly precise and functionally effective pathways can emerge in an adult patient as early as four weeks after injury.[166] There is in fact no fixed area dedicated to any part of the body: if a hand is deafferented or in-activated for any length of time, it will lose its place in the sensory cortex.[167] The emergence of new pathways was also demonstrated in healthy individuals. A study by researchers from the Wellcome Trust found that the brains of longtime London taxi drivers differed structurally from a non-taxi-driving control group.[168] The volume of the posterior hippocampus of the taxi drivers was larger than in the control subjects, and the discrepancy in volume corresponded roughly to the time they had spent as taxi drivers.[169]

The high flexibility of neural circuits, swift absorption of foreign objects, and equally rapid potential disappearance of limbs from the mental body map shows that a neat dichotomous opposition is virtually impossible in practice between the organic body and a prosthesis. As Marquard Smith writes, "the organic and the artificial, meat and machinery, like the normal and the pathological and the ordinary and the monstrous, are always and already of one another."[170] With its highly malleable boundaries, the self is akin to an amoeba, displaying an "uncanny ability to change its shape, alter its margins, reform and regenerate new parts as needed."[171] Not only can prostheses become "organic" and an integral part of the body, but we can push the argument further and consider the "real" limbs as "natural prostheses" employed by the brain to interact with the environment.[172] The body would then be construed as a type of projection—or phantom—a "possibility ready to materialize itself in any number of shapes or forms."[173]

This analysis is in fact consonant with the experience related by Sobchack with respect to her nonamputated right leg. Confronted with the plasticity of her left leg, experienced as a phantom at times telescoped and at times fully extended, she came to the realization that her experience of her right leg also lacked the solidity suggested by visual feedback. While she could see her right leg, she could not feel its contours unless it was in physical contact with surrounding objects. For all its fleshy solidity, she writes, she sensed her right leg as "little more than a generally vague and hardly weighty verticality."[174]

Rita Carter writes that phantom limbs are particular occasions when body maps get stuck "in a configuration that is incongruent with the real body."[175] Usually, however, they seamlessly adapt to changes in the physical body, thereby concealing their illusory nature. This misapprehension also extends to the fantasy of the body (and the nation) as a singular totality—a point on which I elaborate further in chapters 4 and 5. The corporeal discourse that gives so much potency to nationalism rests on the assumption that the body is real, organic, natural, and continuous. Yet the human body is one that is "always and already fragmented, in bits and pieces, a *corps morcelé*."[176]

For Lacan, the subject's desire to view herself as a totality comes at the expense of a misrecognition. As Vivian Sobchack writes, the initial discovery of our bodies is made piecemeal when, as infants, we learn about our bodies through the names of body parts.[177] The mirror stage, which for Lacan constitutes the primary process of identification as an individual through a "specular recognition of bodily integrity," signals the child's jubilant comprehension of its unity, which "gives rise to a *retroactive* (and apprehensive) fantasy of its body as once in pieces."[178] As Smith further elaborates, it is precisely this forced unification, necessary for a "de-alienation from that original fragmentary experience to take place," which requires "this very misrecognition—that it was, is, and will persist as *corps morcelé*."[179]

This fantasy of singularity, integrity, and contiguousness is also something we see in its discursive overlap with political phenomena, namely in the misrecognition of the nation-state as uninterrupted, homogeneous, and evenly operative. Through my discussion of phantomic space, partitions, and prosthetic territories, my overall concern in this chapter has been to address the multiple misalignments between, on the one hand, a totalizing imaginary and, on the other, the specter of territorial fractures and spillovers. As I develop in chapter 4, the denial of the nation-state's deeply fragmentary nature unavoidably leads to cartographic anxieties nestled in boundaries, edges, and remote corners. The fetishization of the border thus indexes a political will seeking to ensure sovereignty and legitimacy, but it also guarantees the continued fantasy of the state as singular.

4

EPIDERMIC STATES

¡Pobre México! ¡Tan lejos de Dios y tan cerca de los Estados Unidos!

—Anonymous

Russia and China laid to rest their remaining territorial disputes in 2004, after decades of hostility and clashes in 1969 that subsequently led to the Sino-Soviet split (*Sovietsko-kitaiskii raskol*; *Zhong-Su jiaowu* 中苏交恶) and the hermetic closure of the border. It had been agreed as early as 1991 that Damansky Island (in Chinese, Zhenbao Dao 珍宝岛) would be ceded to China, but two unresolved disputes still remained: Bolshoi Ussuriisk Island (Heixiazi Dao 黑瞎子岛) and Tarabarov Island (Yinlong Dao 银龙岛), located near the Russian city of Khabarovsk. The two governments finally came to an agreement in 2004 after long talks from which their respective citizens were excluded. In both countries the two islands had played a major symbolic role, and the compromises made by Russia and China were widely perceived on both sides as a betrayal and admission of defeat.[1]

As negotiations were proceeding apace, a rumor started circulating in Russia that some Chinese citizens were surreptitiously throwing rocks and sandbags into the Amur River in an attempt to increase Chinese territory by linking disputed river islands to their side of the river.[2] The majority of commentators were understandably dismissive of these claims—the image of a country as large as China trying to extend its boundaries in such a furtive manner elicited a certain amusement. That so much effort would be expended for the sake of two small islands of no particular significance, and that such attempts should be perceived as a vital threat to Russia, an even larger entity, seemed rather puzzling.[3] Yet these Russian allegations indexed anxieties that ran deep. When I carried out fieldwork in the region a decade later, territorial gains of a few hundred square yards, this time to the advantage of Russia, were again being discussed. As the Russian border town of Blagoveshchensk was reinforcing its embankment—partly in response to the 2013 floods that had inundated several neighborhoods—the excavation works saw vast quantities of earth being dumped all along the bank to reclaim low-lying land. This time, it was the Chinese who complained this construction was impacting the main navigational channel. For Masha, a teacher at a secondary school in Blagoveshchensk, these earthworks were great news—"the land reclamation is actually pushing the river further away towards China. This means Russia is getting bigger!"[4]

That the loss or gain of minute slivers of land should be perceived as crucial concerns to Russia, the world's largest state, seems rather puzzling. Yet disputes over small territorial fragments are very common, with many contemporary conflicts taking place precisely over such minuscule and apparently worthless pieces of real estate. Thus the linchpin of the current conflict between India and Pakistan is the snowy wastes of Siachen, a Himalayan peak as iconic as it is unfit for human life, and where battle is waged primarily between man and mountain.

Other conflicts over tiny specks of land, too barren or too distant to hold economic or material value, have also proven very difficult to solve.[5] The Kuril Islands, between Russia and Japan, or the Pinnacle Islands (in Japanese, Senkaku 尖閣; in Chinese, Diaoyu 钓鱼), between Japan and China, are such examples. Commentators have read these territorial stakes as rational moves, ultimately predicated on economics, geopolitics, or even national pride and patriotism. The Kuril Islands, for instance, most of which are uninhabited, have a significant indirect material value in the fish stocks that surround the archipelago. A transfer of these islands to Japan would signal heavy losses for the Russian fishing industry.[6] In the case of the Senkaku/Diaoyu Islands that sit astride rich oil deposits, the material value is even more explicit. But explanations based purely in material advantages can oversimplify the motives of actors involved, and the material or strategic value of disputed territories frequently seems to be found in the observer's assumption that the state is ultimately a rational actor carefully balancing its books. In fact, the economic fallout of territorial disputes often far exceeds any potential benefits.[7] The lack of a Russo-Japanese resolution over the Kuril Islands, for instance, has embittered relations between the two countries, leading their economic relations to stagnate; despite geographical proximity, Japan lags behind as Russia's eleventh trade partner, and the balance of trade between the two countries is miniscule.[8]

Nations are eager to portray these territorial disputes as steeped in deep history, but struggles over exact lines of demarcation are for the most part very recent. The Paracel and Spratly Islands, currently at the center of an embattled dispute between China, Taiwan, Vietnam, Malaysia, Brunei, and the Philippines, were unoccupied—and largely unclaimed—until the end of World War II. The Siachen Glacier, over which India and Pakistan have lost over two thousand soldiers since 1984—"97 percent of them killed by the weather and the terrain"—was left unmapped at partition, since neither side anticipated it would become a matter of contention.[9] Given the total lack of strategic value, combined with the forbidding physical terrain and weather conditions, it was "mutually agreed that there was little need to go beyond map coordinate NJ9842 on the original cease-fire line."[10]

In chapter 1, I argued that the modern conceptualization of the nation-state as homogenous and evenly operative has led to a condensation of affect around borders. The importance, indeed fetishization, of the border emerges particularly clearly in the context of India, where a draft bill proposes to make an incorrect depiction of the country an offense punishable by a maximum jail term of seven years and a fine up to Rs 1 crore (USD 150,000).[11] The bill also makes it mandatory to obtain permission from a government authority before acquiring, disseminating, publishing, or distributing any geospatial information on India, either inside India or abroad.[12] This bill has primarily been a way to put pressure on Google to depict the territories of Arunachal Pradesh and Jammu and Kashmir as indisputably Indian. Until then, the dotted lines delineating them had shown them as disputed—a practice that had elicited considerable anger from Indian netizens as well as calls for Google to be fined, "dragged to court," or even "blocked like in China."[13]

If the borders of territories that are being disputed are particularly sensitive, even long-settled borders between friendly nations are subject to considerable scrutiny. A new concept of a movable border has thus been recently introduced by the Italian government into national legislation to track the minute changes, in real time, of the Austrian-Italian border due to global warming and shrinking Alpine glaciers. A grid of twenty-five solar-powered sensors has now been fitted on the surface of the glacier at the foot of Mt. Similaun, and every two hours these sensors record data, allowing for an automated mapping of the shifts in the border.[14]

It is in such attempts that we really grasp the desire to contain and account for the nation's tiniest of fragments—even if said fragments are found in frozen, inaccessible, and uninhabitable locations. The point here is in fact not about human appropriation or utilization but about definition, since, to be a fully sovereign nation, all borders must be defined and incontestable. In the case of Kashmir, disputed by India and Pakistan, the struggle is not to make use of the land at the border, but to reconcile the numerous demarcation lines that have been drawn on paper by multiple actors, specifically the Line of Control (LoC) on the western borders of the Himalayas and the Line of Actual Control (LAC), the de facto boundary between India and China. A definitive and unambiguous line of demarcation beyond NJ9842 represents an ideal that both countries are slowly creeping toward with the aid of new technologies such as laser fences, motion sensors, CCTV cameras, and a network of radars. Eventually, it is hoped, the border will be fully mapped, with every single inch accounted for. It will never be manned, nor is that the objective.

In fact, as I develop later in this chapter, the best borders are those left empty of people insofar as the presence of groups straddling the border disturbs the organicist wholesomeness that nation-states seek to project. With languages, kin groups, and human activities seeping across the lines, inhabited borderlands are inherently messy. In Russia, and particularly in the far eastern regions, the border is supplemented by additional zones of separation seeking to disrupt, interrupt, and insulate. These practices directly reinforce the idea that the border is sacred and requires protection.[15] In Russia, access to the actual border line has long been subject to severe restrictions: "Not everyone is granted the right to tread the last meters of Fatherland" goes the epitaph attributed to communist revolutionary Sergey Lazo. For the people living in these sensitive zones, such as the inhabitants of the border town of Blagoveshchensk, residence has long been associated with duty. During the difficult decades dominated by the Sino-Soviet split, slogans such as "You are living on the border, stay vigilant!" (Zhivësh na granitse, bud' bditelen!) and "Border under lock" (Granitsa na zamke) were continually reiterated.

THE FETISHIZED EDGE

Nikolai Gogol's satirical short story "The Nose" tells the story of Major Kovalev, who one day awakens to discover his nose is missing. In his analysis of the story, Alexander Etkind equates the lost appendage with a fetish: "When in its proper place, the nose is just a little part of Kovalev's wholeness, a metonymy of his impeccable functioning as the corporeal and imperial subject. Lost, the nose turns into the all-embracing symbol for Kovalev's unaccomplished dreams and aspirations, the summary metaphor for all those goods, bodies, and statuses . . . which are unreachable for the noseless. The part is made into a fetish only after it has been lost."[16] Just like Kovalev's nose in Gogol's short story, whose sudden disappearance turns it from a small component of a larger whole into a site of unrivaled significance, each small island or peak on a nation's border has the potential to transform into a condensed symbol of the nation itself.[17] The two islands of Bolshoi Ussuriisk and Tarabarov discussed at the beginning of this chapter acted for China precisely as Kovalev's nose did for him, their reintegration into the national map signaling a recomposition of the country's natural shape, namely the "cockerel whose crest had been missing its tip."[18]

Recent research on phantom pains and body mapping again makes for a fascinating analogy. Noting how phantom pains appeared to be relieved when other parts of the body were touched (a patient experienced sensations in his missing index finger when his upper lip was stroked, for instance), neurologist Vilayanur Ramachandran explained these sensory pathway overlaps, or crosstalk, as the result of the so-called Penfield homunculus (figure 4.1). This odd depiction of corporeal mapping represents the way in which different points on the body surface are mapped onto the surface of the brain. In the 1940s and 1950s, Canadian neurosurgeon Wilder Penfield carried out experiments whereby he stimulated specific regions of the brain with an electrode and tracked the sensations experienced by the patients. He discovered in particular a narrow strip running from top to bottom down both sides of the brain where his electrode produced sensations localized in various parts of the body: "This 'sensory homunculus' . . . forms a greatly distorted representation of the body on the surface of the brain, with the parts that are particularly important taking up disproportionately large areas. For example, the area involved with the lips or with the fingers takes up as much space as the area involved with the entire trunk of the body."[19]

Here again, the corporeal map and the national map show several interesting parallels. In the physical body, some organs or parts of the body, such as

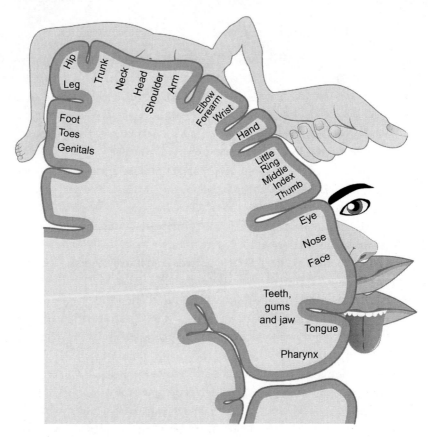

4.1. The Penfield homunculus. Illustration from Betts et al., *Anatomy and Physiology*, chap. 14, "The Somatic Nervous System."

the fingers or the epidermis, are overrepresented and are awash with sensory endings. In the same way, the contours of the nation, insofar as they graphically define the recognizable shape of the nation, are subject to fetishization and tend to be symbolically dominant. For Russia and China, the islands of Bolshoi Ussuriisk and Tarabarov loom large on the nation's mental map. In spite of their small size, they are overrepresented spaces where national affect is condensed, while by contrast the vast expanses of Siberia are frequently perceived as a compressed space.[20] This suggests that while the space of the nation is evenly operative, it is not evenly distributed. In fact, it is often in the "little things" that greater significance resides.[21] Just as the nation-state is reproduced "unobtrusively on the margins of conscious awareness by little words, such as 'the' and 'we,'" the enduring preoccupation with small isles

4.2. Sensory homunculus. Image from Wikimedia Commons, Creative Commons Attribution-ShareAlike 4.0 International (CC-BY-SA 4.0), last updated October 17, 2020.

and peaks should be read not as a misfiring of the nationalist project but in fact as central to national narratives.[22]

The symbolic predominance of borders that is projected by the ubiquitous logomap echoes here the overrepresentation of the hand (and other significant bodily parts such as the lips or the genitals) in the somatosensory cortex. An artist's rendering (see figure 4.2) aptly portrays in three-dimensional form the unequal distribution of libidinal investment in the body, a corporeal view I was excited to also find illustrated in a self-portrait by my five-year-old niece (see figure 4.3). In both representations, the same bodily parts are overrepresented, the hands in particular much inflated in comparison with the rest of the arms—the latter invisible in my niece's drawing—and reflecting the telescoping process described in chapter 3.[23]

In recent years, Penfield's striking visualization has attracted important and valid criticisms insofar as it depicts the human body as static, male,

4.3. Martina (age 5), "Self."

and normative. Significant differences in fact exist between the somatotopic maps of male and female subjects, leading researchers to coin the term *hermunculus* as an alternative to the androcentric *homunculus*.[24] Penfield's "cartography of bodily interiority" also leaves little space for the plastic and dynamic nature of cortical mapping: research has shown that factors such as "changed gender identifications, fluctuations in hormone levels, ovulation, pregnancy, limb amputations, mastectomies, stages in the life cycle, and other alterations to the physicality of the body" all have impactful consequences on somatotopic mapping.[25]

Paradoxically, these very shortcomings make the Penfield homunculus a particularly apt representation of the national body. Echoing predominantly male concerns and projecting a sense of stability and immobility, this "grotesque creature," in the words of sociologist Mark Paterson—a dimension I analyze in more detail in chapter 5 under the moniker of *monstrous*—constitutes the underlying structure of the somatopolitical.[26] Rather than homogeneous, the national body is lumpy, misshapen, unevenly distributed. Consequently, as Itty Abraham discusses in his work, not all territorial loss is equivalent because "national space is unevenly distributed across state territories; . . . not all land or terrain lying within state boundaries matters to the same extent":[27]

When the eastern Indian province of Bengal was partitioned in 1905 for administrative reasons, the huge public outcry in reaction led to its reversal a few years later, a shocking outcome for a powerful colonial state that faced scant public accountability. Yet when Burma was separated from British India in 1931, there was little outcry, in spite of the grave difficulties faced by people of Indian origin, mostly Bengali, Telugu, and Tamil. What distinguished Bengal in 1905 from Burma in 1931 was the meaning of these territories for the nascent Indian nation. Geographically peripheral (to New Delhi), Bengal was deemed a "heartland" of the nation in 1905, while Burma in 1931 [was] little more than [a] periphery whose partition was not construed in terms of national loss, even if many nationals lost everything they owned.[28]

What this example illustrates is that the experience of loss is not always directly mappable to a corresponding economic value. Spatialization of affect and the overrepresentation of particular territories are also impacted by dynamics such as historical experience, ethnic composition, and geopolitical concerns. A further crucial aspect rarely accorded due consideration is the aesthetic dimension of the state's contour. Some parts of the national silhouette are more iconic than others, particularly when they figure prominently in the recognizability of the state. As analyzed in chapter 2 and revisited in chapter 5, an irregular outline constitutes a core aspect of a logo or brand such as Texas; pointy and phallic edges are more potent than round, curved border lines, where loss would be less immediately visible.[29] It is precisely the lopping-off of such regions that tends to prompt narratives of mutilation, dismemberment, and emasculation.

BORDER AS SKIN

In his germinal coinage of the concept of the geobody, Thongchai Winichakul insisted that while a nation can function without the full panoply of state symbols, it cannot be imagined without boundary lines, in that these lines depict the nation-state as a singular entity.[30] Physical boundedness projects a coherence, continuity, and stability—spatially and temporally—which condenses and aligns a vast array of economic, political, and cultural processes.[31] As Timothy Mitchell has convincingly argued, the fact that "the state's boundary never marks a real exterior" does not make that line illusory.[32] The setting up and policing of the border help manufacture the nation-state as a quasi-transcendental entity that emerges and gains palpability through the "powerful, metaphysical effect of practices."[33] In hardening what were initially mere perimeters, Anthony Giddens writes, boundaries have turned states into bordered power containers—as well as "territorial traps," in John Agnew's felicitous phrasing.[34]

This notion of container is one that, again, closely reverberates with conceptualizations of the body and therefore further reinforces the mirroring process between nation and body. In a fascinating study of the cultural meanings of skin as expressed through language, Claudia Benthien identifies two different but complementary meanings that point to divergent cultural imaginings of subject and body. On the one hand, skin is conceptualized as an enclosure, an envelope, or cover—potentially a deceptive one: "What is authentic lies beneath the skin, is hidden inside the body. . . . Skin is conceived of as something other than the self . . . as something foreign and external to it."[35] On the other hand, a second group of sayings equates the skin with the subject, and often has skin stand metonymically for the whole individual. If this conceptualization of skin only survives in a few isolated expressions, it remains a crucial constituent of the concept, finding in fact a new lease on life through the work of Sigmund Freud, Didier Anzieu, and a number of psychoanalytically minded cultural theorists.

This duality is clearly visible at the border between Russia and China. The twinned border towns of Blagoveshchensk and Heihe, separated only by the width of the Amur River, constitute a particularly potent example of this productive tension insofar as the two cities stand as exemplars of their respective nations and civilizations. Their riverside urbanization models—the skin that each presents to the other—differs drastically. Heihe has styled itself as a liminal city, with statues and urban furniture borrowing from Russian popular culture; by contrast, Blagoveshchensk emphasizes its control of the border through military symbols and statues of pioneering Russian explorers. The Russian city thus appears to embody the defensive aspect of skin, turning its riverbank into a protective integument, while its Chinese neighbor makes use of this cutaneous/border surface principally to display the symbols of its newfound modernity, in the form of skyscrapers and urban lighting. Blagoveshchensk—and the Russian Far East (RFE) border overall— is constructed as an impassable line of defense; by contrast, Heihe presents itself as friendly, inviting, indeed an enticing lure for Russian visitors.[36] The two cities are a fitting illustration of the double-sidedness and dual nature of border/skin. In many ways they constitute an extreme case in that their roles hardly overlap. Heihe is liminal, turned outward, with ambitions to become a global city, whereas Blagoveshchensk is symptomatic of a borderland region tightly wrapped in a set of protective layers.

In her work, Benthien underlines a further dimension of skin, namely the dialogue and complementarity that exist between the two opposing facets of protection and communication. Thus while skin constitutes an envelope and closure against the environment, it is also a permeable and breathable membrane.[37] Interestingly, the very same point has also been made by social scientists with respect to national borders. No country, no matter how authoritarian its regime may be, seeks autarchy or hermeticity. All nation-states in fact oscillate between the conflicting aims of making their borders "impenetrable by particular undesirables, and hyper-permeable to desired groups and individuals as well as certain goods and services."[38]

This holds true for both Russia and China, and the contrast I describe above between Heihe and Blagoveshchensk is in fact a more complex set of amorphous practices. If the Russian city embodies in many ways the protective facet of skin, constituting a thick hide difficult for outsiders to penetrate, it remains nonetheless permeable to the gaze. Its riverbank is bare and exposed. By contrast, while Heihe is more permeable and porous to Russian visitors, its exposed face tends to be perceived and described by onlookers as a facade, a mirage. Heihe's riverfront development—the only surface of Heihe visible from the other side of the Amur—was consistently described to me as a Potemkin village, a visual trick performed by the Chinese. It was nothing but *pyl' v glaza*, a sleight of hand, I was told, a show intended to attract Russian customers. A smooth, shiny, and impenetrable surface, it projected an idealized version of successful modernity while simultaneously concealing the real, gritty texture of Chinese social life.[39]

The eye of the observer caresses yet cannot pierce the surface. In fact, the gaze reinforces the very thickness of the surface, transforming it into a skin under its optical caress.[40] This very impenetrability, this resistance to the gaze, speaks of course to the wider cultural trope of Asia as mysterious and impenetrable, a trope Russians share with the rest of Europe. This reflective surface and attendant lack of sensorial feedback is of direct relevance to the current form of the Sino-Russian border. If the skin/border represents an osmotic line between self and other, then we might consider outside stimuli, but also the lack of stimuli, as constitutive of that line. The thickness of Russia's epidermis is thus not simply inseparable from what it is in tactile contact with, but represents a direct result of that contact. Like a callus that bears witness to the palms' labor, history, and friction against rough textures, the border acquires thickness in response to the geobody it happens to be pressing and rubbing against.

TOUCHING FEELING

If the analogy of border as skin is not novel and has been used, albeit somewhat differently, in border literature, its double-sided nature, the sharing of this skin, has not elicited as much discussion.[41] Yet the fact that the nation's geobody does not exist in isolation but finds its shape circumscribed, molded, and directly dependent upon the geobodies of others is theoretically crucial.

I retraced in chapter 1 the cartographic revolution whereby the reconceptualization of the nation-state as homogeneous and evenly operative cohered into an emphasis on borders. From a nucleus surrounded by a set of expanding zones, the nation-state now conceptually resembles an exoskeleton. The nation's edge, as container and separator, constitutes a privileged site "where the legitimacy of its powers is scrutinized" and where sovereignty and legitimacy are emphasized, defended, and contested.[42] Anthropologists have noted how space at the borders has its own specialized aesthetics: "fences, customs posts, flags, road signs . . . whose function is in part to try to leave no doubt as to whom and where one is."[43] But while borders are sites of emphatic state inscription, these inscriptions themselves are subject to countless restrictions: maps of border areas are rarely made freely available to the public, and photography is usually forbidden in airports or at border posts.

These state practices closely reverberate with psychoanalytical views of the body. In *The Ego and the Id*, Sigmund Freud theorized that the ego was "first and foremost a bodily ego": less a self-contained entity than a kind of "bodily tracing," a "cartography of the erotogenic intensity of the body."[44] In his own development of the Freudian concept of bodily ego, psychoanalyst Didier Anzieu noted how the skin is the most vital of all the sense organs: "One can live without sight, hearing, taste or smell, but it is impossible to survive if the greater part of one's skin is not intact."[45] The skin is much more than a simple envelope or membrane; it is also an organ innervated with countless sensory endings.[46] Unlike the eyes, mouth, or ears, which can be closed or stopped, the skin is always switched on, making it one of the body's most crucial sensory receptors.

For Anzieu, this very hypersensitivity of skin is intimately linked to the development of the ego. Expanding on Freud's insight that the ego emerges through the organism's sensual confrontation with the surrounding external world, Anzieu foregrounds the role of tactility, and therefore skin itself, in this gradual process of individuation.[47] For the first few months of life, an infant is unable to differentiate her body from that of her parent. As she becomes aware of her somatic borders, as she "discovers the rind of [her] body," the infant gains a sense of her psychic borders as well.[48] It is thus through the skin, Anzieu argues, that the infant comes to recognize herself as an individual. The significance of the skin as the site of the self has been extensively mined in literature. As Judith Halberstam reminds us, "The vampire will puncture and mark the skin with his fangs, Mr. Hyde will covet white skin, Dorian Gray will desire his own canvas, Buffalo Bill will covet female skin, Leatherface will wear his victim's skin as a trophy and recycle his flesh as food."[49] One may also add to this list Patrick Süskind's novel, *Perfume* (1985), where the central character, Jean-Baptiste Grenouille, endowed with an unsurpassed sense of smell but himself odorless, kills young women to steal the scent that permeates their skin.

Especially relevant to the present argument are the cuts and gaps on the body's surface, which Lacan has described as erotogenic zones. These apertures of ingestion and emission, Susan Stewart writes, "work to constitute the notion of the subject, of the individual body and ultimately the self"—an interpretation that offers significant mileage for the theorization of contemporary borders.[50]

While Winichakul's notion of geobody has proved evocative to many scholars working in a range of ethnographic contexts, interaction between different geobodies has not been given as much attention. The concept has been widely employed to critique and problematize the natural and organic formation of the nation-state, but the imaginary whereby the geobody is dislocated from the regional and international community has remained somewhat undertheorized. Yet geobodies do not exist in isolation: the skin of the geobody is also the skin of another. Geobodies may in fact be better imagined as tightly packed together, rendered immobile by their neighbors, every change, tremor, or frisson of the geobody causing an immediate and mirrored countermovement in its neighbor.[51] This intersensoriality has important repercussions for the ways in which borders are imagined, erected, and managed. It elucidates, for instance, the evolution and survival of forms of spatial separation such as buffer states and buffer zones, no-man's-lands, walls, or cordons sanitaires.

In international relations, buffer states are particular kinds of political animals tethered to "specific eras of history and historically significant rivalries between powerful states."[52] The quintessential textbook buffer state is nineteenth-century Afghanistan, but the label has also been affixed to other countries at other times, like Mongolia, Siam, or Finland, as well as to now-defunct entities such the Far Eastern Republic (insulating Russia from Japan). A buffer state is defined as a state existing in a precarious position contiguous to two or three other states that have a higher than 0.5 probability of defeating it in a conflict, and where the military power of these larger states is comparable.[53] This definition speaks to a fragile, and generally temporary, equilibrium between equally powerful states whose long-term aspiration is to gain additional territory.

This definition is a less satisfactory descriptor of other instances of political buffering. Buffer states can also emerge in order to separate and insulate two states or empires, as in the case of the short-lived Far Eastern Republic. Other examples are Germany and Korea, which were both partitioned and served as double buffers for larger geopolitical blocs. The understanding that buffer states are eventually destined to be incorporated into larger political entities does seem to be supported by history, but I would qualify the premise that conflict avoidance is the only rationale behind the formation of buffer states and buffer zones.

As border theorist Emmanuel Brunet-Jailly observes, the early literature on borders underscored the importance of buffer zones: good borders were preferably not settled by humans and should ideally be desert-like.[54] These liminal regions were thus not zones to be incorporated, but essentially outer layers of separation and insulation.[55] If buffer zones are a much less common occurrence today—at least in their original definition and form—the basic function they served would appear to be sustained by other forms of spatial partitioning. Frontier zones are thus frequently the sites of nature reserves, created to enhance the protection of biodiversity in certain areas. While nature reserves are not always found in borderlands, they often tend to be, and I suggest this is not coincidental. The decision to locate such areas on the edge of the nation is partly pragmatic since a large enclosure situated more centrally would have adverse impacts on communication and transport infrastructures, but it is also a choice that reinforces a core premise concerning the nation-state, namely that it constitutes a discrete organic entity. As the work of Juliet Fall, discussed in chapter 2, elucidates, delineation of these zones remains inflected by biogeographic determinism, the very concept of *ecosystem* presupposing an alignment of different kinds of spaces that is rarely ever found on the ground. A further advantage of this geographic placement, I will argue, is also to reinforce the nation's insulation—though not necessarily isolation—and thereby harness a political imaginary of touch.

I favor the term *haptic* over *tactile* here insofar as its use typically relates to a re-creation of the sensorial experience of touch, that is, a socially inflected rather than merely physiological experience. Used in technologies such as mobile phones, haptics is a feedback technology that recreates the sense of touch by applying forces, vibrations, or motions to the user. I am using it here to refer to deliberate as well as to chance and involuntary epidermic contact, to the pressing together of bodies, to gentle caresses but also to friction, rubbing, and chafing. As an intimate, multidirectional, and fractal force, haptics also evoke the multiplicity of cultural and social practices at work.[56]

The fact that this tactility involves two geobodies, that is, two imagined political bodies, might appear to run counter to my argument, but I suggest that it in fact offers further fodder for analysis. Indeed, if geobodies pertain to the realm of the imaginary, so too do human bodies. The social construction of the body has extensively borrowed from other social practices such as nationalism, and the two are inextricably enmeshed in social imaginaries—I am thinking here in particular of the work of Emily Martin on the ways in which immunology has conceptualized the body as an imperiled nation-state continuously at war to quell alien invaders.[57]

Ultimately, touch relates to the limits of the self. Overall, a state's border practices toward a given neighbor are symptomatic of larger, but more nebulous and constantly shifting, ideas of culture and civilization. The desire to separate and buffer oscillates directly in line with perceived danger to the integrity of national identity and the self. The high-security fence insulating the United States from Mexico is thus not reducible to a simple economic rationale but is instead intimately tied to wider concerns such as ethnic and linguistic purity. Touching the Other, especially when that Other is perceived as economically, culturally, or ethnically "inferior," is not simply an external threat. The very line of contact, this corporeal sharing with the Other, is also reflective of the self. The greatly intimate experience of being bodily pressed against a neighbor, especially when that neighbor is seen as "radically Other," can potentially prove destabilizing.[58]

The four-thousand-kilometer border that constitutes the Sino-Russian interface is a particularly fitting example of uneasy neighboring. The vast region now referred to as the RFE saw its first pioneers in the seventeenth century but was not securely controlled until the nineteenth century. Eager to consolidate its hold, in 1735 the Russian Empire bestowed upon the Cossacks—a group forcibly resettled from western Russia—the exclusive privilege to settle the ten-kilometer-wide strip adjacent to the border. The practice adopted by the empire was thus comparable to other borderlands management systems encountered elsewhere. It shared some features in particular with the medieval and early modern European marches, where different laws applied with the view to defending the border against hostile incursions and regulating border trade. This system was further developed with the establishment of the Soviet Union, when militarization was accompanied by the creation of restricted access (*ogranichenny dostup*) and later forbidden (*zapretnye*) border zones. The paranoia that defined particular moments of the Soviet period, as in the 1930s for instance, saw the emergence of closed cities and a further hardening of border zones. People deemed untrustworthy were evicted from border cities such as Vladivostok, Blagoveshchensk, and Khabarovsk. As Natalia Ryzhova writes, "Border zones had to become clean, diaphanous, sanitized, sterile, and disinfected so that those who stayed behind could be recognized as proper citizens, entrusted with defending sacred Soviet sovereignty." The worsening of the geopolitical balance in 1937 led to the enlargement and ossification of the border zones adjoining Japan, Korea, Manchukuo, and Mongolia. From that date until the Soviet Union's implosion, the RFE's entire territory remained closed, and its border zones were subject to a special regime of exclusion.[59]

In 1991, border exclusion zones (*prigranichnye zony*) were suddenly annulled: barbed wire, checkpoints, and special regimes all practically disappeared. Border zones, renamed "border strips," thinned to a width of five kilometers or less. This evaporation of border control occurred at a particularly difficult transition period and was largely symptomatic of an absence of political control overall. A 2004 decree, followed in 2006 by additional rules, led to a renewed expansion of exclusion zones, occasionally thickening to a width of up to one hundred kilometers.[60]

The example of Russia's oscillating contact zone with China is an apposite illustration of the capacity of the national epidermis to register affect and to respond to external and internal stimuli. The thickness of borders, fluctuating in line with political events, is very revealing of regional dynamic forces.

It is also symptomatic of how a nation-state views itself. The thickness of Russia's epidermis is not, nor has it historically been, equally distributed. While it has fluctuated, it has been consistently thicker on the border with China. The western border with Europe, while also militarized, does not reach depths of a hundred kilometers as it does in the east.[61] On the southern border with Kazakhstan, the border is thinner still. As I develop in the next section, the neighbor's touch is a very intimate experience. Depending on who that neighbor is, depending on the extent of the contact, touch can be akin to a lover's gentle, tender caress. It can also turn into an uncomfortable, at times even traumatic, experience.

The neighbor's caress can also be sexual. A potent mixture of lust, attraction, and aversion is in fact a common feature of colonial and mixed-race encounters where the skin, texture, and smell of the Other—and especially exotic women—is both denigrated and sexually fetishized. The sexual component of cross-border relations is visible at the Sino-Russian border in the form of love, prostitution, but also temporary couplings and other pragmatic arrangements. The loaded and ambivalent nature of these pairings comes through in the reluctance to make them publicly visible. In addition to socially reprehensible sexual practices such as prostitution, romantic and pragmatic cohabitations between Russians and Chinese are also frequently looked down upon. Russian women in a relationship with a Chinese man are seen as desperate and lonely, while for Chinese men, a Russian wife signifies access to a higher social status and permanent residence. The fact that these unions are uncommon and imbalanced (pairings between Russian men and Chinese women are virtually unheard of) speaks to the extent and limit of desirability and touchability of the body of the Other.

As Sartre has shown, the caress is more than a simple interaction between two bodies: it is constitutive of the self.[62] The thickness of Russia's eastern lining might therefore be indicative of more than just fears of territorial encroachment. It also indexes a reluctance to engage and to be associated with an Asian neighbor. In the Russian national imaginary, the figure of Asia has predominantly been a negative one since as early as the time of Catherine II. Perceived as immobile and stagnant, Asia represents the part of Russia that has prevented it from developing into a civilized country on par with Europe. The thick integument separating Russia from its principal Asian neighbor might thus be construed not so much as a border with a different polity but as a layer insulating it from a repressed part of itself always threatening to resurface.[63]

TEXXTURE

In a stimulating essay on Henry James, Renu Bora draws a useful distinction between two kinds of textures. "Texture" indexes "the surface resonance or quality of an object or material," qualities "that can usually be anticipated by looking."[64] By contrast, "texxture"—with two x's—"refers not really to surface or even depth so much as to an intimately violent, pragmatic, medium, inner level . . . of the stuffness of material structure."[65] As Eve Kosofsky Sedgwick later expands, unlike "texture," which "signifies the willed erasure of its history," "texxture" is dense with information about how, historically and materially, it came into being.[66] This very density is, for Bora, signaled by the two x's, which hint at its complex and intrinsically narrative and temporal nature.[67] Intimately associated with sensoriality and sensuality, texxture is thus inherently haptic.

Texxture is important with respect to skin insofar as it is a surface that registers and bears the traces of affect. Even though considerable social pressure exists for skin to be smooth and polished, free of blemishes, wrinkles, and traces of both labor and elapsed time, epidermic surfaces nevertheless always fail to be smooth.[68] Paradoxically, this aspirational drive toward smoothness is supplemented by the desire to socially mark that surface through clothing, makeup, or jewelry as well as through piercings and tattoos. Tattoos of state outlines, such as the one on the cover of this book, are particularly telling of the intimate relation between nation and body in that the logomap, etched upon the body, places the two in direct equivalence. Skin is thus a somewhat contradictory space, constituting both a concealment device and a productive surface where social identity is mobilized and displayed. Like skin, borders are also located at a critical juncture of contradictory desires: a site where identity and sovereignty are strongly and unambiguously inscribed, but also a dividing line that ideally is smooth, unmarked, natural.

Of special significance are the cutaneous openings of the body's surface. As Elizabeth Grosz notes, skin "provides the ground for the articulation of orifices, erotogenic rims, cuts on the body's surface, loci of exchange between the inside and the outside, points of conversion of the outside into the body, and of the inside out of the body."[69] In addition to the liminal aspects of these sites of exchange, Grosz draws attention to libidinal investment in the texxture of skin.[70] These cuts and orifices on the body's surface, she writes, "create a kind of 'landscape' of that surface, that is, they provide it with 'regions,' 'zones,' capable of erotic significance; they serve as a kind of gridding, an uneven distribution of intensities, of erotic investments in the body."[71] Knots, folds, cuts, pleats, and orifices are sites of danger requiring surveillance and control, but they are also sites of attraction and fascination. This enmeshment of two contradictory yet complementary pulls is in fact at the very core of the nature of both skin and political borders.

Skin is commonly imagined as a two-dimensional flat interface, as suggested by expressions such as "skin deep," shorthand for superficiality and lack of depth. It often comes as a surprise to discover that skin is actually the largest organ, weighing as much as 18 percent of the total weight of an adult. Michel Serres compares it to a gigantic, multidimensional, and topological knot, beginning from the very embryonic state with one or more sheets—folded, pleated, rolled, invaginated.[72] Borders are similarly conceptualized as two-dimensional lines, and the common experience of going through security lines at border crossings directly feeds into this imaginary. If the recent work of border studies scholars such as Josiah Heyman, Hilary Cunningham, and others has helped problematize this notion and illuminate the ways in which borders post-9/11 frequently extend deep into nations, the persistent focus on human crossings offers an imaginary of borders that remains flat and linear.[73] Yet, like skin, a border also has depth, with borderlands and liminal zones abutting it on each side.

Both skin and borders are also palimpsests insofar as they register changes in their multilayered textures. Skin, despite being constantly regenerated and shedding dry flakes, bears the material trace of past events and traumas. It continually incorporates into its materiality the passing of time through the "accumulation of marks, wrinkles, lines and creases, as well as in the literal disintegration of skin."[74] It is also a nested set of integuments, in that it is constituted of specialized layers innervated by innumerable sensors. Similarly, insofar as all borders are unnatural, recent, and historically contingent, they are eminently palimpsestic. Frequently slicing across former linguistic and cultural continuums, borders require continual emphasis and reiteration in order to silence former territorial incarnations. As spectral overlays, territories that are located across competing sovereignties must similarly be brought within discursive range through processes of co-opting, rewriting, or erasure. Yet, as discussed earlier, architectural, cultural, historical, and etymological palimpsests form a dense cultural substratum prone to resurface and contest the cultural homogeneity implicit in nationalist narratives.

Texxture of course also matters to contact between geobodies. Pressed against each other, it is through their respective texxtures that nation-states encounter each other. The gritty nature of this contact interface is reminiscent of Anna Tsing's metaphor of friction, which she employs as an analytical prism to attend to the political, social, and economic transformations inherent to the present context of increasing global connectedness.[75] My use of *texxture* is perhaps most congruent with the so-called affective turn and resonates in particular with the work of Yael Navaro-Yashin on Greek and Turkish Cypriot imaginaries of the state.[76] The discursive metaphors used by Navaro-Yashin's informants in relation to their location on the overlapping realms of two different polities are strongly somatic. They speak, for instance, of being "enclosed inside this place," of feeling as if they were "being strangled by our throats."[77] To refer to the "dis-resonating feeling" produced by such environments, Navaro-Yashin uses the term "irritability," which in some ways echoes Sianne Ngai's usage of "irritation."[78] In *Ugly Feelings*, Ngai describes irritation as a "conspicuously weak or inadequate form of anger, as well as an affect that bears an unusually close relationship to the body's surfaces or skin."[79] I would argue that irritability/irritation is a particularly apt metaphor for the uncanny (Navaro-Yashin) and the low-grade yet persistent (Ngai) friction that border encounters represent insofar as it evokes a primarily epidermal response to the presence of the Other. It also speaks to the ambivalent and conflicting desires of tactility and avoidance of that tactility, and to the constant and somewhat pesky presence of the neighbor pressed against one's skin.

This tactile reluctance is traceable in the movement of goods and people that characterizes postsocialist Sino-Russian relations at the border. Although the reopening of the border in 1990, after two decades of hermetic closure, led to a flurry of trade between Russia and China, not a single bridge connects Blagoveshchensk to Heihe—nor indeed any border cities over the long Amur River. Instead, travelers continue to be funneled through the slow and expensive state-managed river transport services, each side using its respective nation's fleet. This division of labor echoes the emphasis on the avoidance of jostling and tactile contact that prevails on the Russian side. From workers to farmhands, Chinese presence in the RFE remains insulated within compounds that are both out of sight and out of touch.

Friction also extends beyond the merely irritating and the shallow, and can cause deeper-tissue wounds. Gloria Anzaldúa has famously described the US-Mexican border as "*una herida abierta* [an open wound] where the Third World grates against the first and bleeds. And before a scab forms it hemorrhages again, the lifeblood of two worlds merging to form a third country—a border culture."[80] Even more than economic and cultural friction, territorial disputes and warfare are notably traumatic. They often lead to permanent scarring, both metaphorically in terms of their social and political repercussions, but also in their actual physical effects on the landscape. The partition of the island of Cyprus and establishment of a demilitarized zone in 1974, for example, has sliced across the capital Nicosia, dividing it into two separate cities. The Green Line, a few meters wide in old Nicosia but with a depth of a few miles at other points, has led the two sides to become increasingly divergent.

If the insulation between Nicosia's two sides is no longer hermetic, with the recent creation of a number of crossings, lines of division such as these tend to leave scars that survive long after the political divides that have led to them. The city of Berlin, sutured back together thirty-five years ago after three decades, is a case in point. Despite a common language and culture prior to the erection of the wall, and despite a comprehensive program of urban renewal after 1989, differences between East and West Berlin have not been effaced. Indeed, insofar as hard divisions lead to structural changes, once cities become divided it becomes virtually impossible to stitch them back together again.[81] In some cases, these fractures are accentuated and fetishized, as I discuss in chapter 5 in the context of the enclave complex of Baarle-Nassau athwart the Dutch-Belgian border.

Political divisions and partitions are frequently expressed through metaphors evoking a wide array of corporeal abrasions and injuries: from minor scuffs, scrapes, and welts, to more damaging cuts and lesions, and to (semi)permanent transformations such as calluses, scabs, and scars. These wounds and abrasions are the lasting consequences of warfare and strife, but they are also consciously inflicted. The infamous quote of Bosnian Serb commander Ratko Mladić that "borders are drawn with blood" speaks to a political will to effect dislocations and somatize partitions that extends well beyond the specific context of mutilation and dismembering of the Yugoslavian body politic. One only needs to think of the established and all-too-frequent practice of laying land mines in border zones.[82] Literally inflicting wounds on foreign bodies, land mines seek to physically dislocate and dislodge the national geobody from the Other's epidermal embrace.[83] By destroying the common skin that binds them together, this violent act is also akin to a birth insofar as it represents a process of individuation. As noted in chapter 3, nation-states' founding acts—whether through scission or fusion—are nearly always bloody and violent.[84]

Some of these cuts and abrasions are open wounds that continue to bleed through the individual bodies of thousands, as in Kashmir, for instance, disputed with India. Older wounds, resolved through bilateral treaties, have formed scar tissue, a fibrous knot that remains long after the event, a "compromise between lesion and healing."[85] I discussed in chapter 3 how partition wrenched apart India and Pakistan in a violent process of exclusion and expulsion. The border that sliced them apart is a potent illustration of such

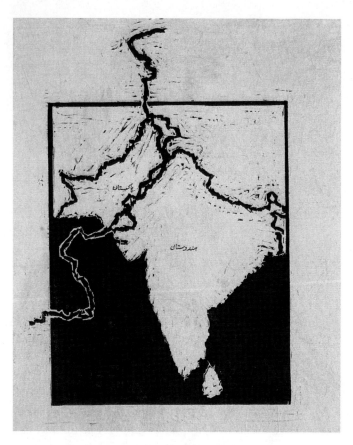

4.4. Zarina Hashmi, *Atlas of My World* (2001).

scar tissue, the graphic trace of a traumatic wound whose incomplete healing continues to haunt the two countries' relationship (see figure 4.4).[86]

TOPOLOGICAL GEOGRAPHIES

The analogy of skin, which I employ here as an extension of a cluster of somatic metaphors that discursively equate the nation with a living body, offers critical theoretical insights. Through its tensile, stretchable, and foldable nature, skin behaves in ways not dissimilar to borders. Further, foregrounding the skin's elasticity and pliability can help reconcile the hardness and immobility of border posts with the multidirectional force of national affect.

I suggest it might be advantageous here to replace the dominant topographical model of borders with a topological one. Unlike the former, which is Euclidean and geographically bound, a topological understanding allows for spatial relations that are primarily vector based. One of the most commonly given examples of a topological structure is the Möbius strip, a three-dimensional shape in which different faces or aspects of a solid are imagined as connecting with each other. For Steven Connor, a topological model speaks to the implicative capacity of skin to be folded in upon itself and to be involved in ambivalent substances and forms that do not have simple superficiality or absolute homogeneity.[87] While a topographical scheme is constricting insofar as it depends upon the simple alternative of inside and outside, a topological model might resemble the shifting surfaces of smoke, clouds, dust, sand, or foam.[88]

Topology, as a "new paradigm of figure and object that is beyond form . . . an object that is constantly in *deformation*," is a useful model for border studies.[89] A topological conceptualization of borders has much mileage in that it hampers visual representations and therefore does not impart borders with an overriding linear vision. Instead, it gives precedence to the relational, to vectors and rhizomes. As a distributed field, it also better accommodates folds, pleats, and crevices than topographical linear geographies.[90] As architectural theorist Stan Allen argues, field configurations constitute a spatial matrix capable of unifying diverse elements while respecting the identity of each: "Form matters, but not so much the forms of things as the forms between things."[91]

A well-known mathematical problem called the Seven Bridges of Königsberg can illustrate the somewhat abstract concept of topological fields.[92] The problem poses the following puzzle: whether it is possible to find a walk through the city that would cross each bridge once and only once. In this conundrum, distances are irrelevant, and the shape of the city can be distorted and twisted at will—as long as the relations between the nodes (here: the bridges) remain constant. As Victoria Blum and Anna Secor clarify, a topological space is "not defined by the distances between points that characterize it when it is in a fixed state but rather by the characteristics that it maintains in the process of distortion and transformation (bending, stretching, squeezing, but not breaking)."[93]

In the context of the Sino-Russian borderlands, the numerous layers that insulate Russia from China are eminently mobile. They expand, contract, and distort under the pressure of political, social, and economic forces. They can be very thin, even nonexistent, as at my current field site—the city of Blagoveshchensk—but they can also extend deep inland. Some segments of these restricted zones are fenced off and patrolled, while others are unmarked, with limits that are both ambiguous and variable.[94] Rather than a mere line of contact, it most resembles an epidermal surface in that it may be stretched taut but can also be folded, wrinkled, and crumpled. It can contain orifices and be marked by abrasions and scars. Cities, boundary markers, and crossings—like the bridges in the Königsberg problem—are fixed nodes, but the borderland itself can be visualized as a pliable ribbon whose shape continually twists and morphs. The location and extent of the restricted zones are in fact difficult to know even for local Russians, as information about them frequently circulates through word of mouth and rumors: certain places are said to be out of bounds, or requiring a permit, but their actual status is more difficult to ascertain. The borderland thus recalls Steven Connor's skin analogy in that, like smoke or dust, its exact topography remains shifting and ungraspable.[95]

NONHOMOGENEITY

I described earlier how the Penfield homunculus, with its disproportionately large areas, forms a distorted representation of the body. A further remarkable feature of the Penfield homunculus map is that it is not entirely continuous. "The face is not near the neck, where it should be, but is below the hand. The genitals, instead of being between the thighs, are located below the foot."[96] If the homunculus was initially imagined as a reduced human figure, new research shows bodily mapping actually follows a different organizational model. The various parts that make up the body are best thought of as elements of a superset whose sequentiality prevails over exact location.[97] Here again, what matters most is the relation that binds these parts together, the only key properties being the ones that survive distortion and stretching.[98]

This nonhomogeneity links back to the issues of telescoping and rerouting discussed in chapter 3. In both cases it is the connection between each point, and their positions relative to each other, that predominate. In the telescoping phenomenon, where the phantom gradually fades away and the arm becomes progressively shorter, the relation between the phantom hand and the rest of the body is unaffected by the reduction of the phantom arm. The sequential nature of their relationship is not qualitatively disturbed by the shorter distance. In the same way, the dynamic rerouting of pathways following the loss of a part of the body has no effect on the relation between the various points of the set in that their relation remains identical irrespective of distortion or distance.

Political boundaries exhibit an analogous tension between connections and pathways, between topography and topology. As with the Königsberg bridges, relations prevail over topography. This does not mean that boundary markers do not matter and that they can be moved at will without consequences. The examples I have given earlier clearly demonstrate that this is not the case. But while the location of border lines remains unchanged, their actual management and control is now often carried out remotely, or even outsourced, as in the case of Frontex, an agency created by the European Union to manage the borders of its member states.[99] The example of the UK-French border, in particular along the path of the Eurostar, is frequently given as an illustration of the fractured and complex nature of modern borders. As passengers board the London-bound train in Paris, they go through UK border control, where they are met with a sign welcoming them to the United Kingdom. Still physically in France, they find themselves in a British enclave of some sort, subject to British authorities and to British law. Should they commit a crime in this zone of exception, they would be deported to the UK, despite being about two hundred miles away from the actual border.

For border scholars such as Hilary Cunningham, such examples demonstrate that borders are "never continuous or juridically self-evident—although they may be imagined, propagated, and mythologized as such."[100] However, if the more complex topographical arrangement of border control in a neoliberal environment may look like a sign of weakening, fracture, or even a harbinger of eventual obsolescence of borders, I would argue that this complexity has in fact no meaningful effect on the actual location or force of national borders. From a topological perspective, the location of UK border control in a train station in Paris is essentially a twisting of the skin that binds the two nations together, not a symptom of leakiness, fluidity, or permeability.[101]

Where Cunningham's argument is especially pertinent is in identifying the tension between a flat and binary imaginary of borders and their actual complexity and multifaceted realities. This tension echoes Wendy Brown's argument that a proliferation of border walls is symptomatic of an erosion of nation-state sovereignty.[102] As I argued in the introduction, if I disagree that the political state is witnessing any kind of erosion, walls are nonetheless indubitably formidable in their projection of an image of stability and clarity. It is in this role that the logomap matters most: as a national homunculus—a graphic confirmation of the nation's bodily integrity, homogeneity, and continuity. Far from anachronistic, the logomap's visual power is especially potent in an increasingly connected world in which the contours of national sovereignty appear ever blurrier.[103]

What this indirectly hints at is that the nation's visual emphasis on containment and hermeticity is actually sustained by a phantasmatic, abjected double. The emergence of the logomap, free from all geographical shackles and dislocated from its neighbors, is made possible through the suppression, indeed repression, of similarities and overlaps. The visually unambiguous logomap is thus paralleled by the uncanny shadowy figure of the monstrous and the concorporate, which threatens to disrupt the idealized portrayal of the nation-state as autonomous and independent. In chapter 5, I turn to an analysis of enclaves, archipelagoes, and other atomized and fractured national spaces where the skin of the nation is being stretched beyond breaking point.

ARCHIPELAGOES, ENCLAVES, AND OTHER CARTOGRAPHIC MONSTERS

It was decided that everything that was found *inside* the dotted line would be colored purple and called France, while everything *outside* the dotted line would be colored differently . . . and would be given a different name (in fact, for quite a few years, there was a strong insistence on coloring purple—and thereby calling France—bits of space that weren't part of that hexagon and were even often quite far away from it, but generally these didn't hold quite as well).

—Georges Perec, *Espèces d'espaces*

FRACTURED SPACE

In the early 1970s, American artist Gordon Matta-Clark discovered that the City of New York periodically auctioned off "gutterspace"—residual parcels resulting from anomalies in zoning, surveying, and public-works expansion. Intrigued by the idea of ownable but unoccupiable (and frequently inaccessible) space, Matta-Clark purchased the deeds to fifteen of these microplots of land—slivers of curbsides and alleyways—for between $25 and $75 apiece.[1] Over the next years, he collected the maps, deeds, and other bureaucratic documentation attached to the slivers, which, combined with maps and montaged images of each site, formed his project *Fake Estates* (figure 5.1). His concept of "anarchitecture"—a conflation of the words *anarchy* and *architecture*, indexing a focus on voids, gaps, and leftover spaces—echoes the attention this chapter places on gaps, fractures, and places that remain unaccounted for.

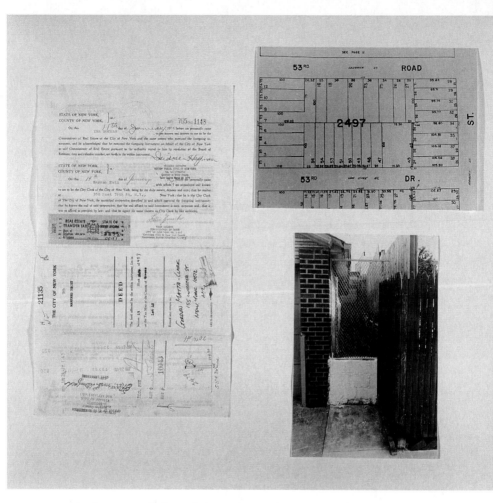

5.1. Gordon Matta-Clark, *Reality Properties: Fake Estates, Little Alley Block 2497, Lot 42.* © Gordon Matta-Clark, 1974 (posthumous assembly, 1992).

Focusing on fractured space such as political enclaves, on auratic and negative spaces like archipelagoes, and finally on what I term the monstrous, this final chapter is concerned with spaces where the logomap resolutely departs from the ideal of the nation-state evoked so far in the book.[2]

Detached and fragmented, enclaves are a remarkably rare phenomenon in contemporary political geography. They are technically a subset of the larger family of political fragments, which are noncontiguous parts of a nation's territory.[3] Fragments can include islands belonging to a larger landmass (such as the state of Hawaii in relation to the US mainland), or to noncontiguous territory (such as the state of Alaska). Enclaves refer specifically to parts of sovereign territory wholly surrounded by another sovereign state. The largest, and most intricate, enclave complex was located, until 2015, across the India-Bangladesh border.[4] Known as the Chitmahals, it consisted of 102 Indian enclaves on Bangladesh territory and of seventy-one Bangladeshi enclaves within India's mainland. This spatial enmeshment was complicated further by the existence of counterenclaves and even—a unique case worldwide—a counter-counterenclave: a tiny piece of Indian territory in a fragment of Bangladesh, itself within a piece of India within Bangladesh.[5]

While these enclaves—just like enclaves elsewhere in the world—were commonly imagined as being walled off or at least clearly demarcated, they were neither territorially isolated nor did they have their boundaries signposted on the ground.[6] This invisibility did not however spell freedom of movement. On the contrary, residents of these enclaves were often described as stateless, since they lived in zones outside of official administration and since officials of one country could not cross a sovereign frontier to administer territory.[7] In September 2011, after decades of attempts at a resolution, the governments of India and Bangladesh finally announced their intention to resolve the issue through a land swap, giving residents a choice of nationality.[8] So extensive was this enclave complex that its resolution caused a reduction of 70 percent in the number of enclaves in the world.[9] While the resolution was largely prompted by the considerable human suffering they caused as well as by the difficulties for both states in administering such labyrinthine geography, there was also the sense that the enclaves were anachronistic and that both India and Bangladesh needed to regularize their border to become fully aligned on modern models.[10]

Enclaves—the anthropologist Madeleine Reeves refers to them poetically as "eruptions of state territorialization"[11]—are anachronistic to the extent that they are the vestiges of political organizations based on patronage that could vary from village to village rather than on territorially defined sovereignty. In the case of the Chitmahals, although many legends have it that the enclaves were the result of tracts of land gambled away by drunken maharajas, their existence was due to an incompatibility between two territorial logics: the feudal political schemes that prevailed in South Asia during the Mogul era, on the one hand, and the territorial organization of the sovereign state system that was introduced by the British, on the other.[12]

This incompatibility between these two logics of sovereignty is one that does not sit well within the contemporary organization of geopolitical space. Terms such as *surreal* and *absurd* that pervaded analyses of the Chitmahals have also

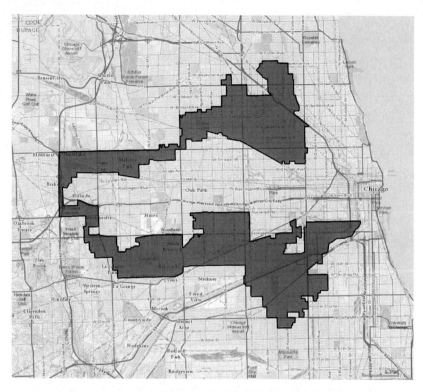

5.2. Fourth Congressional District of Illinois, US Department of the Interior, 1 Million Scale project. Image from Wikimedia Commons, PD Atlas, April 6, 2014.

been used to refer to the complex mosaic of post-Soviet Central Asia—a political geography that evokes similarly negative evaluations.[13] "When this 'indescribable' border is described," anthropologist Madeleine Reeves writes about the latter, "the tone is often one of alarm at the dangers of territorial indeterminacy, or incredulity at the inability of states to sort out where the border 'really' lies."[14] The byzantine geography of the region—a perfect setting for Gary Shteyngart's novel *Absurdistan*—is routinely summarized as symptomatic of a perverse Soviet scheme to make them unworkable, which is not an entirely fair assessment. The drawing of the winding and twisted borders of the Central Asian successor states was in fact the outcome of the Soviet Nationalities Policy, whereby each ethnic group was to have its own eponymous republic, language, and set of cultural attributes.[15] These were effectively administrative and internal boundaries, in this sense not unlike some of the more extreme forms of gerrymandering in the United States (see figure 5.2) and never envisaged to one day become international borders.[16] Regardless of intent, they have caused significant harm in the post-Soviet era, inhibiting human movement and restricting access to natural resources—water in particular.[17]

A very different set of enclave complexes are the ones found in Europe, the most extensive and convoluted of which being Baarle-Hertog and Baarle-Nassau, two towns enmeshed into a single urban entity across the border between Belgium and the Netherlands. Unlike the fraught situation in the Chitmahals, Central Asia, or the fractured Palestinian territory, Baarle is a place devoid of local and colonial anxieties. As a result, Baarle has been largely dismissed as a curious but ultimately irrelevant case study by border theorists. Yet the territorial logic that operates in Baarle is the same we find at work elsewhere, namely that every inch of the territory must be controlled and that borders should be unambiguously marked. In fact, the highly fractured and miniature scale of the environment makes it a truly fascinating place where inconsistencies, breaches, and ambiguities in the ideals of territorial sovereignty are laid bare.

On a total area of 32.35 square miles, the two towns are intertwined into one another. Situated only three miles away from the Belgian mainland, the Belgian town of Baarle-Hertog is made up of twenty-two exclaves, with the remaining territory around it forming the Dutch town of Baarle-Nassau.[18] The situation is complicated further by the presence of seven counterenclaves: plots of Dutch territory located within the Belgian enclaves. Some of the enclaves are truly miniscule, no larger than three thousand square yards. This territorial jigsaw is compounded by the irregularity of the shapes of the enclaves, which means residents may cross the border five or six times on their way to the corner store.[19] Border lines slice seemingly haphazardly across fields, streets, office buildings, and private homes, creating an intricate mosaic of national sovereignties, each with its own specific tax, traffic, and labor laws.

Like other enclaves elsewhere in Europe, Baarle's case is a vestigial relic of a medieval spatial logic premised on vassalage and ties of fealty rather than territoriality.[20] As discussed in chapter 1, the Peace of Westphalia marked a rupture in the way political space was envisioned. By the eighteenth century, geographer Alastair Bonnett writes, enclaves were being seen as a problem, and the "rational world of the Enlightenment tried to sponge away the dark and unmanageable world of enclaves."[21] European states attempted to eradicate many of them through delimitation treaties and conquest, but Baarle, never important or irksome enough to get to the top of anyone's to-do list, remained a notable exception.

In fact, not only was there little incentive to iron out the territorial messiness, but the few attempts at doing so through treaties and land swaps were actively resisted by the residents who found the existing situation to their advantage. Practices of evasion have been central to life in Baarle, and its inhabitants are immensely proud of their ability to navigate the town's tortuous spatiality. "Playing with the border," as it is known locally, had important repercussions during World War I, when Belgium, unlike the Netherlands, was occupied by the German army. With German troops unable to physically occupy Baarle-Hertog without crossing into neutral Dutch territory, the Belgian enclave became a space of resistance and contraband, defiantly erecting a military radio transmitter.[22]

Today, with Belgium and the Netherlands part of the European Union, differences between the two halves have been much attenuated. Baarle-Hertog and Baarle-Nassau share a currency, and many laws and regulations have been standardized, making it more difficult, and less economically rewarding, to play with the border. The two towns work closely together in their provision of services and co-run binational operations such as the fire station and the sewage treatment facility.[23] The readiness of both municipalities to "make it work" is held up by locals as an example of how Europeans can live together in a European Union within which sovereign borders are, ironically, becoming less and less relevant.

Homogenization and standardization across the two municipalities has not, however, led to the disappearance of the borders. On the contrary, in 2000 the two communal councils embarked on a program of marking the location of the boundary lines. They fixed metal disks on roads and footpaths to form dotted lines and also repaved some streets and sidewalks, adding stones inset with the letters B and NL to indicate the nationality of each side of the line. This exercise, paradoxically funded by a European Union eager to efface its own internal borders, was carried out less to make space legible than as part of a drive to rebrand Baarle for tourism purposes. All the local people I spoke to when I visited in 2015 in fact insisted that these lines were there only for visitors, since they themselves, as locals, knew where the boundaries were. While these assertions were somewhat overblown—the exact location of borders having been established through two demarcation projects, in 1974 and 1995—residents were clearly comfortable in inhabiting these in-between spaces. More than comfortable, they relished the ambiguity—an ambiguity only harnessed through an intimate knowledge of local geography.

In his 2014 book *Off the Map*, British geographer Alastair Bonnett speaks of his fascination with spaces located in between nations and of his desire to explore the "further possible distance between the border posts of two contiguous nations" in order to "step outside, if only for a moment, the claustrophobic grid of nations."[24] Paradoxically, Baarle may be one of these places. Although it appears to be a highly demarcated space with every inch accounted for and distributed, it is in fact a complex, messy, and nonlinear entanglement of sovereignties. Instead of stepping outside the grid of nations, it is in the very fractures found in Baarle, highlighting the arbitrary nature of territorial sovereignty, that this "breathing space" is enacted. Baarle's crosshatched spaces are in this sense reminiscent of the Japanese art form of *kintsugi*, in which the fractures in a broken object are first accentuated with multiple coats of lacquer and then covered with a metallic powder, usually gold.[25] Rather than attempting to conceal the nonorganic arbitrariness of territorial borders through somatic narratives, borders in Baarle are marked, accentuated, and persistently—indeed fetishistically—reiterated.[26]

Baarle likes to tout itself as a European laboratory—an example of harmonious cohabitation in a mixed environment. More importantly, Baarle is a sovereignty laboratory in that it shines a light on the very principles and mechanics of territorial sovereignty. The length to which both municipalities go to adhere to this political ideal, despite the challenges imposed by Baarle's fractal geography, makes it fascinating case study. Indeed, if they supply services to their respective residents and dutifully share the costs of road repair and illumination prorated down to the square meter, the two municipalities in fact tacitly agree on the convenient fiction that they are entirely distinct. Yet, despite careful and extensive demarcation, separation is ultimately illusory given that the border bisects numerous dwellings which, for administrative and fiscal purposes, need to be located in only one of the two municipalities. The established practice of determining national affiliation by the location of the front door means that buildings are treated as singular, rather than the spatial hybrids that they actually are. The reality that a given house is not wholly in Belgium or the Netherlands is well understood, but for reasons of convenience it is treated legally and jurisdictionally as if it were. So while Baarle's surface is unambiguously marked, the complex of enclaves is in fact an elastic space, a distorted grid where borders are routinely twisted into a workable space in order to make this very partition possible.

Such distortions, due in Baarle to the physical constraints imposed by the miniaturized nature of the towns' enclaves, are in fact quite common. From special economic zones and corridors to territories that states control but do not have sovereignty over (such as the United States with respect to Guantánamo Bay), and from territories and dependencies where citizens have fewer rights (like Puerto Rico) to islands where the strict religious rules of the mainland do not apply (such as Iran's Kish Island), these are some of the countless folds and kinks in a state's spatial fabric imagined to be, and idealized as, homogenous.[27] These torsions and distortions are spatial but also temporal. Various special exceptions have thus been granted on a temporary basis, as when a Scottish court was established in the Netherlands, on neutral ground, with the explicit aim to rule on the trial of two Libyans in connection with the Lockerbie bombing of Pan Am Flight 103.[28] A more unusual case was Suite 212 at Claridge's Hotel in London—a temporary Yugoslavian enclave that was created for a single day in 1945 to ensure the heir to the throne would be born on Yugoslavian soil.[29]

"Empirical spaces of legal suspension," particularly in relation to migration mechanisms, have proliferated in recent decades.[30] From the Esquimalt Naval Base in British Columbia, which was designated in 1999 as "not-yet-Canada" so that six hundred Chinese migrants could not claim refugee status, to the island of Nauru, which has performed asylum-processing services for payment on behalf of Australia, the gap between the legal definition of territorial sovereignty and actual practices on the ground appears to be widening.[31] Recent border literature has done much to expose the resistant fiction that political borders and territorial sovereignty are coextensive, even if power differentials—specifically when states have sufficient clout to bend the rules—often remain unexamined.[32] Terms such as *unbundled, flexible, aleatory, paternal, graduated,* and *variegated* have been introduced by social science and political scholars as hyphenated qualifiers in order to account for the nonlinearity, nonhomogeneity, and noncontiguity of political borders.[33] While these forms of metastasized sovereignty are useful to unpack the spatial formation of neoliberal economies, interpreting territorial discontinuities through exceptionalism unwittingly reinscribes the Westphalian model as the norm. These kinds of liminal spaces, Sandro Mezzadra and Brett Neilson write, "provide a privileged perspective on globalization and its accompanying tensions, frictions, and conflicts. The bordering technologies that make these spaces possible intertwine with state borders and contribute to the formation of new territorial assemblages for the workings of governmentality and sovereignty."[34] In fact, I would argue that these spatial and temporal exceptions function as instruments designed to work within the agreed system without having to challenge its core tenets. Instead of actual exceptions, then, they constitute internal devices inherent to the inner workings of territorial sovereignty.[35] One of the core points this chapter makes is that territorial ambivalence does not exist in spite of the state; rather, it is structurally folded within it.

Further, like the colonies, far-flung territories, and dependencies I discuss below, spatial and temporal enclaves are extraneous to the logomap and as such remain largely invisible—their ambiguous sovereignty status making them even more difficult to represent graphically. These spaces speak to the central argument developed in this chapter, namely that the visual clarity of the logomap is made possible and sustained through practices that twist and distort the territorial ideal of modern political geography. Operating side by side with the logomap, they constitute its negative doppelgänger. Driven by the unsaid, the unconscious, the repressed, and the monstrous, the actual working of the logomap is discussed in the final part of this chapter. The intervening section, however, first looks at a set of territorial forms and phenomena I bring together under the collective rubric of negative space—spaces that are defined by a lack and an absence: unwanted, unmarked, invisible, as well as spaces traced and delineated by the presence of Others.

NEGATIVE SPACE

The concept of terra nullius (nobody's land) emerged in the eighteenth century on the basis of Roman law res nullius (nobody's thing). By the early twentieth century, it was used productively by various European states to claim land on the basis of first discovery, but often also on the basis of effective occupation—thus enabling European states to claim land on which indigenous populations lived. The fact that only one true terra nullius remains (a section of Antarctica) speaks volumes about the insatiable hunger for territory that has been characteristic of modern geopolitics. Every last parcel of the rest of the terrestrial world, regardless of elevation, climate, or inhabitability, is someone's sovereign territory—nominally if not in actual practice.[36]

This very appetite for territory has paradoxically led to two notable cases where pieces of land have remained unclaimed by their neighbors. Bir Tawil, an eight-hundred-square-mile area along the border between Egypt and Sudan, lies at the intersection of two competing boundary lines. Egypt asserts the straight political boundary, established in 1899, while Sudan asserts the irregular administrative boundary established in 1902—each to their respective advantage.[37]

The other exception is a series of misalignments between Serbia and Croatia along the Danube. Whereas Serbia holds the opinion that the thalweg, the main navigational channel, represents the international border between the two countries in that the border should follow the river, Croatia claims that the international border lies along the boundaries of the cadastral municipalities located along the river. The cadastre-based boundary reflects the course of the Danube that existed in the nineteenth century, before meandering and hydraulic engineering works altered its course. Serbia and Croatia both favor the principle that most benefits them, but over time the shifting geography of the Danube opened a breach between the two states, creating slices of territory beyond either country's sovereignty. Taking advantage of this rare instance of unclaimed *terra*, Czech politician Vít Jedlička proclaimed on April 13, 2015, the Free Republic of Liberland on one of these four pockets of land unclaimed by either nation. A few weeks later, the second largest pocket, a mere thousand-square-foot patch of land, was claimed by another micronation project, the Kingdom of Enclava, and finally the micronation of Verdis, established in 2019 by a fourteen-year-old Australian, claimed the third patch, a tiny sliver of land of barely 0.1 square miles—leaving only an even smaller land discrepancy unclaimed as of this writing.[38]

In both instances, these unclaimed territories are the unlikely outcome of different territorial logics. A claim to sovereignty over Bir Tawil or over the four pockets of land by the Danube would be impossible without challenging the principles each state asserts, to their respective overall advantage. Rather than being unwanted, as some observers have argued, they are, rather, collateral damage in the unbridled ambition of territorial expansion.[39] In this sense, these gaps in the otherwise tight-fitting global political map are similar to Matta-Clark's gutterspace. There too the gaps were the result of shifting spatial usage rather than unwanted plots of land. In Manhattan, breaches had opened as a result of the creation of transport infrastructure like the subway. In the borough of Queens, where the majority of Matta-Clark's plots—perhaps better termed *voids* in that they were negative spaces defined by boundaries—were located, they were largely "accidents of the collision of urbanization and the rural landscape."[40]

True relinquishments of political space are exceedingly rare.[41] While they do not constitute unwanted spaces, buffers constitute nonetheless what I term negative space insofar as they form sacrificial zones from which state presence is seen to retreat. As discussed in chapter 4, in buffer zones states come to the mutual agreement to forsake a contact area of varying depth. A common type are demilitarized zones, such as those running across the island of Cyprus or the Korean Peninsula. At the Korean DMZ, a site to which I return later in this chapter, North and South Korea are separated by a

2.5-mile-wide demilitarized zone. With the exception of one small village in each section, the entire zone is uninhabited.[42] Demilitarized zones, just like the buffer states discussed in chapter 4, feature a strong temporal dimension in that they are conceptualized as transitory phenomena, destined to eventually disappear upon resolution of the conflict that led to their creation. In this sense, buffer zones also echo some of the temporal aspects of the *terrain vague*, a French term notably difficult to translate denoting an urban area both abandoned and slated for future development—a space of decay awaiting eventual gentrification and inclusion into the city's fabric.[43]

Similarly, spatial categories such as no-man's-lands, cordons sanitaires, no-fly zones, and safe zones, even if they all differ in origin, impulse, and aspiration, resemble buffer zones in that they are liminal frontier zones characterized by restricted access—for civilians and nonlocal populations, if not for all. For the sake of the present argument, and seemingly running counter to the important work of geographers who have carefully sought to delineate and distinguish them from one another, I bundle them here instead under the heading of buffer zones, as a special category of negative spaces, in order to focus on their shared attributes.

No-man's-lands, as political geographers Noam Leshem and Alasdair Pinkerton have argued, are very specific kinds of spatial partitioning with a unique history and characteristics. No-man's-lands, they write, are "spaces produced by simultaneous forces of abandonment and enclosure."[44] This very tension, one might argue, is also present in both buffers and border zones.[45] In fact, regardless of intent, the very process of bordering can lead to the creation of buffers and no-man's-lands. In the same way that Russia's layering of its border with China has created zones of varying widths to which foreigners generally do not have access and which even Russian citizens cannot enter without special authorization, the border wall erected between the United States and Mexico has unintentionally created pockets of uncertain status. In South Texas, Miguel Díaz-Barriga and Margaret Dorsey write, the border wall built by the Department of Homeland Security was erected north of the international boundary, the Rio Grande, thereby placing a ribbon of US land of approximately forty thousand acres in an ambiguous position.[46] But unlike in Russia where residents feel responsible for securing the border and largely enjoy the social capital this confers on them, in South Texas residents report feeling trapped in this liminal zone, which they describe as a space of chaos, danger, and fear.[47]

Both cases, like border walls in general, reinforce the notion of the state as bounded, separate, and territorially homogeneous. By contrast, extremely rare are zones that are shared across polities—such as Pheasant Island, an uninhabited river island on the border between France and Spain whose administration alternates every six months between the two nations. From the spatial distortions discussed earlier in the case of Baarle, to the existence of enclaved and ambulatory diplomatic spaces exempt from local taxation and civil jurisdiction, various mechanisms are in place with the explicit goal of sustaining the illusion of the state as container.[48]

Expanding the concept of buffers to all forms of territorial liminalities and articulatory spaces between political states helps underscore the ubiquity of transitional sites that tend to remain invisible in both cartography and the political imagination. The political concept of buffer, too frequently relegated by geographers and social theorists to its narrow historical usage—and still largely undertheorized as a result—speaks to entanglements and overlaps that resemble pre-Westphalian political geographies. Reconfigured in this way, buffers constitute less a space separating two entities than a zone connecting them, leading to productive assemblages that challenge the very ideal of the state as discrete and autonomous. In particular, the idea of backyard discussed below evokes the tension between the apparent stable boundaries of the state and its much more ambiguous incarnation. It allows for a view of the state that is both unmoored from its physical boundaries and that melts into its contiguous neighbors.

As a space that is outside the house yet still within the realm of the domestic, the backyard is a useful metaphor of liminality and buffering. In its primary context of homeownership, a backyard refers to the outdoor, but domestic, space beyond the prying eyes of neighbors. In geopolitics, usage of the concept of backyard to refer to a neighboring area where a state is invested and within which actions by enemy or competing powers might be feared or seen as provocative originated with the Monroe Doctrine in the nineteenth century. That the concept should have been adopted in political geography to designate spaces beyond the sovereign reach of a state—instead of a less loaded term such as *neighborhood*—is noteworthy. It appropriates those extraterritorial spaces into the realm of the domestic, thus directly running counter to the cartographic practices characteristic of the post-Westphalian political order. The dimension of ownership present in the original context also deserves notice in that it endures in the selective mobilization of the term: routinely used for world powers such as the United States, Russia, or the European Union, speaking of a backyard in the context of a smaller country would sound absurd. Similarly, the area designated as backyard tends to denote a state comparatively weaker, thus in the context of the United States clearly referring to the unequal relations with Central and South America rather than Canada.

While not precisely equivalent, the Russian concept of *near abroad* (*blizhnee zarubezh'e*) covers semantic ground similar to the US *backyard*. In the context of postsocialist Russia, *near abroad* has come to denote, from a Russian perspective, the fifteen independent states that emerged after the breakup of the Soviet Union in 1991. As for the United States, this blurry zone between the domestic and the (here, newly) foreign is a zone, strategically vital to Russian interests, where outside interference is perceived to constitute a direct existential threat. As Gerard Toal notes, many in the West hear the phrase *near abroad* as a reluctance on the part of Russia to acknowledge the full sovereignty of the new post-Soviet states. The semantic range of the term extends, however, beyond that: it does denote a long-standing spatial entanglement but also acknowledges a "new arrangement of sovereignty and an old familiarity" as well as indexing a range of geopolitical emotions.[49]

The territorial extensions beyond the state proper that *backyard* and *near abroad* gesture at add a further layer of complexity to the cutaneous dimension discussed in chapter 3, notably the ways in which objects such as a cane or a vehicle can effortlessly become incorporated into an individual's bodily map. They also hint at an auratic dimension of geopolitics I have explored more fully elsewhere and which I define as the spaces that extend beyond the edges of the political state in ways that are not cartographically visible, yet are securely tied to a spatial referent (the political state) and anchored in the material realities of that state.[50]

Linked to the spatial edges, fragments, and remainders discussed at the beginning of the chapter in the context of Matta-Clark's anarchitecture in New York, the question of backyard in its aerial urban form has been primarily linked to property overhangs and unobstructed views.[51] In a hot property market, the empty space above a building can translate into tens of millions of dollars. In New York, where every building is zoned to be a certain height, a building that does not use its full allotment of vertical space can sell that right to a neighboring building.[52] Once the "air right" has been sold and the opportunity to grow surrendered, the adjacent building is then in a position to guarantee its residents unobstructed vistas.[53] As a result, the air above, behind, or to the left or right might be worth far more than the building that carries the rights to it.[54]

Thinking of urban space in this way is helpful, since the notion of backyard that was smuggled into geopolitics also carries this dimension of extensibility beyond a state's physical footprint. Noncontiguous territorial fragments and

5.3. "We Can Do This." Slogan of the national campaign to increase confidence among Americans in the coronavirus vaccine. US Department of Health and Human Services, Office of the Assistant Secretary for Public Affairs.

overseas military bases, as well as dependent territories (without representation and with reduced sovereign rights) complicate political cartography's unambiguous representations. The visually tidy logomap that Benedict described as free of neighbors and geographical context is an ideal more easily supported by those states that are standalone (such as islands), without colonial extensions, and of somewhat regular shape.[55] As discussed in chapter 1, noncontiguous fragments, including fetishized ones such as Russia's Kuril Islands, frequently fall out of political maps. Similarly, colonies and overseas possessions are difficult if not impossible to represent. France's spatially neat hexagon is only the tip of the spatial iceberg that the country constitutes.[56] Its numerous overseas territories or DOM-TOM (*départements et régions d'outre-mer et territoires d'outre-mer*) make the country a truly global entity, with a territorial footprint accounting for 18 percent of the mainland's territory and with an exclusive economic zone representing 96.7 percent of the total.[57] Even fragments closer to the mainland and fully integrated in terms of sovereignty bear a fragile visual relationship to the state they're attached to. Akin to diacritics, their relationship to their continental state feels additive and impermanent. A quick Google search for images of the "USA logomap" brings up outlines of the mainland without Alaska or Hawaii. In the rare instances where the two states are included, it often feels like an afterthought: reduced in size, they are tucked in where space allows (see figure 5.3, which unusually also includes Puerto Rico).[58]

Visual representation matters. When territories are left out, they fall out of mind.[59] The fact that the United States' outline never includes distant territories such as American Samoa or Guam has clear repercussions on the place of these territories in American consciousness.[60] US representatives themselves are not necessarily aware that these islands are American: in March 2021 Congresswoman Marjorie Taylor Greene argued that hard-earned tax dollars should go for America, not for foreign countries like China, Russia, or Guam. More embarrassingly, an official statement from the State Department in 1935 announced it was annexing Baker, Howland, and Jarvis Islands in the Pacific, only to rescind the announcement a couple of days later when a consultation of records revealed these islands already belonged to the United States.[61]

Of course there are also undeniable advantages to this invisibility and territorial ambiguity, and the earlier point about offshore bases where different rules apply or islands that serve as airlocks for the processing of migrants is an important one to bear in mind.[62] But from a purely practical visual design standpoint, states that are fractured, dispersed, or with unwieldy shapes, such as Chile, are notably difficult to logomap, and this has an impact on the imaginary of the state.[63]

Especially awkward is logomapping a fractured territory such as an archipelagic state or a state containing numerous islands. Japan's outline, for design reasons, tends to be reduced to its five main islands, since an inclusion of all its northern and southern islands would dilute the country's iconic recognizability, the important logo component of its logomap. In the case of Canada, its exact number of islands is ambiguous on account of their land/ice composition, thus making the Canadian north visually blurry. Likewise, the Philippines archipelago is too vast to be represented in its multitude of islands and requires simplification. As in Canada, the exact number of islands is ultimately reliant on the definition of what constitutes an island. So while the official number is 7,107, it may in fact be more: the country's mapping agency announced in 2016 that they had found 534 others.[64]

Fractured yet connected, archipelagic states hang together as a cluster. Their geographical and visual coherence relies on an unspoken premise of gravitational pull—the assumption that proximity bespeaks kinship and belonging.[65] Archipelagic logomaps thus work best with groups of islands that are tightly clustered together—another reason why a dispersive archipelago such as Japan tends to be reduced to its core islands, despite the affective prominence of disputed islands such as Senkaku or Takeshima in Japanese political consciousness.[66]

In the modern cartographic imagination, geographic rather than hydrographic, what is holding the archipelago together is a negative space, an absence.[67] The watery expanse breaks the archipelago into its constituent fragments, but at the same time it is the negative space that holds them together. In recent years China has attempted to make this explicit by giving equal weight to land and water. Unlike previous maps that depicted noncontiguous territories in cutaway boxes, the new, so-called vertical map is singular and continuous, and includes the vast body of water south of Hainan Island. In the new map, the land, islands, and claimed waters in the South China Sea are all featured on the same scale in one complete map, thereby placing the islands, but also the entirety of the maritime space, in direct visual equivalence with the mainland. As the Hunan Map Press editor in chief, Lei Yixun, told the state media agency Xinhua News, this new map helps "correct misconceptions that territories carry different weights, and fosters a raised territorial awareness and marine consciousness with the public."[68]

More dramatically, in 2016 the Japanese Ministry of Foreign Affairs launched a visual campaign about its disputed borders. A poster titled "Do you know the shape of Japan?" (Nihon no katachi shitte imasu ka?) highlights three tension points: the Northern Territories, Takeshima, and Senkaku Islands, disputed with Russia, Korea, and China, respectively (figure 5.4). What is radical about this map is less the territorial claims that it stakes than the confident demarcation of a terraqueous entity neatly defined against an undifferentiated background. The poster's outline distinguishes between Japanese and non-Japanese waters, gives equal visual weight to both land and sea, and seeks, through explicitly pedagogical means, to foster affective attachment to these more-than-human geographies.

These deployments of territorial claims beyond *terra* frequently overlap with other states' attempts to embrace the terraqueous. China's so-called nine-dash line self-demarcation encompasses vast swaths of maritime Southeast Asia, impinging on the territorial waters and exclusive economic zones of others.[69] The decision by the United National Convention on the Law of the Sea (UNCLOS) to grant coastal states sovereign rights over extended continental shelves up to 350 nautical miles from the coastal baseline has led to further entanglements. Relating to the subsurface only, these sovereign rights have no effect on the legal status of the superjacent water column or airspace above those waters, thereby creating a complicated layering of three-dimensional space. A similar volumetric entanglement has been described by architect Eyal Weizman in the context of the Israel-Palestine interface, where part of Israeli territory, in the form of a road linking Jewish Jerusalem and

5.4. "Do you know the shape of Japan?" (日本のカタチ知っていますか.)

the West Bank settlement of Gush Etzion, finds itself alternatively above and below Palestinian territory.[70]

Qualifying in fact as archipelago on account of its highly fractured and dispersive nature, the Palestinian territory is a visually potent example of the relationship between fractured territory and the negative (but all-defining) space that surrounds it. Broken up into numerous fragments and enclaves and increasingly perforated by Israeli settlements, Palestine's geobody contains within itself the phantomic presence of Israel in that its logomap continues to represent it as a single uninterrupted space. Fascinatingly, the same iconic logomap is also used to represent Israel—making it, in the words of Yair Wallach, a "picture of a geographic schizophrenia: two adversary and asymmetrical nation-selves inhabiting a single geo-body."[71] Recalling China Miéville's fictional towns of Besźel and Ul Qoma that share the same geographical footprint but whose inhabitants have learned to carefully disentangle themselves from one another, the two logomaps appear identical only to outsiders. Israelis and Palestinians themselves can easily distinguish between the two through visual and textual cues such as legend, place names, and coloring.[72]

The two logomaps are also incomplete, nostalgic, and aspirational. Palestine's logomap is increasingly divergent from the realities on the ground, where territory is interrupted by an ever greater number of illegal settlements, roadblocks, and border walls; Israel's, by contrast, inches toward isomorphism as more and more Palestinian enclaves are being assimilated. Yet even then, this Palestinian space is never fully absorbed and remains liminal and phantom-like. *Palimpstine*, a portmanteau term coined by Salman Rushdie, is especially apposite here in evoking the historically layered nature of Palestine and the partially effaced territorial phantoms that constitute it.[73] In its erasure of Israel's colonial violence and transformation of border walls and no-man's-lands into beaches, camping sites, natural reserves, and marinas, Julien Boussac's evocative *Archipelago of Eastern Palestine* (figure 5.5) recalls here some of the fantasy maps discussed earlier. It also echoes my deployment of negative space—concealing (and highlighting at the same time) the violence of Israel's settler colonialism in the redacted geography through gaps, silences, and watery expanses.[74]

While this political concorporation of two geobodies enmeshed into one is quite unique, it nonetheless speaks to a central premise of the book, namely that all states, irrespective of their outwardly discreteness, are never independent or autonomous entities. In fact, as I argue in the final section of this chapter, the more borders and separations are made explicit, the more the Other is repressed, suppressed, and pushed out of sight, the more entanglement comes to structure a state's identity. The very separation and erasure enacted by the logomap and by cartographic and reiterative visual practices, such as weather maps, mobilizes the phantomatic presence of the other, the monster under the bed. As mentioned in chapter 4, the limits of the state are also the limits of its neighbor—every kink and bend of its terrestrial outline having its negative counterpart across the border. Sometimes the logomap contains within itself the presence of the other, as in the case of Greece's outline, whose islands hug the (cartographically excised) Turkish

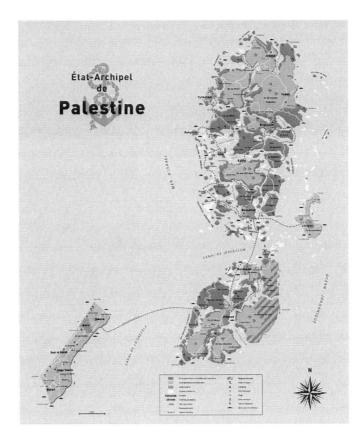

5.5. Julien Boussac, *L'archipel de Palestine Orientale*. Image from Wikimedia Commons, Creative Commons Attribution-NoDerivatives 4.0 International (CC-BY-ND 4.0), 2009.

coast.[75] But entanglements also occur across insulated and seemingly unambiguous demarcation lines, like that between North and South Korea, whose respective continued existences are predicated on the negation of the other.

MONSTROUS SPACE

A few years ago, after a public presentation I had just given on the enclave complex of Baarle-Hertog/Baarle-Nassau, a member of the audience explained over drinks that the talk had been interesting but had made him angry. "Why do they still have this mess? Why can't they sort it out? I hate it." For this individual, deviance from established norms of territorial sovereignty had no place in the modern political system. It jarred with the cartography we have all become accustomed to and constituted a prime example of what I term the territorial monstrous.

Having summoned monsters at various points in this chapter, time has come to clarify what I mean, and do not mean, by the term. Unlike the statement above, my use of *monster* does not smuggle in any derogatory dimension—a perhaps self-evident, but nonetheless crucial, point to make given that some of the monsters discussed here refer to real, existing subjects. They are the individuals whose bodies have been designated throughout history as frightening, obscene, animalistic, or impure: freaks, queers, Blacks, women, trans people.[76] Feared, rejected outcasts, but also envied and fetishized, these monstrous selves open up realms of alternative worlds.[77] In films and graphic novels featuring superheroes, vampires, or werewolves, the hero is in fact increasingly the physically/socially deviant imbued with preternatural powers, whereas the real monster is a socially sclerotic, and frequently immoral, human society.[78]

Following the publication of Jeffrey Cohen's *Monster Theory* in 1996, the figure of the monster has proven a very fertile notion for scholars in a range of disciplines, notably in literature and film studies. As Cohen writes in the collection and in later work, the monster is a transgressive figure and category violator.[79] Blurring the "binary oppositions that govern our basic concepts and modes of self-definition," the monster evokes an intolerable ambiguity.[80] Athwart human and animal, male and female, inside and outside, singular and plural, known and unknown, other and same, alive and dead, the monster must be exiled or destroyed to keep the system pure, yet it always returns in the guise of the repressed.[81] On the cusp between the frightening and the marvelous, and in spite of its organic nature, the monster is eminently cultural.[82] In evoking the dominant fears of a particular time and place, it is "constructed as monstrous through the influence of social conventions, expectations, and attitudes."[83] As such, the monster serves as a useful analytical figure to further our understanding of what it means to be human.[84]

I suggest that the territorial monstrous can serve a similar purpose here. In this chapter, I use the productive figure of the monster to examine territorial forms divergent from the ideals of cohesiveness, integrity, and autonomy that are inherent in the ideal of Westphalian territorial sovereignty. Previously appearing in maps at the edge of the known world in the form of sea monsters and so-called monster races, and associated with the exotic and (in the context of pre-sixteenth-century Europe) the non-Christian universe, the territorially monstrous is now tied to the temporary (the refugee camp), the illusory (the de facto state, the micronation), and the extraterritorial

(Guantánamo, black sites) as well as to the forms of territorial discontinuities and misalignments discussed throughout the book such as phantoms and prosthetics.[85] Enclaves are especially monstrous in that they expose both the ways in which states are fitted into each other and how their outer limits are also those of their neighbors (see chapter 4). They reveal, through their enmeshed nature, the enmeshed nature of all states.

By its very nature, the monstrous is ubiquitous and territorially amorphous. Uncontainable, it is associated with the sprawling, the excessive, the gigantic.[86] Perhaps, Elizabeth Grosz ponders, "our fear of the immersion or loss of identity with another is greater or more pervasive than our fear of bodily incompletion," thereby explaining why the monsters recognized throughout history are largely monsters of excess.[87] Similarly excessive is the imperial/colonial project: a territorial monster that is boundless, unrestrained, and anthropophagous—blurring the line between self and other.[88] Unfinished, outgrowing itself, and transgressing its own limits, the territorially monstrous recalls the grotesque body of Rabelais's Pantagruel discussed in chapter 2—a grotesque body that Bakhtin locates in the hinterland of discourse.[89]

True to its dual etymological origin of *monstrare* (show or reveal) and *monere* (warn or portend), the monster inhabits in fact a remarkable in-between space. Pushed out of sight, its existence nonetheless speaks to the fictive nature of the visible, and it is here, perhaps, that lie the greatest "promises of monsters."[90] Banished but always threatening to return, the monster is the uncanny doppelgänger—the messy, the entangled, repressed side of the logomap that necessarily structures the nonmonstrous.

A powerful depiction of this spatial duality is found in a scene of *My Winnipeg*, a surrealist mockumentary directed and written by Guy Maddin.[91] In Winnipeg, the narrator reports, the city's streets are supplemented by back lanes: "The lanes are illicit things, best not discussed, shameful. They receive the breach ends of houses, the side of the homes not meant for polite company. They're the weedy landscapes of shameful abandonment, conduits of refuse removal. Here we strew what we no longer want to acknowledge." The opposition between front and back lanes speaks, of course, to the hierarchical arrangement of social space, with imposing public-facing frontages supplemented by the more modest entrances and living quarters of domestics and support personnel.[92] It recalls also the Black and queer geographies found in the spaces of possibility afforded by white hegemonic power.[93] Existing in parallel but made invisible and voiceless, these geographies are intricately woven into—and indeed sustain—represented spaces.[94] A potent contemporary example is the way in which majority white communities have used "prison gerrymandering" to count Black and brown inmates as residents in order to inflate their census numbers and thereby their legislative power in Washington, "while simultaneously disempowering the black communities the inmates left when they were incarcerated."[95] Similarly problematic are spaces that elude neat classification, the ambiguous zones athwart categories such as race or gender. In Maddin's Winnipeg, this is exemplified by "the strange case of Lorette. A hermaphrodite street—half front street, half back lane. No-one speaks of Lorette."[96]

The blurring of gender and racial boundaries is always troublesome, but perhaps especially monstrous are cases where the very notion of individuality appears to be at stake. Conjoined twins blur that line in fundamental ways that jar with ideals of autonomy and body integrity, and are "highly disruptive of western notions of individual agency."[97] The first course of action considered in such births is separation, even though survival is not guaranteed.[98] In the case of Eilish, a conjoined twin born in Ireland in 1988 and who lost her sister Katie when they were separated at age three, the experience was highly traumatic, and for a long time she barely spoke. Reexperiencing trauma at the age of six when her prosthesis was taken away in order to fit a new one, she decided to name the new prosthesis Katie—a way for her to make the prosthetic a full part of her body and reintegrate her missing, phantom, twin.[99]

Choosing to embrace concorporation is clearly a challenging proposition for a parent, but it can prove extremely rewarding. For conjoined twin sisters Abigail and Brittany Hensel, the subject of a number of television documentaries, separation would have led to gross impairment of mobility and independent function, whereas their lateral symmetry—not a common occurrence in conjoined twins—provides them with full, unhindered mobility.[100] The Hensel sisters each has her own heart, stomach, spine, lungs, and spinal cord, but share a bladder, large intestine, liver, diaphragm, and reproductive organs. Each twin fully controls her half of the body—one leg and one arm on either side—which means that physical activities like running, biking, driving, or swimming must be a joint team effort, and the twins have learned to collaborate—each sister anticipating and responding to incipient movements in the other.[101] A situation such as this complicates our understanding of an individuality resting on bodily separateness. As their family doctor explains, individuality is a hard concept to embrace for conjoined twins who have grown together. "While they are considered separate people, they are always interlinked and intertwined."[102] Intellectually and legally, the two sisters are two separate individuals, each with her own personality, likes, and dislikes.

Yet they remain physically and emotionally attuned to one another in ways that seemingly blur this distinction.

Such forms of concorporation echo in fascinating ways some of the arguments made earlier in the book. Notably, the ways in which each sister anticipates and responds to her twin's incipient movements recall the intersensoriality of geobodies where a common skin binds two states together. What I want to argue here is that concorporation in the form of conjoined twinness makes for a better organizing metaphor than the zero-sum game predicated on competition and rivalry between entirely autonomous entities that informs geopolitical imaginaries. Rather than rejecting the somatic analogy as illusory and simplistic, I suggest political geography might draw inspiration from the rich literature, discussed in chapter 3, that has challenged the fiction of the discrete autonomous body to reveal its entangled, labile, and multiple nature. Taking that kind of corporeal model as analogy helps view territorial misalignments not as exceptions or hyphenated spatial hybrids but as true representations of territorial sovereignty. Indeed, political anthropologists Rebecca Bryant and Madeleine Reeves have recently made the germane argument that "the more closely we examine a map of the world, the more we see that it is covered with exceptions."[103] Historian Lauren Benton has similarly argued that through various patterns and practices, colonial powers produced "political geographies that were uneven, disaggregated, and oddly shaped—and not at all consistent with the image produced by monochrome shading of imperial maps."[104] A number of scholars in other disciplines have also made the case that so-called phantom states, hovering above a Westphalian cartography, "display some of the internal characteristics of statehood, such as de facto control over a distinct territory and population, a claim to external independence as well as a modicum of popular legitimacy" yet are unrecognized—and may indeed prefer to remain unrecognized.[105] And yet, if geographers and cultural theorists have acknowledged the Westphalian model as fiction, we seem unable to fully jettison the viscerally experienced somatic representations of the state as discrete container and somehow continue to be taken aback by the breach between de jure and de facto, and the attendant nonlinearity, nonhomogeneity, and noncontiguity of neoliberal political borders.

Entanglements are found at all political borders, including at the DMZ, the demilitarized zone between South and North Korea, which may be the most hermetic and fraught of international borders. Separate and wholly distinct political states yet historically, linguistically, and culturally singular, the two halves of the Korean Peninsula recall the concorporation of the Hensel sisters in that their functioning requires fine attuning to the other. Like conjoined twins, they are intimately intertwined: organically singular, their destiny is imagined in terms of reconciliation and reconstitution.[106]

This intermeshing is visible in the structural opposition between the two—with South Korea depicted as successful, democratic, and modern while North Korea stands for nonmodernity, economic failure, and authoritarianism. This relation is not merely one of opposition, it is also one of mimetic complementarity, with each half structured through the very existence of the other.[107] As cultural theorist Margrit Shildrick writes, "monstrous" and "normal" are two concepts "locked in a mutually constitutive relationship" insofar as the monstrous is "a necessary signifier . . . of normality, of a self that is constructed discursively against what it is not."[108] South Korean depictions of North Korea as a dystopian nation effectively posit the south as utopian: the more authoritarian and despotic the north is, the more the south appears democratic and free. This dichotomization also means that each side of the Korean Peninsula plays a crucial role in the definition and identity of its counterpart. Since each half constitutes the other's "negative space," every change in one produces a change in the other. As Shildrick explains, the "apparent security of the binary self/non-self that guarantees the identity of the selfsame is irrevocably displaced by the necessity that the subject be defined by its excluded other."[109] As such, it is not that "the monster represents the threat *of* difference, but that it threatens to interrupt difference."[110]

As its doppelgänger, each side stands for the other's body double, both complete opposite and uncanny semblant. In an attempt to move away from this mimetic embrace, just like twins seeking to assert their uniqueness and individuality, the two Koreas tend to use two different names to refer to the Korean Peninsula.[111] However, this will to distinguish is much weakened by the two sides' strong emotional and symbolic investment in the DMZ, the skin that binds them together. Ironically, the more the DMZ is emphasized as the buffer keeping them apart, the more it defines their twinlike relation.

The case of the Korean Peninsula is admittedly exceptional in its decades-long partition and hermetic border, but the notion of concorporation can also be productive to describe other forms of somatic entanglement. Speaking of the colonizer/colonized relation between France and Algeria, Étienne Balibar described it as more than one, yet not quite two. To the concept of hybridity, which is "still too fluid, not confrontational or dialectical enough," he preferred to speak of fractals, which open a breach between whole numbers and may better reflect the ways in which Algeria and France "always already contributed a part of the other."[112]

Cross-border entanglements are, unsurprisingly, even more extensive elsewhere. The tension between neat cartographic representations of discrete boundaries and the messy realities on the ground has perhaps been one of the most crucial contributions made by border studies scholars. This literature has underscored the dry, abstract nature of a political geography detached from cultural, linguistic, and social entanglements. Working in a different discipline, political geographers have been paying increasing attention to the elemental, looking at the significance of materialities such as air and water for political space, and for borders in particular. Here as well, the tension between a well-ordered cartographic world and the recalcitrance of the material world has opened up productive spaces for scholarly exploration.[113] A third, largely separate, conversation within philosophy has emphasized the significance of entanglements and symbioses between life-forms—thereby blurring the borders of species and challenging the assumption of competition as the main driver of evolution. Bringing these three germane interests into dialogue with each other can be helpful in mining the meaningfulness of liminal spaces in ways that are both dynamic and productive.

Prompted in part by the global effects of climate change, we are witnessing an increasing acknowledgment of, and respect for, all kinds of planetary connections. No longer mistaking the forest for the tree, a number of influential books have successfully shifted focus from the individual to the amorphous entities across scales that sustain those individuals.[114] From biotic entities organized into clusters of genomes with unstable group boundaries (in the case of some influenza strains) to organisms such as certain fungi where the concept of species is largely irrelevant, there is increasingly a sense that coevolution, rather than a Darwinian competition between species, might be a more useful model.[115] A classic example is lichen. Neither green algae nor fungi, as was initially presumed, lichen is the coevolution of at least three distinct species.[116] A more extreme example is superorganisms, such as the *Armillaria* root rot that spreads across whole forests and may well be the largest organism in the world. As Tsing notes, "differentiating 'individuals' becomes difficult, as these individuals contain many genetic signatures, helping the fungus adapt to new environmental situations. Species are open-ended when even individuals are so molten, so long-lived, and so unwilling to draw lines of reproductive isolation."[117] It is not just that mutual dependencies are a common feature of most organisms, writes Shildrick, but that they operate at the most fundamental level of cellular life. Microchimerism, occurring at the cellular level and with limited impact on visible morphology, presents serious challenges to the fundamental doxa of Western medicine.

Unlike a hybrid, in which each cell consists of a combination of genes, in a chimera each individual cell will contain genes from only one of the originating organisms.[118]

As the notion of the individual as fixed and bounded is now questioned—Nigel Thrift suggests, evocatively, it "might be more accurate to liken humans to schools of fish briefly stabilized by particular spaces, temporary solidifications which pulse with particular affects"[119]—it is perhaps an opportune time to destabilize certain assumptions we continue to hold about the state. Taking cooperation rather than competition as a primary model, idealist and utopian as it may be, posits the border not as a violent device of separation but as a permeable membrane.

Of immediate relevance to the concerns of this book, particular reimaginings of individuality, autonomy, and bodily integrity can cast bodily boundaries and phantoms in a new light. Karen Barad's discussion of the brittlestar—an echinoderm closely related to starfish that will break off its exposed body part when in danger of being captured—demonstrates how individuality is not necessarily contingent on the illusion of the fixity of bodily boundaries.[120] While the ability to distinguish self from other is crucial to its own survival, these categories do not need to be fixed. On the contrary, Barad argues, their survival "depends on their capacity to discern the reality of their changing and relational nature."[121] Pondering further the ontological nature of separated limbs that continue to wiggle and emit light after breaking off, Barad asks, "When is a broken-off limb only a piece of the environment and when it is an offspring? At what point does the 'disconnected' limb belong to the 'environment' rather than the 'brittlestar'? Is contiguity of body parts required in the specification of a single organism? Can we trust visual delineations to define bodily boundaries? . . . Imagine the possibilities for lost limb memory trauma when it comes to brittlestars."[122]

Intriguing as it might be, the use of the brittlestar as an analogy for the state, just like the other monsters mobilized here, can only take us so far. The monsters featuring here as figures of othering are primarily intended as inspirational models, suggestive of ways of doing politics differently. They are potent reminders, as Barad notes, that differentiating is not necessarily about othering or separating but about making connections and commitments. There are nonetheless clear dangers inherent in utopian narratives of entanglement, as Eva Giraud reminds us. Acknowledging that the notion of entanglement grasps something crucial about the world, she nonetheless insists on the importance of paying attention to the "frictions, foreclosures, and exclusions that play a constitutive role in the composition of lived reality."[123]

This last point takes me to the second usage I want to make of monsters. If my summoning of monsters is tied, in part, to this scholarly focus on entanglements, arguing for the collaborative and complex nature of geopolitics to finally take center stage, the monster is also, importantly, a harbinger of a time of reckoning. A point I have made at several junctures in this book is that the iterative representational practice of the state as a logomap is powerful on account of its simplicity. It depicts the state in a binary opposition of inside/outside and, more importantly, portrays it as internally homogeneous. This very homogeneity is however deleterious, indeed lethal, to many citizens in a given state given that, as Jens Bartelson writes, the quest for sovereign agency tends to circumscribe the autonomy of other actors.[124] As the many examples provided in this book make clear, the somatic state that dominates the nationalist imagination tends to be cisgender, heteronormative (with a patriotic male rescuing a female in danger) and, in a Euro-American context, white. Publicly grievable lives are rarely gay, while the differentials in the value of Black and white lives is not a point that needs further belaboring.[125] It is in this context, I suggest, that the resentment elicited by the fragmented and disjointed body of Baarle's enclave complex should be read as an exclamation of cisgender heteronormative anger.

Ken Jennings writes that the "awesome stuff" on old maps continually gets pushed to the edge of the paper. Thus the Garden of Eden, originally located in Asia Minor, "kept drifting over the horizon until finally it landed outside the map altogether."[126] Yet the monsters that lurked on the edges of medieval maps have not disappeared. They have been relegated farther away in the form of aliens and extraterrestrials, migrating in the genres of science fiction, fantasy, and horror to the confines of the universe—"relocated to a galaxy far, far away," as Jeffrey Weinstock notes.[127] At the same time, he adds, monstrous races have often been mapped onto real-world ethnic groups, suggesting an entrenched perniciousness of stereotypes.[128] Embracing the monsters can bring back into the open the body located at the hinterland of national discourse—a body that is multiple, complex, and includes deviations of shape, color, and gender.[129] But while it may be time to give the monsters the center stage they rightfully deserve, we should nonetheless remain mindful of the danger of co-optation and selective cultural appropriation. In the same way that medieval cartography, in placing monsters at the very edge of the map, could tap into the marvelous while simultaneously condemning monstrous bodies closer to home as the outcome of transgressive sexual relations or the overly fertile maternal imagination, Black, queer, and female bodies have long cohabited as objects of both desire and fear.[130] Film, music, and other forms of media have served as vehicles to explore nonnormative bodies and experiences safely while simultaneously silencing them.

As rapper Azealia Banks explains in an interview, dominant white culture has a history of fetishizing Black culture through caricature and stereotypes.[131] From minstrel shows to hip-hop music, white performers have selectively adopted certain aspects of Black culture, incorporating them into the mainstream, thereby making them acceptable. As she perceptively adds, it's like "white people are running out of whiteness, so they're like lashing onto everything else." Her point is fully consonant here with Hortense Spillers's assessment that the history of Black people has been something that could be used as a note of inspiration while at the same time failing to generate new discourse.[132] Worse, as Sylvia Wynter has remarked, the record industry has turned Black music—the outcome of the sustained experience of African Americans' social marginality—into "the raw material of its profit production"—the bourgeoisie order thereby creating "the condition of possibility of its own subversion."[133] This is because, Imani Perry writes, "neoliberal capitalism loves to absorb and co-opt 'difference.' It feeds on novelty in the form of a particular transgression as long as said novelty submits to overarching market logics. New products sell. They don't disrupt the market."[134] Even within the Academy, Ruth Wilson Gilmore writes, the object status of African Americans is that of "decorative beasts": merely "living symbols whose occasional display is contingent on the Academy's need to illustrate certain ideological triumphs: capitalism, for example, or Christianity, equality, democracy, multiculturalism."[135]

Bearing in mind these pitfalls of cultural appropriation, it remains nonetheless crucial to ensure that a multiplicity of voices continues to shape cultural and geopolitical narratives. In recent decades, queer, feminist, and Black geographers have challenged patriarchal modes of writing that for too long have silenced and stereotyped minorities. If discursive violence has, at least in part, been deliberate and intentional, it has also been the unfortunate, often unreflected, cultural product of entrenched systemic hierarchies. Similarly, disability studies scholars have successfully pushed back against ideas of a body aligned on constricting notions of gender expression, sexuality, and corporeal integrity, shifting the very ground of nationalist narratives tied to the body.[136] These initially peripheral viewpoints have gained significance and recognition and can no longer be ignored.[137] As McKenzie Wark writes, "When monsters speak, their voices echo."[138]

Sumathi Ramaswamy has argued that the logomap's abstract nature is devoid of content and is therefore a poor support of national sentiment.[139]

But perhaps its potency comes from its very simplicity. Since it is not over-laid with explicit meaning, it is not semantically overdetermined and can be vehicular of a wider range of affect. In fact, the logomap coexists with other forms of space mapping, notably maps as tools of navigation. While the two share little overlap in either usage or iconicity, they are nonetheless placed in a relation of complementarity—a complementarity recently accentuated and made explicit through technologies such as Google Maps, which, depending on the level of magnification selected, toggles from logomap to detailed map, and to street view. Detailed bird's-eye and ego-centered maps are not (yet) available in real time; however, their regular updates (and the ability to go back in time and access earlier versions) bring them a palimpsest-like quality that runs counter to the fixity of the logomaps to which they are attached. In turn, this suggests the logomap itself is not immune to a certain temporal plasticity.

I turn more explicitly to these questions of plasticity in the short coda that follows. I explore in particular how military technologies, and specifically their capacity to map in real time a three-dimensional space, are transforming the relation we have to space and, by extension, to territorial sovereignty. Taking here again the body as dominant metaphor—though this time an entomological-technological amalgam—these new technologies are increasingly detached from the human experience. Whereas maps played an instrumental role in colonizing new territories by portraying, ahead of actual exploration, entire continents (see chapter 1), the promissory role of cartography has now lost much of its force. With a management of sovereignty increasingly carried out through nonhuman assemblages, in spaces and at speeds that are more and more beyond human comprehension and mental modeling, we find ourselves at a critical juncture. Whereas traditional logographic representations of the state remain powerful as affective vehicles for demagogic purposes, actual border work is managed by algorithmic computations increasingly reliant on artificial intelligence.[140]

Coda

BEYOND THE MAP?

We all share the sense that we live in a transformative moment of territoriality. The ground is shifting under our feet.

—Charles Maier, *Once within Borders*

After numerous complaints and threats of legal action concerning its depictions of national borders—notably by India with respect to the province of Kashmir (see chapter 4)—Google has come up with a creative way to deal with contention and is offering localized versions of its maps to its different users. An Indian user will now see Kashmir as fully part of India whereas someone in Pakistan will see it as a disputed territory (figure C.1). Similarly, the Sea of Japan will display as the East Sea for South Korean users, Western Sahara will vanish from view for Moroccan users, and, quite contentiously in view of the events that have unfolded since, Google Maps has shown the Crimean Peninsula since 2014 with a dotted-line border for Ukrainians and others, but as a full-line border when viewed in Russia.[1]

Beyond the political and ethical issues at stake in producing parallel cartographic versions, this multiplicity of views weakens the logomap insofar as its potency has relied on its fixity and simple inner/outer dichotomy. No longer unquestionably there, detached from its geographic context, the logomap instead becomes mutable, contextual, highly personal. These practices speak to a newfound plasticity, enabled by a democratization of technology, that allows anyone to easily create their own maps. Previously suppressed and rendered invisible, stateless entities, spectral geographies, phantom territories, breakaway provinces, and de facto states can emerge as logomaps in their own right, challenging dominant power structures. Countercartographies can also propose alternative or supplemental territorial models by mapping cultural and religious territories, or by subverting orientation, as discussed in chapter 1 with the south-up Hobo-Dyer map (figure 1.8).

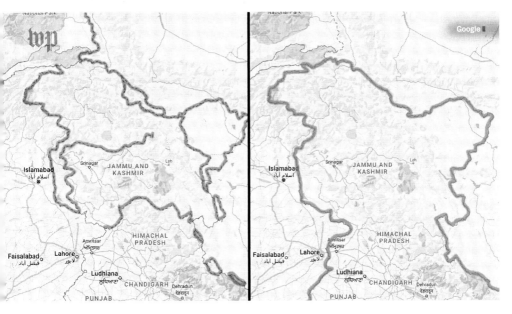

C.1. Pakistan versus India Google Maps views. Screen grab from video by Greg Bensinger / *Washington Post*.

In addition to an ever more detailed view from above, immersive cartography such as Google Street View offers to a user an ego-centered and embodied perspective, refinable through scale, zooming levels, and orientation. The contrast between the map ("a plane projection totalizing observations") and the itinerary ("a discursive series of operations") drawn by Michel de Certeau is now a simple matter of toggling between viewing modes.[2] Yet these are starkly distinctive ways of orientation. The God's-eye view of space, flattened and homogeneously distributed, is an acquired map-reading technique on which the logomap is ultimately reliant. By contrast, ego-centered wayfinding utilizes landmarks that, like magnetic poles, vectorize the space of orientation.[3] In that sense, Google Maps GPS systems resemble premodern navigation methods where space was conceptualized as lines of passage, skeins, and pathways across land and sea—confirming once again the argument made by Laura Benton, Jordan Branch, and others that the Westphalian treaty marked less of a fault line than a gradual (and incomplete) shift in territorial management and the imaginary of space.[4]

Digital plasticity also offers numerous opportunities to register the passing of time in maps. And while we should remain attentive to the ways in which geographic information system visualizations "risk imposing a linear ordering of events onto time periods or places in which the idea of Newtonian time . . . was not yet hegemonic," digital mapping offers undeniable advantages over the representational fixity of maps.[5] Older maps, frozen in time, are being replaced by digital ones that enable "dynamic, interactive visualisations where map readers can track changes or make changes over time."[6] Versions of maps can also be stored and retrieved rather than supersede one another, enabling a user to go back in time. This can be especially useful to monitor changes to the environment caused by climate change. I discussed in chapter 4 the concept of a movable border, tracking the shrinking of Alpine glaciers and their consequent shifting of the Austrian-Italian border.[7] The Greenland coastline has similarly witnessed rapid shifts, and it occasionally happens that GPS navigation devices will alert users of imminent collision with nonexistent obstacles. The retreat rate of the ice shelf has been so rapid that the coordinates of the former extent of glaciers are out of date: what the system is tracking is the digital phantom left behind by the ice.[8]

This materiality of terrain poses significant challenges to traditional cartographic practices that lack dynamism, and which are therefore poorly suited to keep track of shifts in the environment. Cartography, as Matthew Edney has argued, is an idealized practice—construing maps in "certain confined and quite unrealistic ways," smothering the "actual messiness of mapping with a thick, fluffy, warm, and comforting blanket of cartographic uniformity and transcultural universality."[9] Rivers are conventionally represented in blue, regardless of their actual color or levels of pollution, while the all-seeing bird's-eye satellite view is in fact a composite image, shorn of all forms of weather.[10] And with increasing forays into spaces beyond the horizontal and the earthbound, mapping techniques (both paper and digital), insofar as they privilege and overemphasize the ground, are becoming progressively inadequate to delineate novel forms of territorial sovereignty. Aerial, maritime, orbital, polar, and subterranean environments are the new sites of geopolitical adventurism and resource grabs, but they remain challenging to represent cartographically given their spatial configurations and recalcitrant materiality.[11] Voluminous, fragmented, and scattered, they are also difficult to visualize mentally in their totality. Firmly "beyond the visceral worlds of everyday experience and visibility," these sites increasingly depend upon machine intelligence and algorithmic computations.[12]

Traditional cartography is also woefully inadequate to represent complex planetary processes such as climate change and phenomena that philosopher of science Tim Morton terms *hyperobjects*.[13] If climate modeling projections have undeniably made remarkable progress thanks to machine learning, the cartographic imaginary remains essentially unchanged. The 1884 satirical no-vella *Flatland: A Romance of Many Dimensions* by Edwin A. Abbott, in which inhabitants are unable to perceive the existence of three-dimensional shapes, makes for a good allegory. Originally written as a critique of Victorian society and its lack of vision for a more socially complex world, notably gender equal-ity, it speaks today to the threats humanity is facing. As Morton spells out in his book, "If an apple were to invade a two-dimensional world, first the stick people would see some dots as the bottom of the apple touched their universe, then a rapid succession of shapes that would appear like an expanding and contracting circular blob, diminishing to a tiny circle, possibly a point, and disappearing."[14] Such partial views epitomize the prevailing view of the state as flat, bound, and autonomous. They also point to the enduring metaphoric role of maps in conceptualizing more-than-human phenomena. Recalling the image of the chromosome island opening chapter 1 (figure 1.1), the framing of climate change as "uncharted territory" in fact remains common to imagine the future.[15]

Territorial sovereignty is complicated further by forms of border manage-ment increasingly remote and automated. A typical traveler to the United States from Europe, for instance, will go through U.S. passport control at the European airport before boarding. As of this writing, operating at fifteen lo-cations worldwide, US Customs and Border Protection preclearance allows travelers to bypass inspections upon arrival. Similar (though not quite as ex-tensive) arrangements exist in European countries where biometric passports also facilitate entry and expedite passport control. Globally, biometric data and biographical material are becoming crucial in the control of human movement. As Matthew Longo argues, there has been a "strategic shift *away from a focus on nation-states and sub-state actors and toward the individual.*"[16] This may foretell, he continues, a dissolution of the individual into data points, a move from an enumerated to a pixelated subject, whereby the "individual is no lon-ger a meaningful category, except as the aggregation of those data-points."[17]

While not entirely deterritorialized, these new forms of bordering man-agement practices—often invisible and ephemeral—challenge assumptions of a neat correspondence between border and territory.[18] As I flesh out below, this shift is having dramatic repercussions for the body-state equation dis-cussed in this book. Corporeal metaphors had provided solidity and tangibil-ity to an abstract, disembodied, and historically contingent logomap—even if this body was itself always and already fragmented (see chapter 3).[19] The ongoing dissolution of the national body through algorithmic computations, accelerated through automated forms of monitoring and surveillance found beyond the human perceptual realm, are making the logomap feel quaint, perhaps even irrelevant to contemporary concerns. Already in the early 1990s John Agnew drew attention to the tacit assumptions bundled in the modern geopolitical imaginary of the nation-state—a "container" imagined to hold discrete societies within them and representing a fixed unit of sovereign space. This "territorial trap," he argued, rendered invisible the numerous economic, cultural, and political dynamics that had no place in this imaginary.[20] Given that these dynamics have increased even further in both spatial complexity and velocity, has the logomap become irrelevant as an object of study? Are we, in other words, . . .

. . . BEYOND THE MAP?

In a recent study, Agnew seeks to recapture the term *geopolitics*, demonstrating that this geography of power continues to structure and govern the political economy both nationally and globally.[21] His timing is especially prescient given Russia's war on Ukraine, formulated and waged along an "old geopolitics" model that many political analysts had pronounced dead. Indeed, the war hitherto fought against the West by Russia, through fake news and cyberattacks, had suggested the neoliberal landscape had given way to new tactics and strategies. But while, as Agnew contends, we need to understand the messy and turbulent entanglements of finance, business, energy, and electoral politics, the old logics of spatial expansionism and territorial domination remain crucial. In fact, these have proven key to win at least some of Russia's popular opinion (to the extent that we can tell), in spite of economic sanctions and global condemnation.

Along the same lines, the clamorous calls for more border walls—a significant factor in the election of a new crop of populist leaders both in the United States and elsewhere in the world—complicate the claims of numerous scholars that borders are now everywhere (and nowhere).[22] Of course, these statements refer to a delocalization of bordering processes (or "border work," as Madeleine Reeves has phrased it) rather than to the physical location of borders, which is in fact continually reinforced and reinscribed with border walls and deforestation zones.[23] The notion of a boundary as a line has been extensively challenged by border studies scholars who have demonstrated borders to be permeable to varying degrees.[24] We now have, Madeleine Reeves argues, an inverse correlation between sovereignty and bordering practices, and proliferating forms of bordering and control can occur far from the geographical edges of the state, as I discussed in chapter 5 with the case of "not yet Canada" and Australia's outsourcing of asylum processing on the island of Nauru.[25] The situation is further complicated by the proliferation of different legal spaces, ranging from free ports to tax havens and special economic zones, from 176 globally in 1986 to 5,400 by 2018.[26]

We must nonetheless be careful of casual statements about the deterritorialization of borders given that more than fifty thousand migrants have died worldwide since 2014 trying to cross borders.[27] The invisibility of borders also betrays a very privileged view of border crossing, whose unequal practices are especially stark at the Mexico-US border: endless lines to cross into the United States, versus a simple reminder to take your US passport or green card with you before you step into Mexico. Indeed, Agnew reminds us, territorial sovereignty is ultimately contingent rather than absolute, with some actors always more sovereign than others.[28] Borders have in fact been typically more important to smaller and weaker states, which see them as offering a form of protection from the outside. Larger and more powerful states, by contrast, often view them as impediments. Testament to this asymmetry, in the postwar period small states were the main proponents of human rights, whereas the larger states all vetoed any international mechanisms of enforcement against their sovereignty.[29]

Control is also exerted by nonstate actors, as in the case of the International Monetary Fund and the World Bank, over supposedly sovereign states, like many in sub-Saharan Africa.[30] This specific tension, between the fixity of borders, on the one hand, and the fluid nature of a political power circulating topologically and obeying a different spatial logic, on the other, speaks to the dual nature of political borders. This duality is frequently misinterpreted rather as the supersession of one logic by another than as their essentially complementary nature. The monochrome simplicity of the logomap certainly does not reflect the complex entanglements of state and nonstate actors in the contemporary world, but this is in fact nothing new.[31] As I have illuminated through the concepts of phantoms, prosthetics, and territorial monsters, the jigsaw-like visuals of political geography conceal and suppress dynamics that exist beyond the cartographic representations of political geography. These dynamics may be symptomatic of the contemporary neoliberal system, but they have been around for a while. Agnew suggests that even during the golden age of geopolitics, in the first half of the twentieth century, the term was more a "rhetorical reference point" than an accurate guide to the actual workings of state powers.[32] Similarly, royal alliances, marriages, and kinship ties have long been woven across European state borders—creating sovereign arrangements supplementary to (and frequently running roughshod over) the border lines of political maps and nation-bound affect. In other words, our jigsaw-like world geography is only, at most, a partial representation of political realities.

And yet, the central argument I make in this book is that the logomap deserves more sustained scholarly attention. It may well be a fiction, but it is a potent one, with very real consequences. It is, in this sense, reminiscent of race—scientifically unsound as a concept but a social fact nonetheless, and a lethal one at that. And just like statements about being colorblind index a position of privilege unavailable to Black and brown subjects, "border-blindness" is similarly skewed in favor of citizens of countries where borders are not at stake. For newly emerging countries (such as the independent states formerly part of Yugoslavia or the Soviet Union) and countries engaged in territorial disputes with others (India and Pakistan, for example), graphic representations in the form of logomaps are crucial, both to their respective citizens and to global publics.[33] For all intents and purposes, as I argue in chapter 1, the contour of the state *is* the state. It is the familiar face of the nation (see discussion on pareidolia in chapter 2) familiar to its citizens, imbued with affect, and suffused with corporeal metaphors.

The logomap also reifies the state in a world geography imagined as a jigsaw-like mosaic—where every state occupies a specific portion of the earth's surface and where there are no blank spaces nor overlaps. Unambiguous borders are essential for both recognition and commensurability, as discussed earlier in the context of Thailand. As a result, entities with an amorphous territorial footprint—such as empires, cultural, religious, and linguistic communities, or breakaway and unrecognized states—constitute at best spectral overlays that lack both visibility and effective resonance. A further example is the Euro-region, composed of small chunks of territory from three or four different countries, created and nurtured by proponents of European integration with the aim of erasing Europe's long-standing national boundaries. But despite considerable efforts by the European Union, Catherine Dunlop concludes, only a small group of Europeans is aware of the presence of these Euro-regions, which remain "strange and unfamiliar to most people," lacking the brand recognition of national logomaps.[34]

The political events that have accompanied me in the writing of this book, and that are likely to accompany future readers (I am thinking specifically about Russia's war on Ukraine, Israel's war on Gaza, and the vast proliferation of border walls), betray the continued affective force of the logomap and the bounded state that it indexes. Even where borders feel unimportant—or when there is an explicit political will to efface them, such as within the European Union—the logomap imaginary is never very deep below the surface.[35] This was shown very clearly with early responses to the COVID-19 pandemic. As northern Italy was suddenly transforming into the principal site of infection in Europe—prompting several countries, including the United States, to issue advisory restrictions for the whole of Italy—countries bordering Italy were largely absent from news headlines. In an echo of familiar weather map visuals where atmospheric conditions appear to be neatly bounded by state outlines, Italy was presented suspended in the air—virally tied to distant Wuhan and Iran yet "wholly detached from its geographic context."[36]

The force of these visuals was evident as it translated into a slow response from Italy's neighbors. France, whose borders with Italy lie only a couple of hundred miles from Lombardy, went into lockdown on March 17, that is, eight days after Italy. Switzerland, only thirty miles from the European epicenter of the outbreak, did not close its schools or stores until March 16, a full week after Italy's lockdown. This jigsaw-puzzle spatial imaginary unsurprisingly led to a domino effect whereby European countries started implementing measures nationally, but only as their own situation deteriorated. The very same scenario unfolded in the United States.[37] Starting with California and Washington, the states of Connecticut, Delaware, Illinois, Louisiana, New York, and New Jersey later followed suit. But the majority of states that were unimpacted did not impose meaningful (often not even any) restrictions—as if their borders were somehow able to keep them entirely separate, and thus safe.

These political decisions speak to the interpretive framework of the logomap, itself the product of a view of the state as a container. These frequently unconscious frameworks that organize our knowledge of the world—frameworks that Martin Lewis and Kären Wigen have termed metageographies—play an outsize role in "formulating global constructs for the public imagination." They inform diplomats, politicians, and military strategists, as well as academics and journalists, and shape "studies of history, sociology, anthropology, economics, political science, and natural history."[38] These metageographies are dominant to such an extent that it has proven very difficult to think outside of the realm of the nation-state, outside of the "territorial trap."[39] The state, Stephanie Fishel summarizes pithily, continues to hold our collective political imagination.[40]

BIFURCATIONS

Critical cartographers and historians have convincingly argued that the map preceded the territory. They have demonstrated that imperial maps in particular played a key role in colonizing new territories by portraying, ahead of actual exploration, entire continents as blank spaces or, alternatively, as places inhabited by monsters or fantastical creatures.[41] We are now witnessing a critical reversal of this chronology. Except for a few corners of the globe still inaccessible to humans unaided by technology, the territory has now largely caught up with the map, and it is the map, having lost its earlier promissory role, that is struggling to keep up with the territory.[42] Cartography's newest challenge is to devise new ways to represent the spaces that are being explored (and mined) beyond the horizontal, the enclosed, and the surface.

In a thought-provoking essay, Wayne Chambliss tracks this dialogic evolution of mapping and exploration in the context of subterranean geographies. State actors, he writes, have been relying on new technologies—such as magnetometers and other metal detectors, electromagnetic induction, electrical resistivity, gravity measurement technology, and seismic and acoustic sensors—to map the subsurface. Of all these techniques, gravity measurement technology shows the most promise. Because the Earth's composition is not homogeneous, the force of gravity varies at every point of the Earth's surface by a tiny amount. The US military, he explains, is currently mapping the subterranean to create a baseline. Subsequent changes in the gravitational fields, such as the creation of underground bunkers or a military facility, will alter the structure's gravitational signature, making the structure visible. While it is feasible in theory to spoof these mapping technologies (by adding heavy material to counterbalance the missing soil), it will nonetheless prove increasingly difficult to do so as the technology becomes more sophisticated.[43]

His account illustrates the meretricious nature of territorial sovereignty and the ultimate futility of attempting to pursue a perfect alignment between the map and the territory. In this sense, Japan's endeavors, discussed in chapter 5, to draw out a terraqueous outline feel ineffectual given the increasing military and economic incursions into three-dimensional space and beyond.[44] The treatment of maritime territory through a terrestrial framework—by creating a bloated logomap encompassing territorial waters—also fails to take into account the different materiality of ocean space, which challenges traditional forms of containment and is fundamentally at odds with the placement of fixed boundaries.[45]

New technologies are creating an ever wider breach between the logomap as established vector of national sentiments, on the one hand, and future forms of territorial management and state contours, on the other. New representations may thus need to be devised to reflect the emergent pluriterritorial, polycentric, and multiscalar geographies of globalization as well as the three-dimensional territorial incursions beyond the terrestrial.[46] Military objectives have increasingly been to find new ways to address state security beyond human geographies and through technologies that would extend—indeed supersede—human capabilities. In many ways these are not recent developments, as Packer and Reeves show.[47] As early as the 1890s, new forms of technical media, such as photography for instance, were already being mobilized to fine-tune the capacities of artillery and create superior weapons. In its ever-evolving search for technological superiority, the US military is adopting modes of information, communication, and mobility that gradually require less and less human input. In fact, seen as "inherently undependable" and with "highly unreliable data collection, storage, and processing capacities," humans essentially introduce noise and errors into a given system.[48] As a result, foreshadowing what Packer and Reeves term "humanectomy," the US military is experimenting with "taking humans out of as many links in the chain of command as possible."[49] There is now a genuine risk that humans may eventually be entirely taken out of geopolitical assemblages. With its limited vision, juvenile data-processing capacities, and highly vulnerable communications processes, the human component—or "wetware" in the phrasing of Friedrich Kittler—is the ultimate source of the fog of war.[50] As sophisticated systems for processing battlefield data are being developed, the human has suddenly emerged as an epistemological hindrance.[51]

At the same time, and this is a point that bears repeating, this evolution is taking place in parallel to a geopolitical imaginary that remains very much aligned on traditional forms of territorial control. While military emphasis on "full spectrum dominance"—an ambition for the total occupation and control of land, sea, outer space, and cyberspace[52]—may suggest as much, this breach is not a neat disjunction between military and civilian imaginaries. The challenge to imagine territorial sovereignty in other ways is one that is shared across publics. Thus the 1991 statement by Russian military theorist Vladimir Slipchenko that the very spatial categories of war were changing, that area-based military concepts such as front, rear, and flank would be irrelevant in the future, and that "there will be no need to occupy enemy territory" appears premature in the current context of the Russian war on Ukraine.[53] While interstate conflicts, and indeed much of neoliberal economies, operate on different spatial logics, military decisions continue to be made on the basis of classical geopolitical imaginaries and logomap-bound affect. And so we find ourselves at a critical juncture, with an ever-widening breach between the fixity and simplicity of the logomap, on the one hand, and a labile, voluminous, multi-material, all-encompassing, and increasingly unmappable sovereign territory, on the other.

This gap is widening to the point of having created two irreconcilable spatial imaginaries. This divergence is significant in that it signals a rupture between the discrete logomap and the body of the citizen—a powerful analogy that has played a defining role in modeling and structuring national affect. I have explored in this book the common bodily metaphors and analogies that have helped naturalize state outlines and weave affective ties between the citizen and her logomap. New organizational models based on biological architectures are privileging, however, very different bodies, such as swarms, that give precedence to autonomy, emergence, and distributed functioning. Comparing favorably with human cognitive intelligence, swarms require no planning, central representation, or traditional modeling.[54] As organizations continuously on the verge of materialization and dissolution, swarms are both radically heterogeneous and consistent.[55] Military strategists have now begun to imagine the emergence of a "swarmanoid"—a "heterogeneous assemblage of bots that each perform unique epistemological and kinetic functions."[56] As technology develops further, components of such assemblages are likely to involve scales at the very limit of human perception and detectability. Nanotechnology in particular promises to enter the domain of the microbial—worlds and microcosms "inaccessible to prosthetic-free human experience, zones hard to apprehend as connected to our own forms of life."[57]

But while this makes them a superior model to face challenges to territorial sovereignty beyond the horizontal, they constitute a poor vector of patriotic affect. Not only are swarms difficult to represent spatially, but they also feel very alien in their lack of autonomous individuality. Lacking spatial representations evoking containment, contiguity, and physical integrity, the model of the swarm fails to elicit the same kind of recognition, and the corporeal metaphors it elicits are no longer human but avian, possibly entomological.

In its fractured and dispersive nature, the swarm nonetheless echoes a psychoanalytical view of the body as a dismembered body—a *corps morcelé*, "always and already fragmented, in bits and pieces," as discussed in chapter 3.[58] The model of the swarm also defies the fiction of the body as real, organic, natural, and continuous. The corporeal discourse undergirding nationalism and imaginaries of the state relies on the assumption that the body is unitary and discrete. Yet, as I argue in chapter 5, the body is increasingly being recognized as the product of entanglements across life-forms. As such, fragmented and dispersive models—of a corporeality otherwise—may help reconfigure understandings and metaphors of the state in line with its actual spatiality and modes of operation.

A POSTGEOGRAPHIC IMAGINARY?

In *After the Map*, William Rankin argues that electronic navigation systems are increasingly displacing previous mapping practices and that, as a result, the tight relationship between geographic legibility and political authority has been lost. Because electronic coordinates are explicitly designed to exceed the boundaries of individual states, he writes, there is no longer a requirement of a "long-term geographic commitment or sustained control over a contiguous expanse of land."[59] While, as I argue above, we are certainly witnessing a transformation in the practice of sovereignty, his contention that it has become "possible to imagine territory as something separate from sovereignty" is, in my view, supported neither by the global rise in populist ethnonationalism, nor by the enduring forms of traditional warfare to acquire territory.

Where we may be seeing an incipient change, however, is in the use of nonfigurative symbols, out of a recognition that logomaps are fundamentally incomplete (in leaving out islands, territories, and territorial fragments) and misleading (in their use of full colors). Here the case of the United Kingdom might serve as a useful example. In addition to the difficulty of representing the state as a logomap given that it involves various concatenated legal entities both within the state and adjacent to it—such as Crown Dependencies (the Isle of Man, Guernsey, and Jersey), Overseas Territories, and Commonwealth Realms—the UK's own territorial arrangement of four components (England, Wales, Scotland, and Northern Ireland) across two main islands adds further complexity. Perhaps out of a reluctance to split Ireland, the UK rarely uses its logomap, opting instead for a flag.

Not only does this visual rupture between territory and sovereignty not appear to have lessened national attachment, but the very nonterritorial representation is in fact more inclusive since it is no longer making claims to geographical accuracy. We can see similar incipient developments elsewhere, notably with the French hexagon, represented in more stylized ways in the colors of the flag. Unlike a logomap aligned on an ideal of territorial container, these abstract logos offer membership to a more geographically malleable entity, aligned on civic and participatory rather than ethnic forms of belonging. There are nonetheless dangers inherent to such visual practices in that they can obscure further the control that states such as Britain or France continue to exert on countries only nominally postcolonial, thereby rendering completely invisible the numerous territorial specks and "confetti" that bestow a truly global footprint on these former colonial powers.[60]

These shifts are, however, unlikely to displace entrenched visualizations of the state as a logomap. As I argued above, alternative visuals (in the form of a flag or stylized logomap) are symptomatic of privilege insofar as they are largely available to states that do not need reiterative emphasis of their outline. By contrast, in countries where borders are unstable or felt to be under threat (such as India and Pakistan, or Israel and Palestine), logomaps remain ubiquitous, and incorrect mapping will often result in hefty fines.

Forecasts of a weakening or supersession of the logomap by alternatives are thus premature and unconvincing. What we can expect, however, is a further concatenation of spatial logics. What if, Quinn Slobodian asks, "the end of history was not the checkerboard of two-hundred-plus nation-states existing under conditions of liberal democracy, but tens of thousands of jurisdictions of various political systems in constant competition?"[61] Benjamin Bratton has drawn attention to the ways in which the internet is emerging as "a living, quasi-autonomous . . . transterritorial civil society that produces, defends, and demands rights on its own" beyond the body of the state. This does not portend, he insists, the demise of the state, but does imply its ongoing redefinition "in relation to network geographies that it can neither contain nor be contained by."[62] Bratton envisions, for instance, the possible scenario of a quasi-state actor, religious polity, or Cloud platform offering more secure levels of digital identity than a state—leading to the coexistence of overlapping realms of sovereignty (national, political, economic, fiscal, etc.) in ways that resemble the pre-Westphalian order.[63] Having seen premodern frontiers turn into inflexible borders, we are now witnessing the reemergence of new kinds of frontiers. Perhaps we have come full circle after all.

Notes

INTRODUCTION

Epigraphs: Donald J. Trump, political campaign ad, January 2016, archived January 27, 2016, at Archive.org, https://archive.org/details/PolAd_DonaldTrump _5iqfp; Longo, *The Politics of Borders*, xii.

1. Iyengar, "India Bans al-Jazeera."
2. In this book I occasionally use shortcuts for nation-states: *India, Russia, China*, and so on. This stylistic shorthand should not distract the reader from the multivocal and inherently messy nature of the state.
3. According to the draft bill, "No person shall depict, disseminate, publish or distribute any wrong or false topographic information of India including international boundaries through internet platforms or online services or in any electronic or physical form. Whoever acquired any geospatial information of India in contravention of the law shall be punished with a fine ranging from RS 1 crore to RS 100 crore and/or imprisonment for a period up to seven years" (*Indian Express*, "Up to RS 100 cr Fine, 7 YRS in Jail").
4. Callahan, *China*, 122.
5. Hayton, *The South China Sea*, 250. The U-shaped line is in fact ambiguous in that the PRC has neither clearly defined the exact location coordinates of the line nor what it means legally and politically. It has its origin, not in the graticular network of latitudes and longitudes on which modern maps are based, but in the more normative and aesthetic map-making practice of early modern China (Callahan, *Sensible Politics*, 151).
6. Perec, *Espèces d'espaces*, 147, my translation.
7. Agnew, "The Territorial Trap."
8. Similarly, the exchange of territory between states is "almost always portrayed as a net loss to state power even when the objective benefits of resolving territorial disputes include a mutual improvement in bilateral relations and greater regional peace and stability" (Abraham, *How India Became Territorial*, 143–45).

9. Bukh, *These Islands Are Ours*, 96.
10. Bukh, *These Islands Are Ours*, 1.
11. Bukh, *These Islands Are Ours*, 158.
12. Bukh, *These Islands Are Ours*, 157–58.
13. Bukh, *These Islands Are Ours*, 157.
14. Bukh, *These Islands Are Ours*, 3.
15. Brown, *Walled States*.
16. Agnew, *Hidden Geopolitics*, 84.
17. Hansen and Stepputat, introduction to *States of Imagination*, 10, 2.
18. Jones, *Violent Borders*, 67.
19. Agnew, *Hidden Geopolitics*.
20. On electronic terraforming, see Engelhardt, "On Space and Territory in Cyberwar."
21. Neocleous, *Imagining the State*, 126.
22. Brown, *Statelessness*, 3.
23. Koch, "Introduction: Spatializing Authoritarianism," 5.
24. Murphy, "The Sovereign State System," 107.
25. Lewis and Wigen, *The Myth of Continents*, ix, 2.
26. Lewis and Wigen, *The Myth of Continents*, xiii, 9.
27. Moisio et al., "Changing Geographies of the State," 3–4.
28. Mongia, *Indian Migration and Empire*, 5. Mark Neocleous reports that the tiny proportion of conflicts between two sovereign territorial states receives the majority of media and academic attention (*Imagining the State*, 106).
29. Writing in 2007, Liam O'Dowd noted that only 3 percent of the world's population were currently living outside the state where they were born (cited in Paasi, "A Border Theory," 21). These numbers will almost certainly continue to swell under the pressure of climate change and economic inequalities, placing undue stress on asylum seekers and refugees in particular.
30. Billé and Humphrey, *On the Edge*.
31. Alesina and Spolaore, *The Size of Nations*, 199–200.
32. Billé, "Doughnut"; Ryzhova, "Freedoms, the State and Security."
33. Pew Research Center for the People and the Press, cited in Díaz-Barriga and Dorsey, *Fencing in Democracy*, 17.
34. Mitchell, "The Limits of the State," 94. Rebecca Bryant has discussed how this transcendental entity is then materialized and reproduced synecdochally. In her discussion of national airlines, she argued that the abstract notion of the stateless becomes embodied: airplanes turn into "containers that become small pieces of the homeland outside the homeland itself" (Bryant, "Sovereignty in the Skies," 23).
35. For some dramatic contrasts, see Egoshin, "The Countries' Borders." The starkest difference is perhaps at night, between North and South Korea, while another fascinating contrast is between the former East and West halves of Berlin, whose electrical systems have not changed—the latter using mercury vapor or metal halide lights, and the former yellow sodium lights.
36. Edney, *Cartography*, 103.
37. Edney, *Cartography*, 1, 66.

38. Agnew, "No Borders, No Nations," 398. On Japanese and Chinese maps, see, respectively, Wigen, *A Malleable Map*; and Akin, *East Asian Cartographic Print Culture*.

39. Edney, *Cartography*, 5.

40. See for instance Sahlins (*Boundaries*) on the formation of French and Spanish national identities in the Pyrenees, and Dunlop (*Cartophilia*) on the search for identity in Alsace. Dunlop (*Cartophilia*, 129) notes that "maps trained people to see their national identity in their local surroundings: their village streets, bell towers, fields, and classrooms" and that it became crucial for nationalists to develop techniques of visual training and pedagogy that would tie these images of local and regional space to a universal image of the nation.

41. Anderson, *Imagined Communities*, 175.

42. Anderson, *Imagined Communities*, 185.

43. France, discussed at several junctures in the book, is a good example of the latter.

44. Reeves, "Signs of Sovereignty," 225.

45. Reeves, "Signs of Sovereignty," 225. In 1988 Soviet geographers admitted publicly that most of the maps that had been sold to the public since the 1930s had been willfully falsified and deformed (Vadrot, cited in Jacob, *The Sovereign Map*, 274).

46. Graham, *Vertical*, 45.

47. See Brook, *Mr. Selden's Map of China*, 5.

48. 18 U.S. Code § 700 stipulates that a person who knowingly mutilates, defaces, physically defiles, burns, maintains on the floor or ground, or tramples upon any flag of the United States shall be fined under this title or imprisoned for not more than one year, or both. As per the code, the term "flag of the United States" means any flag of the United States, or any part thereof, made of any substance, of any size, in a form that is commonly displayed.

49. Léopold Lambert (*États d'urgence*, 82–83) recalls the case of Yasmina Benson, who was sentenced to ten months in jail for holding up the Algerian flag in Paris during the Algerian War. On alternative logomaps, see Yıldırım ("Space, Loss and Resistance"), discussed in chapter 3, with the example of the Kurdish logomap, whose use is illegal in Turkey.

50. Brook, *Mr. Selden's Map of China*, 5.

51. Brook, *Mr. Selden's Map of China*, 5.

52. Shanghaiist, "Gap Apologizes for T-Shirt Design," emphasis added.

53. Korzybski, "A Non-Aristotelian System."

54. A compendium of somatic metaphors of the state and their cultural underpinnings and relevance can be found in the survey by Andreas Musolff, *National Conceptualisations of the Body Politic*. Many of these metaphors, in particular the rape metaphor, are expressed in heavily gendered language, as I discuss in the course of the book.

55. TallBear, *Native American DNA*.

56. Neocleous, *The Politics of Immunity*, 299.

57. Winichakul, *Siam Mapped*. This is discussed in detail in chapter 2.

58. Ramaswamy, "Maps and Mother Goddesses in Modern India."

59. Lakoff, *Women, Fire, and Dangerous Things*.

60. Gibbs, *The Poetics of Mind*, 126.

61. Gibbs, *The Poetics of Mind*, 5, 17.

62. Jennifer Terry writes that an invading and occupying force, "staged metaphorically as an expert medical team whose main task is to rid the occupied society of a diseased insurgency," can transform the alleged patient "into a compliant subject of the new occupying regime" (*Attachments to War*, 28).

63. Psychologist Robert Epstein argues that the metaphor of the brain as computer, for instance, is a deeply flawed one. But it is "sticky" and as such "encumbers our thinking with language and ideas" we have trouble thinking beyond. He recounts challenging researchers at one of the world's most prestigious research institutes to account for intelligent human behavior without reference to any aspect of the concept of information processing. Although they saw the problem with the metaphor, they were unable to come up with a working alternative (Epstein, "The Empty Brain"). But even sticky metaphors are not static. Over the past two thousand years, writes George Zarkadakis, people have used six core metaphors to try to explain human intelligence (*In Our Own Image*).

64. Kurgan, *Close Up at a Distance*, 14.

65. Porteous, *Landscapes of the Mind*, 70.

66. Stewart, *On Longing*, 101–2.

67. Douglas, *Purity and Danger*.

68. Winichakul, *Siam Mapped*.

69. See, in particular, the argument made by Sumathi Ramaswamy discussed in chapter 1.

70. In the context of India, Sumathi Ramaswamy writes that the logomap was too abstract and unhomely and that it was accompanied at first with what she calls "barefoot cartography" ("Maps and Mother Goddesses in Modern India"). Similarly, maps produced in France and Germany lacked the "local perspective necessary to connect with the emotions or life experiences of ordinary Alsatians and Lorrainers" and gave rise to "vernacular" maps (Dunlop, *Cartophilia*, 14).

71. See Broers, *Armenia and Azerbaijan*.

72. I have been careful in this book to use *state* and *nation* appropriately, but for stylistic purposes I have sometimes taken liberties. This may be seen as a metacommentary on the ways in which the two are frequently confused and amalgamated in common speech.

73. Brown, *Walled States*, 118–19, paraphrased in Olson, *Imagined Sovereignties*, 12.

74. Olson, *Imagined Sovereignties*, 26–27.

75. Bukh, *These Islands Are Ours*, 5–14.

76. Anthony Smith, cited in Paasi, *Territories, Boundaries and Consciousness*, 48.

77. Lewis and Wigen, *The Myth of Continents*, 1997.

78. See for instance Callahan, *China*, 116; and Chung, *Domestic Politics*, 6–9.

79. Toal, *Near Abroad*, 251.

80. Both Poland and Hungary are regional examples where popular engagement with lost territories is particularly strong. Hungary's political discourse has been molded as a result of the Treaty of Trianon (June 1920) that saw the loss of two-thirds of its territory. In Poland, governments since World War II have continually emphasized the importance of good neighborly relations and future

peace, and have sought to silence dissenting voices. Occasional rumblings (see chapter 2) suggest that these borders may not be as stable as geopolitical maps indicate.

81. Laszczkowski and Reeves, "Introduction: Affect and the Anthropology of the State," 8.

82. Hutchison, *Affective Communities in World Politics*, 13–16.

83. Itty Abraham writes that the loss of the province of Bengal led to such an outcry that the decision was reversed a few years later. By contrast, the separation of Burma from British India did not produce the same reaction, even though it led to much human strife. "Bengal was deemed a 'heartland' of the nation in 1905, while Burma in 1931 was little more than periphery whose partition was not construed in terms of national loss, even if many nationals lost everything they owned" (Abraham, *How India Became Territorial*, 36–37).

84. Reeves, "Signs of Sovereignty," 222; and Agnew, *Hidden Geopolitics*, 61.

85. Lambert, *États d'urgence*, 41.

86. In a large-scale study, Musolff reports several instances, from Saudi and Pakistani citizens, to analogize the Muslim community (*ummah*) as a body, suggesting that the corporeal metaphor may apply to groups beyond the constraints of the nation-state (*National Conceptualisations of the Body Politic*, 147).

87. Bernstein, *Religious Bodies Politic*, 35–36, 8.

88. Simpson, *Mohawk Interruptus*.

89. The Haudenosaunee (or Iroquois) passport, in use since 1977, evolved from negotiations with the US State Department and other countries. While it has been successfully used for international travel in some cases, it is generally not accepted as a valid documentation, most notably by Canada.

90. Goeman, *Mark My Words*, 117, 206, and 117.

91. Or at least, not the national (logo)map. Simpson (*Mohawk Interruptus*, 33) speaks of a "cartography of refusal," which suggests the map remains at the core of spatial understandings of belonging.

92. Anderson, *The Nation on No Map*, 2, 5, and 23, emphasis in the original.

93. Sharpe, *In the Wake*, 14; Anderson, *The Nation on No Map*, 142. For an example of a violent suppression of collective attempts at Black economic autonomy, see Lewis, *Violent Utopia*.

94. Spillers, "Mama's Baby, Papa's Maybe"; Perry, *Vexy Thing*, 154.

95. Brenner, *Confounding Powers*, 26.

96. Brenner, *Confounding Powers*, 28.

97. Ajami, "The End of Pan-Arabism," cited in Brenner, *Confounding Powers*, 205.

98. Gilmore (*Abolition Geography*, 420) prefers the term *syncretic*, which "downplays any presumption of prior purity" and "avoids suggesting technical intervention." I discuss these points further in chapter 5.

99. Tsing, *Friction*, 7.

100. Tsing, *Friction*, 122. Mindful not to "exoticize alterity for its own sake," Ramaswamy teases out the different trajectories of cartography outside Europe, thereby highlighting both overlaps and innovations ("Conceit of the Globe in Mughal Visual Practice," 754).

101. Scott, *The Art of Not Being Governed*. The term *Zomia* and the original development of its concept are attributable to Willem van Schendel ("Geographies of Knowing").

102. Hansen and Stepputat, introduction to *States of Imagination*, 10. One must also recall that full sovereignty was previously seen as the privilege of European nations alone (with partial exceptions made for some countries, like Turkey, Siam, Persia, and Japan). "This immediately excluded from consideration political formations that were nomadic or itinerant, or whose control over territory followed modes other than the prevailing organicist metaphor of territory as the state's body" (Abraham, *How India Became Territorial*, 65).

103. Bartelson, "Three Concepts of Recognition," 116, cited in Bryant and Hatay, *Sovereignty Suspended*, 14–15.

104. Andreas, *Border Games*, 129.

105. Bryant, "Sovereignty in Drag," 60. See also chapter 5.

106. Bryant, "Sovereignty in Drag," 75, emphasis added.

107. Dunn, *No Path Home*, 195; and Dunn and Frederiksen, "Uncanny Valleys," 24.

108. As of 2009, the CIA assessed at around fifty the number of countries containing stateless zones, where the "local government has lost all effectiveness or simply given up" (Singer, *Wired for War*, 286).

109. Bryant and Reeves, "Introduction: Toward an Anthropology of Sovereign Agency," 5.

110. Amilhat Szary, *Géopolitique des frontières*, 88. Writing about special zones and enclaves, Mezzadra and Neilson argue that these territorial excisions are not spaces of legal voidness but are instead saturated by competing norms and calculations (*Border as Method*, 208–9).

111. On three-dimensional approaches to the state, see Billé, *Voluminous States*.

112. Callahan, *Sensible Politics*, 222.

113. Benton, *A Search for Sovereignty*, 279.

114. See, respectively, Benton, *A Search for Sovereignty*; Cocks, *On Sovereignty and Other Political Delusions*; Krasner, *Sovereignty*.

115. This reverberates a point James Scott has made in his work. A planned institution, he writes, "generates an unofficial reality—a 'dark twin'—that arises to perform many of the various needs that the planned institution fails to fulfill" (*Seeing Like a State*, 261). I make a germane argument in my discussion of the territorial monster (see chapter 5).

116. Bartelson, *Sovereignty as Symbolic Form*, 63.

117. Bartelson, "Epilogue: The Ironies of Misrecognition," 241; and Cocks, *On Sovereignty*, 26.

118. Chatterjee, *The Nation and Its Fragments*, 5.

119. Bryant and Hatay, *Sovereignty Suspended*, 111.

120. Bryant and Hatay, *Sovereignty Suspended*, 4–5. Bryant and Hatay compare this performance to a "kind of metaphysical trick that makes something that is really only an idea seem like a real thing in the world." Ferguson and Gupta ("Spatializing States," 983–84) have drawn attention to how states invest much effort in developing practices to ensure that they are imagined in specific ways, employing rituals and procedures to "animate and naturalize metaphors." See also Billig (*Banal Nationalism*) on ordinary practices that reproduce the nation on a daily basis.

121. Dunn, *No Path Home*, 174.

122. Paasi, *Territories, Boundaries and Consciousness*, 51.

123. Arjun Chowdhury (*The Myth of International Order*) points out that the majority of states in the international system—about two-thirds of them—are weak states, resembling Libya more than Denmark or the United States. The language of weakness and failure, he writes, suggests an aberration from a norm, yet strong states are the exception.

124. See Bodin, "Russian Geopolitical Discourse"; Greenberg, "Divided Lands, Phantom Limbs"; von Hirschhausen et al., *Phantom Grenzen*; von Löwis, "Phantom Borders."

125. Anthropologist Liisa Malkki has argued, for instance, that the primary metaphor of nationhood is botanical ("National Geographic," 27). While a wider range of ethnographic contexts would be necessary to make the argument fully persuasive, its organic nature intuitively feels right. Malkki's notion of the refugee as someone extraneous, displaced, out of place, certainly reverberates with my argument about phantom territories and spectral presences.

126. In her exploration of the relation between the body and the city, Elizabeth Grosz has argued that the isomorphism in representational models is not a "mirroring of nature in artifice," but rather "a two-way linkage which could be defined as an *interface*, perhaps even a cobuilding" ("Bodies-Cities," 33–34, emphasis in the original).

127. Lury, *Prosthetic Culture*, 1.

128. Mitchell, "Picturing Terror," 917.

129. Stoler, *Haunted by Empire*, 1.

130. See Ahmed, *The Cultural Politics of Emotion*; Dixon, *Feminist Geopolitics*; Enloe, *Bananas, Beaches, and Bases*.

131. Weheliye, *Habeas Viscus*, 6–7. In fact, the Western model of the state and its territory was perfected "in a purer form" in the colonies, before being exported to the rest of the world (Elden, *The Birth of Territory*, 326). Weheliye (*Habeas Viscus*, 35–36) also notes that the German concentration camp has "its point of origin in German Southwest Africa at the turn of the twentieth century" before being subsequently reconstituted as an industrialized killing machine in Europe during the Third Reich.

132. Tomaini and Mittman, *Sea Monsters*.

133. Barad, *Meeting the Universe Halfway*, ix.

134. Bennett, *Vibrant Matter*, 120.

135. Parikka, *Insect Media*, 59.

136. Smith, "The Uncertainty of Placing," 2.

CHAPTER 1. CARTOGRAPHIC REVOLUTIONS

Epigraph: Monmonier, *How to Lie with Maps*, 88.

1. Baltimore et al., "Mapping the Genome," 70.

2. Baltimore et al., "Mapping the Genome."

3. For more on medieval sea monsters, see Hill, *Cartographical Curiosities*, 34; and especially Nigg, *Sea Monsters*; and Van Duzer, *Sea Monsters on Medieval and Renaissance Maps*.

4. Simone Pinet notes that the very concept of space was for a very long time melded with the similar concept of time, and it is not "until the thirteenth century . . . that time began to be unsutured from space." Spatial metaphors for time endure, largely unreflected: "behind" and "forward" indicate past and future respectively (Pinet, *Archipelagoes*, xviii). I return to orientation and kinesthetic metaphors in chapter 2.

5. Charting, another cartographic term, is similarly shorthand for all kinds of explorations, spatial or intellectual.

6. Kurgan, *Close Up at a Distance*, 16.

7. Not coincidentally, Europe's first scientific institutions were two bureaucracies created to regulate all geographical knowledge of their burgeoning empires: Spain's Casa de la Contratación, and Portugal's Casa da Mina (Turnbull, "Cartography and Science in Early Modern Europe," 6–7).

8. Turnbull, "Cartography and Science in Early Modern Europe," 6.

9. Pickles, *A History of Spaces*, 12.

10. Rachel Hewitt (*Map of a Nation*, 167) recounts the difficulties encountered by an Ordnance Survey mapmaker in 1830s Ireland who found that to describe his purpose, he first needed to enquire, "Do you know what a *map* is?" and to carefully explain that it was "a representation of the land on paper."

11. Wood, *Rethinking the Power of Maps*, 20.

12. Wood, *Rethinking the Power of Maps*, 17–18.

13. Edney, *Cartography*, 1.

14. Turnbull, "Cartography and Science in Early Modern Europe," 7.

15. Harley and Woodward, *The History of Cartography*, vol. 1, xvi. The Marshallese stick charts represented major ocean swell patterns, where island locations were shown by shells tied to the framework, or by the lashed junction of two or more sticks (Woodward and Lewis, *The History of Cartography*, vol. 2, bk. 3, 475–85).

16. Wood, *Rethinking the Power of Maps*, 26.

17. Harley, *The New Nature of Maps*, 36.

18. Klinghoffer, *The Power of Projections*, 78.

19. Klinghoffer, *The Power of Projections*, 123.

20. Monmonier, *How to Lie with Maps*, 96–98.

21. Monmonier, *How to Lie with Maps*, 99.

22. Anderson, *Imagined Communities*.

23. Buisseret, *Monarchs, Ministers, and Maps*, 1.

24. Wood, *Rethinking the Power of Maps*, 8, emphasis in the original.

25. Helgerson, *Forms of Nationhood*, 51.

26. Buisseret, *Monarchs, Ministers, and Maps*, 1.

27. In China, Kären Wigen and Caroline Winterer write, the introduction of European cartography in the sixteenth century opened whole new worlds of understanding but did not "literally reset East Asian calendars" (Wigen and Winterer, "Pacific Asia," 35). In Japan, as in China, cartography is among the oldest forms of place writing, but practices differed from European ones. Japanese maps "generalized and symbolized landscape elements," but they did not "deploy a regular scale, nor did they plot the region or the nation onto a gridded globe." As a result, the

cartographic practices of early modern Japan "defy a simple premodern/modern polarity" (Wigen, *A Malleable Map*, 122–23).

28. P. D. A. Harvey notes that before the Renaissance there was no term for *map* in any European language, and that the terms used in contemporary languages can all denote other things besides *map*, thus resulting in various ambiguities (*The History of Topographical Maps*, 10). For a fuller discussion of the lexical landscape of cartographic terms in European languages, see Jacob, *The Sovereign Map*, 18–21.

29. King, *Mapping Reality*, 23.

30. Hilde De Weerdt also draws attention to the term *ditu* (地圖, map) also being used metaphorically in the sense of *territory* during the Song dynasty, suggesting that empire maps had by this time become a familiar object in the lives of Song readers (*Maps and Memory*, 158).

31. Wood, *Rethinking the Power of Maps*, 26. See also Akin, *East Asian Cartographic Print Culture*.

32. Padrón, *The Spacious Word*, 96. Simon Ferdinand makes the important caveat that an insistence on a history of mapmaking narrated in terms of rupture and transformation masks the varied, halting, and complex processes that informed this paradigm shift (*Mapping beyond Measure*, 18). The spectral bodily imaginaries I describe in later chapters in fact suggest that this transformation remains incomplete.

33. Helgerson, *Forms of Nationhood*.

34. Charles Maier asserts that alternative concepts for forms of territorial stability without fixed frontiers exist, and he provides as examples nomadic and confederated groups who have staked out territories with varying perimeters and are able to live in a parallel relationship with their settled neighbors (*Once within Borders*, 5). While this was true historically, it no longer holds.

35. Agnew, "No Borders, No Nations," 398.

36. Agnew, "No Borders, No Nations," 398.

37. Buisseret, *Monarchs, Ministers, and Maps*, 2.

38. Mary Louise Pratt (*Imperial Eyes*) has famously spoken of "planetary consciousness" to refer to Europe's development of global categories and displacement of older (native) forms.

39. Agnew, "No Borders, No Nations," 398.

40. Agnew, "No Borders, No Nations," 398. As Raymond Craib reminds us, this does not mean that colonial subjects were mere passive recipients of European boundary-making exercises. In the context of Mexico, surveyors were the "objects of intense scrutiny, constantly subject to the influences, pressures, and threats of an array of rural inhabitants (Craib, *Cartographic Mexico*, 12). However, "the basic premises of modern land surveying left little room for forms of engaging with the land that did not conform to the specifics of nominally Western property norms. Different ways of understanding, occupying, and working space were made to disappear—largely through the law—and different ways of representing space dismissed in courts as unscientific, unreliable, or simply illegible" (Craib, "Cartography and Decolonization," 32).

41. The previous lack of knowledge about non-Western cartographies was due, in part, to the difficulty in reconciling them with the linear and teleological history of

cartography as ever-more accurate and scientific representation of the landscape (Crampton, *Mapping*, 10).

42. Antrim, *Mapping the Middle East*, 9, 15.

43. *Siam Mapped*, the frequently cited study by Thai historian Thongchai Winichakul, retraces the complex processes whereby a non-European nation emerged politically and cartographically between 1850 and 1910. Traditionally, several types of maps had coexisted in the country, the most prominent of which was the Traiphum map, a symbolic representation of Buddhist cosmology. Diagrammatic guides for military campaigns and maritime commerce also existed that were practice oriented and secular in nature. These maps represented multiple and overlapping sovereignties and showed Siamese subjects bound primarily to a specific lord rather than the state. Since the Siamese court's concerns were located primarily in tax-paying subjects rather than in territory, borders were seen as a matter for the local people to decide. In fact, the question of boundaries is completely absent from the 1826 treaty with Britain (Winichakul, *Siam Mapped*, 64).

44. Hostetler, "Qing Connections," 626.

45. Song, *Making Borders in Modern East Asia*; Hostetler, "Qing Connections"; Kivelson, "Cartography, Autocracy and State Powerlessness."

46. Song, *Making Borders in Modern East Asia*, 2–3.

47. Ricardo Padrón's book *The Spacious Word* similarly tracks "a story of how the old lingers long after the initial emergence of the new" and how "a central aspect of modernity slinks into existence" (12).

48. Shoemaker, *A Strange Likeness*, 3–4.

49. Shoemaker, *A Strange Likeness*, 4. Barry Lopez similarly notes that early European travelers were surprised by the highly accurate Inuit maps of the coastal and interior regions (*Arctic Dreams*, 287).

50. Benton, *A Search for Sovereignty*, xii, 3.

51. Branch, *The Cartographic State*, 169.

52. Branch, *The Cartographic State*, 125, 7. Branch relies here in part on the work of Andreas Osiander, who argues that the idea that a system of states was created in 1648 is a fallacy (Osiander, *The States System of Europe*).

53. Branch, *The Cartographic State*, 83.

54. Branch, *The Cartographic State*, 94.

55. Dunlop, *Cartophilia*, 5.

56. Dunlop, *Cartophilia*, 6–7. The very rise of nationalism, she writes, "depended on the creation of powerful relationships among local, regional, and national feelings of territorial attachment" (10).

57. Lauren Benton writes that the change from portolan charts to modern maps, with the consequent removal of compasses and rhumb lines, led to world maps that portrayed the oceans as a blank expanse (*A Search for Sovereignty*, 105). In order to fill an increasingly void and undifferentiated space, sea monsters and ships came to be integrated. Largely optional decorative elements, they were included only if requested by the commissioning client (Van Duzer, *Sea Monsters on Medieval and Renaissance Maps*, 10).

58. Padrón, *The Spacious Word*, 53.

59. Eventually these various strands were brought together through Ptolemy's grid as a universal idiom. Indeed, the grid was able to map the earth, chart the seas, and depict a single city or the entire globe (Padrón, *The Spacious Word*, 71).

60. Jacob, *The Sovereign Map*, 131. East was usually at the top, since it was associated with paradise in Genesis 2:8. This association endured until the sixteenth century, coding India as a source of marvels (and occasionally the origin of poisonous animals, polluted waters, and death; Wittkower, *Allegory and the Migration of Symbols*, 60; Helms, *Ulysses' Sail*, 216).

61. Padrón, *The Spacious Word*, 35.

62. Garfield, *On the Map*, 694–95. They were also representations of space and time, telling a story at a particular time but also the story of its origins (Massey, *For Space*, 107).

63. Birkholz, *The King's Two Maps*, xvii.

64. Woodward, *Art and Cartography*, cited in Monmonier, *How to Lie with Maps*, 57.

65. Monmonier, *How to Lie with Maps*, 54–55.

66. One might also suggest that the very modern and abstract logomap shares with the T-O map a role of social and cultural orientation. Madeleine Reeves argues that the outline of the state functions as icon rather than tool of navigation. Analogous to the image of the flag, the visage of the president, or the coat of arms, it is to be viewed and committed to memory rather than carried or used (Reeves, "Signs of Sovereignty," 225).

67. Traub, "Mapping the Global Body," 59.

68. As an example of the now conventional equivalence between the national territory and the body of the citizen, Palestinian families who have lost their children in the conflict with Israel often display a photo of the child superimposed over the map of Palestine (Wallach, "Trapped in Mirror-Images," 365).

69. Maier dates this "cadastral century" from around 1680 to 1820 (*Once within Borders*, 10–11).

70. Norman Thrower (*Maps and Civilization*, 24) points out that while Ptolemy was the ultimate authority on cartography and astronomy, it may be exaggerated to attribute all these developments specifically to him. It may be preferable to "think of a Ptolemaic corpus—similar to the Hippocratic tradition in medicine—to which a number of workers contributed."

71. King, *Mapping Reality*, 44.

72. Helgerson, *Forms of Nationhood*, 107.

73. Helgerson, *Forms of Nationhood*, 112.

74. Helgerson, *Forms of Nationhood*, 112.

75. Helgerson, *Forms of Nationhood*. As discussed further in chapter 2, the association between land and royal power had itself displaced an earlier corporeality that was primarily religious.

76. Helgerson, *Forms of Nationhood*, 117.

77. Helgerson, *Forms of Nationhood*, 128.

78. Helgerson, *Forms of Nationhood*, 135.

79. Helgerson, *Forms of Nationhood*, 131. As Kären Wigen describes, a parallel situation in Japan saw the cartographic depiction of current events—particularly

natural disasters or public affairs such as protests and uprisings—fall under strict censorship. Wigen, "Orienting the Past in Early Modern Japan," 54–55.

80. Harley, *The New Nature of Maps*, 111.

81. Akerman, "The Structuring of Political Territory," 144, 141.

82. Hale, *Renaissance Europe*, 52. As James Akerman remarks ("The Structuring of Political Territory," 153), the eagerness of Americans to publish their own atlases so soon after independence is a clear indication of the power of atlases in defining and molding the geopolitical imagination.

83. Conley, *The Self-Made Map*, 2.

84. Branch, *The Cartographic State*, 7.

85. Branch, *The Cartographic State*, 88.

86. Branch, *The Cartographic State*, 168–69.

87. Song, *Making Borders in Modern East Asia*, 86. Historian Alexander Akin also demonstrates that the cartographic publishing boom in the late Ming dynasty was much more than simply an influence of European practices. A very large proportion of Chinese maps were simply copied from earlier work, and the transformation was mostly about how maps were deployed, contrasted, and combined rather than in their nature or technique. If late Ming maps were embedded in a wider East Asian sphere, the flow of cartographic texts was also multidirectional, "linking nodes of cartographic and geographic synthesis within a broader web of influence" (Akin, *East Asian Cartographic Print Culture*, 12–17). In the African context, as Achille Mbembe writes, the situation was similar: "Attachment to the territory and to the land was entirely relative. In some cases, political entities were not delimited by boundaries in the classical sense of the term, but rather by an imbrication of multiple spaces constantly joined, disjoined, and recombined through wars, conquests, and the mobility of goods and persons. . . . In other cases, mastery over spaces was based on controlling people or localities, and sometimes both together. . . . In still other cases, the spatial dynamics tending to make the boundary a genuine physical limit went hand in hand with the principle of dispersing and deterritorializing allegiances" (Mbembe, "At the Edge of the World," 263).

88. Nail, *Theory of the Border*, 91.

89. Scott, *The Art of Not Being Governed*, 68.

90. Branch, "Mapping the Sovereign State," 16. Branch also points out that the Peace of Westphalia, generally seen as marking an epistemological break with premodern political geography, in fact "used no cartographic language and made no mention of maps for reference or for the demarcation of boundaries."

91. Anderson, *Imagined Communities*, 19. The practical aspects of territorial management show far more heterogeneity. In the context of Russia, geographer Boris Rodoman argues, national territory is of an anisotropic nature—meaning that it has different properties in different directions, similar to wood, stronger along the grain than across it. In contemporary Russia, vertical links are strong, and its horizontal ones weak. Thus the "vertical" roads linking the metropolis to the regional capitals are extensive and well maintained. By contrast, the roads running "horizontally" between small towns or villages are neglected—often becoming

impassable in bad weather—or simply do not exist (Billé and Humphrey, *On the Edge*, 27–28).

92. Woodward, "Maps and the Rationalization of Geographic Space," 87, cited in Traub, *Mapping the Global Body*, 49. Jordan Branch also draws attention to the high degree of differentiation among diverse places in a particular territory, with French kings, for instance, holding some parts of France as personal possessions and other parts through feudal vassals (*The Cartographic State*, 24).

93. Ludden, "Maps in the Mind," 1058.

94. Hewitt, *Map of a Nation*, 42.

95. See Branch, "Mapping the Sovereign State," 21.

96. Anderson, *Imagined Communities*, 175.

97. Biggs, "Putting the State on the Map," 374.

98. Gellner, *Nationalism*, 139–40.

99. Pickles, *A History of Spaces*, 20.

100. Bryant also adds national airlines as a source of pride and national identification—"a sense of nation-state unity wrapped up in pride in command of modern technology" ("Sovereignty in the Skies," 26).

101. Anderson (*Imagined Communities*, 195) describes how nationalism has drawn on the metaphor of sleep and awakening to resolve the discontinuity between, on the one hand, the recent creation of the nation and, on the other, the myth of the nation as timeless. The metaphor explains why, despite its absence on older maps, the nation has always existed. It had merely been asleep until then.

102. These forms of geographical isolation are frequently there to help visualize a particular state, as I discuss in chapter 5, but they can also be politically motivated. The omission of Israel from Palestinian maps, notes Yair Wallach, is paralleled by a similar failure of Israeli maps to mark the Palestinian territories under military occupation ("Trapped in Mirror-Images," 361).

103. Jacob, *The Sovereign Map*, 315.

104. Benoît, "Des enfants dessinent la carte de France," 22–23, cited in Jacob, *The Sovereign Map*, 316.

105. Pinet, *Archipelagoes*, 2011, 45. See also Ramaswamy, *The Lost Land of Lemuria*.

106. Jacob, *The Sovereign Map*, 286. Thus Brazil and California were originally designated as islands, even after this was known not to be the case (Pinet, *Archipelagoes*, 139). By contrast, history books for children in the Turkish Republic of Northern Cyprus claim that Cyprus was originally geographically attached to Anatolia but that "geological transformations caused it to break away to become an island" (Navaro-Yashin, *The Make-Believe Space*, 53).

107. Steinberg, "Insularity, Sovereignty and Statehood," 261. In fact, this association remains, as I discuss further in chapter 5, and the boundary line between Northern Ireland and the Republic of Ireland, for instance, "appears as an insult to the idea of territorial holism" (263).

108. Steinberg, "Insularity, Sovereignty and Statehood," 263.

109. Succinctly put: "We don't get our image of the world from running around and looking at the world. We get it from some diagram or map" (Saarinen, "Centering of Mental Maps").

110. Anderson, *Imagined Communities*, 175.

111. Christian Jacob notes that France's "logo of the hexagon, in its geometrical perfection, is frequently used by organizations of territorial management—government ministries and political parties, but also insurance companies or supporters of nationwide causes" (*The Sovereign Map*, 348–49).

112. Winichakul, *Siam Mapped*, 138.

113. Borges, "Del rigor en la ciencia," 137.

114. Carroll, *Sylvie and Bruno Concluded*, 169.

115. Eco, "Dell'impossibilità di costruire la carta dell'impero 1 a 1," 158.

116. Korzybski, "A Non-Aristotelian System." The full quote, rarely given, is as follows: "A map is not the territory it represents, but, if correct, it has a similar structure to the territory, which accounts for its usefulness." As Bernhard Siegert writes, maps are not representations of space but spaces of representation. As such, they "contain less information about a territory than about the way it is observed and described" (*The Map Is the Territory*).

117. Jacob, *The Sovereign Map*, 14.

118. Jacob, *The Sovereign Map*, 23.

119. Harley, *The New Nature of Maps*, 35.

120. Foucault, *This Is Not a Pipe*, 17.

121. Jacob, *The Sovereign Map*, 322.

122. Think, for instance, of the expression "wiping off the map," which posits the map as document of record and, ultimately, as more real than the reality it purports to represent.

123. Baudrillard, *Simulacres et simulation*, 17.

124. Baudrillard, *Simulacres et simulation*, 10.

125. King, *Mapping Reality*, 89.

126. As Stephen Greenblatt has argued in the context of European explorers encountering the Americas, the monstrous in fact frequently cohabited with the marvelous. At the same time as the unknown, "primitive," and "uncivilized" American continent frightened the colonizers, its mineral wealth and exotic fauna also fascinated them. These mysterious spaces inhabited by fantastical, outsized, and grotesque creatures were also places of self-discovery and renewal. They fed a longing for what seemed to be missing in the explorers' own subjectivity (Greenblatt, *Marvelous Possessions*, 76, 92). I continue this exploration of the monstrous in chapter 5.

127. Medvedev, "A General Theory of Russian Space," 24–25. The mention of Stalitex, a "light, firm plastic," a material named after Stalin, is clearly a facetious addition, but it also speaks to the importance of technology—a technology that has been instrumental for the development of cartography itself.

128. Bodin, "Russian Geopolitical Discourse," 178. Dugin, whose views are widely characterized as fascist, has advocated for Ukraine to become "a purely administrative sector of the Russian centralized state" (Burbank, "The Grand Theory Driving Putin to War").

129. Andrukhovych, *My Final Territory*, 113. This imaginary echoes my discussion of the *corps morcelé* in chapters 3 and 4.

130. One might even go further and argue that the logomap is more real than the territory since it is able to capture and possess distant and physically inaccessible remote corners that remain elusive to the technologies of the state. See Harris, "Lag." Catherine Dunlop has argued along similar lines that it is only thanks to maps that "places that had once felt remote and culturally estranged from European capitals became visible, and even knowable" (*Cartophilia*, 19).

131. King, *Mapping Reality*, 142. A somewhat similar situation is the unusual case of Null Island, an imaginary one-square-meter plot of land located at 0°N 0°E in the South Atlantic Ocean, intended to help analysts flag errors in geocoding processes. Misspelled street names, nonexistent building numbers, and other errors leads to a coordinate output of 0,0. Since "0,0" is an actual location on the Earth's surface in the system, the feature will be mapped there, adding to an island of misfit data. "This shared experience among geographers has fed the mystique of Null Island, with GIS enthusiasts creating fantasy maps, a 'national' flag, and articles detailing Null Island's rich (and fake) history online" (St. Onge, "Null Island").

132. Pickles, *A History of Spaces*, 21.

133. Butler, *Precarious Life*, 34–35.

134. Cathal McCall has described how the imagined borders of the UK often retreat to those of Britain and related an event when in a debate in the House of Lords the then security minister referred to people traveling from Northern Ireland "to the United Kingdom" ("Debordering and Rebordering," 222–23). These slips speak to the visual sense of wholeness and unity projected by islands, and the cultural reluctance toward divided islands or archipelagoes, as discussed further in chapter 5.

135. The medieval practice of placing east at the top remains sedimented in the word *orientation*. The Hobo-Dyer map is thus disorienting in more ways than one.

136. A fascinating worldwide study from the late 1980s looked at mental maps drawn by respondents from Europe, Asia, and North and South America, and particularly whether these maps would be Eurocentric (placing Europe at the center, like a Mercator map) or whether they would be Sinocentric or Americentric. It found Sinocentric maps were prevalent in Indonesia, Papua New Guinea, Australia, and New Zealand. However, highly indicative of the hold of European educational systems, in Hong Kong, Singapore, the Philippines, and Thailand, most students sketched Eurocentric maps even though it placed their countries in peripheral positions (Saarinen, "Centering of Mental Maps of the World," 37–40).

137. Francaviglia, *The Shape of Texas*, 69.

138. Tyner, "Persuasive Cartography," 140.

139. Tyner, "Persuasive Cartography," 140.

140. Monmonier, *How to Lie with Maps*, 50–51.

141. The most unusual case might be the fictitious town of Agloe in upstate New York, created by Otto G. Lindberg, director of the General Drafting Co., and his assistant, Ernest Alpers, in the 1930s, using a mix of the first letters in their names. A few years later, Lindberg tried to sue another map company, as the town of Agloe appeared on their map. They were surprised to discover the place now existed, a store having opened at that location. "The owners had seen Agloe on

a map distributed by Esso, which owned scores of gas stations. Esso had bought that map from Lindberg and Alpers. If Esso says this place is called Agloe, the store folks figured, well, that's what we'll call ourselves" (Krulwich, "An Imaginary Town Becomes Real"). Sometimes, elements are concealed in official maps for more anodyne reasons—a cartographic inside joke. A good example is the inclusion of figures such as a spider, a naked woman, a fish, or a marmot in Switzerland's remote mountainous regions. See Poll, "For Decades, Cartographers Have Been Hiding."

142. Tyner, "Persuasive Cartography," 140.

143. Speir, "Magic Geography."

144. In the 1960s, the position of Soviet cities deemed militarily sensitive was systematically distorted, and it was only in 1988 that "Soviet geographers finally admitted publicly that most of the maps that had been sold to the public since the 1930s had been willfully falsified and deformed." Jacob, *The Sovereign Map*, 274.

145. Klinghoffer, *The Power of Projections*, 31. Soviet cartographic disinformation also affected city maps. For instance, detailed street maps of large Soviet cities frequently failed to identify principal thoroughfares, and Soviet street maps of Moscow "suppressed the imposing KGB building on Dzerzhinski Square, as well as other important buildings" (Monmonier, *How to Lie with Maps*, 117–18). Such cartographic censorship, widely practiced, is usually justified on the grounds of national security, political expediency, or commercial necessity (Harley, *The New Nature of Maps*, 64).

146. Cartier, "What's Territorial about China?," 73.

147. For some additional examples, see Monmonier, *How to Lie with Maps*, 44–45; Speir, "Magic Geography," 321–22; King, *Mapping Reality*, 26.

148. The phenomenon of cartographic anxiety is discussed in more depth in chapter 3.

149. Harley, *The New Nature of Maps*, 57.

150. Garfield, *On the Map*, 214; see also Conrad, *Heart of Darkness*.

151. Jacob, *The Sovereign Map*, 264.

152. Harley, *The New Nature of Maps*, 138.

153. Garfield, *On the Map*, 214.

154. Harley, *The New Nature of Maps*, 144.

155. Mignolo, *The Darker Side of the Renaissance*, 262.

156. Scott, *The Art of Not Being Governed*, 12.

157. A visible consequence of internal colonialism is the massive reduction in localisms and vernaculars of all kinds, from linguistic diversity to indigenous practices (Scott, *The Art of Not Being Governed*, 13).

158. Fortna, *Imperial Classroom*; Fortna, "Change in the School Maps."

159. Fortna, "Change in the School Maps," 23.

160. Fortna, "Change in the School Maps," 26.

161. See also Yavuz, *Nostalgia for the Empire*.

162. Ramaswamy, "Maps, Mother/Goddesses, and Martyrdom," 825.

163. Ramaswamy, "Maps and Mother Goddesses in Modern India," 100; see also Ramaswamy, "Maps, Mother/Goddesses, and Martyrdom," 824.

164. Ramaswamy, "Maps, Mother/Goddesses, and Martyrdom," 824.

165. Harley, "Silences and Secrecy," 66.

166. Ramaswamy, "Maps, Mother/Goddesses, and Martyrdom," 828.
167. Ramaswamy, "Maps, Mother/Goddesses, and Martyrdom," 829.
168. Ramaswamy, "Maps and Mother Goddesses in Modern India," 98.
169. Ramaswamy, "Maps and Mother Goddesses in Modern India," 99. See also Wigen, "Orienting the Past."
170. The logomap looks deceptively simple but is a form of representation that could only have emerged and been understood once the core tenets of state and territory had become stable.
171. Jacob, *The Sovereign Map*, 2.

CHAPTER 2. THE GODDESS, THE BOOT, AND THE SQUARE

The title of this chapter riffs on George Lakoff's groundbreaking book *Women, Fire, and Dangerous Things*, for reasons that will become clear as the argument unfolds. Epigraph: Orton, *From Head to Toe*, 102.

1. Šír, "Cult of Personality," 204.
2. On the latter, see Yurchak, "Bodies of Lenin."
3. David Markus notes that Trump is a figure "whose sense of personhood appears intimately connected to [his] lavish dwellings"—the gold and gaudy decor a materialization of business and personal success, and in this sense not unlike the Niyazov's gilded statue. Markus, *Notes on Trumpspace*, 50.
4. Turits, *Foundations of Despotism*, cited in Koch, "On the Cult of Personality."
5. Koch, "On the Cult of Personality."
6. Reeves, "#Trumpistan." See also Masco, "The Condition of Our Condition."
7. Azoulay, "When a Demolished House Becomes a Public Square," 215–16.
8. Santner, *The Royal Remains*, 33.
9. Santner, *The Royal Remains*, 245. Thongchai Winichakul makes a similar point with respect to Thailand. Although the modern geobody "displaced the premodern non-bounded, hierarchical realm, the manifestation of the royal body emerged in a new form. But it was still very much the royal body" (Winichakul, *Siam Mapped*, 134).
10. Kantorowicz, *The King's Two Bodies*, 210.
11. Santner, *The Royal Remains*, 36.
12. Along similar lines, Mark Neocleous notes that "most states find that the king's robes really do fit rather well, even if they also feel obliged to dress them up with some liberal democratic accessories" (*The Politics of Immunity*, 343).
13. Writing about this somatic undercarriage, Pheng Cheah notes that an earlier dominant understanding of collective existence in mechanical terms gave way to a vision of the political body as an organism. Whereas "a machine is organized from the top down," he explains, "a living being is organized from within and self-perpetuating"—a better analogy for the reform of the absolute state (Cheah, *Spectral Nationality*, 25–26).
14. Jeffrey Cohen writes, the "body is hybrid category, part cultural and part material, in which interior and exterior are always enfolded, always crossing into each other" (*Of Giants*, xvii).

15. This in fact tracks with the analysis of metaphors by cognitive linguists like Lakoff and Johnson, who have argued that all human thought is metaphorical, whether or not there is an objective physical reality out there or not (Marks, *Metaphors in International Relations Theory*, 16).

16. Martin, "Toward an Anthropology of Immunology"; Cohen, *A Body Worth Defending*. The bias noted by Martin toward militaristic metaphors remains prevalent, even though the science reveals a high degree of cooperation and mutual benefit between the human host and its multitudes of passengers. In fact, Shildrick writes, "Many microbes are unable to survive outside the body, just as the human being herself could not survive and develop without maintaining an active microbial viscera" (*Visceral Prostheses*, 79).

17. Rape has been a familiar military metaphor, from "the Rape of Belgium" at the beginning of World War I, to the "Rape of Nanjing" in World War II, and the "rape of Kuwait" during the Gulf War in 1991. The association between war and rape extends of course beyond the lexical, with actual rapes commonly committed as part of an attack. But Elden also draws attention to the origin of the term, "from the Latin word *rapere* meaning to seize, to abduct, to capture" ("Outside Territory," 133).

18. Neocleous, *The Politics of Immunity*, 2–3. Jennifer Terry gives the example of "surgical strike" as a term that describes both precision in targeted bombing and a medical operation removing "a tumor or other deleterious agent through a penetrating incision and extraction" (*Attachments to War*, 35).

19. Neocleous, *The Politics of Immunity*, 57–58.

20. Indeed, as Pheng Cheah argues, we are still "very far from having renounced organicism in contemporary political discourse" (*Spectral Nationality*, 34). Jussi Parikka goes further and argues that the idea of seeing the state as a living organism became consolidated by the twentieth century. No longer just metaphorical, the "new rationalization of life referred to how the forms of organization could take nature as their object and 'incorporate and reproduce nature's original characteristics'" (Parikka, *Insect Media*, 114, citing Roberto Esposito).

21. Winichakul, *Siam Mapped*, 77.

22. A large-scale study of the metaphor of the nation-as-body, carried out across thirty linguistic and cultural backgrounds, has shown how the metaphor is culturally mediated and therefore embedded differently depending on the cultural context (Musolff, *National Conceptualisations of the Body Politic*).

23. Gyatso, "Down with the Demoness," 38. In a resonant manner, anthropologist Tâm Ngô writes that Vietnamese spiritualists believe that China has over millennia hexed Vietnam by planting objects or human bodies in the important "dragon vein" of Vietnam in order to cut off the vital force of Vietnamese national sovereignty (Ngô, "Between a Rock and a Hard Place"). Ananya Kabir also mentions the legend of the demon Jalodhbhava, whose excesses were kept in check through the draining of an immense lake in the Kashmir Valley (*Territory of Desire*, 91).

24. Lessing, "The Topographical Identification," 89.

25. Douglas, *Purity and Danger*.

26. For Mongolian, see Billé, *Sinophobia*, 109–10. A more extreme case is Great Andamanese, in which nouns, verbs, adjectives and adverbs are used with markers derived from seven zones of the body (Abbi, "This Ancient Language").

27. Porteous, *Landscapes of the Mind*, 70. In a study noting the similarities that existed between European colonialists and indigenous populations in North America, Nancy Shoemaker argues that both groups shared a basic understanding of space that had emerged in a corporeal, sensory experience of travel: "They knew what it was like to move physically through a landscape made up of valleys, mountains, rivers, and boulders, and they could extend those feelings metaphorically to describe other, more abstract situations" (*A Strange Likeness*, 4).

28. Lakoff and Johnson, *Metaphors We Live By*. See also Fishel, *The Microbial State*.

29. I am thinking for instance of the difference in how time is mapped in English and Chinese. English conceptualizes past and future events in a horizontal way (past is behind us, and future in front) while Chinese includes a vertical orientation—*shang xingqi*, last week, versus *xia xingqi*, next week, where *shang* and *xia* respectively mean top and bottom, thus visualizing time as moving down.

30. Many conceptual metaphors are also unique to particular subcultures because of differences in social-cultural context, history, and concerns. Kövecses, *Where Metaphors Come From*, 13.

31. Musolff identifies five main similes: "the state as a body" (with various parts of the state corresponding to various organs), "the state as a geobody" (where the capital is the head or heart of the state), "the state as a person" ("Italy is a beautiful woman" or "Austria is a middle-aged man"), "the state as a bodily part of the world" ("New Jersey is the armpit of the country"), and "the state as part of ego" ("Italy is like the leg of my body"). These similes all coexist in any given context but in different ratios. See Musolff, *National Conceptualisations of the Body Politic*.

32. Marks, *Metaphors in International Relations Theory*, 5.

33. Hill, *Cartographical Curiosities*, 46.

34. Garfield, *On the Map*, 164.

35. De Baecque, *The Body Politic*, 12. As discussed in chapter 1, cartographic representations were vehicles of symbolic instruction at the same time as they were meant to reflect a physical reality. A number of these early maps also conceived the world in a way that was both religious and corporeal, such as the thirteenth-century Ebstorf map from Germany, which represented the world as Christ's embodiment, with Jerusalem as geographic and symbolic navel. In such maps, the body of Christ is circumscribed within a T-O map, with his head, hands, and feet marking the four cardinal directions. His corporeal presence was also sometimes extended through the bodies of his twelve disciples, who presided over more distant regions. As Valerie Traub has noted, from the fifteenth century onward, the body of the monarch increasingly superseded that of Christ and became a crucial resource in articulations of monarchical power ("Mapping the Global Body," 78–80). The Ditchley portrait discussed in chapter 1, in which Elizabeth I stands atop Saxton's map of England and Wales, is perhaps one of the clearest examples of this evolution (see fig. 1.4).

36. Anthropomorphic maps have also been employed when the identity, rather than the borders, of a state were seen as at risk. Claude Gandelman reminds us that in "sixteenth-century France the image of French territory as the body of a woman ripped open was used by the Protestant writer Agrippa d'Aubigné as effective political propaganda during the religious wars" (*Reading Pictures, Viewing Texts*, 78–79).

37. This appears in fact to be supported by the emphasis on corporealized logomaps in situations of perceived threats or at the birth of new nations, when it is critical to emphasize the organic nature of the state.

38. Sinelschikova, "How the Bear Became the Symbol of Russia."

39. The Russian animated television series *Masha and the Bear* can similarly be seen as an exercise in soft power. The cartoon portrays the bear as a warm, fatherly figure, who takes care of a disobedient little girl, Masha.

40. Kommersant, "Putin."

41. Wishnick, "Why a 'Strategic Partnership?,'" 58.

42. Songster, *Panda Nation*, 11.

43. Maxwell, "Zoomorphic Maps."

44. Meier, "The Octopus, a Motif of Evil."

45. It reappeared first in 2014 as Russia invaded Crimea (Isabella, "Attack of the Cartographic Land Octopus"). It has also recently been used to refer to China, in the context of the Belt and Road Initiative.

46. Psychologist Raymond Gibbs in fact criticized the mistaken "assumption that things in our cognition that are most alive and most active are those that are conscious" (*The Poetics of Mind*, 22).

47. Leslie Hepple writes that the two components of the metaphor (state and body) are sufficiently rich and complex for "only selected linkages to have been exploited: there always exists the possibility of new, original insights into different linkages, or of cross-fertilization from alternative forms of the metaphor in other areas of social theory" ("Metaphor, Geopolitical Discourse and the Military," 143).

48. DNA has also become the principal somatic marker of belonging in Native American self-identifications, replacing earlier uses of "blood," as Kim TallBear points out (*Native American DNA*, 8).

49. In a decade-long study across five continents and a dozen languages, cognitive linguist Andreas Musolff reports a slew of others: x-ray, clone, immunosuppressants, neurosis, steroids, transplant, genes, pandemic, root canal treatment (*National Conceptualisations of the Body Politic*, 37–38).

50. Hale, *The Body Politic*, 15.

51. The fable of Aesop was also popular at that time, appearing in several collections, in English and Latin translations (Hale, *The Body Politic*, 119). Its appearance in Shakespeare's *Coriolanus* may have contributed, in part, to its renewed popularity.

52. Grosz, "Bodies-Cities," 34.

53. Harris, *Foreign Bodies and the Body Politic*, 2. Hobbes, later followed by Rousseau, also equates the circulation of money with the blood of the sovereign (see Nail, *Theory of the Border*, 129).

54. Musolff, *National Conceptualisations of the Body Politic*, 25.

55. De Baecque, *The Body Politic*. See also Kantorowicz, *The King's Two Bodies*.
56. De Baecque, *The Body Politic*, 29. This shift has also been traced through the concept of treason by historian D. Alan Orr. The law of treason in Great Britain was "at the time of its statutory declaration in 1352 as much a personal crime against the monarch as the unlawful usurpation of his sovereign authority." It is only later, as new demands emerged, that it increasingly referred to the unlawful seizure of sovereign or state power. "It was a crime against the king not merely in respect of his person but in his role as the lawful wielder and guardian of sovereign power" (Orr, *Treason and the State*, 1–2).
57. Ryan, "Trump's Dick Reportedly Looks Like Toad." I discuss monstrous corporealities in more detail in chapter 5.
58. Gandelman, *Reading Pictures, Viewing Texts*, 19.
59. Gandelman, *Reading Pictures, Viewing Texts*.
60. This point is also made by Neocleous (*Imagining the State*, 35).
61. Cohen, *Of Giants*, 12. It also recalls Borges's map, tattered and slowly disintegrating across the land.
62. Hale, *The Body Politic*, 12, 131.
63. Neocleous, *Imagining the State*, 9.
64. Abrahamsson, *Radikalkonservatismens rötter*, 32.
65. Abrahamsson, *Radikalkonservatismens rötter*, 28–29.
66. Abrahamsson, *Radikalkonservatismens rötter*, 48–49.
67. In Sweden, writes Abrahamsson, Kjellén appears as a threatening echo from the past, and his name is once again being used across the entire political spectrum (*Radikalkonservatismens rötter*, 18–19). Mark Bassin makes the important argument that while contemporary parallels to Ratzel's writings are striking, they operate in very different political and intellectual worlds. The affinity across the centuries, he writes, is found on a more general and structural level, namely an ideological argument from nature deployed toward a recognizably programmatic end (Bassin, "Politics from Nature," 27).
68. Gumilev, *Etnogenez i biosfera zemli*, 16.
69. Gumilev, *Etnogenez i biosfera zemli*, 231, 239, 33.
70. If an individual with two Mongolian parents will be automatically Mongolian, a prolonged residence abroad will dilute this Mongolianness. They may be less likely, for instance, to pass on to their progeny the so-called Mongolian spot—a birthmark on the lower back that fades over the first couple of years (Billé, *Sinophobia*).
71. The Soviet experience was also formative of its own conceptualization of place-bound ethnicity, notably through the nationalities policy formulated by Stalin, whereby an official nationality required a common language, a common economic base, a common psychological makeup, and a common territory—effectively tying groups to discrete patches of land.
72. To describe the genesis and evolution of ethnic groups, Gumilev introduced the concept of "passionarity" (*passionnarnost'*). He argued that ethnic groups go through the stages of birth, development, inertia, and death.
73. Beer and De Landtsheer, *Metaphorical World Politics*.

74. On dismemberment, see Fortna, "Change in the School Maps," 24; on maiming, Ramaswamy, "Midnight's Line," 30; Nelson, "Stumped Identities," 315; on mutilation, Paasi, "Boundaries as Social Practice and Discourse"; on strangulation, Navaro-Yashin, "'Life Is Dead Here,'" 110. In the mid-nineteenth century the Ottoman Empire was known as the "sick man of Europe." In the early twentieth century, China was described as the "sick man of Asia," whose life needed to be saved (Lynteris, "Yellow Peril Epidemics"). "Can a political system have a nervous breakdown?" asks Neocleous (*The Politics of Immunity*, 299), providing a slew of examples of headlines published in the space of a few months in 2018 and 2019 where the concept of nervous breakdown was applied to Brexit Britain, Spain, China, Russia, Australia, and Ireland, among others.

75. The nation, Hobsbawm reminds us, is in fact a very recent invention (*Nations and Nationalism since 1780*).

76. Gellner, *Nationalism*, 8.

77. Agnew, "The Territorial Trap."

78. Ludden, "Maps in the Mind," 1058.

79. Massey, "Geography on the Agenda," 10–11.

80. Longo, *The Politics of Borders*, 50; Jones, *Violent Borders*, 155. Jones notes the irony in the name of the United Nations, which is in fact run by and through sovereign states.

81. Garfield, *On the Map*, 160.

82. My inspiration here is the felicitous title of a 1998 article by Matthew Sparke ("The Map That Roared") on contemporary Canada.

83. Kosonen, "Maps, Newspapers, and Nationalism," 97.

84. Jacobs, "Meet the Maiden Hidden Inside."

85. Prescott, *Political Frontiers and Boundaries*, 110.

86. Fall, *Drawing the Line*, 17.

87. Fall, "Artificial States?," 140.

88. Fall, "Artificial States?," 143.

89. Wood, *Rethinking the Power of Maps*, 33.

90. Fall, "Artificial States?," 143.

91. Robert Lloyd ("The Caprivi Strip of Namibia," 69) notes that the shape of states in West Africa, often narrow and deep, reflects European colonial efforts to tap into interior markets. It is important nonetheless to bear in mind the complex history of these borders. As Achille Mbembe writes, views of African boundaries as having been imposed by colonialism tends to ignore local imaginaries and autochthonous practices of space. If boundaries inherited from colonization were not defined by Africans themselves, it does not necessarily mean that they were entirely arbitrary (Mbembe, *At the Edge of the World*, 261–64).

92. Not only are they mobile, but natural features are also cartographically and discursively created. Rivers may seem unambiguous in the political imagination and appear in the bluest of hues on maps, but in reality they may be shallow, diminutive, meandering, or swamplike.

93. Cunningham, "Necrotone." On the notion of ecosystem, John Prescott noted that "even if the changes in vegetation, climate, drainage, elevation, structure, mor-

phology, and geology could each be reduced to a single line, these lines would not coincide with each other" (*Political Frontiers and Boundaries*, 109).

94. On international peace parks and transnational conservation areas, see Büscher, *Transforming the Frontier*.

95. In their introduction to a collection on partitions, Dubnov and Robson write that "one notable aspect of the rhetoric of partition is its frequent naturalization through a language of biology and science." They note in particular the "much-repeated medical metaphor depicting partition as a surgery" (Dubnov and Robson, "Drawing the Line, Writing beyond It," 4).

96. See International Boundary Commission, http://www.internationalboundarycom mission.org.

97. France's national animal is the lowly rooster, but it is imagined nonetheless to embody certain national qualities. The French will joke about the rooster's crowing on a pile of manure—a tongue-in-cheek acknowledgment of a national arrogance that is not always warranted.

98. Ritvo, *The Platypus and the Mermaid*, 45.

99. Ritvo, *The Platypus and the Mermaid*, 72.

100. Fall and Matthey, "De plantes dignes et d'invasions barbares," 634. See also Tamminen (*Biogenetic Paradoxes of the Nation*) on the contemporary concept of "national genetic sovereignty."

101. Fall, *Drawing the Line*, 251. In the course of my research in the Russian Far East, I heard similar narratives about Siberian tigers that weave in and out of the Russia-China border (Billé and Humphrey, *On the Edge*, 226–27).

102. Liisa Malkki has, for instance, drawn attention to the belief about the sacredness of "national soil" that naturalizes the relationship between people and land ("National Geographic"). Dirk Moses also points to the ways in which botanical metaphors express a similar linkage, underscored by the language of "uprooting" from native lands in which people live ("Partitions, Hostages, Transfer," 263).

103. On the latter, see introduction to the collection by Billé and Urbansky, *Yellow Perils*, 1–34.

104. Storey, *Territories*, 88.

105. Lang Ho, "World in Motion/The Other Final," 236. However, stereotypes can evolve. Jews are stereotyped in the United States as nerdy and unathletic; yet many of basketball's early stars were Jewish. See Stark, *When Basketball Was Jewish*.

106. Billig, *Banal Nationalism*.

107. Packaged by consultants and PR agencies, and utilizing similar tools as corporations, nation-branding exercises began in the early 2000s to distill the qualities and virtues of countries into easily digestible sound bites. As Quin Slobodian notes, "A famous early example of nation branding was Britain, where the idea of Cool Britannia became closely linked to Tony Blair and New Labour after 1997. Another was Hong Kong, which crafted a campaign billing itself as Asia's World City, launched in 2001. Uniquely Singapore was launched in 2004, Incredible India in 2005" (*Crack-Up Capitalism*, 182–83).

108. Garfield, *On the Map*, 162.

109. Ramaswamy, "Maps and Mother Goddesses in Modern India," 97.

110. See, for instance, Nash, "Remapping the Body/Land"; Lewes, *Nudes from No-where*; and Rose, *Feminism and Geography*. As I discuss in chapter 5, Black and brown, queer, and differently abled bodies are routinely coded as monstrous—offering a potential for thinking about territorial sovereignty differently.

111. On geographical features and bodily organs, see Fall, "Embodied Geographies, Naturalised Boundaries," 665–66. On the geographic and the pornographic, see Edney, "Mapping Empires, Mapping Bodies," 85.

112. Fall, *Drawing the Line*, 653. The coinage of *gynocartography* is attributable to Darby Lewes (*Nudes from Nowhere*).

113. Das, *Life and Words*, 55.

114. Enloe, *Bananas, Beaches, and Bases*, 87.

115. Kauanui, *Paradoxes of Hawaiian Sovereignty*, 113–14.

116. Das, *Life and Words*, 13.

117. Fluri and Lehr, *The Carpetbaggers of Kabul*, 14.

118. Ramaswamy, "Maps and Mother Goddesses in Modern India," 104.

119. Agulhon, *Marianne into Battle*.

120. Harvey, "The City as a Body Politic," 32.

121. Branch, *The Cartographic State*, 150. Branch adds that the emphasis in the 1790 reorganization of the country into *départements* was on equal area (defined in terms of travel time) rather than rectilinear shape (161).

122. Fall, *Drawing the Line*, 19–20.

123. Dunlop, *Cartophilia*, 60. Germans disagreed on the merits of rivers, mountains, and other three-dimensional geographic features. Instead, they interpreted a natural border to mean a "line of cultural demarcation between human popula-tions based on barriers of language, ethnicity, or history" (52–53).

124. Dunlop, *Cartophilia*, 60.

125. Foucher, *Fronts et frontières*, 97.

126. A roundish island, self-contained, self-sufficient, and without any neighbors, is the archetypal nation-state. In the typology of fictive maps, Christian Jacob writes, island maps occupy a privileged place. A utopian space, the island is "well suited to all the dreams of the microcosm" (Jacob, *The Sovereign Map*, 286). I develop this more fully in chapter 5.

127. As a self-confessed "maphead," Ken Jennings was seduced by the evocative power held by the outlines of countries and states: "Alaska was a chubby profile smiling benevolently toward Siberia. Maine was a boxing glove. Burma had a tail like a monkey. I admired roughly rectangular territories like Turkey and Portugal and Puerto Rico, which seemed sturdy and respectable to me, but not more precisely rectangular places like Colorado or Utah, whose geometric perfection made them false, uneasy additions to the national map" (*Maphead*, 4–5).

128. Francaviglia, *The Shape of Texas*, 18.

129. Francaviglia, *The Shape of Texas*, 30.

130. Foucault, discussing the writings of Alexandre Le Maitre, noted that "a good country is one that . . . must have the form of a circle, and the capital must be right at the center of the circle" (*Security, Territory, Population*, 13–14, cited in Longo, *The Politics of Borders*, 110).

131. Gibbs, *The Poetics of Mind*, 225.

132. Moronuki, "The Unreasonable Effectiveness of Metaphor."

133. Francaviglia, *The Shape of Texas*, 30.

134. Stein, *Developmental Time, Cultural Space*, 7.

135. Ozturk, Krehm, and Vouloumanos, "Sound Symbolism in Infancy."

136. The experiment was repeated in 2001 by Vilayanur Ramachandran and Edward Hubbard with American college undergraduates and Tamil speakers in India using the words *kiki* and *bouba*. In both groups, 95 to 98 percent selected the curvy shape as *bouba* and the jagged one as *kiki*.

137. Pareidolia resembles in this sense *cartocacoethes*, a term coined by John Krygier to denote the "mania, uncontrollable urge, compulsion or itch to see maps everywhere." Both psychological conditions cause the mind to perceive meaning where it does not exist. Krygier, cited in Edney, *Cartography*, 62.

138. Francaviglia, *The Shape of Texas*, 69.

139. Francaviglia, *The Shape of Texas*, 31.

140. Francaviglia, *The Shape of Texas*, 18–19.

141. Putz, *Metaphor and National Identity*. Recently, a far-right Hungarian commentator referred to contemporary Hungary as a "mutilated, blood-soaked remainder of the homeland" (Balogh, "A New Declaration of War").

142. Today, the territory of the Eastern Borderlands (Kresy), which included the major cities of Lviv, Vilnius, and Grodno, is divided between Ukraine, Belarus, and Lithuania. The Eastern Borderlands are still home to a Polish minority, and historical memory of the region is maintained by many.

143. Personal communication with anthropologist Ivan Peshkov.

144. Two weeks before Putin's annexationist speech, a map had already appeared on *Russia Today*, depicting Crimea as part of Novorossiya (New Russia). Seegel, "Any Lessons Learned?," 125.

145. Dunn, *No Path Home*, 27.

146. Svyatenkov, "Nyneshnyaya Rossiya." The historical and cultural entanglement of Russia and Ukraine made the loss of the latter extremely traumatic. The Central Asian republics, by contrast, did not cause similar phantom pains in spite of their much larger territorial footprint.

147. Bachelard, *La poétique de l'espace*, 32–33.

148. Balibar, "La forme nation," 126.

149. Garfield, *On the Map*, 429.

150. Lines and motifs tattooed on the bodies of the Mortlock group of the Middle Caroline Islands in the western Pacific were used to represent the arrangement of islands and archipelagos (Harvey, *The History of Topographical Maps*, 29–31). National and state outlines are also common tattoos in contemporary Europe, the United States, and elsewhere, as a way to display corporeal belonging. In the novel *Dolly City*, by the Israeli novelist Orly Castel-Bloom, a mother makes incisions on the back of her adopted son in the shape of the country's map—a symptom of nationalist mapping turning into pathological obsession (Wallach, "Trapped in Mirror-Images," 364).

151. Francaviglia, *The Shape of Texas*, 66.

152. Wallach, "Trapped in Mirror-Images," 364.

153. Toal, *Near Abroad*, 46.

154. Leanne Betasamosake Simpson speaks, for instance, of maps elders "carried in their bodies as two-dimensional representations of the networks they live and their parents and grandparents lived" (Simpson, *As We Have Always Done*, 16).

155. Nail, *Theory of the Border*, 37.

156. Sobchack, *Carnal Thoughts*, 73.

157. Sobchack, *Carnal Thoughts*, 73, emphasis in the original.

158. Haggard, "From Bodily Sensations to Sense of Self."

159. See discussion in King, *Mapping Reality*, 76–77.

160. Gibbs, *The Poetics of Mind*, 1994, 10.

161. Searle, "Metaphor," 88.

162. Searle, "Metaphor," 99.

163. Searle, "Metaphor," 84.

164. Searle, "Metaphor," 98.

165. Gibbs, *The Poetics of Mind*, 5.

166. Searle, "Metaphor," 98.

167. Lakoff, *Women, Fire, and Dangerous Things*, 383.

168. Lakoff, *Women, Fire, and Dangerous Things*, 381. Similarities across languages and cultures would appear to support Lakoff's thesis. This particular metaphor is found, in slightly different guises, in languages as different as Hungarian, Japanese, Chinese, Zulu, Polish, Wolof, and Tahitian.

169. Gibbs, *The Poetics of Mind*, 8–9.

170. Sharifian et al., "Culture and Language."

171. Kövecses, *Where Metaphors Come From*.

172. Lutz, *Unnatural Emotions*.

173. Lakoff, *Moral Politics*, 31.

174. Oushakine, *The Patriotism of Despair*, 125.

175. Keller, *Refiguring Life*, xi–xii.

176. Yu, "The Chinese Heart," 148.

177. Aretxaga, *States of Terror*, 201–3.

178. Thibodeau and Boroditsky, "Metaphors We Think With." Similarly, vocabulary borrowed from war and violence to frame cybercrimes tends to "activate our imaginations" in certain ways and affect risk perception. "The use of this terminology is harmful," Alice Hutchings argues, insofar as "executing code is not a direct analogy to a violent or aggressive act" (*The Amplification of Online Deviancy*, 82).

179. Boyer, "Human Cognition and Cultural Evolution."

180. Zinken and Musolff, "A Discourse-Centred Perspective."

181. In *Sovereignty in China*, Carrai demonstrates that if the Chinese neologism for *sovereignty* only appeared in the nineteenth century, it does not mean that Chinese international law is merely a Chinese variation on a European grand narrative.

182. Le Breton, *Anthropologie du corps et modernité*, 84.

183. Boyer, "Human Cognition and Cultural Evolution," 217–18.

CHAPTER 3. TERRITORIAL PHANTOM PAINS

Epigraph: Borges, "Epílogo," 146–47.

1. Benjamin, "Moscow Diary," 50–51. The SRF, or RSFSR ([Russian] Soviet [Federative] Socialist Republic) was the precursor to the Soviet Union (USSR), 1922–90.

2. A similar situation is reported by anthropologist Tone Bringa in the context of the war in Bosnia-Herzegovina, where maps played a dominant role. Printed in newspapers and displayed on daily televised news bulletins, maps and outlines were also discussed in the country's living rooms and coffee shops. "For most Bosnians and Herzegovinians, the maps represented a new way of imagining belonging and perceiving the political landscape." They "exposed people to alternative spatial logics and which spatial logics a person adopted depended on one's ethnicity as well as where one lived in Bosnia-Herzegovina" (Bringa, "From Boundaries to Borders," 225).

3. Widdis, "Russia as Space," 30.

4. With Russia's invasion of Ukraine, this equivalence is finally being challenged in academia. The Center for European, Russian, and Eurasian Studies is considering changing its name—challenging the rationale behind listing just one country by name (Russia), in a geographical remit spanning two continents and reaching from the Atlantic to the Pacific (Prince, "Moscow's Invasion of Ukraine").

5. Toal, *Near Abroad*, 251. An important part of Russia's rationale has been the notion that its conationals were stranded across the border, in temporarily occupied historically indigenous territories—a narrative far from exclusive to Russia. See Moses, "Partitions, Hostages, Transfer," 264.

6. This also tapped into Russia's desire to reestablish itself as a world power and to reemerge from the humiliation of post-Soviet collapse (Dunn, *No Path Home*, 27).

7. In a blog post, Pavel Svyatenkov argues that Russia has become a stump (*obrubok*) of the former USSR, a shell without content (*obolochka bez soderzhania*). Russia has failed to acquire its own symbols and holidays, maintaining those of its former incarnation, but without the other republics it is merely its defective heir (*ego nepolnotsennyi naslednik*; Svyatenkov, "Nyneshnyaya Rossia").

8. The impossibility of reintegrating the missing limb, as the status of Russia's war on Ukraine as of late 2024 suggests, may transform into the resignation to cut it off completely (see Ries, "Cruel Speech"). Both strategies, while diametrically opposed, effectively seek to achieve bodily integrity at all costs.

9. Toal, *Near Abroad*, 3.

10. Pew Research Center, "Europeans Divided." Hungarian post-1945 political identity debates have been largely framed around the idea of a territorial loss conceptualized as mutilation. See, for example, Zeidler, *Ideas on Territorial Revision in Hungary*; Putz, *Metaphor and National Identity*; Musolff, *National Conceptualisations of the Body Politic*. In an interview of Vladimir Putin by Tucker Carlson, the Russian president discusses Hungarian territorial losses and leaves the door open as to whether Hungary may in the future seek to reintegrate territories lost to Ukraine (Carlson, "Interview to Tucker Carlson").

11. As he added, "We're only demanding that which was taken from us. If Poland had not experienced the years between 1939 and 1945, it would today be a country of 66 million if you look at the demographic data" (*Deutsche Welle*, "Voting Debate").

12. The afterlives of former borders thus reemerge in a host of social practices such as voting behavior (see von Löwis, "Phantom Borders").

13. Ramaswamy, "Maps and Mother Goddesses in Modern India," 98.

14. Yıldırım, "Space, Loss and Resistance," 442.

15. Above I discussed Russian forms of nostalgia for the loss of the Soviet Union. Similar feelings are described by Hakan Yavuz in the case of Turkey. As Turkey became more secular, a sense of emptiness ensued, and its long Ottoman past provided a seemingly boundless reservoir of "experiences, lessons, possibilities, and imaginings about a past path traveled that now is being rediscovered for the future" (Yavuz, *Nostalgia for the Empire*, 2).

16. Chung, *Domestic Politics, International Bargaining*, 6–9.

17. Ivy, *Discourses of the Vanishing*, 10.

18. Green, *Notes from the Balkans*, 136.

19. Stewart, *On Longing*, 23.

20. On architectural palimpsests, see Huyssen, *Present Pasts*; Leshem, "Repopulating the Emptiness"; and Navaro-Yashin, *The Make-Believe Space*.

21. Green, "A Sense of Border," 585. This is especially true in the case of frontiers where, according to J. R. Prescott, even after the region becomes settled, it continues to "partake of the frontier characteristic" (*Political Frontiers and Boundaries*, 39).

22. See Brown, *A Biography of No Place*.

23. Lattimore, *Pivot of Asia*.

24. Nianshen Song writes that Chinese, Korean, and Japanese scholars all sought to rewrite history in order to justify an exclusive sovereign claim over Manchuria. In Japan, the school of "Manchurian-Korean history" (*mansenshi*) formed a crucial part of Japanese Oriental historiography. In response, Chinese historians initiated historical studies of northeast China (*dongbeishi*), while Korean historians also sought to revive Korean national spirit in Manchuria (Song, *Making Borders in Modern East Asia*, 8).

25. Kim, "The Emergence of Siberia," 307.

26. Koreans also share numerous cultural and linguistic affinities with the Manchu as well as other groups in the region, such as the Mongols.

27. In the late 1930s, Japan implemented a policy to relocate peasants to Manchuria (Park, "Korean Manchuria," 196). The majority of these relocated Koreans were landless peasants who "escaped poverty and debt and came to Manchuria to seek new land or job opportunities" (195).

28. This negative image acts as an apt spatial metaphor for the traumatic events of World War II. I am grateful to Professor Song-Yong Park for drawing my attention to this phantasmatic doppelgänger.

29. Schmid, "Looking North toward Manchuria."

30. Song, *Making Borders in Modern East Asia*, 216.

31. Yamamuro contests the term *puppet state* and argues that the horrifying details of mass extermination by the Japanese army might better deserve the name of "Auschwitz state" (*Manchuria under Japanese Dominion*, 4).

32. Itoh, *Japanese War Orphans in Manchuria.*

33. Sixty thousand Japanese remained in Manchuria after the war. In the 1950s, half of them were repatriated. For the remaining thirty thousand, repatriation resumed in the early 1980s.

34. Young, *Japan's Total Empire*, 5. As Yukiko Koga points out, the loss of the utopia linked to Manchuria cannot be mourned since it is inextricably linked to World War II imperial violence. At the same time, Manchuria is the focus of a veritable obsession, with an "enormous and persistent cultural production of books, films, comics, and commentaries on Japan's Manchuria," while the facts of war are silenced. As a result, we witness an "interplay of amnesia and obsession" whereby Japanese repatriates' loss is fused with feelings of guilt (Koga, *Inheritance of Loss*, 74–75).

35. Duara, *Sovereignty and Authenticity*, 62.

36. Tamanoi, *Memory Maps*, 2.

37. Bassin, *Imperial Visions*, 2.

38. Bassin, *Imperial Visions*, 8.

39. See Billé and Humphrey, *On the Edge*, 228–29.

40. As Mark Elliott points out, the name "Manju" never gained acceptance as an orthodox place name in Chinese, nor did it acquire a geographical sense in Manchu itself ("The Limits of Tartary," 605).

41. Fairbank, *The Chinese World Order*; Tu, "Cultural China"; Fiskesjö, "On the 'Raw' and the 'Cooked.'"

42. Potter, "Theoretical and Conceptual Perspectives," 240.

43. Callahan, *China*, 92–93.

44. Callahan, *China*, 105; see fig. 3.3. These cartographic practices are not exclusive to China. Catherine Dunlop mentions similar usage in turn-of-the-century France, where most classroom wall maps continued to include lost provinces in representations of French national territory: "Alsace-Lorraine was simply colored purple, to signify mourning, or white, to signify absence" (Dunlop, *Cartophilia*, 120). For similar representations in Thailand, see Winichakul, *Siam Mapped*; and Strate, *The Lost Territories.*

45. Prescott, *Political Frontiers and Boundaries*, 14.

46. Logvinchuk, "Val Chingis-Khana."

47. Béatrice von Hirschhausen terms "phantom borders" those lines left behind by "defunct imperial territorialities." Like specters, she writes, they are unpredictable by nature: they may suddenly materialize on maps as different voting behaviors or as forms and modes of social action and practices, but may remain invisible in many other realms (von Hirschhausen, "De l'intérêt heuristique du concept de fantôme géographique," 107). See also von Hirschhausen et al., *Phantom Grenzen*; von Löwis, "Phantom Borders."

48. Szmagalska-Follis, "Repossession," 337.

49. Similarly inspired by Miéville's novel, Deborah Cowen makes a germane point in an article on urban infrastructure ("The City and the City"). Her reflections on what Miéville terms "grosstopicality"—the status of being in the same place in absolute space, but in entirely different urban worlds—echo the racialized layers of spatial experience I explore in chapter 5.

50. Elizabeth Cullen Dunn proposes the term "insiles" rather than "exiles," given that the vast majority of refugees live in camps that are located within the borders of their own country (*No Path Home*, 3). Migrants, writes Alison Mountz, "haunt the international state system as ghostly figures out of place, in various states of not belonging, refusing either to adapt to the territorial desires of nation-states or to disappear from view" (*The Death of Asylum*, 222).

51. In *White Sight*, Nicholas Mirzoeff addresses precisely these radicalized forms of seeing and unseeing, arguing that "white sight" is a learned operating system created collectively. Mirzoeff calls the systemic failure to notice these entrenched politics of vision "blanking." Ways of seeing also vary, as Denis Cosgrove has noted, "with individuals, genders, cultures and so on, and there are histories and historical geographies of seeing" (*Geography and Vision*, 5).

52. Miéville, "The City and the City," 80.

53. Navaro-Yashin, *The Make-Believe Space*, 13, 15.

54. On this aspect of ruins, see Navaro-Yashin, *The Make-Believe Space*, 147–52. See also Gordillo, *Rubble*. In *Imperial Debris*, Ann Laura Stoler notes that rot, like debris, ruin, and trash, "contains an active substance. It is hard to wipe out. Like debris, it is not where one always expects it to be. Nor is it always immediately visible" (x). A phantasmatic layer, it recalls the map of the Soviet Union discussed in chapter 1 that conceals the reality rotting underneath it.

55. Gordon, *Ghostly Matters*, xix. "In the venerable U.S. tradition of naming places for the people who have been driven from them," writes Daniel Immerwahr, we have the example of Oklahoma, a Choctaw word meaning "red people" (*How to Hide an Empire*, 44).

56. Alexseev, "Migration, Hostility, and Ethnopolitical Mobilization," 111. To an extent, the surviving usage of these Chinese names has been due to the difficulty for Chinese speakers of pronouncing the Russian names. A long-term resident of Blagoveshchensk, Lisha, uses the abbreviated form Bu-shi (布市), that is, "B town," as she feels that using the Chinese "Hailanpao" is not culturally sensitive.

57. Until recently, official PRC maps indicated transliterated names only, whereas maps published in unofficial publications almost always used the Chinese names instead of the poorly known Russian versions (Ministry of Natural Resources, China, "Circular of the Ministry of Natural Resources on Printing and Distributing the 'Specifications for the Display of Public Map Contents'").

58. The Manchu in China number ten million and are the largest minority after the Zhuang, at sixteen million. In terms of culture and language, however, they have become virtually assimilated to the Han majority, except for a small offshoot community descending from a Manchu garrison in Xinjiang. With the exception of this forty-thousand-strong group, the Xibo (锡伯), the Manchu language is essentially moribund.

59. Boym, *The Future of Nostalgia*, 33.
60. Dyatlov, "'The Blagoveshchensk Utopia'"; Qi, *Heihe Shihua*, 76–79; Zatsepine, "The Blagoveshchensk Massacre of 1900."
61. See Massumi, *Parables for the Virtual*; and Ngai, *Ugly Feelings*.
62. Dyatlov, "'The Blagoveshchensk Utopia.'"
63. The will to eliminate the phantomic presence of others in the context of postwar Bosnia saw houses burned down, their remnants hauled away, and the infrastructure such as pipes dug out of the ground so that "no trace remained of the people who had lived there" (Bakke, *The Likeness*, 3).
64. A similar argument might be made about the victims of European colonization, particularly in the Americas, where the presence of the settlers forcibly silences indigenous populations. See, for instance, Gastón Gordillo's point about the phantomlike presence of Indians in Argentina (Gordillo, *Rubble*, 41). The spectral historical Chinese presence in the Russian Far East also has echoes in displaced populations elsewhere in the world. Elizabeth Dunn's work on internal displaced persons (IDPS) illuminates the way in which IDPS constitute bodily reminders of territorial phantoms (*No Path Home*). As she also writes, in an article coauthored with Martin Frederiksen, camps are themselves "often inhabited by the ghosts of the villages and towns the residents have left behind" (Dunn and Frederiksen, "Uncanny Valleys," 21).
65. The Sixty-Four Villages East of the River were a group of Manchu and Han Chinese–inhabited villages located on the north bank of the Amur River, opposite Heihe, and on the east bank of the Zeya River, opposite Blagoveshchensk. Recognized as Chinese enclaves in Russia according to the Aigun Treaty, they were annexed by Russia during the Boxer Rebellion. Their inhabitants were expelled and suffered the same fate as the Chinese living in Blagoveshchensk. The town of Aihui itself was destroyed during the events, making the location of the museum symbolically potent.
66. Dyatlov, "'The Blagoveshchensk Utopia,'" 16.
67. Derrida, *Spectres de Marx*, 31.
68. This echoes in some ways the work by Heonik Kwon on ghosts in Vietnam. In *After the Massacre*, Kwon analyzes how tragic events such as the massacre of civilians in the villages of My Lai and Ha My have been assimilated into everyday ritual life, and how the restless dead—those not properly buried or commemorated—continue to exert their presence over the living.
69. Derrida, "I Have a Taste for the Secret," 49.
70. Navaro-Yashin, *The Make-Believe Space*, 13.
71. Billé and Urbansky, *Yellow Perils*. For an extended discussion of this in the case of Mongolia, see Billé, *Sinophobia*.
72. Carter, *Creating a Chinese Harbin*.
73. Carter, *Creating a Chinese Harbin*, 12.
74. On these "past futures," see Pulford, *Past Progress*.
75. Manchuria, Nianshen Song notes, was also symbolically crucial to claims of progress and modernity for China, Korea, and Japan. For China, it was integral to its state formation. For Japan, Manchuria was a testing ground of the Japanese

dream for building a pan-Asianist empire. "With multiple players competing for and transforming the space in turns and together, the history of this frontier was synchronous to the winding path of East Asian history as it twisted its way through the twentieth century" (Song, *Making Borders in Modern East Asia*, 10–11).

76. Dostoyevsky, *A Writer's Diary*, 1374.

77. As recounted by a Chinese friend at school in Guangzhou in the 1980s. The entomological metaphor has also been used in the context of prepartition India, described as having to choose between a unified Indian state or a "maimed, mutilated and moth-eaten" territorial entity.

78. Borneman, *Belonging in the Two Berlins*, 1.

79. Appadurai, "Caressing the Phantom Limb"; Bodin, "Russian Geopolitical Discourse"; Gaidar, *Collapse of an Empire*; Greenberg, "Divided Lands, Phantom Limbs"; von Hirschhausen et al., *Phantom Grenzen*; von Löwis, "Phantom Borders."

80. As S. Weir Mitchell noted at the time, in the vast majority of cases, an individual losing a limb will experience the phenomenon and "carry about with him a constant or inconstant phantom of the missing member, a sensory ghost of that much of himself . . . faintly felt at times, but ready to be called up to his perception by a blow, a touch, or a change of wind" (*Injuries of Nerves and Their Consequences*, 348).

81. Grosz, *Volatile Bodies*, 70.

82. Bishop, "Dreams, Phantom Limbs and Virtual Reality."

83. Bishop, "Dreams, Phantom Limbs and Virtual Reality." Vivian Sobchack facetiously writes that prosthetic users like herself are frequently startled to read about "all the hidden powers that their prostheses apparently exercise both in the world and in the imaginations of cultural theorists" ("A Leg to Stand On," 20). As she notes in an earlier text, it is especially startling, she says, "since my prosthetic leg can barely stand on its own and certainly will never go out dancing without me" (Sobchack, *Carnal Thoughts*, 205).

84. Melzack, "Phantom Limbs, the Self and the Brain," 9.

85. Melzack, "Phantom Limbs, the Self and the Brain," 2.

86. Sacks, foreword to *Phantoms in the Brain*, vii.

87. Melzack, "Phantom Limbs, the Self and the Brain," 3.

88. Ramachandran and Hirstein, "The Perception of Phantom Limbs," 1606.

89. Ramachandran and Blakeslee, *Phantoms in the Brain*, 46.

90. Brugger, "Phantomology," 8. See also Ramachandran and Blakeslee, *Phantoms in the Brain*, 270.

91. Diamond, "The Phantom Limb," 5.

92. A study by Simmel ("The Reality of Phantom Sensations") reported phantoms in 20 percent of amputees under the age of two, in 25 percent of children between two and four, 61 percent between four and six, 75 percent between six and eight, and 100 percent in children older than eight.

93. Ramachandran and Blakeslee, *Phantoms in the Brain*, 46.

94. Geoch and Ramachandran, "The Appearance of New Phantom Fingers," 95.

95. Hill, "Phantom Limb Pain," 134; Richardson, "Phantom Limb Pain," 151.

96. Sacks, foreword to *Phantoms in the Brain*, viii.

97. Grosz, *Volatile Bodies*, 73.

98. Lacan, "The Mirror-Phase as Formative."
99. Schilder (*The Image and Appearance*, 197–98), discussed in Grosz, *Volatile Bodies*, 32–33. On the basis of vestibular experiments and observations of amputees, Schilder goes so far as to suggest that the body itself may be a phantom (*The Image and Appearance*, 297, cited in Weiss, *Body Images*, 35).
100. Diamond, "The Phantom Limb," 6.
101. French, "The Political Economy of Injury," 69.
102. French, "The Political Economy of Injury," 80–81.
103. See Terry, *Attachments to War*; and Açıksöz, *Sacrificial Limbs*.
104. O'Connor, "'Fractions of Men,'" 744.
105. In his work, visual artist Kader Attia has explored this parallel between bodily wounds and cultural wounds, notably in the context of colonization, genocide, or slavery. As he argues in a television interview with France 24, the more a society tries to repress these traumas, the more specters and phantoms will continue to haunt it, accruing force in the process (Simon, "Kader Attia"). See also the work of Alexa Wright, another artist who has explored the visuals of phantom limbs. See in particular her exhibition called *After Image* (Alexa Wright, *After Image*, 1997, https://www.alexawright.com/after-image).
106. Anthropologist Matteo Benussi points out that the loss of Istria has not led to phantom pains for Italy. He suggests, correctly in my opinion, that it is because Italy's own national shape was still in flux at the time of the loss (personal communication).
107. Dunn, *No Path Home*, 175.
108. Shteyngart, "Out of My Mouth."
109. O'Leary, "Partition," 29. The term *vivisection* to refer to partition is credited to Mahatma Gandhi—the carving-up of the body politic and bloody dismemberment of the motherland eventually leading to phantom limbs in the nation's identity (Greenberg, "Divided Lands, Phantom Limbs," 7–8). Writing in the context of Cyprus, Rebecca Bryant notes that the mapping of the fissure in the body politic onto bodies, and especially the analogy of partition to a wound, has molded interpretations of history and imaginations of political futures ("Partitions of Memory," 337).
110. Krishna, "Oppressive Pasts and Desired Futures," 858.
111. Krishna, "Oppressive Pasts and Desired Futures," 858, 859.
112. Krishna, "Oppressive Pasts and Desired Futures," 865.
113. Etkind, "Post-Soviet Russia," 155–56.
114. Harris, *Untimely Matter in the Time of Shakespeare*, 4; Bryant, "History's Remainders," 683.
115. Reeves, "Fixing the Border," 911. See also Fortna, "Change in the School Maps"; and Ramaswamy, "Midnight's Line."
116. Dubnov and Robson, "Drawing the Line," 27, 2.
117. Dubnov and Robson, "Drawing the Line," 25.
118. Dubnov and Robson, "Drawing the Line," 15.
119. Nasar, "Lines of Control," 10. Stuart Elden also reminds us that rape, "while today having primarily a sexual sense, comes from the Latin word *rapere* meaning to seize, to abduct, to capture" ("Outside Territory," 133).

on, *Imagined Communities*, 7.

na, "Cartographic Anxiety," 509.

ue creation of India through territorial loss, Abraham writes, would nonetheless see the trope of the "phantom limb of territorial nostalgia" run through Indian literature and foreign policies for decades to come (*How India Became Territorial*, 71). There was, Butalia also notes, "a deep sense of shame, almost of inadequacy, that India had allowed a part of itself, a part of its body, to be lost to the other nation" (*The Other Side of Silence*, 149).

123. Kristeva, *Pouvoirs de l'horreur*. Arjun Appadurai speaks of the common forms of bodily violence where people are mutilated, their arms or legs cut off, in a politics of amputation that predominantly targets the stranger, the migrant, the minor. "This form of political violence stops short of killing so as to leave the scarred body behind, a living victim of sacrifice. . . . The victims were literally left with phantom limbs while they were themselves converted into phantoms of national memory. The phantom limb of the minority or the migrant is a reminder of the place of amputation in the imagining of the national body" (Appadurai, "Caressing the Phantom Limb"). See also Salih Açıksöz's *Sacrificial Limbs* for an analysis of the place of the prosthetic in the context of contemporary Turkey.

124. Butalia, *The Other Side of Silence*, 34–35. Relatedly, it made the recovery of women held by the "other" side a point of concern, with women in their reproductive years being prioritized over old women or little children (Das, *Life and Words*, 26).

125. Prescott, *Political Frontiers and Boundaries*, 110.

126. See further discussion in Lee (*Orientals*, 109). The same resistance was encountered with respect to Alaska, with Andrew Johnson's administration reluctant to integrate "Exquimaux fellow citizens." In the end, writes historian Daniel Immerwahr, the deal went through because "there weren't that many 'Exquimaux,' and there was quite a lot of Alaska" (*How to Hide an Empire*, 78). Similarly, in the case of Mexico, the United States "annexed the thinly populated northern part of Mexico (including present-day California, Utah, New Mexico, and Arizona) but let the populous southern part go. This carefully drawn border gave the United States, as one newspaper put it, 'all the territory of value that we can get without taking the people'" (Immerwahr, *How to Hide an Empire*, 77).

127. Bassin, *Imperial Visions*, 14.

128. Bassin, *Imperial Visions*, 14.

129. Bayne and Levy, "Amputees by Choice."

130. Proprioception is the sense of the relative position of neighboring parts of the body and strength of effort being employed in movement.

131. Bennett, "It's but a Flesh Wound," 158.

132. Elliott, "A New Way to Be Mad."

133. Understandably, doctors have been resistant to the idea of amputating a healthy limb—a surgical operation that would make the patient disabled. In 2000, Robert Smith, a British surgeon at Falkirk and District Royal Infirmary in Scotland, decided to amputate the legs of two patients at their request, and was planning to carry out a third amputation before he was stopped by the hospital's trust.

134. Bennett, "It's but a Flesh Wound," 158.

135. Diamond, "The Phantom Limb." The expressed conviction of being in the wrong body echoes the discourse of transsexuals who also locate in surgical procedures the possibility of corrective realignment. In his discussion of the many reverberations between these two desires, feminist scholar Alexandre Baril ("Transformations corporelles et analyses intersectionnelles") suggests the notion of "transableism" (*transcapacité*) may be a useful approach to understanding apotemnophilia.

136. Bennett, "It's but a Flesh Wound," 159.

137. Bennett, "It's but a Flesh Wound," 159.

138. Diamond, "The Phantom Limb."

139. Brown, "Somatoparaphrenia."

140. Individuals who lose considerable weight find themselves still enveloped in the skin of their larger phantom selves, a "cruel, perpetual reminder" enveloping them "like a living shroud" (Lyall, "Losing 650 Pounds").

141. O'Leary, "Partition," 31.

142. Bassin, *Imperial Visions*, 57.

143. Bassin, *Imperial Visions*, 65–66.

144. Moustafine, "The Harbin Connection," 80. A similar situation is seen in the case of the Tibetan Government in Exile in Dharamsala. See, for instance, McConnell, *Rehearsing the State*. Writing about the western Sahara, anthropologist Alice Wilson suggests that exile may also have a transformative role, serving "as an incubator for transformations that perhaps, outside exile, might have struggled to take off" (*Sovereignty in Exile*, 10).

145. Boym, *The Future of Nostalgia*, xvi.

146. Boym, *The Future of Nostalgia*, 353.

147. The location of important cultural sites outside of a state's borders is not a situation unique to Russia. Serbian cultural geography includes numerous places that are not found in present-day Serbia. Serbian territorial claims concerning Kosovo hinged upon the cultural and historical significance of that province, but other places in the region—in Croatia, Bosnia-Herzegovina, Albania, and even Greece— are mentioned in Serb folk songs as well (White, "Place and Its Role in Serbian Identity"). This is also the case in India, where Bengal has traditionally been seen as the "heartland of India" (Abraham, *How India Became Territorial*, 36–37).

148. Juxtaposing the manipulation of older borders by political actors and spiritism séances, Béatrice von Hirschhausen notes that instrumentalizations can easily escape control and take on a life of their own ("De l'intérêt heuristique du concept de fantôme géographique," 108).

149. See also Brahm and Driscoll, *Prosthetic Territories*, for other applications of this term.

150. The term *prosthetic* in fact spans a wide register, since it can index an extension, an augmentation, or an enhancement as well as an addition or replacement (Smith and Morra, introduction to *The Prosthetic Impulse*, 2). In the same volume, Marquard Smith notes that male amputees are "often presented utilizing their prosthetic limbs as model examples of the enhancing potential of human-machine synergy," whereas "letters in the archives of the Science Museum and elsewhere from female amputees emphasize the need for continued disguise"—a fascinat-

ed articulation between the two main meanings of the term *prosthetic*
Vulnerable Articulate," 54).

sing Nationalism Casts Shadow."

lexical phantom has recently been reactivated by Azerbaijan with the re-
g of one of its regions as Eastern Zangezur, thereby hinting at the existence
a Western Zangezur beyond the border. This veiled message was later made
more overtly on social media, with tweets "evoking Zangezur as a lost fragment of
a wider Azerbaijani homeland" (Broers, "Augmented Azerbaijan?").

153. Steinberg, *The Social Construction of the Ocean*, 171–72.

154. Billé, *Voluminous States*.

155. Grosz, *Volatile Bodies*, 80. This process helps explain how national accoutrements
can come to be experienced in visceral ways. Bryant and Hatay relate how Turkish
Cypriots have experienced the collapse of the Cyprus Turkish Airline (CTA) as a
physical loss, akin to the loss of a limb (*Sovereignty Suspended*, 185–87).

156. Head, *Studies in Neurology*, 606.

157. These social extensions of the body also have a formative impact on how the body
is experienced, lived, and used. The use of clothing or shoes will affect a person's
gait and posture. The wearing of glasses not only adjusts vision, it also "changes
the comportment of the head and neck and over years changes the contour of the
muscular-skeletal infrastructure" (Jain, "The Prosthetic Imagination," 41). Interestingly, so-called super-added sensations, such as the feeling that the phantom
limb is clothed, or wearing a watch, testify to the lasting inclusion of external
objects in an individual's body image (Richardson, "Phantom Limb Pain," 138).

158. Grosz, *Volatile Bodies*, 80.

159. Jennifer González uses the term "autotopography" to refer to those personal items
such as clothing or footwear that, over the years, "receive the imprint of a human
trace as the autonomy of their purely functional status is worn away by time" and
that "cannot be replaced or removed without a subversion of the physical body
itself" ("Autotopographies," 133).

160. Sobchack, "Living a 'Phantom Limb,'" 52, emphasis in original.

161. Sobchack, "Living a 'Phantom Limb,'" 62, emphasis in original.

162. Sobchack, "Living a 'Phantom Limb,'" 57.

163. Sobchack, "Living a 'Phantom Limb,'" 57.

164. Sobchack, "Living a 'Phantom Limb,'" 63.

165. See Hill, "Phantom Limb Pain," 127; Melzack, "Phantom Limbs, the Self and the
Brain," 4–5.

166. Ramachandran and Blakeslee, *Phantoms in the Brain*.

167. Sacks, *A Leg to Stand On*, 193. Inactivation can occur after an accident or a stroke.
Though intact, a limb ceases to be seen as part of the body and the self and is
simply ignored by the patient. Neglect, as it is known in neuroscientific literature, may affect a whole side of the body, which then becomes invisible to the
patient—who typically will shave, comb, or apply makeup to only one side of his
or her body. When, often after a stroke, neglect affects a single limb, that limb is
misapprehended as belonging to someone else—the patient then typically kicks it
off the bed, claiming it is another person's, often a relative's. Neglect differs from

apotemnophilia, where the patient is aware that the limb is part of her body but feels it should not be.

168. To obtain their license, London taxi drivers go through stringent training and need to pass what is referred to as "The Knowledge," a test requiring the knowledge of every single street, landmark, museum, park, police station, and school, as well as the quickest route between any two points within a six-mile radius of Charing Cross. This requires the storage of an enormous amount of data, as the area includes a total of 25,000 streets and approximately 20,000 landmarks and places of public interest.

169. Maguire, Woollett and Spiers, "London Taxi Drivers and Bus Drivers." As Victoria Pitts-Taylor notes, however, the prevailing conception of the brain as naturally plastic has its limits. Plasticity is constrained by the limited neural real estate available in the brain, and as a result, adding connections in one area appears to reduce them in others. It is also important to bear in mind that a higher number of neural connections or greater volume does not necessarily equate with greater ability. Finally, not everyone exhibits the same plastic capabilities, which suggests genetic disparities between individuals (Pitts-Taylor, *The Brain's Body*, 30).

170. Smith, "The Uncertainty of Placing," 2.

171. Feinberg, *Altered Egos*, 50.

172. Brugger, "Phantomology," 9.

173. Weiss, *Body Images*, 36. Arnold Modell goes so far as to suggest that the phenomenology of phantom limbs might be "a miscarried attempt to restore the integrity of the body image by providing hallucinatory sensory inputs"—perpetuating "painful sensation in order to support the illusion of the continuity of the self" ("The Sense of Agency," 4).

174. Sobchack, "Living a 'Phantom Limb,'" 59. In fact, as biomechanical engineer Hugh Herr explained to Jennifer Terry, bionics are so profound in their augmentation "that when a normal healthy person wears the device for more than 40 minutes and then takes it off, their own biological legs feel ridiculously heavy and awkward" (Terry, *Attachments to War*, 118).

175. Carter, *Exploring Consciousness*, 217.

176. Smith, "The Uncertainty of Placing," 2.

177. Sobchack, "Living a 'Phantom Limb,'" 55.

178. Sobchack, "Living a 'Phantom Limb,'" 55, emphasis in original.

179. Smith, "The Uncertainty of Placing," 2.

CHAPTER 4. EPIDERMIC STATES

1. In August 2023, the Chinese Ministry of Natural Resources published its yearly edition of the National Map of China, a document largely seen as the official reference regarding China's national sovereignty. In addition to the now habitual territorial claims impinging on India, Malaysia, Vietnam, the Philippines, and Taiwan, the 2023 map also depicted the inclusion of part of Russia's territory. While Bolshoi Ussuriisk Island had been divided equally between China and Russia since 2004, it appears fully within China on the new map. In the current context of

unprecedentedly excellent relations between the two countries, Russian specialists have been eager to downplay this cartographic inclusion as an insignificant oversight (Aleksandrov, "Kitai vklyuchil v svoi novye karty chast' territorii Rossii").

2. Lomanov, "Hu Jintao, mon Amur." The Amur River's islands regularly change size and location, increase, and disappear depending on water levels, thereby affecting the location of the main navigable channel, or *thalweg* (*farvater* in Russian), used as the line demarcating the international boundary. This had in fact major consequences for the resolution of the territorial dispute concerning Damansky Island in the early 1990s, when the lowering of the river levels resulted in the island becoming attached to the Chinese bank, which rendered the dispute moot (Kuhrt, *Russian Policy towards China and Japan*, 33).

3. By *Russia*, I mean here both the Russian government and a substantial section of the public. Of course, not every Russian citizen will feel similarly concerned about this particular issue.

4. Masha, interview with the author, Blagoveshchensk, April 18, 2014.

5. Chung, *Domestic Politics, International Bargaining*, 2.

6. Kuhrt, *Russian Policy towards China and Japan*, 73.

7. In the case of the Balkan wars that tore up Yugoslavia in the 1990s, Serbian claims to Bosnia-Herzegovina, Kosovo, and Macedonia are just as difficult to account for insofar as, geostrategically and economically, they are some of the least valuable territories in the Balkans (White, "Place and Its Role in Serbian Identity," 40). Similarly, in her study on the Valley of Kashmir, Ananya Kabir (*Territory of Desire*, 1) makes a similar observation that the region has emerged as a bone of contention for three nationalisms—Indian, Pakistani, and aspirant Kashmiri—in spite of being "bereft of mineral wealth" and "locked within inhospitable terrain."

8. Simmons, "Rules over Real Estate," 829.

9. Krishna, "Cartographic Anxiety," 511.

10. Abraham, *How India Became Territorial*, 142.

11. The Geospatial Information Regulation Bill, introduced in 2016, has not yet been enacted into law as of this writing. India is not alone in making it an offense to publicize incorrect maps. Argentina makes it "illegal to show a map of the country that does not include the Malvinas, the South Atlantic Islands, and the section of Antarctica that the nation claims is theirs" (Holmes, "Counter Cartographies").

12. Dabas, "Showing PoK or Arunachal Pradesh Outside India." The following statutory warning is also stamped on every foreign publication featuring a map of South Asia: "The external boundaries of India as depicted on this map are neither correct nor authentic" (Kabir, *Territory of Desire*, 9).

13. Such were some of the comments left on the *Economic Times* (Sharma, "7-Year Jail") website when the story broke.

14. Ferrari, Pasqual, and Bagnato, *A Moving Border*. See also Italian Limes, http://italianlimes.net.

15. In Russia, this protection has been ensured by the Cossacks, who from the eighteenth century have occupied, and defended, Russia's buffer zones.

16. Etkind, *Internal Colonization*, 14. These fetishized fragments are also strongly sexualized (see Jasieński, *The Legs of Izolda Morgan*). Logomaps thus frequently

align with female bodily shapes, in the same way that discursive elaborations of nationalism posit the nation as a helpless mother or daughter requiring the protection of patriotic males.

17. This condensation evokes the concept of fractals, whose operation disrupts the relation between the part and the whole, and between the edge and the body.

18. *Economist*, "The Sino-Russian Border."

19. Ramachandran and Blakeslee, *Phantoms in the Brain*, 26.

20. Similarly, American anthropologist Edmund Carpenter noticed that while the maps prepared for him by his Inuit interlocutors were highly accurate, "the only distortions appeared in areas that were hunted very intensively. These regions were drawn larger than those visited less frequently" (Lopez, *Arctic Dreams*, 289).

21. Thrift, "It's the Little Things."

22. Shotter and Billig, "A Bakhtinian Psychology," 20.

23. Diane Ackerman makes a similar point, noting that "children often draw people with big heads and hands, because that is the way their body feels to them" (*A Natural History of the Senses*, 95). A homunculus map of the geobody would similarly look very different, with some parts of the outline overemphasized. Indeed, when asked to draw their country's geobody, people will produce outlines that are deformed and not consistent in terms of ratio. My colleague Natalya Ryzhova drew for me an affective map of Russia as seen from the RFE, where she is from. In her drawing, Russia was elongated like a snake, the entire Far East and Siberia flattened into a ribbon, while Moscow was inflated and taking most of the space in the west.

24. Paterson, *How We Became Sensorimotor*, 30. The very referents of *male* and *female* also show variation due to factors such as fluctuation of hormone levels, menstruation, and other physiological changes (79).

25. Paterson, *How We Became Sensorimotor*, 27, 82.

26. Paterson, *How We Became Sensorimotor*, 65.

27. Abraham, *How India Became Territorial*, 14–15.

28. Abraham, *How India Became Territorial*, 36–37.

29. Francaviglia, *The Shape of Texas*.

30. Winichakul, *Siam Mapped*, 56.

31. Handler, *Nationalism and the Politics of Culture*, 6.

32. Mitchell, "The Limits of the State," 90.

33. Mitchell, "The Limits of the State," 94.

34. Giddens, *The Nation-State and Violence*; Agnew, "The Territorial Trap."

35. Benthien, *Skin*, 17.

36. This structural contrast also reflects an imbalance in terms of population movement. While Russians can travel to Heihe and stay there without a visa for up to thirty days, Chinese borderlanders wishing to cross to the other side are subject to a strict visa regime and to annual quotas.

37. Benthien, *Skin*, 237.

38. Mountz and Hiemstra, "Spatial Strategies for Rebordering Human Migration," 455. According to David Harvey, borders find themselves at the juncture between two different orders, the "capitalist" and the "territorial," which are driven by different motivations: "capitalists want to accumulate more capital, politicians or

state managers want to sustain or augment the power of their own state. The two logics are distinctive and in no way reducible to each other, though they are tightly interwoven" (Harvey, "The City as a Body Politic").

39. Billé and Humphrey, *On the Edge*, 240.

40. Lingis, *Excesses*, 10.

41. In the sense that the outside of the nation is another nation's inside. I am borrowing here the title of Eve Kosofsky Sedgwick's book, one of the theoretical inspirations behind this chapter.

42. Foucher, *L'obsession des frontières*, 26.

43. Donnan and Wilson, *Culture and Power at the Edges*, 15.

44. Freud, *The Ego and the Id*, 26; Grosz, *Volatile Bodies*, 34, 33.

45. Anzieu, *Le moi-peau*, 35–36.

46. Some of these nerve cells are highly sensitive to specific types of stimulation and may be "sensitive only to stroking the surface of a body part in one single direction, or at a specific frequency" (Field, *Touch*, 80).

47. As Steve Pile ("Spatialities of Skin," 65) notes, more than a container, this skin ego is "lumpy, misshapen and unevenly developed," thus reflecting the unequally distributed and uneven weight of national borders.

48. Kaplan, *Oneness and Separateness*, 102.

49. Halberstam, *Skin Shows*, 7.

50. Stewart, *On Longing*, 104.

51. Gearóid Ó Tuathail has argued that the modern geopolitical imaginary emerged at the moment when "the last pockets of unclaimed and un-stated space were surrounded and enclosed within the colonizing projects of expansionist empires and territorializing states" (*Critical Geopolitics*, 15). Sara Ahmed also notes the implicit analogy of the border as skin in the context of asylum policies in the UK, where the government has been reluctant to be seen as a "soft touch." The metaphor of soft touch, she writes, "suggests that the nation's borders and defences are like skin; they are soft, weak, porous and easily shaped or even bruised by the proximity of others" (Ahmed, *The Cultural Politics of Emotion*, 2).

52. Valeriano and Van Benthuysen, "When States Die," 1167.

53. Partem, "The Buffer System in International Relations."

54. Brunet-Jailly, "Securing Borders in Europe and North America," 101.

55. The narrow Wakhan Corridor in Afghanistan guaranteed, for instance, that the British and Russian empires would not touch at any point (Rowe, "The Wakhan Corridor," 64). Afghanistan, like Tibet, epitomized the buffer state. They were "weakly administered political entities occupying huge areas of land with little or no modern infrastructure" and in harsh environments "inhabited by fierce and belligerent native peoples" (Abraham, *How India Became Territorial*, 121).

56. As anthropologist Sarah Green argues with respect to the Balkans, border politics do not always follow a Euclidian geometry. They can also operate as fractals: "breaking fractals down into parts simply gives you more parts and more wholes; however small you break it up, each part is still a complete replication of the whole" (Green, *Notes from the Balkans*, 136). As Laura Marks notes, fractal algorithms

make a "very good model for the act of haptic criticism, because rather than staying on a flat plane . . . they become so complex that they build into depth, attaining spongelike dimensions. . . . Fractals fill up the space between two hierarchically related elements" (*Touch*, xv).

57. Martin, "Toward an Anthropology of Immunology."

58. Žižek, "Neighbors and Other Monsters." As liminal spaces, buffer zones are inherently associated with ideas of violation, pollution, contamination, aversion, and anxiety. Dixon speaks of a geopolitics of abhorrence, which for her indexes "a corporeal situatedness (more often than not sexuated and raced) to the monster that is understood to be the singular expression of the Other, the unnatural, and the abnormal, all of which have a substantial role in the fulmination of geopolitical relations" (*Feminist Geopolitics*, 114).

59. Ryzhova, "Freedoms, the State and Security," 23–25.

60. Ryzhova, "Freedoms, the State and Security," 7. Less well known is a similar situation in the United States where "a technical definition in federal regulations established in 1953 has resulted in 100-mile 'border zones,' sometimes encompassing entire states" (Guy-Ryan, "The Long History").

61. Pisano and Simonyi, "Post-Soviet or Eurasian Lands?"

62. Sartre, *L'être et le néant*, 430.

63. A similar argument might be made for the European Union's southeastern border. The EU's reluctance to accept Turkey as full member may be a way of avoiding a too intimate proximity with its radical, Muslim Other. Rather than being corporeally pressed against countries such as Iran, Iraq, and Syria, it may be preferable for the EU to retain Turkey as a buffer.

64. Bora, "Outing Texture," 98.

65. Bora, "Outing Texture," 99.

66. Sedgwick, *Novel Gazing*, 14–15.

67. Bora, "Outing Texture," 99.

68. McClintock, *Imperial Leather*, 219. As Jay Prosser has argued, "the cultural ideal of skin should be skin that forgets" ("Skin Memories," 54). Ahmed and Stacey, "Introduction: Dermographies," 2.

69. Grosz, *Volatile Bodies*, 36.

70. On liminality with respect to sites of exchange, see Douglas, *Purity and Danger*.

71. Grosz, *Volatile Bodies*, 36.

72. Serres, *The Five Senses*, 80.

73. Heyman, "Culture Theory and the US-Mexico Border"; Cunningham, "Permeabilities, Ecology and Geopolitical Boundaries."

74. Ahmed and Stacey, "Introduction: Dermographies," 2.

75. Tsing, *Friction*.

76. Navaro-Yashin, *The Make-Believe Space*.

77. Navaro-Yashin, *The Make-Believe Space*, xvi.

78. Navaro-Yashin, *The Make-Believe Space*, 20.

79. Ngai, *Ugly Feelings*, 35.

80. Anzaldúa, *Borderlands/La Frontera*, 3.

81. Pullan, "Spatial Discontinuities," 19.
82. For an excellent ethnography of human experiences in mined border zones, see Kim, "Toward an Anthropology of Landmines."
83. Díaz-Barriga and Dorsey (*Fencing in Democracy*, 11) argue that bordering manifests sovereign practices based on the state's power to perpetrate violence. Forms of violence are both ubiquitous and multifarious, including electrified fences (Jones, *Violent Borders*), the redirection of migrants through remote and desolate areas (De León, *The Land of Open Graves*), or the prevention of boats from reaching the coast (Mountz, *The Death of Asylum*).
84. In the context of the US-Mexico border, Ronald Rael (*Borderwall as Architecture*, 134) writes that fences, built with concrete and steel, are meant to tear flesh. This is by no means specific to that international border. The killing, wounding, and abducting of Bangladeshis crossing the border is similarly a routine part of India's border life (Jones, "Agents of Exception," 890). On the Zimbabwe-Botswana border, a fence built in 2003 carries 220 volts of electricity (Díaz-Barriga and Dorsey, *Fencing in Democracy*, 9).
85. Connor, *The Book of Skin*, 52.
86. Rebecca Bryant and Mete Hatay (*Sovereignty Suspended*, 31–32) similarly mention maps issued by the Greek Cypriot Public Information Office that depict the island of Cyprus with a gash through the middle and dripping blood.
87. Connor, *The Book of Skin*, 40.
88. Connor, *The Book of Skin*, 37. In a fascinating article, Victoria Blum and Anna Secor also consider the usefulness of the topological model in their discussion of a psychoanalytic understanding of space. They show how Freud often got mired in topographical models that were spatially evocative but ultimately constrained by the metrics of Euclidean space. By contrast, Lacan used topological operations, which enabled him to build an understanding of space that reconciled the psychic and the material "without being limited to surfaces that have an orientation, are defined by invariant distances, or are fully graphable in three-dimensional space" (Blum and Secor, "Psychotopologies," 1030, 1035).
89. Lash, "Deforming the Figure," 262.
90. On fields, see Allen, "From Object to Field." See also Deleuze, *Foucault*.
91. Allen, "From Object to Field," 24.
92. See Barr, *Experiments in Topology*, 120–22.
93. Blum and Secor, "Psychotopologies," 1034.
94. Billé, "Doughnut."
95. The work of Lisa Meierotto ("A Disciplined Space") suggests that this situation is in fact not specific to Russia. Cabeza Prieta, on the US-Mexico border, is both a nature conservation area and a militarized zone. It is utilized and crisscrossed by different groups in very different ways: border patrol agents, military personnel, hikers, and wildlife conservationists, but also undocumented migrants from Mexico, all enter it at different angles and along different axes. Cabeza Prieta's topographical contours are therefore drastically different depending on who is entering the area and for what motives.
96. Ramachandran and Blakeslee, *Phantoms in the Brain*, 27.

97. This is of course a simplification in that the fragmented body (*corps morcelé*) cannot be neatly divided into discrete components.

98. Barr, *Experiments in Topology*, 2–3.

99. Frontex, from the French *frontières extérieures* (external borders).

100. Cunningham, "Permeabilities, Ecology and Geopolitical Boundaries," 373.

101. While I conceptualize skin here as a spatial container of some kind, its capacity to sustain torsion and distortion nonetheless helps accommodate the notions of phantom and prosthetics laid out in chapter 3.

102. Brown, *Walled States, Waning Sovereignty*.

103. Similarly, as Nicholas De Genova's research has shown, US immigration enforcement efforts have consistently and disproportionately targeted the US-Mexico border, "sustaining a zone of relatively high tolerance within the interior." This "spectacle of enforcement at the border" is required precisely because of the elusive nature of the law and its relative invisibility in its effects (De Genova, *Working the Boundaries*, 242).

CHAPTER 5. ARCHIPELAGOES, ENCLAVES, AND OTHER CARTOGRAPHIC MONSTERS

1. As a poor artist, Matta-Clark was also fascinated by the idea of owning pieces of Manhattan—a city "where every patch of dirt is assumed to be a highly valuable, fungible commodity" (Kastner, Najafi, and Richard, *Odd Lots*, 4). For many other buyers, the hope was to get in the way of future urban redevelopment projects and gain enormous value as a result. These slivers could then turn into what have been called "nail households" (钉子户) in the context of Chinese urban projects.

2. I refer here exclusively to political enclaves, not to the extended and metaphoric usage of *enclave* as an ethnic or cultural subunit.

3. Whyte, "'En Territoire Belge et à Quarante Centimètres,'" 1.

4. *Enclave complex* refers to a grouping of enclaves such as the one described across the Bangladesh-India border, or the one at Baarle described in this chapter.

5. Dahala Khagrabari was one of the smallest—seven thousand square meters (1.7 acres)—of the Indo-Bangladesh enclaves. It was completely encircled by the Bangladeshi village of Upanchowki Bhajni, itself contained in the Indian village of Balapara Khagrabari, itself contained in the Debiganj, Rangpur Division, Bangladesh. For more on the sociopolitical complexities of these enclaves, see Cons, *Sensitive Space*.

6. As Jason Cons writes, borders in both India and Bangladesh are areas of official anxiety. In India, as mentioned in chapter 4, borders are "spaces of intense restriction of information, where unsanctioned possession of detailed maps is a jailable offense" (Cons, *Sensitive Space*, 36).

7. Cons, "Narrating Boundaries," 38. The situation for residents of these enclaves echoes the ways in which people in refugee camps are "caught in the interstices of an emerging system of humanitarian governance that confounds territorial boundaries" (Dunn, *No Path Home*, 3).

8. On the history and afterlife of this territorial exchange, see Ferdoush, *Sovereign Atonement*.

9. Bonnett, *Off the Map*, 224.

10. Residents of enclaves needing to go to the "mainland," to go to school, hospital, or the market, were constrained to cross the border(s) illegally (Jacobs, *Strange Maps*, 125).

11. Reeves, *Border Work*, 242.

12. Jones, "The Border Enclaves of India and Bangladesh," 18.

13. Cons, *Sensitive Space*, 45.

14. Reeves, *Border Work*, 3–4.

15. The same logic led to the establishment in 1928 of the Jewish Autonomous Oblast in the Russian Far East, initially under the name of Birobidzhan Jewish National Raion.

16. Gerrymandering has created shapes that are described as "highly irregular," "tortured and dramatically irregular," "bizarre," and "irrational" and that jar with ideals of state outlines, as described in chapter 2 (Branch, "How Should States Be Shaped?," 20–21). Working toward fairness of representation, Stacey Abrams notes that the core standards for fair districts include "compactness (not creating sprawling, oddly shaped districts to pick up favored voters); contiguity (keeping cities or counties intact and not splitting neighborhoods or universities); equal population (all districts have the same number of people); preservation of existing political communities; partisan fairness . . . and racial fairness" (Abrams, *Our Time Is Now*, 182–83).

17. Reeves, *Border Work*. Gerrymandering in the United States is also far from benign in its rationale and application through its active exclusion and disempowerment of Black voters (Anderson, *The Nation on No Map*, 9).

18. The difference between enclaves and exclaves is essentially one of perspective. An exclave is a piece of territory separated from the mainland and fully surrounded by foreign territory, that is, landlocked without access to the sea. Unlike enclaves, exclaves can be surrounded by more than one foreign state. Nakhchevan, for instance, is an exclave of Azerbaijian, but is not an enclave since it is not wholly contained within another state (Nakhchevan is hemmed in by Armenia, Iran, and Turkey). Lesotho, fully contained within South Africa, is an enclave, but is, however, not an exclave as "there is no other territory to be exclaved *from*" (Jacobs, *Strange Maps*, 114–15). Finally, Kaliningrad qualifies as neither enclave nor exclave since it is separated from the rest of Russia but has access to the sea. It is known as a fragment.

19. See Billé, "Jigsaw."

20. The case of Baarle harks back to the late twelfth century, namely to the creation of two charters, between Godfrey, Lord of Breda, and Henry, Count of Louvain and Duke of Brabant. Over time, the continual exchange, purchase, and inheritance of land and land rights contributed to the patchwork nature of Baarle. But it is only with the Peace of Münster in 1648 that the enclaves took on a national character: the portion of Baarle under the Count of Nassau was added to the United Provinces (Generaliteitslanden) while the part belonging to the Duke of Brabant remained with Spanish Netherlands (present-day Belgium). For a more detailed history, see Whyte, "'En Territoire Belge et à Quarante Centimètres.'"

21. Bonnett, *Off the Map*, 219. As discussed in chapter 1 and analyzed extensively by Jordan Branch, if the Peace of Westphalia marked some kind of rupture, "the shift to modern uniformly territorial states was not complete until more than a century after 1648" (*The Cartographic State*, 30).

22. Vinokurov, *A Theory of Enclaves*, 204.

23. For more on the contemporary administration of Baarle's services, see Billé, "Jigsaw."

24. Bonnett, *Off the Map*, 87–89. Micronations have served a similar purpose, carving out spaces of utopia between and outside recognized nations.

25. Perry (*Vexy Thing*, 240) describes *kintsugi* as an archive of injury—like scar tissue marking the process of being put back together and back to use.

26. An art project in Austria similarly sought to make borders visible by running a red ribbon through the town of St. Jakob im Rosental/Šentjakob v Rožu, on the Slovenian border (Brunner, "Kärnten").

27. As Alison Mountz points out, islands function as key sites of territorial struggle where nation-states use distance, invisibility, and subnational jurisdictional status to operationalize what Aihwa Ong has termed "graduated zones of sovereignty" (Mountz, "The Enforcement Archipelago"). Permanent detention of prisoners in Guantánamo Bay has relied on the fact that the territory was leased from Cuba and therefore not under US sovereignty. Lawyers representing the detainees argued, however, that with a shopping mall, a McDonald's, a Baskin-Robbins, a Boy Scout contingent, and a *Star Trek* fan club, Guantánamo Bay was in effect an American enclave. In addition, they argued that Fidel Castro refused to recognize the lease (Immerwahr, *How to Hide an Empire*, 389).

28. Dutch law still theoretically applied to the area, but, barring an emergency, the Dutch authorities were banned from entering the premises, and the court had the authority to enact regulations that superseded Dutch law when necessary for the execution of the trial and to jail people for contempt of court. See also "High Court of Justiciary," UK Statutory Instruments, 1998, no. 2251.

29. Vinokurov, *A Theory of Enclaves*, 41.

30. Reeves, "Signs of Sovereignty," 236.

31. See Baldacchino, *Island Enclaves*, 26–29.

32. As Godfrey Baldacchino notes, "The Nauru and Kiribati cases suggest that some sovereign states are . . . 'less equal than others,' since they demonstrate that the practice of hierarchical subservience can exist within the realm of political possibility, fueled by dire economic expediency" (*Island Enclaves*, 38–39). Along similar lines, Reece Jones notes that after the reserves of phosphorus that drove Nauru's economy were exhausted, the government welcomed aid from Australia in exchange for hosting the migrants (*Violent Borders*, 66).

33. Aihwa Ong coined the terms "variegated sovereignty" and "graduated sovereignty" (see in particular Ong, "Graduated Sovereignty in South-East Asia"), while the qualifiers "aleatory" and "paternal" are attributable to Dunn and Cons ("Aleatory Sovereignty and the Rule of Sensitive Spaces") and Dodds and Kirby ("Resurrecting the Vigilante") respectively.

34. Mezzadra and Neilson, *Border as Method*, 211–12.

35. In the context of the United States, territories are classified as organized or unorganized, incorporated or unincorporated—denoting varying degrees of integration, political representation, and citizenship rights. People born in American Samoa, an unorganized and unincorporated territory, are US nationals but not US citizens (nor citizens of any country). As such, when on the mainland, finding employment is difficult because they are not citizens, yet, as nationals, they are not eligible for a green card either. They are also not allowed to vote in elections nor are they allowed to serve on jury duty. To gain these rights, they have to become naturalized, like any other immigrant, despite having been born in the United States (Mack, *The Not-Quite States of America*, 71).

36. Gearóid Ó Tuathail argues that the modern geopolitical imaginary in fact emerged when "the last pockets of unclaimed and un-stated space were surrounded and enclosed within the colonizing projects of expansionist empires and territorializing states" (*Critical Geopolitics*, 12).

37. For more on Bir Tawil, see Bonnett, *Off the Map*, 92–96. Another interesting territorial relinquishment is the land that came to form the Oklahoma Panhandle. Originally part of Texas, it was surrendered when Texas sought to enter the Union in 1845 as a slave state but as per the so-called Missouri Compromise, slavery was prohibited north of 36°30′ parallel. The 170-mile strip, officially called the "Public Land Strip," was left with no state or territorial ownership from 1850 until 1890.

38. Squires, "Welcome to the World's Newest Country"; Buzzara, "Liberland 2.0."

39. Alastair Bonnett writes of Bir Tawil that "no one wants it" and that it is "actively spurned" (*Off the Map*, 92–93).

40. As Jeffrey Kastner further notes ("Gordon Matta-Clark's Moment," 34–36), rural lines reflected water, elevation, and soil conditions, whereas the urban grid rationalized the landscape and obliterated topographic obstacles and oddities. In fact, so uncompromising was the new grid system of blocks and lots in a section of Astoria that in a few instances slivers were created just to maintain the uniform 25 × 100-foot lot size.

41. A few years ago, a group of Norwegians campaigned to gift Mount Halti to Finland to mark its one hundred years of independence from Russia in 2017. With most of the mountain already part of Finland, the change would have seen the 4,478-foot summit change hands—a change that would have shifted the border by just a few hundred feet but that made Halti the tallest mountain in Finland. After months of deliberations and in spite of more than seventeen thousand supporters, the Norwegian prime minister rejected the proposal, stating that "the alteration of borders between countries causes too many judicial problems that could affect, for example, the Constitution" (Withnall, "Norway Refuses to Give Mountain to Finland").

42. Daeseong-dong, in the south, is administered under the terms of the DMZ. Its residents are classified as Republic of Korea citizens but are exempt from paying taxes and from other civic requirements such as military service. In the north, Kijŏng-dong is a model village, constructed and designed to be viewed from the border. See "Daeseong-dong," *Wikipedia*, last modified August 14, 2024, https://en .wikipedia.org/wiki/Daeseong-dong.

43. Unintegrated socially, *terrains vagues* are also zones of danger, violence, and illicit activities. For a fascinating discussion of this term, see de Solà-Morales Rubió, "Terrain Vague."

44. Leshem and Pinkerton, "Re-inhabiting No-Man's Land."

45. Paradoxically, this very abandonment has opened up spaces of opportunity for nonhuman animals such as birds, helping make former wastelands environmentally lush. See E. Kim, "Invasive Others and Significant Others."

46. Díaz-Barriga and Dorsey, *Fencing in Democracy*, 12.

47. Ryzhova, "Freedoms, the State and Security"; Díaz-Barriga and Dorsey, *Fencing in Democracy*, 45.

48. An enclaved space will typically be an embassy, whereas an ambulatory entity might be a diplomatic pouch—or even an individual diplomat. For Godfrey Baldacchino (*Island Enclaves*, 8), an "agent of extraterritoriality" such as a resident ambassador is essentially an extension of the principle of sanctuary into the secular world. Rebecca Bryant also gives the example of the national airline whose aircrafts "become small pieces of the homeland" and as "mobile containers," come to synecdochally "stand for the state itself" (Bryant, "Sovereignty in the Skies," 23, 28).

49. Toal, *Near Abroad*, 3.

50. Billé, "Auratic Geographies." On the materiality of the state, see also Billé, *Voluminous States*.

51. "Not in my backyard" (NIMBY) opposition movements have also often been linked to the construction of airports, whose flight paths would negatively alter property prices as well as the quality of life of its residents. Quinn Slobodian also notes the emergence since the 2010s of "vertical secession," with the "podium building" arrangement placing "a second-floor courtyard—featuring amenities such as artificial ponds and outdoor bars—above the ground floor, an ersatz street above the street" (*Crack-Up Capitalism*, 56).

52. These deals are usually restricted to properties that share at least ten feet of lot line. Further, the restrictions are defined by the ratio of floor area to lot size. This ratio determines a building's permissible bulk and varies by zone as well as by its position on a block or boulevard. "Corner and boulevard sites have fewer restrictions than side streets, particularly in matters of height" (Finn, "The Great Air Race").

53. Herships, "The Air Up There."

54. Finn, "The Great Air Race."

55. As Brian Roberts has reminded us, the island has traditionally been taken as "the world writ small, with its circumscribing shoreline evoking a sense of autonomy" (*Borderwaters*, 108). As a result, the drawing of boundaries across islands often feels like "an insult to the idea of territorial holism" (Steinberg, "Insularity, Sovereignty and Statehood," 263). This reluctance is seen in the vanishingly small number of divided islands—only ten worldwide (Baldacchino, "Only Ten").

56. Even Corsica, a few miles off France's southern coastline and generally included in the logomap, is absent from the graphic imaginary of the hexagon.

57. Overseas French territorial administration is made up of four different categories: overseas departments or regions, overseas collectivities, the territory of

New Caledonia, and uninhabited territories—all with varying legal status and levels of autonomy.

58. Clamorous calls for a reinforcement of the border wall relies, and plays, upon this imaginary of the United States reduced to its mainland. With America the beautiful stretching from sea to shining sea, as the patriotic song goes, and "the border" shorthand for its southern border with Mexico, the US-Mexico border becomes the sole line of interaction.

59. In his study of the United States' dependent territories, Doug Mack makes a germane point. He argues that the very imaginary of America, which relies so heavily on the trope of states ("on the flag, in the maps, in the songs, in our very name"), makes territories invisible and ultimately forgettable (Mack, *The Not-Quite States of America*, 252).

60. Well aware of this, the Ottoman Empire began producing maps that represented the empire in its entirety. Whereas older maps based on European models had depicted the Ottoman domains as marginal lands clinging to the fringes of Europe, Asia, and Africa, new maps showed the empire's far-flung territory within a single unified frame (Fortna, "Change in the School Maps," 23).

61. Immerwahr, *How to Hide an Empire*, 341.

62. In terms of US immigration, Ellis and Angel Islands, on the East and West Coasts, functioned as such airlocks. See also Paglen (*Blank Spots on the Map*) on the Pentagon's black sites, forming a dark parallel geography.

63. This design aspect is more than a consequence or afterthought. Benjamin Bratton notes that "the partition of India . . . was a design decision, and the image and map of Pakistan that would result was constituent of a design imaginary" ("On Geoscapes and the Google Caliphate," 5).

64. Bonnett, *Beyond the Map*, 39. In recent years, China has claimed uninhabited rocks and shoals, some barely above water, and transformed them through terraforming into proper islands in order to extend its maritime footprint. Recalling the Tibetan goddess discussed in chapter 2, these small reefs and outcrops are acting as anchor points to pin down the limits of China's newly reimagined terraqueous geobody.

65. Britain's claim to the Falklands Islands (Malvinas) was made more difficult because of its distance from the mainland and the compounding fact that it fitted "naturally" within the Argentinian logomap. As Geoff King writes, even the most creative mapmakers would be hard pressed to make a cartographic case for the British claim to the islands (*Mapping Reality*, 26).

66. On the symbolism of these islands, see Bukh, *These Islands Are Ours*. The Kuril Islands, in spite of the vociferous Russian insistence on preserving Russia's territorial integrity, are similarly frequently forgotten and left out of weather maps (Richardson, *At the Edge of the Nation*, 101).

67. As Alice Te Punga Somerville writes, the "division between land and sea is so deeply understood as a natural border in European and Euro-American culture that . . . the sea operates as an empty border space—an absence—between presence (land) and other presence (other land)" ("The Great Pacific Garbage Patch," 326). These hydrophobic views have of course not been shared by island, archi-

pelago, and littoral societies. Tongan intellectual Epeli Hau'ofa noted, "There is a world of difference between viewing the Pacific as 'islands in a far sea' and as 'a sea of islands.' The first emphasizes dry surfaces in a vast ocean far from the centers of power. . . . The second is a more holistic perspective in which things are seen in the totality of their relationships" (cited in Craib, "Cartography and Decolonization," 19). In Vietnam, the duality of water and land is not a contradiction—the word *nước* indeed meaning "water" as well as "nation," "country," and "homeland" (Gandhi, *Archipelago of Resettlement*, 10).

68. Florcruz, "China's New Vertical Map."

69. China's new passport design, issued in 2012, included watermarks of disputed areas and territories on its visa pages. In protest, Vietnamese immigration officials refused to issue entry stamps on these passports, stamping separate piece of paper instead (Florcruz, "China's New Vertical Map").

70. As Weizman explains, "When the bridge's columns rest on Palestinian ground, the 'border' runs, presumably, through the thermodynamic joint between the column and the beams" (*Hollow Land*, 180). Early in 2023, Prime Minister Benjamin Netanyahu proposed building a network of underground highway systems across the West Bank in order to ensure territorial contiguity for both Israeli settlements and Palestinian towns (Yerushalmi, "Netanyahu Aims to Fill West Bank").

71. Wallach, "Trapped in Mirror-Images," 360.

72. Wallach, "Trapped in Mirror-Images," 358.

73. A number of writers have also emphasized the multiple and contested nature of Jerusalem, choosing to pluralize the name in acknowledgment of the different ways it is experienced by Arabs or Jews (Musa Budairi, discussed in Wallach, "Trapped in Mirror-Images," 366) and of the overall slippage "between the original and its simulacra, between territory and map, between the 'thing itself' and its representation" (Azoulay, "Save as Jerusalems," 142).

74. On redaction, see Min, Billé, and Makley, ■■■■■ *[Redacted]*. On the nature/settler colonialism interface, see Braverman, *Settling Nature*.

75. A similar negative space is the outline of Mongolia, missing from China's contemporary outline. See discussion in chapter 3.

76. On trans people and the embrace of the monstrous, see Stryker, *When Monsters Speak*.

77. Noting this ambivalence, Rosemary Thomson suggests that the fascinated publics of nineteenth-century freak shows "longed in some sense to be extraordinary marvels instead of mundane, even banal" onlookers, and that "the privileged state of disembodiment that the freak show conferred upon its spectators, however fraudulent, must have been seductive" ("Introduction: From Wonder to Error," 10–11).

78. Also mobilizing the monster as a device to reflect on cultural values—and giving voice to the apotemnophilic drive discussed in chapter 3—the novel *Geek Love* by Katherine Dunn recounts the story of a traveling carnival whose owners have bred their own freak show, using drugs and radioactive material to alter the genes of their children. One of them, Arturo, a boy with flippers for hands and feet, becomes the leader of a cult, Arturism. Fascinated by Arturo and desperate to

resemble him, a growing number of followers have their limbs amputated. As they rise in the hierarchy of the cult, they start with toes and fingers, aiming to lose increasingly significant parts of their bodies.

79. Cohen, *Of Giants*, 134.

80. Grosz, "Intolerable Ambiguity," 274. The monster, Cohen writes, "appears to be outside the human body, as the limit of its coherence; thus he threatens travelers and errant knights with dismemberment or anthropophagy: with the complete dissolution of their selfhood. But closer examination reveals that the monster is also fully within, a foundational figure" (*Of Giants*, xii).

81. Cohen, *Of Giants*, 16.

82. *Teras*, the Greek stem in *teratology* (the science of monsters), means "portent, marvel, monster."

83. Weinstock, "Introduction: A Genealogy of Monster Theory," 27. Jeffrey Weinstock ("Invisible Monsters," 359) notes how the figure of the monster in film and literature has recently evolved. Decoupled from physical deformity, the monstrous is linked to antithetical moral values. Further, "In film ostensibly targeted at children, such as *Shrek* and *Monsters, Inc.* franchises, the 'true monster' is shown not to be the fairy tale creature or exotic beast but rather the human society that demonizes somatic difference. Such narratives—products of twentieth- and twenty-first-century civil right movements—clearly convey a message of tolerance and the valuing of diversity" (Weinstock, "Introduction: A Genealogy of Monster Theory," 28).

84. McKenzie Wark reminds us, "All human bodies are in some way unnatural, in the sense that they all require some kind of technics to endure and thrive. But some have to be held as abject—as unassimilable, as other—to sustain the fiction of the normative body as natural" (introduction to *When Monsters Speak*, 12–13).

85. The "monstrous races," ranging from the unusual to the truly fabulous, "were not supernatural or infernal creatures, but varieties of men, whose chief distinction from the men of Europe was one of geography. The monstrous races were always far away, in India, Ethiopia, Albania, or Cathay, places whose outlines were vague to the medieval mind but whose names evoked mystery. As geographical knowledge grew, and the existence of many of these races began to appear unlikely, they were shifted to regions less well known—the Far North and ultimately the New World" (Friedman, *The Monstrous Races*, 1). As Alexa Wright notes, the "monstrous races" point to an established history, in Western cultures, "of articulating narratives of self and other visually, in the form of strange bodies and unconventional behaviors" ("Monstrous Strangers at the Edge," 174). In a germinal text, Rudolf Wittkower notes the similarity of this imagery in Arabic literature, suggesting a wider geographical scope than usually imagined (*Allegory and the Migration of Symbols*, 54).

86. Elsewhere, I have suggested that anxieties about China's footprint are found in two particular cartographic gaps: on the one hand, in the misalignment between People's Republic of China and Republic of China maps (with the latter claiming Mongolia and parts of today's Russia) and, on the other, in the proliferation of cultural-historical maps of China that portray large swaths of northern Asia as regions formerly inhabited by Chinese. See Billé, "Cartographic Embrace."

87. Grosz, "Intolerable Ambiguity," 284. Alphonso Lingis also noted this particular connection between the excessive and the monstrous. Unlike a dog with a missing leg, which might evoke a surge of care and tenderness, he writes, an "excess of body parts initially provokes nothing but repugnance and horror" (Lingis, "The Physiology of Art," 77).

88. As mentioned in chapter 3, this blurring is especially palpable in territorially continuous entities such as Imperial Russia's expansion or the enlargement of the European Union. In the British, French, or Dutch colonial enterprises, the line between self and other was in fact strictly policed.

89. Bakhtin, *Rabelais and His World* (cited in Neocleous, *Imagining the State*, 35). On transgressing its own limits, see Stallybrass, "Patriarchal Territories," 124.

90. I am borrowing this wording from the title of a pivotal 1992 article by Donna Haraway, "The Promises of Monsters." Perry (*Vexy Thing*, 96–97) reminds us that in 1987 Hortense Spillers had already enjoined us to "embrace the monstrosity, not the celebrity; the monstrosity, not the representative; the monstrosity, not the ideal."

91. Maddin, *My Winnipeg*.

92. William C. Anderson opens his book with a powerful statement, speaking from the position of someone who worked as a janitor for most of his life: "As a janitor, you learn intimately what's wrong with this society because you have to clean it up. You get to know society very well through its messes. How much someone despises you or fails to see you is apparent in what they leave behind for you to clean up. . . . Day after day we labor, dealing with the dirt of empire, which works to maintain its dominance through violence against oppressed people" (*The Nation on No Map*, 2).

93. The *Green Book*, a travel guide published between 1936 and 1962, provided a list of safe establishments for Black travelers where they could eat and spend the night safely. These restaurants and hotels formed a parallel network of support invisible to the white majority. For more, see Taylor, *Overground Railroad*.

94. Katherine McKittrick terms these spaces "demonic grounds": a very different geography "genealogically wrapped up in the historical spatial unrepresentability of black femininity" (*Demonic Grounds*, xxv).

95. Taylor, *Overground Railroad*, 296–97.

96. Maddin, *My Winnipeg*.

97. Shildrick, "'You Are There, Like My Skin,'" 163. See also Pingree, "The 'Exceptions That Prove the Rule.'" On the ways in which first peoples and indigenous communities become invisible in accounts that privilege majority groups, see Schaeffer, *Unsettled Borders*; and Billé and Humphrey, *On the Edge*.

98. In an essay about Thai conjoined twins Dao and Duan, David Clark and Catherine Myser write that "the compulsion to assume a properly singular corporeality . . . has a tremendous, even killing force in our culture. This constraint is perhaps no more apparent than in the case of conjoined twins, whose surgical separation marks the extent to which the medical regime is willing to go to (re)construct the body so that it more closely approximates what is posited as ideal and reiterated as normal" ("Being Humaned," 350–51).

99. Galloway, "Eilish."
100. See in particular Pihlaja's television documentary "The Twins Who Share a Body."
101. Although they finish each other's sentences and speak in striking harmony, they never use the singular to talk about themselves. In emails, by contrast, they write as one person, using the pronoun *I*—similar in this respect to the practice of the "Siamese twins" Chang and Eng, who signed their correspondence "ChangEng" (Grosz, "Intolerable Ambiguity," 281). Their handling of writing, with each sister controlling one hand, with little spoken communication, continues to baffle their doctors.
102. Pihlaja, "The Twins Who Share a Body."
103. Bryant and Reeves, "Introduction: Toward an Anthropology of Sovereign Agency," 5. In the same collection, Alice Wilson further remarks that "even nation-states that do not fall into the category of anomalies operate nonterritorial forms of sovereignty, such as taxing citizens located abroad (e.g., the United States, Eritrea) or extending political representation in national institutions to citizens living abroad (e.g., France)" ("Everyday Sovereignty in Exile," 139).
104. Benton, *A Search for Sovereignty*, 2.
105. Bartelson, "Epilogue: The Ironies of Misrecognition," 243. Daniel Byman and Charles King make a point germane to my argument in this chapter, namely, that enclave complexes and other territorial "monsters" offer important insights into the workings and aspirations of orthodox political geography. They write, "The encouraging news about phantom states is that they function in many ways like recognized countries, and in most cases should be treated as such by political analysts. Especially for phantom states that have proven to be the longest-lasting—places such as Northern Cyprus, Abkhazia, South Ossetia, and Nagorno-Karabakh—there is much to learn about how states are made and how they survive" (Byman and King, "The Mystery of Phantom States," 55).
106. A more common instance of concorporation is pregnancy, which Gail Weiss calls intercorporeality. The integrity of the pregnant body is undermined not only by an externality of the inside, but also by the fact that the boundaries of the expectant body are themselves in flux (Weiss, *Body Images*, 52). In the case of pregnancy, temporality is similarly crucial, with the pregnant body split between past and future (Young, *Throwing Like a Girl*, 161).
107. The visual artist Jane Jin Kaisen (*Apertures|Specters|Rifts*) speaks of the DMZ as a mimetic semblant but also as a rift, a wound, a specter—echoing the multiple analytical positions of the border deployed in the book.
108. Shildrick, *Embodying the Monster*, 29–30.
109. Shildrick, *Embodying the Monster*, 30.
110. Shildrick, *Embodying the Monster*, 45, emphasis in the original.
111. South Koreans use *Hanguk* whereas North Koreans use *Chosŏn*. *Hanguk*, the land of the Han, references the Three Han Kingdoms (57 BCE to 668 AD), in roughly the same geographical area as today's South Korea. *Chosŏn* refers to the eponymous kingdom that existed from the fourteenth century to 1910 and expanded the Korean territory to the entire peninsula.

112. Balibar, "Algeria, France," 164. In the context of the early twentieth-century
     United States, the fascination with concorporation—prompted here by the famous
     "Siamese twins" Chang and Eng—was similarly tied to reflections about Ameri-
     ca's "own configurations of government (divided states within a united nation),"
     whereby "connecting the states too closely was 'monstrous' and excessive" (Pin-
     gree, "America's 'United Siamese Brothers,'" 94–95). The disappearance of the
     portent aspect of monsters did not, Dixon notes, spell the disappearance of tera-
     tology from geopolitics. The eugenics movement indeed testifies to the survival of
     linkages between the body and the state (Dixon, *Feminist Geopolitics*, 125).
113. Billé, *Voluminous States*.
114. Popularly nicknamed the Wood Wide Web, the vast underground network of
     microbes that connects individual trees has helped reframe forests in a more
     collaborative way (Wohlleben, *The Hidden Life of Trees*). On fungal connec-
     tions, see Sheldrake, *Entangled Life*. On the microbial world, see Yong, *I Contain
     Multitudes*.
115. Ed Cohen ponders, "Imagine what might have happened if 'community' had
     achieved the same biological status that immunity did. . . . How might we experi-
     ence ourselves as organisms if we imagined that coexistence rather than self-
     defense provides the basis for our well-being?" (Cohen, *A Body Worth Defending*,
     281). Along similar lines, Neocleous (*The Politics of Immunity*, 40–41) writes that
     endocrinologists frequently speak of an endocrine orchestra, "implying an inter-
     reaction between the various components of the system which determines overall
     endocrine function." So used are we to "imagining our bodies as spaces of war and
     strategic fields of battle" that these alternative metaphors strike us as odd.
116. Fishel, *The Microbial State*, 65.
117. Tsing, *The Mushroom at the End of the World*, 231.
118. Shildrick, *Visceral Prostheses*, 72–73, 85. Cases of chimerism have surfaced when
     blood tests showed a mother's DNA not matching that of her biological children.
     "Current research indicates that tetragametic chimerism may develop quite com-
     monly as a result of what is known as the vanishing twin syndrome in which a twin
     embryo may fuse with the other." Originally conceived as dizygotic twins, these
     women had absorbed the other embryonic twin, but while one fetus disappeared,
     its DNA did not (Shildrick, *Visceral Prostheses*, 152–53).
119. Thrift, *Non-representational Theory*, 236.
120. Barad, "Invertebrate Visions." Shildrick notes that "one consequence of seeking to
     maintain the *illusion* of the separation and distinction necessary to the sovereign
     subject is that all encounters between self and other are potentially risky, and
     must be negotiated within a strict set of normative rules and regulations that con-
     struct the parameters of safety and danger" (*Dangerous Discourses of Disability*,
     83–84).
121. Barad, "Invertebrate Visions," 228.
122. Barad, "Invertebrate Visions," 230.
123. Giraud, *What Comes after Entanglement?*, 2–3.
124. Bartelson, "Epilogue: The Ironies of Misrecognition," 241–42.

125. Butler, *Precarious Life*, 34–35.
126. Jennings, *Maphead*, 85.
127. Weinstock, "Freaks in Space," 330.
128. Weinstock, "Introduction: A Genealogy of Monster Theory," 17. Taking only a couple of examples from *Star Wars*, the character Jar Jar Binks speaks a Caribbean-flavored pidgin English, while the evil Viceroy of the Federation, Nute Gunray, appears to be based on Asian stereotypes.
129. For Bakhtin (*Rabelais and His World*), as mentioned earlier, the body located "at the hinterland of discourse" was the grotesque body. On thinking with monsters, see also Musharbash and Gershon, *Living with Monsters*.
130. Wright, "Monstrous Strangers at the Edge," 183–84. On the maternal imagination, see Huet, *Monstrous Imagination*.
131. Channel 4 News, "Azealia Banks on White Hip-Hop."
132. Spillers, "Whatcha Gonna Do?," cited in Weheliye, *Habeas Viscus*, 39.
133. Wynter, "Black Metamorphosis," 896, cited in McKittrick, *Dear Science and Other Stories*, 161.
134. Perry, *Vexy Thing*, 111. Thus "the ascent of President Barack Obama and the political career of Hillary Clinton . . . are metaphors for social transformations that are not actualized for the overwhelming majority of people in the groups they represent" (111). Similarly, we "witness the coexistence of the queer celebrity and the persistence of anti-queer violence" (203).
135. Gilmore, *Abolition Geography*, 51–52.
136. As Margrit Shildrick argues, disability runs counter to "modernist discourses that figure the human body—or at least the white male body—as ideally closed and invulnerable." Noteworthy is how the female form was perceived by Aristotle as an intrinsic deformity. Shildrick, "Vulnerable Bodies and Ontological Contamination," 155–56.
137. This move from periphery to center is actually how science develops, with novel theories frequently seen as outlandish before they become mainstream.
138. Wark, introduction to *When Monsters Speak*, 17.
139. Ramaswamy, "Maps, Mother/Goddesses, and Martyrdom," 824. See discussion in chapter 2.
140. Bratton, *The Stack*; Shaw, *Predator Empire*.

CODA. BEYOND THE MAP?

Epigraph: Maier, *Once within Borders*, 13.
1. Bensinger, "Google Redraws the Borders." Mike Duggan (*All Mapped Out*) draws attention to the ways in which Washington's interests are fully embedded in Google Maps, which has, for instance, "never used the word 'Palestine' to demarcate Palestinian territory, instead opting for 'the West Bank' and 'the Gaza Strip,' which even so have a history of periodically disappearing from the map" (91).
2. This smooth zooming in and out is actually anything but. The overhead view in Google Earth is "a patchwork of archived aerial and satellite images of varying ori-

gins, sources, motivations, and resolutions." Google generates no overhead images of its own but accesses them from various sources and then assembles a composite map of these images, regardless of origin or resolution (Kurgan, *Close Up at a Distance*, 20). See also discussion in Jacob, *The Sovereign Map*, 307.

3. Massumi, *Parables for the Virtual*, 180.
4. Benton, *A Search for Sovereignty*; Branch, *The Cartographic State*.
5. Winterer and Wigen, "Introduction: Maps Tell Time," 4.
6. Turk, "Maps as Foams," 197.
7. Ferrari, Pasqual, and Bagnato, *A Moving Border*.
8. Macfarlane, *Underland*, 344.
9. Edney, *Cartography*, 1.
10. Robinson, *The Look of Maps*, 10–11; Ellis, *Aeroscopics*, 5.
11. See Chambliss, "Spoofing"; Dodds, "Fissure."
12. Graham, *Vertical*, 26.
13. Morton, *Hyperobjects*.
14. Morton, *Hyperobjects*, 70.
15. See Ripple et al., "The 2023 State of the Climate Report."
16. Longo, *The Politics of Borders*, 223–24, emphasis in the original.
17. Longo, *The Politics of Borders*, 223–24.
18. Vaughan-Williams, *Border Politics*, 33. Anne-Laure Amilhat Szary (*Géopolitique des frontières*, 123–24) notes in this respect that a traveler to the United States from Canada, having gotten through the preclearance control, will remain on Canadian territory but now fall under US law, all the while within a perimeter frequently managed by a private operator.
19. Smith, "The Uncertainty of Placing," 2.
20. Agnew, "The Territorial Trap."
21. Agnew, *Hidden Geopolitics*. As Stuart Elden had already argued as early as 2005 in "Missing the Point" (9), territory remains of paramount importance, and equations of globalization with deterritorialization are misconceptions of the very basis of this crucial term.
22. Balibar, *Politics and the Other Scene*. Balibar nonetheless notes that the fictive nature of borders does "not make them any less real" (76).
23. Reeves, *Border Work*. So extensive is this staggered and delocalized process that "transnational journeys no longer resemble a border crossing as a singular event but rather a proliferating series of spaces of confinement and limbo that migrants move through for years: the camp, the ship, the detention center, the island" (Mountz, *The Death of Asylum*, xx).
24. Cunningham, "Permeabilities," 373.
25. Reeves, "Time and Contingency," 165–66.
26. Slobodian, *Crack-Up Capitalism*, 94.
27. Data provided in Missing Migrants Project, *50,000 Lives Lost during Migration*.
28. Agnew, *Hidden Geopolitics*, 8–9. With respect to preclearance infrastructures, Ayelet Shachar notes that while the United States is seeking to further expand its reach into new regions and continents, no other country operates its immigration control on US soil (*The Shifting Border*, 27–28).

29. Longo, *The Politics of Borders*, 127–28.

30. Lewis and Wigen, *The Myth of Continents*, 191.

31. On very early globalization, see Billé, Mehendale, and Lankton, *The Maritime Silk Road*.

32. Agnew, *Hidden Geopolitics*, 4.

33. A notable exception is the state of Israel, which in early Zionist maps "did not show political borders at all, leaving undefined the exact territorial limits of the Land of Israel"—a pragmatic approach in order to extend into territories in Transjordan, Lebanon, and Sinai. And even "after the establishment of Israel, geography textbooks remained ambiguous on the question of the country's borders, always presenting borders which were wider than the actual extent of Jewish settlement" (Wallach, "Trapped in Mirror-Images," 363). Similarly, Pakistan's official map lacks an eastern edge, representing the "unfinished business" of Kashmir (Kabir, *Territory of Desire*, 8).

34. Dunlop, *Cartophilia*, 193.

35. This erasure of internal borders has been of course paralleled by a reinforcement of Europe's external borders.

36. Anderson, *Imagined Communities*, 175.

37. As discussed earlier in the book, while logomaps of the United States are rare, state logomaps, to the extent that they work well as visual symbols, are commonly used.

38. Lewis and Wigen, *The Myth of Continents*, ix, xiii.

39. Agnew, "The Territorial Trap."

40. Fishel, *The Microbial State*, 9.

41. See in particular Benton, *A Search for Sovereignty*, as well as the discussion in chapter 1.

42. On one of the few remaining gaps, see Harris, "Lag."

43. Chambliss, "Spoofing."

44. See Billé, *Voluminous States*; Au, "Data Centres on the Moon."

45. The symbolic planting of a flag, if attempted at the surface of the North Pole, would not take place on "solid, spatially fixed land but on a mathematically determined spot marked on a maze of mobile and shifting ice floes" (Steinberg, Tasch, and Gerhardt, *Contesting the Arctic*, 40).

46. Branch, *The Cartographic State*, 180.

47. Packer and Reeves, "Taking People Out," 262.

48. Packer and Reeves, "Taking People Out," 264.

49. Packer and Reeves, "Taking People Out," 263.

50. Packer and Reeves, *Killer Apps*, 23.

51. A former principal advisor on national security and intelligence to Senator McCain, Christian Brose, argues that the "problem is not that the US military is on the verge of taking humans 'out of the loop' of the kill chain but that the US military today has way too many loops and way too many humans in the middle of all of them" (Brose, *The Kill Chain*, 147–48). Similarly, the concept of "unmanned" conceals vast numbers of humans enabling the functioning of "autonomous" machines (Chandler, *Unmanning*). As Brose further notes, "For years, the US military has supplied only a fraction of the drone missions that its commanders in combat

have demanded. The problem has not been a lack of drones, but a lack of people" (*The Kill Chain*, 144).

52. Shaw, *Predator Empire*, 22.
53. Quoted in Immerwahr, *How to Hide an Empire*, 379.
54. Parikka, *Insect Media*, xi.
55. Parikka, *Insect Media*, 59.
56. Packer and Reeves, "Taking People Out," 275.
57. Helmreich, *Alien Ocean*, 16.
58. Smith, "The Uncertainty of Placing," 2.
59. Rankin, *After the Map*, 4.
60. France's sustained political control over its former colonies in Africa is a complex entanglement known as Françafrique. "By formally returning their 'international sovereignty' to the colonies while voiding it to a large extent of its content, and by ensuring that the presidency of the new states reverts to carefully selected and strictly supervised leaders, the former metropolis kills two birds with one stone: it sheds its colonial 'burdens,' in de Gaulle's phrasing, and conceals the perpetuation of imperial mechanisms behind an 'indigenous' façade" (Borrel et al., *L'Empire qui ne veut pas mourir*, 17).
61. Slobodian, *Crack-Up Capitalism*, 8–9.
62. Bratton, *The Stack*, 10–11.
63. Bratton, *The Stack*, 316.

Bibliography

Abbi, Anvita. "This Ancient Language Has the Only Grammar Based Entirely on the Human Body." *Scientific American*, June 1, 2023. https://www.scientificamerican.com/article/this-ancient-language-has-the-only-grammar-based-entirely-on-the-human-body.

Abbott, Edwin A. *Flatland: A Romance of Many Dimensions.* London: Seeley, 1884.

Abraham, Itty. *How India Became Territorial.* Stanford, CA: Stanford University Press, 2014.

Abrahamsson, Christian. *Radikalkonservatismens rötter: Rudolf Kjellén och 1914 års idéer.* Stockholm: Timbro Förlag, 2021.

Abrams, Stacey. *Our Time Is Now: Power, Purpose, and the Fight for a Fair America.* New York: Henry Holt, 2019.

Açıksöz, Salih Can. *Sacrificial Limbs: Masculinity, Disability, and Political Violence in Turkey.* Oakland: University of California Press, 2020.

Ackerman, Diane. *A Natural History of the Senses.* New York: Vintage, 1995.

Agnew, John. *Hidden Geopolitics: Governance in a Globalized World.* Lanham, MD: Rowman and Littlefield, 2023.

Agnew, John. "No Borders, No Nations: Making Greece in Macedonia." *Annals of the Association of American Geographers* 97, no. 2 (June 2007): 398–422.

Agnew, John. "The Territorial Trap: The Geographical Assumptions of International Relations Theory." *Review of International Political Economy* 1 (1994): 53–80.

Agulhon, Maurice. *Marianne into Battle: Republican Imagery and Symbolism in France, 1789–1880.* Cambridge: Cambridge University Press, 1981.

Ahmed, Sara. *The Cultural Politics of Emotion.* Edinburgh: Edinburgh University Press, 2004.

Ahmed, Sara, and Jackie Stacey. "Introduction: Dermographies." In *Thinking through the Skin,* edited by Sara Ahmed and Jackie Stacey. London: Routledge, 2001.

Ajami, Fouad. "The End of Pan-Arabism." *Foreign Affairs* 57, no. 2 (Winter 1978–79): 355–73.

Akerman, James R. "The Structuring of Political Territory in Early Printed Atlases." *Imago Mundi* 47 (1995): 138–54.

Akin, Alexander. *East Asian Cartographic Print Culture: The Late Ming Publishing Boom and Its Trans-regional Connections.* Amsterdam: Amsterdam University Press, 2021.

Aleksandrov, Semyon. "Kitai vklyuchil v svoi novye karty chast' territorii Rossii. Chem eto grozit otnosheniami RF i KNR?" *Lenta.ru*, August 29, 2023. https://lenta.ru /news/2023/08/29/china_russia_ostrov.

Alesina, Alberto, and Enrico Spolaore. *The Size of Nations.* Cambridge, MA: MIT Press, 2003.

Alexseev, Mikhail A. "Migration, Hostility, and Ethnopolitical Mobilization: Russia's Anti-Chinese Legacies in Formation." In *Rebounding Identities: The Politics of Identity in Russia and Ukraine*, edited by Dominique Arel and Blair A. Ruble, 116–48. Baltimore, MD: Johns Hopkins University Press, 2006.

Allen, Stan. "From Object to Field." *Architectural Design* 67, no. 5/6 (May/June 1997): 24–31.

Amilhat Szary, Anne-Laure. *Géopolitique des frontières: Découper la terre, imposer une vision du monde.* Paris: Le Cavalier Bleu, 2020.

Anderson, Benedict. *Imagined Communities: Reflections on the Origin and Spread of Nationalism.* London: Verso, 1991.

Anderson, William C. *The Nation on No Map: Black Anarchism and Abolition.* Chico, CA: AK, 2021.

Andreas, Peter. *Border Games: Policing the U.S.-Mexico Divide.* Ithaca, NY: Cornell University Press, 2009.

Andrukhovych, Yuri. *My Final Territory: Selected Essays.* Toronto: University of Toronto Press, 2018.

Antrim, Zayde. *Mapping the Middle East.* London: Reaktion, 2018.

Anzaldúa, Gloria. *Borderlands/La Frontera: The New Mestiza.* San Francisco: Aunt Lute, 1999.

Anzieu, Didier. *Le moi-peau.* Paris: Dunod, 1995.

Appadurai, Arjun. "Caressing the Phantom Limb. 'Heimat'—Progression, Regression, Stagnation?" Keynote lecture, Savvy Contemporary, Laboratory of Form-Ideas, June 1, 2018. Available on YouTube, https://www.youtube.com/watch?v=6Yvm9LVYeVM.

Aretxaga, Begoña. *States of Terror.* Reno: University of Nevada Press, 2005.

Au, Yung. "Data Centres on the Moon and Other Tales: A Volumetric and Elemental Analysis of the Coloniality of Digital Infrastructures." *Territory, Politics, Governance* 12, no. 1 (2024): 12–30. https://doi.org/10.1080/21622671.2022.2153160.

Azoulay, Ariella. "Save as Jerusalems." In *Giving Ground: The Politics of Propinquity*, edited by Joan Copjec and Michael Sorkin, 131–61. London: Verso, 1999.

Azoulay, Ariella. "When a Demolished House Becomes a Public Square." In *Imperial Debris: On Ruins and Ruination*, edited by Ann Laura Stoler, 194–224. Durham, NC: Duke University Press, 2013.

Bachelard, Gaston. *La poétique de l'espace.* Paris: Presses universitaires de France, 1961.

Bakhtin, Mikhail. *Rabelais and His World.* Translated by Helene Iswolsky. Cambridge, MA: MIT Press, 1971.

Bakke, Gretchen. *The Likeness: Semblance and Self in Slovene Society.* Oakland: University of California Press, 2020.

Baldacchino, Godfrey. *Island Enclaves: Offshoring Strategies, Creative Governance, and Subnational Island Jurisdictions.* Montreal: McGill-Queen's University Press, 2010.

Baldacchino, Godfrey. "Only Ten: Islands as Uncomfortable Fragmented Polities." In *The Political Economy of Divided Islands: Unified Geographies, Multiple Polities,* edited by Godfrey Baldacchino, 1–17. Houndmills, UK: Palgrave Macmillan, 2013.

Balibar, Étienne. "Algeria, France: One Nation or Two?" In *Giving Ground: The Politics of Propinquity,* edited by Joan Copjec and Michael Sorkin, 162–72. London: Verso, 1999.

Balibar, Étienne. "La forme nation: Histoire et idéologie." In *Race, nation, classe: Les identités ambiguës,* edited by Étienne Balibar and Immanuel Wallerstein. Paris: La Découverte, 1988.

Balibar, Étienne. *Politics and the Other Scene.* London: Verso, 2002.

Balogh, Eva S. "A New Declaration of War: Justice for Hungary!" *Hungarian Spectrum,* June 4, 2017. Archived June 9, 2017, at Archive.org. https://web.archive.org/web/20170609044357/http://hungarianspectrum.org/2017/06/04/a-new-declaration-of-war-justice-for-hungary.

Baltimore, David, David Botstein, David R. Cox, David J. Galas, Leroy Hood, Robert K. Moyzis, Maynard V. Olson, Nancy S. Wexler, and Norton D. Ziner. "Mapping the Genome: The Vision, the Science, the Implementation; What Is the Genome Project?" *Los Alamos (National Laboratory) Science* 20 (1992): 68–102.

Barad, Karen. "Invertebrate Visions: Diffractions of the Brittlestar." In *The Multispecies Salon,* edited by Eben Kirksey, 221–41. Durham, NC: Duke University Press, 2014.

Barad, Karen. *Meeting the Universe Halfway: Quantum Physics and the Entanglement of Matter and Meaning.* Durham, NC: Duke University Press, 2007.

Baril, Alexandre. "Transformations corporelles et analyses intersectionnelles: Repenser les amputations volontaires (transcapacité) à la lumière des apports théoriques et politiques des études trans." Unpublished paper presented at the twelfth European Association of Social Anthropologists Biennial Conference, Nanterre, France, July 12, 2012.

Barr, Stephen. *Experiments in Topology.* New York: Dover, 1964.

Bartelson, Jens. "Epilogue: The Ironies of Misrecognition." In *The Everyday Lives of Sovereignty: Political Imagination beyond the State,* edited by Rebecca Bryant and Madeleine Reeves, 240–51. Ithaca, NY: Cornell University Press, 2021.

Bartelson, Jens. *Sovereignty as Symbolic Form.* London: Routledge, 2014.

Bartelson, Jens. "Three Concepts of Recognition." *International Theory* 5, no. 1 (2013): 107–29.

Bassin, Mark. *Imperial Visions: Nationalist Imagination and Geographical Expansion in the Russian Far East, 1840–1865.* Cambridge: Cambridge University Press, 1999.

Bassin, Mark. "Politics from Nature: Environment, Ideology, and the Determinist Tradition." In *A Companion to Political Geography,* edited by John Agnew, Katharyne Mitchell, and Gerard Toal, 13–29. Malden: Blackwell, 2003.

Baudrillard, Jean. *Simulacres et simulation.* Paris: Galilée, 1981.

Bayne, Tim, and Neil Levy. "Amputees by Choice: Body Integrity Identity Disorder and the Ethics of Amputation." *Journal of Applied Philosophy* 22, no. 1 (2005): 75–86.

Beer, Francis A., and Christ'l De Landtsheer. *Metaphorical World Politics*. Lansing: Michigan State University Press, 2004.

Benjamin, Walter. "Moscow Diary." *October* 35 (Winter 1985): 9–135.

Bennett, Jane. *Vibrant Matter: A Political Ecology of Things*. Durham, NC: Duke University Press, 2010.

Bennett, Theodore. "It's but a Flesh Wound: Criminal Law and the Conceptualisation of Healthy Limb Amputation." *Alternative Law Journal* 36, no. 3 (July 2011), 158–62.

Benoît, Monique. "Des enfants dessinent la carte de France à main levée d'après leur souvenir des informations météo à la télévision." *Mappemonde* 3 (1990): 22–27.

Bensinger, Greg. "Google Redraws the Borders on Maps Depending on Who's Looking." *Washington Post*, February 14, 2020. https://www.washingtonpost.com/technology/2020/02/14/google-maps-political-borders.

Benthien, Claudia. *Skin: On the Cultural Border between Self and the World*. New York: Columbia University Press, 2002.

Benton, Lauren. *A Search for Sovereignty: Law and Geography in European Empires, 1400–1900*. Cambridge: Cambridge University Press, 2010.

Bernstein, Anya. *Religious Bodies Politic: Rituals of Sovereignty in Buryat Buddhism*. Chicago: University of Chicago Press, 2013.

Betts, J. Gordon, Kelly A. Young, James A. Wise, Eddie Johnson, Brandon Poe, Dean H. Kruse, et al. *Anatomy and Physiology*. Houston: OpenStax, 2013. https://openstax.org/books/anatomy-and-physiology/pages/14-2-central-processing.

Biggs, Michael. "Putting the State on the Map: Cartography, Territory, and European State Formation." *Comparative Studies in Society and History* 41, no. 2 (April 1999), 374–405.

Billé, Franck. "Auratic Geographies: Buffers, Backyards, Entanglements." *Geopolitics* 29, no. 3 (2021): 1004–26. https://doi.org/10.1080/14650045.2021.1881490.

Billé, Franck. "Cartographic Embrace: A View from China's Northern Rim." *Cross-Currents: East Asian History and Culture Review*, no. 21 (2016): 88–110.

Billé, Franck. "Doughnut." *Cultural Anthropology: Fieldsights*, September 30, 2019. https://culanth.org/fieldsights/doughnut.

Billé, Franck. "Jigsaw: Micropartitioning in the Enclaves of Baarle-Hertog/Baarle-Nassau." In *Voluminous States: Sovereignty, Materiality, and the Territorial Imagination*, edited by Franck Billé, 217–29. Durham, NC: Duke University Press, 2020.

Billé, Franck. *Sinophobia: Anxiety, Violence, and the Making of Mongolian Identity*. Honolulu: University of Hawai'i Press, 2015.

Billé, Franck. *Voluminous States: Sovereignty, Materiality, and the Territorial Imagination*. Durham, NC: Duke University Press, 2020.

Billé, Franck, and Caroline Humphrey. *On the Edge: Life along the Russia-China Border*. Cambridge, MA: Harvard University Press, 2021.

Billé, Franck, Sanjyot Mehendale, and James Lankton. *The Maritime Silk Road: Global Connectivities, Regional Nodes, Localities*. Amsterdam: Amsterdam University Press, 2022.

Billé, Franck, and Sören Urbansky. *Yellow Perils: China Narratives in the Contemporary World*. Honolulu: University of Hawai'i Press, 2018.

Billig, Michael. *Banal Nationalism*. London: Sage, 1995.

Birkholz, Daniel. *The King's Two Maps: Cartography and Culture in Thirteenth-Century England*. New York: Routledge, 2004.

Bishop, Mark. "Dreams, Phantom Limbs and Virtual Reality: Challenges to the Singularity of Space?" *Journal of Neuro-Aesthetics*, no. 4 (2004). https://www.artbrain.org/journal-of-neuroaesthetics/journal-neuroaesthetics-4/dreams-phantom-limbs-and-virtual-reality-challenges-to-the-singularity-of-space.

Blum, Virginia, and Anna Secor. "Psychotopologies: Closing the Circuit between Psychic and Material Space." *Environment and Planning D: Society and Space* 29 (2011): 1030–47.

Bodin, Per-Arne. "Russian Geopolitical Discourse: On Pseudomorphosis, Phantom Pains, and Simulacra." In *Eurasia 2.0: Russian Geopolitics in the Age of New Media*, edited by Mikhail Suslov and Mark Bassin, 167–81. Lanham, MD: Lexington, 2016.

Bonnett, Alastair. *Beyond the Map: Unruly Enclaves, Ghostly Places, Emerging Lands and Our Search for New Utopias*. Chicago: University of Chicago Press, 2018.

Bonnett, Alastair. *Off the Map: Lost Spaces, Invisible Cities, Forgotten Islands, Feral Places, and What They Tell Us about the World*. London: Aurum, 2014.

Bora, Renu. "Outing Texture." In *Novel Gazing: Queer Readings in Fiction*, edited by Eve Kosofsky Sedgwick, 94–127. Durham, NC: Duke University Press, 1997.

Borges, Jorge Luis. "Del rigor en la ciencia" (1946). In *El Hacedor*, 137. New York: Vintage Español, 2012.

Borges, Jorge Luis. "Epílogo" (1960). In *El Hacedor*, 146 47. New York: Vintage Español, 2012.

Borneman, John. *Belonging in the Two Berlins: Kin, State, Nation*. Cambridge: Cambridge University Press, 1992.

Borrel, Thomas, Amzat Boukari-Yabara, Benoît Collombat, and Thomas Deltombe. *L'Empire qui ne veut pas mourir: Une histoire de la Françafrique*. Paris: Le Seuil, 2021.

Boyer, Pascal. "Human Cognition and Cultural Evolution." In *Anthropological Theory Today*, edited by Henrietta Moore. Cambridge: Polity, 1999.

Boym, Svetlana. *The Future of Nostalgia*. New York: Basic Books, 2001.

Brahm, Gabriel, Jr., and Mark Driscoll. *Prosthetic Territories: Politics and Hypertechnologies*. Boulder, CO: Westview, 1995.

Branch, Jordan. *The Cartographic State: Maps, Territory, and the Origins of Sovereignty*. Cambridge: Cambridge University Press, 2014.

Branch, Jordan. "How Should States Be Shaped? Contiguity, Compactness, and Territorial Rights." *International Theory* 8, no. 1 (2016): 1–28.

Branch, Jordan. "Mapping the Sovereign State: Technology, Authority, and Systemic Change." *International Organization* 65, no. 1 (January 2011): 1–36.

Bratton, Benjamin H. "On Geoscapes and the Google Caliphate: Except #Mumbai." *Theory, Culture and Society* 26, no. 7–8 (2009): 329–43.

Bratton, Benjamin H. *The Stack: On Software and Sovereignty*. Cambridge, MA: MIT Press, 2015.

Braverman, Irus. *Settling Nature: The Conservation Regime in Palestine-Israel*. Minneapolis: University of Minnesota Press, 2023.

Brenner, William J. *Confounding Powers: Anarchy and International Society from the Assassins to Al Qaeda.* Cambridge: Cambridge University Press, 2016.

Bringa, Tone. "From Boundaries to Borders: Spatial Practices and State-Making; the Case of Bosnia-Herzegovina." In *Eurasian Borderlands: Spatializing Borders in the Aftermath of State Collapse,* edited by Tone Bringa and Hege Toje, 213–39. New York: Palgrave Macmillan, 2016.

Broers, Laurence. *Armenia and Azerbaijan: Anatomy of a Rivalry.* Edinburgh: Edinburgh University Press, 2019.

Broers, Laurence. "Augmented Azerbaijan? The Return of Azerbaijani Irredentism." *Eurasianet,* August 5, 2021. https://eurasianet.org/perspectives-augmented -azerbaijan-the-return-of-azerbaijani-irredentism.

Brook, Timothy. *Mr. Selden's Map of China: Decoding the Secrets of a Vanished Cartographer.* Toronto: House of Anansi, 2013.

Brose, Christian. *The Kill Chain: Defending America in the Future of High-Tech Warfare.* New York: Hachette, 2020.

Brown, Joshua. "Somatoparaphrenia: Europe's Next Phase." *Forbes,* May 6, 2012. http://www.forbes.com/sites/joshuabrown/2012/05/06/somatoparaphrenia -europes-next-phase.

Brown, Kate. *A Biography of No Place: From Ethnic Borderland to Soviet Heartland.* Cambridge, MA: Harvard University Press, 2005.

Brown, Tony C. *Statelessness: On Almost Not Existing.* Minneapolis: University of Minnesota Press, 2022.

Brown, Wendy. *Walled States, Waning Sovereignty.* New York: Zone, 2010.

Brugger, Peter. "Phantomology: The Science of the Body in the Brain." *Journal of Neuro-Aesthetics,* no. 4 (2004). https://www.artbrain.org/ journal-of-neuro aesthetics/journal-neuroaesthetics-4/phantomology-the-science-of-the-body-in -the-brain.

Brunet-Jailly, Emmanuel. "Securing Borders in Europe and North America." In *A Companion to Border Studies,* edited by Thomas M. Wilson and Hastings Donnan, 100–118. Chichester: Wiley-Blackwell, 2012.

Brunner, Katharina. "Kärnten: 'Grenz'-Band zieht sich durch Ort." *Der Standard,* July 31, 2020. https://www.derstandard.at/story/2000119093717/kaernten-grenz -band-zieht-sich-durch-ort.

Bryant, Rebecca. "History's Remainders: On Time and Objects after Conflict in Cyprus." *American Ethnologist* 41, no. 4 (2014): 681–97.

Bryant, Rebecca. "Partitions of Memory: Wounds and Witnessing in Cyprus." *Comparative Studies in Society and History* 54, no. 2 (2012): 332–60.

Bryant, Rebecca. "Sovereignty in Drag: On Fakes, Foreclosure, and Unbecoming States." *Cultural Anthropology* 36, no. 1 (2021): 52–83.

Bryant, Rebecca. "Sovereignty in the Skies: An Anthropology of Everyday Aeropolitics." In *The Everyday Lives of Sovereignty: Political Imagination beyond the State,* edited by Rebecca Bryant and Madeleine Reeves, 19–43. Ithaca, NY: Cornell University Press, 2021.

Bryant, Rebecca, and Mete Hatay. *Sovereignty Suspended: Building the So-Called State.* Philadelphia: University of Philadelphia Press, 2020.

Bryant, Rebecca, and Madeleine Reeves. "Introduction: Toward an Anthropology of Sovereign Agency." In *The Everyday Lives of Sovereignty: Political Imagination Beyond the State*, edited by Rebecca Bryant and Madeleine Reeves, 1–18. Ithaca, NY: Cornell University Press, 2021.

Buisseret, David. *Monarchs, Ministers, and Maps: The Emergence of Cartography as a Tool of Government in Early Modern Europe*. Chicago: University of Chicago Press, 1992.

Bukh, Alexander. *These Islands Are Ours: The Social Construction of Territorial Disputes in Northeast Asia*. Stanford, CA: Stanford University Press, 2020.

Burbank, Jane. "The Grand Theory Driving Putin to War." *New York Times*, March 22, 2022. https://www.nytimes.com/2022/03/22/opinion/russia-ukraine-putin-eurasianism.html.

Büscher, Bram. *Transforming the Frontier: Peace Parks and the Politics of Neoliberal Conservation in Southern Africa*. Durham, NC: Duke University Press, 2013.

Butalia, Urvashi. *The Other Side of Silence: Voices from the Partition of India*. Durham, NC: Duke University Press, 2000.

Butler, Judith. *Precarious Life: The Powers of Mourning and Violence*. London: Verso, 2004.

Buzzara. "Liberland 2.0: Kako jedan četrnaestogodišnjak stvara državu između Hrvatske i Srbije." June 3, 2019. Archived August 11, 2019, at Archive.org. https://web.archive.org/web/20190811034512/https://www.rtl.hr/buzzara/virealno/3500391/liberland-20-kako-jedan-cetrnaestogodisnjak-stvara-drzavu-izmedju-hrvatske-i-srbije.

Byman, Daniel, and Charles King. "The Mystery of Phantom States." *Washington Quarterly* 35, no. 3 (2012): 43–57.

Callahan, William A. *China: The Pessoptimist Nation*. Oxford: Oxford University Press, 2010.

Callahan, William A. *Sensible Politics: Visualizing International Relations*. Oxford: Oxford University Press, 2020.

Carlson, Tucker. "Interview to Tucker Carlson." Kremlin, Moscow, February 9, 2024. http://en.kremlin.ru/events/president/news/73411.

Carrai, Maria Adele. *Sovereignty in China: A Genealogy of a Concept since 1840*. Cambridge: Cambridge University Press, 2019.

Carroll, Lewis. *Sylvie and Bruno Concluded*. London: Macmillan, 1893.

Carter, James H. *Creating a Chinese Harbin: Nationalism in an International City, 1916–1932*. Ithaca, NY: Cornell University Press, 2002.

Carter, Rita. *Exploring Consciousness*. Berkeley: University of California Press, 2002.

Cartier, Carolyn. "What's Territorial about China? From Geopolitical Narratives to the 'Administrative Area Economy.'" *Eurasian Geography and Economics* 54, no. 1 (2013): 57–77.

Chambliss, Wayne. "Spoofing: The Geophysics of Not Being Governed." In *Voluminous States: Sovereignty, Materiality, and the Territorial Imagination*, edited by Franck Billé, 64–77. Durham, NC: Duke University Press, 2020.

Chandler, Katherine. *Unmanning: How Humans, Machines and Media Perform Drone Warfare*. New Brunswick, NJ: Rutgers University Press, 2020.

Channel 4 News. "Azealia Banks on White Hip-Hop and #blacklivesmatter." Posted on YouTube, March 2, 2015. https://www.youtube.com/watch?v=8PIgbeVC6hQ.

Chatterjee, Parha. *The Nation and Its Fragments: Colonial and Postcolonial Histories.* Princeton, NJ: Princeton University Press, 1993.

Cheah, Pheng. *Spectral Nationality: Passages of Freedom from Kant to Postcolonial Literatures of Liberation.* New York: Columbia University Press, 2003.

Chowdhury, Arjun. *The Myth of International Order: Why Weak States Persist and Alternatives to the State Fade Away.* Oxford: Oxford University Press, 2018.

Chung, Chien-peng. *Domestic Politics, International Bargaining and China's Territorial Disputes.* New York: Routledge, 2004.

Clark, David L., and Catherine Myser. "Being Humaned: Medical Documentaries and the Hyperrealization of Conjoined Twins." In *Freakery: Cultural Spectacles of the Extraordinary Body*, edited by Rosemary Garland Thomson, 338–55. New York: New York University Press, 1996.

Cocks, Joan. *On Sovereignty and Other Political Delusions.* London: Bloomsbury, 2014.

Cohen, Ed. *A Body Worth Defending: Immunity, Biopolitics, and the Apotheosis of the Modern Body.* Durham, NC: Duke University Press, 2009.

Cohen, Jeffrey Jerome. *Monster Theory: Reading Culture.* Minneapolis: University of Minnesota Press, 1996.

Cohen, Jeffrey Jerome. *Of Giants: Sex, Monsters, and the Middle Ages.* Minneapolis: University of Minnesota Press, 1999.

Conley, Tom. *The Self-Made Map: Cartographic Writing in Early Modern France.* Minneapolis: University of Minnesota Press, 1996.

Connor, Steven. *The Book of Skin.* London: Reaktion, 2009.

Conrad, Joseph. *Heart of Darkness.* London: Blackwood's Magazine, 1899.

Cons, Jason. "Narrating Boundaries: Framing and Contesting Suffering, Community, and Belonging in Enclaves along the India-Bangladesh Border." *Political Geography* 35 (2013): 37–46.

Cons, Jason. *Sensitive Space: Fragmented Territory at the India-Bangladesh Border.* Seattle: University of Washington Press, 2016.

Cosgrove, Denis. *Geography and Vision: Seeing, Imagining and Representing the World.* London: I. B. Tauris, 2008.

Cowen, Deborah. "The City and the City (and the City): Infrastructure in the Breach." *Society + Space*, October 10, 2017. https://www.societyandspace.org/articles/the -city-and-the-city-and-the-city-infrastructure-in-the-breach.

Craib, Raymond B. *Cartographic Mexico: A History of State Fixations and Fugitive Landscapes.* Durham, NC: Duke University Press, 2004.

Craib, Raymond B. "Cartography and Decolonization." In *Decolonizing the Map: Cartography from Colony to Nation*, edited by James R. Akerman, 11–71. Chicago: University of Chicago Press, 2017.

Crampton, Jeremy W. *Mapping: A Critical Introduction to Cartography and GIS.* Chichester: Wiley-Blackwell, 2010.

Cunningham, Hilary. "Necrotone: Death-Dealing Volumetrics at the US-Mexico Border." In *Voluminous States: Sovereignty, Materiality, and the Territorial Imagination*, 131–45. Durham, NC: Duke University Press, 2020.

Cunningham, Hilary. "Permeabilities, Ecology and Geopolitical Boundaries." In *A Companion to Border Studies*, edited by Thomas M. Wilson and Hastings Donnan, 371–86. Chichester: Wiley-Blackwell, 2012.

Dabas, Maninder. "Showing PoK or Arunachal Pradesh Outside India on a Map Might Earn You 1 Crore RS. Fine and 7 Years in Jail!" *India Times*, May 5, 2016. http://www.indiatimes.com/news/india/showing-pok-or-arunachal-pradesh-outside-india-on-a-map-might-earn-you-1-crore-rs-fine-and-7-years-in-jail-254583.html.

Das, Veena. *Life and Words: Violence and the Descent into the Ordinary*. Berkeley: University of California Press, 2007.

de Baecque, Antoine. *The Body Politic: Corporeal Metaphor in Revolutionary France, 1700–1800*. Translated by Charlotte Mandell. Stanford, CA: Stanford University Press, 1997.

De Genova, Nicholas. *Working the Boundaries: Race, Space, and "Illegality" in Mexican Chicago*. Durham, NC: Duke University Press, 2005.

De León, Jason. *The Land of Open Graves: Living and Dying on the Migrant Trail*. Oakland: University of California Press, 2015.

Deleuze, Gilles. *Foucault*. Paris: Les Éditions de Minuit, 1986.

Derrida, Jacques. "I Have a Taste for the Secret." In *A Taste for the Secret*, edited by Giacomo Donis and David Webb. Cambridge: Polity, 2001.

Derrida, Jacques. *Spectres de Marx: L'État de la dette, le travail du deuil et la nouvelle Internationale*. Paris: Galilée, 1993.

de Solà-Morales Rubió, Ignasi. "Terrain Vague." In *Anyplace*, edited by Cynthia C. Davidson, 118–23. Cambridge, MA: MIT Press, 1995.

Deutsche Welle. "Voting Debate." June 21, 2007. https://www.dw.com/en/polish-prime-minister-brings-world-war-two-into-eu-vote-debate/a-2618555.

De Weerdt, Hilde. "Maps and Memory: Readings of Cartography in Twelfth- and Thirteenth-Century Song China." *Imago Mundi: The International Journal for the History of Cartography* 61, no. 2 (2009): 145–67.

Diamond, Nicola. "The Phantom Limb: Body and Language, Cultural Expression and Difference." *Journal of Neuro-Aesthetics*, no. 4 (2004). https://www.artbrain.org/journal-of-neuroaesthetics/journal-neuroaesthetics-4/the-phantom-limb-body-and-language-cultural-expression-and-difference.

Díaz-Barriga, Miguel, and Margaret E. Dorsey. *Fencing in Democracy: Necrocitizenship and the US-Mexico Border Wall*. Durham, NC: Duke University Press, 2020.

Dixon, Deborah P. *Feminist Geopolitics: Material States*. London: Routledge, 2016.

Dodds, Klaus. "Fissure: Cracking, Forcing, and Covering Up." In *Voluminous States: Sovereignty, Materiality, and the Territorial Imagination*, edited by Franck Billé, 105–18. Durham, NC: Duke University Press, 2020.

Dodds, Klaus, and Philip Kirby. "Resurrecting the Vigilante: Paternal Sovereignty, Exceptionality and Familial Security in *Taken* (2008) and *Taken 2* (2013)." *Critical Studies on Security* 2, no. 3 (2014): 245–61. https://doi.org/10.1080/21624887.2014.887512.

Donnan, Hastings, and Thomas Wilson. *Culture and Power at the Edges of the State: National Support and Subversion in European Border Regions*. Münster: Lit Verlag, 2005.

Dostoyevsky, Fyodor. *A Writer's Diary*. Translated by K. Lantz. Evanston, IL: Northwestern University Press, 1993.

Douglas, Mary. *Purity and Danger: An Analysis of Concepts of Pollution and Taboo.* London: Routledge and Kegan Paul, 1966.

Duara, Prasenjit. *Sovereignty and Authenticity: Manchukuo and the East Asian Modern.* Lanham, MD: Rowman and Littlefield, 2003.

Dubnov, Arie, and Laura Robson. "Drawing the Line, Writing beyond It: Toward a Transnational History of Partitions." In *Partitions: A Transnational History of Twentieth-Century Territorial Separatism*, edited by Arie Dubnov and Laura Robson, 1–27. Stanford, CA: Stanford University Press, 2019.

Duggan, Mike. *All Mapped Out: How Maps Shape Us.* London: Reaktion, 2024.

Dunlop, Catherine Tatiana. *Cartophilia: Maps and the Search for Identity in the French-German Borderland.* Chicago: University of Chicago Press, 2015.

Dunn, Elizabeth Cullen. *No Path Home: Humanitarian Camps and the Grief of Displacement.* Ithaca, NY: Cornell University Press, 2017.

Dunn, Elizabeth Cullen, and Jason Cons. "Aleatory Sovereignty and the Rule of Sensitive Spaces." *Antipode* 46, no. 1 (2014): 92–109. https://doi.org/doi:10.1111/anti .12028.

Dunn, Elizabeth Cullen, and Martin Demant Frederiksen. "Uncanny Valleys: Unheimlichkeit, Approximation and the Refugee Camp." *Anthropology Today* 34, no. 6 (December 2018): 21–24.

Dunn, Katherine. *Geek Love*. New York: Vintage, 1989.

Dyatlov, Viktor Innokentievich. "'The Blagoveshchensk Utopia': Historical Memory and Historical Responsibility." *Sensus Historiae, Studia interdyscyplinarne* 8, no. 3 (2012): 115–40.

Eco, Umberto. "Dell'impossibilità di costruire la carta dell'impero 1 a 1." In *Il secondo diario minimo*. Milano: Bompiani, 1992.

Economist. "The Sino-Russian Border: The Cockerel's Cropped Crest." July 24, 2008. http://www.economist.com/node/11792951.

Edney, Matthew H. *Cartography: The Ideal and Its History.* Chicago: University of Chicago Press, 2019.

Edney, Matthew H. "Mapping Empires, Mapping Bodies: Reflections on the Use and Abuse of Cartography." *Treballs de la Societat Catalana de Geografia* 63 (2007): 83–104.

Egoshin, Alex. "The Countries' Borders That Are Visible from Space." Vivid Maps, December 3, 2021. https://vividmaps.com/borders-visible-from-space.

Elden, Stuart. *The Birth of Territory.* Chicago: University of Chicago Press, 2009.

Elden, Stuart. "Missing the Point: Globalization, Deterritorialization and the Space of the World." *Transactions of the Institute of British Geographers*, n.s., 30 (2005): 8–19.

Elden, Stuart. "Outside Territory." In *Extraterritorialities in Occupied Worlds*, edited by Maayan Amir and Ruti Sela, 123–38. Earth, Milky Way: punctum, 2016.

Elliott, Carl. "A New Way to Be Mad." *Atlantic*, December 2000. https://www .theatlantic.com/magazine/archive/2000/12/a-new-way-to-be-mad/304671.

Elliott, Mark C. "The Limits of Tartary: Manchuria in Imperial and National Geographies." *Journal of Asian Studies* 59, no. 3 (August 2000): 603–46.

Ellis, Patrick. *Aeroscopics: Media of the Bird's-Eye View*. Oakland: University of California Press, 2021.

Engelhardt, Anna. "On Space and Territory in Cyberwar: The Case of Electronic Terraforming." In *Cyberwar Topologies*, edited by Svitlana Matviyenko and Kayla Hilstob. Unpublished manuscript.

Enloe, Cynthia. *Bananas, Beaches, and Bases: Making Feminist Sense of International Politics*. Berkeley: University of California Press, 2014.

Epstein, Robert. "The Empty Brain." *Aeon*, May 18, 2016. https://aeon.co/essays/your-brain-does-not-process-information-and-it-is-not-a-computer.

Etkind, Alexander. *Internal Colonization: Russia's Imperial Experience*. Cambridge: Polity, 2011.

Etkind, Alexander. "Post-Soviet Russia: The Land of the Oil Curse, Pussy Riot, and Magical Historicism." *boundary 2* 41, no. 1 (2014): 171–201.

Fairbank, J. *The Chinese World Order: Traditional China's Foreign Relations*. Cambridge, MA: Harvard University Press, 1968.

Fall, Juliet J. "Artificial States? On the Enduring Geographical Myth of Natural Borders." *Political Geography* 29 (2010): 140–47.

Fall, Juliet J. *Drawing the Line: Nature, Hybridity and Politics in Transboundary Spaces*. Aldershot: Ashgate, 2005.

Fall, Juliet J. "Embodied Geographies, Naturalised Boundaries, and Uncritical Geopolitics in *La Frontière Invisible*." *Environment and Planning D: Society and Space* 24 (2006): 653–69.

Fall, Juliet J., and Laurent Matthey. "De plantes dignes et d'invasions barbares: Les sociétés au miroir du végétal." *VertigO*, September 27, 2011. https://journals.openedition.org/vertigo/11046.

Feinberg, Todd E. *Altered Egos: How the Brain Creates the Self*. Oxford: Oxford University Press, 2001.

Ferdinand, Simon. *Mapping beyond Measure: Art, Cartography, and the Space of Global Modernity*. Lincoln: University of Nebraska Press, 2019.

Ferdoush, Md Azmeary. *Sovereign Atonement: Citizenship, Territory, and the State at the Bangladesh-India Border*. Cambridge: Cambridge University Press, 2024.

Ferguson, James, and Akhil Gupta. "Spatializing States: Toward an Ethnography of Neoliberal Governmentality." *American Ethnologist* 29, no. 4 (2002): 981–1002.

Ferrari, Marco, Elisa Pasqual, and Andrea Bagnato. *A Moving Border: Alpine Cartographies of Climate Change*. New York: Columbia University Press, 2018.

Field, Tiffany. *Touch*. Cambridge, MA: MIT Press, 2001.

Finn, Robin. "The Great Air Race." *New York Times*, February 22, 2013. https://www.nytimes.com/2013/02/24/realestate/the-great-race-for-manhattan-air-rights.html.

Fishel, Stefanie R. *The Microbial State: Global Thriving and the Body Politic*. Minneapolis: University of Minnesota Press, 2017.

Fiskesjö, Magnus. "On the 'Raw' and the 'Cooked' Barbarians of Imperial China." *Inner Asia* 1/2 (1999): 139–68.

Florcruz, Michelle. "China's New Vertical Map Gives Extra Play to Disputed South China Sea Territories." *International Business Times*, June 25, 2014. http://www.ibtimes.com/chinas-new-vertical-map-gives-extra-play-disputed-south-china-sea-territories-1611550.

Fluri, Jennifer L., and Rachel Lehr. *The Carpetbaggers of Kabul and Other American-Afghan Entanglements: Intimate Development, Geopolitics, and the Currency of Gender and Grief.* Athens: University of Georgia Press, 2017.

Fortna, Benjamin C. "Change in the School Maps of the Late Ottoman Empire." *Imago Mundi* 57, no. 1 (2005): 23–34.

Fortna, Benjamin C. *Imperial Classroom: Islam, the State, and Education in the Late Ottoman Empire.* Oxford: Oxford University Press, 2002.

Foucault, Michel. *Security, Territory, Population: Lectures at the College de France, 1977–1978.* Translated by G. Burchell. Edited by M. Senellart. New York: Picador, 2007.

Foucault, Michel. *This Is Not a Pipe.* Translated by James Harkness. Berkeley: University of California Press, 1983.

Foucher, Michel. *Fronts et frontières: Un tour du monde géopolitique.* Paris: Fayard, 1991.

Foucher, Michel. *L'obsession des frontières.* Paris: Librairie Académique Perrin, 2007.

Francaviglia, Richard V. *The Shape of Texas: Maps as Metaphors.* College Station: Texas A&M University Press, 1995.

French, Lindsay. "The Political Economy of Injury and Compassion: Amputees on the Thai-Cambodia Border." In *Embodiment and Experience: The Existential Ground of Culture and Self*, edited by Thomas J. Csordas, 69–99. Cambridge: Cambridge University Press, 1994.

Freud, Sigmund. *The Ego and the Id.* New York: Norton, 1923.

Friedman, John Block. *The Monstrous Races in Medieval Art and Thought.* Syracuse, NY: Syracuse University Press, 2000.

Gaidar, Yegor. *Collapse of an Empire: Lessons for Modern Russia.* Washington, DC: Brookings Institution Press, 2007.

Galloway, Mark, dir. "Eilish: Life without Katie." *Network First.* Yorkshire Television, August 29, 1995.

Gandelman, Claude. *Reading Pictures, Viewing Texts.* Bloomington: Indiana University Press, 1991.

Gandhi, Evyn Lê Espiritu. *Archipelago of Resettlement: Vietnamese Refugee Settlers and Decolonization across Guam and Israel-Palestine.* Oakland: University of California Press, 2022.

Garfield, Simon. *On the Map: Why the World Looks the Way It Does.* London: Profile, 2012.

Gellner, Ernest. *Nationalism.* London: Phoenix, 1997.

Geoch, Paul D., and V. S. Ramachandran. "The Appearance of New Phantom Fingers Post-amputation in a Phocomelus." *Neurocase: The Neural Basis of Cognition* 18, no. 2 (2012): 95–97.

Gibbs, Raymond W., Jr. *The Poetics of Mind: Figurative Thought, Language, and Understanding.* Cambridge: Cambridge University Press, 1994.

Giddens, Anthony. *The Nation-State and Violence.* Cambridge: Polity, 1985.

Gilmore, Ruth Wilson. *Abolition Geography: Essays towards Liberation*. Edited by Brenna Bhandar and Alberto Toscano. London: Verso, 2022.

Giraud, Eva Haifa. *What Comes after Entanglement? Activism, Anthropocentrism, and an Ethics of Exclusion*. Durham, NC: Duke University Press, 2019.

Goeman, Mishuana. *Mark My Words: Native Women Mapping Our Nations*. Minneapolis: University of Minnesota Press, 2013.

González, Jennifer A. "Autotopographies." In *Prosthetic Territories: Politics and Hypertechnologies*, edited by Gabriel Brahm Jr. and Mark Driscoll. Boulder, CO: Westview, 1995.

Gordillo, Gastón R. *Rubble: The Afterlife of Destruction*. Durham, NC: Duke University Press, 2014.

Gordon, Avery F. *Ghostly Matters: Haunting and the Sociological Imagination*. Minneapolis: University of Minnesota Press, 2008.

Graham, Stephen. *Vertical: The City from Satellites to Bunkers*. London: Verso, 2016.

Green, Sarah F. *Notes from the Balkans: Locating Marginality and Ambiguity on the Greek-Albanian Border*. Princeton, NJ: Princeton University Press, 2005.

Green, Sarah. "A Sense of Border." In *A Companion to Border Studies*, edited by Thomas M. Wilson and Hastings Donnan, 573–92. Chichester: Wiley-Blackwell, 2012.

Greenberg, Jonathan D. "Divided Lands, Phantom Limbs: Partition in the Indian Subcontinent, Palestine, China, and Korea." *Journal of International Affairs* 57, no. 2 (Spring 2004): 7–27.

Greenblatt, Stephen, *Marvelous Possessions: The Wonder of the New World*. Chicago: University of Chicago Press, 1991.

Grosz, Elizabeth. "Bodies-Cities." In *Places through the Body*, edited by Heidi J. Nast and Steve Pile, 31–38. London: Routledge, 1998.

Grosz, Elizabeth. "Intolerable Ambiguity: Freaks as/at the Limit." In *The Monster Theory Reader*, edited by Jeffrey Andrew Weinstock, 272–85. Minneapolis: University of Minnesota Press, 2020.

Grosz, Elizabeth. *Volatile Bodies: Toward a Corporeal Feminism*. Bloomington: Indiana University Press, 1994.

Gumilev, Lev N. *Etnogenez i biosfera zemli*. Moscow: Izdatel'stvo Akt, 2005.

Guy-Ryan, Jessie. "The Long History of America's Constitutionally-Challenged 'Border Zones.'" *Atlas Obscura*, August 1, 2016. http://www.atlasobscura.com/articles/the-long-history-of-americas-constitutionallychallenged-border-zones.

Gyatso, Janet. "Down with the Demoness: Reflections on a Feminine Ground in Tibet." *Tibet Journal* 12, no. 4 (1987): 38–53.

Haggard, Patrick. "From Bodily Sensations to Sense of Self in the Human Brain." Lecture given at Peterhouse College, Cambridge, February 1, 2012.

Halberstam, Judith. *Skin Shows: Gothic Horror and the Technology of Monsters*. Durham, NC: Duke University Press, 1995.

Hale, David George. *The Body Politic: A Political Metaphor in Renaissance English Literature*. The Hague: Mouton, 1971.

Hale, John R. *Renaissance Europe: 1480–1520*. Chichester: Wiley-Blackwell, 2000.

Handler, Richard. *Nationalism and the Politics of Culture in Quebec*. Madison: University of Wisconsin Press, 1988.

Hansen, Thomas Blom, and Finn Stepputat. Introduction to *States of Imagination: Ethnographic Exploration of the Postcolonial State*, edited by Thomas Blom Hansen and Finn Stepputat, 1–38. Durham, NC: Duke University Press, 2001.

Haraway, Donna. "The Promises of Monsters: A Regenerative Politics for Inappropriate/d Others." In *Cultural Studies*, edited by Laurence Grossberg, Cary Nelson, and Paula Treichler, 295–337. New York: Routledge, 1992.

Harley, J. B. *The New Nature of Maps: Essays in the History of Cartography*. Baltimore, MD: Johns Hopkins University Press, 2001.

Harley, J. B. "Silences and Secrecy: The Hidden Agenda of Cartography in Early Modern Europe." *Imago Mundi* 40 (1988): 57–76.

Harley, J. B., and G. Malcolm Lewis, eds. *The History of Cartography*. Vol. 2, bk. 3, *Cartography in the Traditional African, American, Arctic, Australian, and Pacific Societies*. Chicago: University of Chicago Press, 1998.

Harley, J. B., and David Woodward, eds. *The History of Cartography*. Vol. 1, *Cartography in Prehistoric, Ancient, and Medieval Europe and the Mediterranean*. Chicago: University of Chicago Press, 1987.

Harris, Jonathan Gil. *Foreign Bodies and the Body Politic: Discourses of Social Pathology in Early Modern England*. Cambridge: Cambridge University Press, 1998.

Harris, Jonathan Gil. *Untimely Matter in the Time of Shakespeare*. Philadelphia: University of Pennsylvania Press, 2009.

Harris, Tina. "Lag: Four-Dimensional Bordering in the Himalayas." In *Voluminous States: Sovereignty, Materiality, and the Territorial Imagination*, edited by Franck Billé, 78–90. Durham, NC: Duke University Press, 2020.

Harvey, David. "The City as a Body Politic." In *Wounded Cities: Destruction and Reconstruction in a Globalized World*, edited by Jane Schneider and Ida Susser. Oxford: Berg, 2003.

Harvey, P. D. A. *The History of Topographical Maps: Symbols, Pictures and Surveys*. London: Thames and Hudson, 1980.

Hayton, Bill. *The South China Sea: The Struggle for Power in Asia*. New Haven, CT: Yale University Press, 2014.

Head, Henry. *Studies in Neurology*. London: Hodder and Stoughton, 1920.

Helgerson, Richard. *Forms of Nationhood: The Elizabethan Writing of England*. Chicago: University of Chicago Press, 1992.

Helmreich, Stefan. *Alien Ocean: Anthropological Voyages in Microbial Seas*. Berkeley: University of California Press, 2009.

Helms, Mary W. *Ulysses' Sail: An Ethnographic Odyssey of Power, Knowledge, and Geographical Distance*. Princeton, NJ: Princeton University Press, 1988.

Hepple, Leslie W. "Metaphor, Geopolitical Discourse and the Military in South America." In *Writing Worlds: Text, Language and Discourse in Geography*, edited by Trevor J. Barnes and James S. Duncan, 136–54. London: Routledge, 1992.

Herships, Sally. "The Air Up There." *Marketplace*, November 7, 2013. https://www.marketplace.org/2013/11/07/air-there.

Hewitt, Rachel. *Map of a Nation: A Biography of the Ordnance Survey*. London: Granta, 2010.

Heyman, Josiah McC. "Culture Theory and the US-Mexico Border." In *A Companion to Border Studies*, edited by Thomas M. Wilson and Hastings Donnan. Chichester: Wiley-Blackwell, 2012.

High Court of Justiciary (Proceedings in the Netherlands) (United Nations) Order 1998. UK Statutory Instruments, 1998, no. 2251. https://www.legislation.gov.uk /uksi/1998/2251/contents/made.

Hill, Anne. "Phantom Limb Pain: A Review of the Literature on Attributes and Potential Mechanisms." *Journal of Pain and Symptom Management* 17, no. 2 (1999): 125–42.

Hill, Gillian. *Cartographical Curiosities*. London: British Library, 1978.

Hobsbawm, Eric. *Nations and Nationalism since 1780: Programme, Myth, Reality*. Cambridge: Cambridge University Press, 1992.

Holmes, Brian. "Counter Cartographies." In *Else/Where: Mapping New Cartographies of Networks and Territories*, edited by Janet Abrams and Peter Hall. Minneapolis: University of Minnesota Press, 2006.

Hostetler, Laura. "Qing Connections to the Early Modern World: Ethnography and Cartography in Eighteenth-Century China." *Modern Asian Studies* 34, no. 3 (July 2000): 623–62.

Huet, Marie Hélène. *Monstrous Imagination*. Cambridge, MA: Harvard University Press, 1993.

Hutchings, Alice. "The Amplification of Online Deviancy through the Language of Violent Crime, War, and Aggression." *IEEE Security and Privacy*, no. 22 (2024): 81–84. https://www.doi.org/10.1109/MSEC.2024.3353428.

Hutchison, Emma. *Affective Communities in World Politics: Collective Emotions after Trauma*. Cambridge: Cambridge University Press, 2016.

Huyssen, Andreas. *Present Pasts: Urban Palimpsests and the Politics of Memory*. Stanford, CA: Stanford University Press, 2003.

Immerwahr, Daniel. *How to Hide an Empire: A History of the Greater United States*. New York: Farrar, Straus and Giroux, 2019.

Indian Express. "Up to RS 100 cr Fine, 7 YRS in Jail for Wrong Depiction of India Map." May 6, 2016. https://indianexpress.com/article/india/india-news-india/india-map -100-crore-fine-7-years-jail-2786257.

Isabella, Jude. "Attack of the Cartographic Land Octopus." *Hakai Magazine*, September 16, 2016. https://hakaimagazine.com/article-short/attack-cartographic-land -octopus.

Itoh, Mayumi. *Japanese War Orphans in Manchuria: Forgotten Victims of World War II*. New York: Palgrave Macmillan, 2010.

Ivy, Marilyn. *Discourses of the Vanishing: Modernity, Phantasm, Japan*. Chicago: University of Chicago Press, 1995.

Iyengar, Rishi. "India Bans al-Jazeera for 5 Days for Showing 'Incorrect' Maps of Kashmir." *Time*, April 23, 2015. https://time.com/3832585/india-al-jazeera-suspended -kashmir-dispute-maps.

Jacob, Christian. *The Sovereign Map: Theoretical Approaches in Cartography throughout History*. Chicago: University of Chicago Press, 2006.

Jacobs, Frank. "Meet the Maiden Hidden Inside the Map of Finland." *Strange Maps* (blog), July 6, 2010. http://bigthink.com/strange-maps/473-a-map-of-one-arm -waving-suomi-neito.

Jacobs, Frank. *Strange Maps: An Atlas of Cartographic Curiosities.* New York: Viking Studio, 2009.

Jain, Sarah S. "The Prosthetic Imagination: Enabling and Disabling the Prosthesis Trope." *Science, Technology, and Human Values* 24, no. 1 (Winter 1999): 31–54.

Jasieński, Bruno. *The Legs of Izolda Morgan: Selected Writings.* Translated by Soren A. Gauger and Guy Torr. Prague: Twisted Spoon, 2014.

Jennings, Ken. *Maphead: Charting the Wide, Weird World of Geography Wonks.* New York: Scribner, 2012.

John of Salisbury. *Policraticus: On the Frivolities of Courtiers and the Footprints of Philosophers.* Edited and translated by Cary J. Nederman. Cambridge: Cambridge University Press, 1990.

Jones, Reece. "Agents of Exception: Border Security and the Marginalization of Muslims in India." *Environment and Planning D: Society and Space* 27, no. 5 (2009): 879–97.

Jones, Reece. "The Border Enclaves of India and Bangladesh: The Forgotten Lands." In *Borderlines and Borderlands: Political Oddities at the Edge of the Nation-State,* edited by Alexander C. Diener and Joshua Hagen, 15–32. London: Rowman and Littlefield, 2010.

Jones, Reece. *Violent Borders: Refugees and the Right to Move.* London: Verso, 2017.

Kabir, Ananya Jahanara. *Territory of Desire: Representing the Valley of Kashmir.* Minneapolis: University of Minnesota Press, 2009.

Kaisen, Jane Jin. *Apertures | Specters | Rifts.* Leeum Samsung Museum of Art, ARTSPECTRUM, Korea, 2016. https://janejinkaisen.com/apertures-specters-rifts.

Kantorowicz, Ernst H. *The King's Two Bodies: A Study in Mediaeval Political Theology.* Princeton, NJ: Princeton University Press, 1957.

Kaplan, Louise. *Oneness and Separateness: From Infant to Individual.* New York: Simon and Schuster, 1998.

Kastner, Jeffrey. "Gordon Matta-Clark's Moment." In *Odd Lots: Revisiting Gordon Matta-Clark's "Fake Estates,"* edited by Jeffrey Kastner, Sina Najafi, and Frances Richard, 30–37. New York: Cabinet Books, Queens Museum of Art, White Columns, 2005.

Kastner, Jeffrey, Sina Najafi, and Frances Richard. *Odd Lots: Revisiting Gordon Matta-Clark's "Fake Estates."* New York: Cabinet, Queens Museum of Art, White Columns, 2005.

Kauanui, J. Kēhaulani. *Paradoxes of Hawaiian Sovereignty: Land, Sex, and the Colonial Politics of State Nationalism.* Durham, NC: Duke University Press, 2018.

Keller, Evelyn Fox. *Refiguring Life: Metaphors of Twentieth-Century Biology.* New York: Columbia University Press, 1995.

Kim, Eleana. "Invasive Others and Significant Others: Strange Kinship and Interspecies Ethics near the Korean Demilitarized Zone." *Social Research: An International Quarterly* 84, no. 1 (Spring 2017): 203–20.

Kim, Eleana. "Toward an Anthropology of Landmines: Rogue Infrastructure and Military Waste in the Korean DMZ." *Cultural Anthropology* 31, no. 2 (2016): 162–87.

Kim, Hakjoon. "The Emergence of Siberia and the Russian Far East as a 'New Frontier' for Koreans." In *Rediscovering Russia in Asia: Siberia and the Russian Far East*, edited by Stephen Kotkin and David Wolff, 302–11. Armonk, NY: M. E. Sharpe, 1995.

King, Geoff. *Mapping Reality: An Exploration of Cultural Cartographies*. Houndmills, UK: Macmillan, 1996.

Kivelson, Valerie A. "Cartography, Autocracy and State Powerlessness: The Uses of Maps in Early Modern Russia." *Imago Mundi* 51 (1999): 83–105.

Klinghoffer, Arthur Jay. *The Power of Projections: How Maps Reflect Global Politics and History*. Westport, CT: Praeger, 2006.

Koch, Natalie. "Introduction: Spatializing Authoritarianism." In *Spatializing Authoritarianism*, edited by Natalie Koch, 1–21. Syracuse, NY: Syracuse University Press, 2022.

Koch, Natalie. "On the Cult of Personality and Its Consequences: American Nationalism and the Trump Cult." In *Spatializing Authoritarianism*, edited by Natalie Koch, 194–221. Syracuse, NY: Syracuse University Press, 2022.

Koga, Yukiko. *Inheritance of Loss: China, Japan, and the Political Economy of Redemption after Empire*. Chicago: University of Chicago Press, 2016.

Kommersant. "Putin: Rossia 'zuby vyb'ët' vsem, kto poprobuet chto-to u neë otkusit'." May 20, 2021. https://www.kommersant.ru/doc/4818400.

Korzybski, Alfred. "A Non-Aristotelian System and Its Necessity for Rigor in Mathematics and Physics." Paper presented at the Proceedings of the American Mathematical Society, New Orleans, Louisiana, December 28, 1931.

Kosonen, Katariina. "Maps, Newspapers, and Nationalism: The Finnish Historical Experience." *GeoJournal* 48, no. 2 (1999): 91–100.

Kövecses, Zoltán. *Where Metaphors Come From: Reconsidering Context in Metaphor*. Oxford: Oxford University Press, 2015.

Krasner, Stephen D. *Sovereignty: Organized Hypocrisy*. Princeton, NJ: Princeton University Press, 1999.

Krishna, Sankaran. "Cartographic Anxiety: Mapping the Body Politic in India." *Alternatives: Global, Local, Political* 19, no. 4 (Fall 1994): 507–21.

Krishna, Sankaran. "Oppressive Pasts and Desired Futures." *Futures* 24 (1992): 858–66.

Krishnan, Ananth. "Rising Nationalism Casts Shadow on China's Border Disputes." *Hindu*, March 21, 2013. http://www.thehindu.com/news/national/rising-nationalism-casts-shadow-on-chinas-border-disputes/article4530599.ece.

Kristeva, Julia. *Pouvoirs de l'horreur: Essai sur l'abjection*. Paris: Éditions du Seuil, 1980.

Krulwich, Robert. "An Imaginary Town Becomes Real, Then Not. True Story." *Krulwich Wonders*, NPR, March 18, 2014. https://www.npr.org/sections/krulwich/2014/03/18/290236647/an-imaginary-town-becomes-real-then-not-true-story.

Kuhrt, Natasha. *Russian Policy towards China and Japan: The El'tsin and Putin Periods*. London: Routledge, 2007.

Kurgan, Laura. *Close Up at a Distance: Mapping, Technology, and Politics*. New York: Zone, 2013.

Kwon, Heonik. *After the Massacre: Commemoration and Consolation in Ha My and My Lai*. Berkeley: University of California Press, 2006.

Lacan, Jacques. "The Mirror-Phase as Formative of the I." Translated by J. Roussel. *New Left Review* 51 (September–October 1968): 71–77.

Lakoff, George. *Moral Politics: How Liberals and Conservatives Think*. Chicago: University of Chicago Press, 2002.

Lakoff, George. *Women, Fire, and Dangerous Things: What Categories Reveal about the Mind*. Chicago: University of Chicago Press, 1987.

Lakoff, George, and Mark Johnson. *Metaphors We Live By*. Chicago: University of Chicago Press, 1980.

Lambert, Léopold. *États d'urgence: Une histoire spatiale du continuum colonial français*. Paris: Premiers matins de novembre, 2021.

Lang Ho, Cathy. "World in Motion / The Other Final." In *Else/Where: Mapping New Cartographies of Networks and Territories*, edited by Janet Abrams and Peter Hall. Minneapolis: University of Minnesota Press, 2006.

Lash, Scott. "Deforming the Figure: Topology and the Social Imaginary." *Theory, Culture and Society* 29 (2012): 261–87.

Laszczkowski, Mateusz, and Madeleine Reeves. "Introduction: Affect and the Anthropology of the State." In *Affective States: Entanglements, Suspensions, Suspicions*, edited by Mateusz Laszczkowski and Madeleine Reeves, 1–14. Oxford: Berghahn, 2018.

Lattimore, Owen. *Pivot of Asia: Sinkiang and the Inner Asian Frontiers of China and Russia*. Boston: Little, Brown, 1950.

Le Breton, David. *Anthropologie du corps et modernité*. Paris: Presses Universitaires de France, 1998.

Lee, Robert G. *Orientals: Asian Americans in Popular Culture*. Philadelphia: Temple University Press, 1999.

Leshem, Noam. "Repopulating the Emptiness: A Spatial Critique of Ruination in Israel/Palestine." *Environment and Planning D: Society and Space* 31 (2013): 522–37.

Leshem, Noam, and Alasdair Pinkerton. "Re-inhabiting No-Man's Land: Genealogies, Political Life and Critical Agendas." *Transactions of the Institute of British Geographers* 41 (2016): 41–53.

Lessing, Ferdinand D. "The Topographical Identification of Peking with Yamāntaka." In *Ritual and Symbol: Collected Essays on Lamaism and Chinese Symbolism*. Taipei: Chinese Association for Folklore, 1976.

Lewes, Darby. *Nudes from Nowhere: Utopian Sexual Landscapes*. Lanham, MD: Rowman and Littlefield, 2000.

Lewis, Jovan Scott. *Violent Utopia: Dispossession and Black Restoration in Tulsa*. Durham, NC: Duke University Press, 2022.

Lewis, Martin W., and Kären Wigen. *The Myth of Continents: A Critique of Metageography*. Berkeley: University of California Press, 1997.

Lingis, Alphonso. *Excesses: Eros and Culture*. Albany, NY: State University of New York Press, 1984.

Lingis, Alphonso. "The Physiology of Art." In *The Prosthetic Impulse: From a Posthuman Present to a Biocultural Future*, 73–89. Cambridge, MA: MIT Press, 2006.

Lloyd, Robert. "The Caprivi Strip of Namibia: Shifting Sovereignty and the Negotiation of Boundaries." In *Borderlines and Borderlands: Political Oddities at the Edge of the Nation-State*, edited by Alexander C. Diener and Joshua Hagen. London: Rowman and Littlefield, 2010.

Logvinchuk, Arkadii. "Val Chingis-Khana—Gosudarstvennaya granitsa imperii Aisin Gurun (Zolotaya Imperia)." *Nauka i priroda Dalnego Vostoka* 2 (2006).

Lomanov, Aleksandr. "Hu Jintao, mon Amur: Rossia i Kitai zavershili pogranichnoe razmezhevanie." *Vremya Novostei*, October 15, 2004. http://www.vremya.ru/2004/189/4/109852.html.

Longo, Matthew. *The Politics of Borders: Sovereignty, Security, and the Citizen after 9/11*. Cambridge: Cambridge University Press, 2018.

Lopez, Barry. *Arctic Dreams*. New York: Vintage, 2001.

Ludden, David. "Maps in the Mind and the Mobility of Asia." *Journal of Asian Studies* 62, no. 4 (November 2003): 1057–78.

Lukin, Alexander. *The Bear Watches the Dragon: Russia's Perceptions of China and the Evolution of Russian-Chinese Relations since the Eighteenth Century*. Armonk, NY: M. E. Sharpe, 2003.

Lury, Celia. *Prosthetic Culture: Photography, Memory and Identity*. London: Routledge, 1998.

Lutz, Catherine A. *Unnatural Emotions: Everyday Sentiments on a Micronesian Atoll and Their Challenge to Western Theory*. Chicago: University of Chicago Press, 1988.

Lyall, Sarah. "Losing 650 Pounds, and Preparing to Shed a Reminder of That Weight." *New York Times*, April 23, 2015, A14.

Lynteris, Christos. "Yellow Peril Epidemics: The Political Ontology of Degeneration and Emergence." In *Yellow Perils: China Narratives in the Contemporary World*, edited by Franck Billé and Sören Urbansky, 35–49. Honolulu: University of Hawai'i Press, 2018.

Macfarlane, Robert. *Underland: A Deep Time Journey*. New York: Norton, 2019.

Mack, Doug. *The Not-Quite States of America: Dispatches from the Territories and Other Far-Flung Outposts of the USA*. New York: Norton, 2017.

Maddin, Guy, dir. *My Winnipeg*. Canada: Buffalo Gal Pictures, 2007.

Maguire, Eleanor A., Katherine Woollett, and Hugo J. Spiers. "London Taxi Drivers and Bus Drivers: A Structural MRI and Neuropsychological Analysis." *Hippocampus* 16, no. 12 (2006): 1091–1101.

Maier, Charles S. *Once within Borders: Territories of Power, Wealth, and Belonging since 1500*. Cambridge, MA: Belknap, 2016.

Malkki, Liisa. "National Geographic: The Rooting of Peoples and the Territorialization of National Identity." *Cultural Anthropology* 7, no. 1 (1992): 24–44.

Marks, Laura U. *Touch: Sensuous Theory and Multisensory Media*. Minneapolis: University of Minnesota Press, 2002.

Marks, Michael P. *Metaphors in International Relations Theory*. New York: Palgrave, 2011.

Markus, David. *Notes on Trumpspace: Politics, Aesthetics, and the Fantasy of Home*. Earth, Milky Way: punctum, 2023.

Martin, Emily. "Toward an Anthropology of Immunology: The Body as Nation State." *Medical Anthropology Quarterly*, n.s., 4, no. 4 (December 1990): 410–26.

Masco, Joseph. "The Condition of Our Condition." In *Sovereignty Unhinged: An Il-lustrated Primer for the Study of Present Intensities, Disavowals, and Temporal Derangements*, edited by Deborah A. Thomas and Joseph Masco, 277–96. Durham, NC: Duke University Press, 2023.

Massey, Doreen. *For Space*. London: Sage, 2005.

Massey, Doreen. "Geography on the Agenda." *Progress in Human Geography* 25 (2001): 5–17.

Massumi, Brian. *Parables for the Virtual: Movement, Affect, Sensation*. Durham, NC: Duke University Press, 2002.

Maxwell, Rebecca. "Zoomorphic Maps: Imagining Maps as Animals." *Geography Realm*, March 31, 2014. https://www.geographyrealm.com/zoomorphic-maps -imagining-maps-animals.

Mbembe, Achille. "At the Edge of the World: Boundaries, Territoriality, and Sover-eignty in Africa." Translated by Steven Rendall. *Public Culture* 12, no. 1 (Winter 2000): 259–84.

McCall, Cathal. "Debordering and Rebordering the United Kingdom." In *A Compan-ion to Border Studies*, edited by Thomas M. Wilson and Hastings Donnan, 214–29. Chichester, UK: Wiley-Blackwell, 2012.

McClintock, Anne. *Imperial Leather: Race, Gender and Sexuality in the Colonial Con-test*. London: Routledge, 1995.

McConnell, Fiona. *Rehearsing the State: The Political Practices of the Tibetan Government-in-Exile*. Chichester: Wiley Blackwell, 2016.

McKittrick, Katherine. *Dear Science and Other Stories*. Durham, NC: Duke University Press, 2021.

McKittrick, Katherine. *Demonic Grounds: Black Women and the Cartographies of Struggle*. Minneapolis: University of Minnesota Press, 2006.

Medvedev, Sergei. "A General Theory of Russian Space: A Gay Science and a Rigor-ous Science." In *Beyond the Limits: The Concept of Space in Russian History and Culture*, edited by Jeremy Smith. Helsinki: Finnish Literature Society, 1999.

Meier, Allison. "The Octopus, a Motif of Evil in Historical Propaganda Maps." *Hy-perallergic*, May 8, 2017. https://hyperallergic.com/375900/the-map-octopus-a -propaganda-motif-of-spreading-evil.

Meierotto, Lisa. "A Disciplined Space: The Co-evolution of Conservation and Milita-rization on the US-Mexico Border." *Anthropological Quarterly* 87, no. 3 (2014): 637–64.

Melzack, Ronald. "Phantom Limbs, the Self and the Brain." *Canadian Psychology* 30, no. 1 (1989): 1–16.

Mezzadra, Sandro, and Brett Neilson. *Border as Method: Or, the Multiplication of Labor*. Durham, NC: Duke University Press, 2013.

Miéville, China. *The City and the City*. London: Pan, 2009.

Mignolo, Walter D. *The Darker Side of the Renaissance: Literacy, Territoriality, and Colonization*. Ann Arbor: University of Michigan Press, 1995.

Min, Lisa, Franck Billé, and Charlene Makley. ■■■■■■ *[Redacted]: Writing in the Negative Space of the State*. Earth, Milky Way: punctum, 2024.

Ministry of Natural Resources, China. "Circular of the Ministry of Natural Resources on Printing and Distributing the 'Specifications for the Display of Public Map Contents'" [自然资源部关于印发《公开地图内容表示规范》的通知自然资规]. February 6, 2023. http://www.gov.cn/zhengce/zhengceku/2023-02/17/content_5741977.htm.

Mirzoeff, Nicholas. *White Sight: Visual Politics and Practices of Whiteness.* Cambridge, MA: MIT Press, 2023.

Missing Migrants Project. *50,000 Lives Lost during Migration: Analysis of Missing Migrants Project Data 2014–2022.* November 23, 2022. https://missingmigrants.iom.int/50k-deaths.

Mitchell, S. Weir. *Injuries of Nerves and Their Consequences.* Philadelphia: J. B. Lippincott, 1872.

Mitchell, Timothy. "The Limits of the State: Beyond Statist Approaches and Their Critics." *American Political Science Review* 85, no. 1 (March 1991): 77–96.

Mitchell, W. J. T. "Picturing Terror: Derrida's Autoimmunity." *Cardozo Law Review* 27, no. 2 (2005): 913–25.

Modell, Arnold H. "The Sense of Agency and the Illusion of the Self." *Journal of Neuro-Aesthetics*, no. 4 (2004). https://www.artbrain.org/journal-of-neuroaesthetics/journal-neuroaesthetics-4/the-sense-of-agency-and-the-illusion-of-the-self.

Moisio, Sami, Natalie Koch, Andrew E. G. Jonas, Christopher Lizotte, and Juho Luukkonen. "Changing Geographies of the State: Themes, Challenges and Futures." In *Handbook on the Changing Geographies of the State*, 1–28. London: Edward Elgar, 2020.

Mongia, Radhika. *Indian Migration and Empire: A Colonial Genealogy of the Modern State.* Durham, NC: Duke University Press, 2018.

Monmonier, Mark. *How to Lie with Maps.* Chicago: University of Chicago Press, 1991.

Moronuki, Julie. "The Unreasonable Effectiveness of Metaphor." Keynote lecture, Compose :: Melbourne, August 27, 2018. https://argumatronic.com/posts/2018-09-02-effective-metaphor.html.

Morton, Timothy. *Hyperobjects: Philosophy and Ecology after the End of the World.* Minneapolis: University of Minnesota Press, 2013.

Moses, A. Dirk. "Partitions, Hostages, Transfer: Retributive Violence and National Security." In *Partitions: A Transnational History of Twentieth-Century Territorial Separatism*, edited by Arie Dubnov and Laura Robson, 257–95. Stanford, CA: Stanford University Press, 2019.

Mountz, Alison. *The Death of Asylum: Hidden Geographies of the Enforcement Archipelago.* Minneapolis: University of Minnesota Press, 2020.

Mountz, Alison. "The Enforcement Archipelago: Detention, Haunting, and Asylum on Islands." *Political Geography* 30, no. 3 (2011): 118–28.

Mountz, Alison, and Nancy Hiemstra. "Spatial Strategies for Rebordering Human Migration at Sea." In *A Companion to Border Studies*, edited by Thomas M. Wilson and Hastings Donnan, 455–72. Chichester, UK: Wiley-Blackwell, 2012.

Moustafine, Mara. "The Harbin Connection: Russians from China." In *Beyond China: Migrating Identities*, edited by Shen Yuanfang and Penny Edwards, 75–87. Canberra: Australian National University, 2002.

Murphy, Alexander B. "The Sovereign State System as Political-Territorial Ideal: Historical and Contemporary Considerations." In *State Sovereignty as Social Construct*, edited by Thomas J. Biersteker and Cynthia Weber, 81–120. Cambridge: Cambridge University Press, 1996.

Musharbash, Yasmine, and Ilana Gershon. *Living with Monsters: Ethnographic Fiction about Real Monsters*. Earth, Milky Way: punctum, 2023.

Musolff, Andreas. *National Conceptualisations of the Body Politic: Cultural Experience and Political Imagination*. Singapore: Springer, 2021.

Nail, Thomas. *Theory of the Border*. Oxford: Oxford University Press, 2016.

Nasar, Hammad. "Lines of Control: Partition as a Productive Space." In *Lines of Control: Partition as a Productive Space*, edited by Iftikhar Dadi and Hammad Nasar, 9–16. London: Green Cardamom; Ithaca, NY: Herbert F. Johnson Museum of Art, 2012.

Nash, Catherine. "Remapping the Body/Land: New Cartographies of Identity, Gender, and Landscape in Ireland." In *Writing Women and Space: Colonial and Postcolonial Geographies*, edited by Alison Blunt and Gillian Rose, 227–50. New York: Guilford, 1994.

Navaro-Yashin, Yael. "'Life Is Dead Here': Sensing the Political in 'No Man's Land.'" *Anthropological Theory* 3 (2003): 107–25.

Navaro-Yashin, Yael. *The Make-Believe Space: Affective Geography in a Postwar Polity*. Durham, NC: Duke University Press, 2012.

Nelson, Diane M. "Stumped Identities: Body Image, Bodies Politic, and the Mujer Maya as Prosthetic." *Cultural Anthropology* 16, no. 3 (2001): 314–53.

Neocleous, Mark. *Imagining the State*. Maidenhead, UK: Open University Press, 2003.

Neocleous, Mark. *The Politics of Immunity: Security and the Policing of Bodies*. London: Verso, 2022.

Ngai, Sianne. *Ugly Feelings*. Cambridge, MA: Harvard University Press, 2005.

Ngô, Tâm. "Between a Rock and a Hard Place: Sinophobia and Spiritual Warfare in Contemporary Vietnam." Paper presented at the panel "Religion Circulations at China's Borderlands." China Research Seminar Series (virtual). Faculty of Asian and Middle Eastern Studies, University of Cambridge, Easter Term 2021.

Nigg, Joseph. *Sea Monsters: A Voyage around the World's Most Beguiling Map*. Chicago: University of Chicago Press, 2013.

O'Connor, Erin. "'Fractions of Men': Engendering Amputation in Victorian Culture." *Comparative Studies in Society and History* 39, no. 4 (October 1997): 742–77.

O'Leary, Brendan. "Partition." In *A Companion to Border Studies*, edited by Thomas M. Wilson and Hastings Donnan. Chichester, UK: Wiley-Blackwell, 2012.

Olson, Kevin. *Imagined Sovereignties: The Power of the People and Other Myths of the Modern Age*. Cambridge: Cambridge University Press, 2016.

Ong, Aihwa. "Graduated Sovereignty in South-East Asia." In *Anthropologies of Modernity: Foucault, Governmentality, and Life Politics*, edited by Jonathan Xavier Inda, 81–104. Malden, MA: Blackwell, 2008.

Orr, D. Alan. *Treason and the State: Law, Politics, and Ideology in the English Civil War*. Cambridge: Cambridge University Press, 2002.

Orton, Joe. *Head to Toe*. London: Methuen, 1971.

Osiander, Andreas. *The States System of Europe, 1640–1990: Peacemaking and the Conditions of International Stability*. Oxford: Clarendon, 1994.

Ó Tuathail, Gearóid. *Critical Geopolitics: The Politics of Writing Global Space*. London: Routledge, 1996.

Oushakine, Serguei Alex. *The Patriotism of Despair: Nation, War, and Loss in Russia*. Ithaca, NY: Cornell University Press, 2009.

Ozturk, Ozge, Madelaine Krehm, and Athena Vouloumanos. "Sound Symbolism in Infancy: Evidence for Sound-Shape Cross-Modal Correspondences in 4-Month-Olds." *Journal of Experimental Child Psychology* 114, no. 2 (2013): 173–86.

Paasi, Anssi. "A Border Theory: An Unattainable Dream or a Realistic Aim for Border Scholars?" In *The Ashgate Research Companion to Border Studies*, edited by Doris Wastl-Walter, 11–31. Farnham, UK: Ashgate, 2011.

Paasi, Anssi. "Boundaries as Social Practice and Discourse: The Finnish-Russian Border." *Regional Studies* 33, no. 7 (1999): 669–80.

Paasi, Anssi. *Territories, Boundaries and Consciousness: The Changing Geographies of the Finnish-Russian Border*. Chichester: John Wiley and Sons, 1996.

Packer, Jeremy, and Joshua Reeves. *Killer Apps: War, Media, Machine*. Durham, NC: Duke University Press, 2020.

Packer, Jeremy, and Joshua Reeves. "Taking People Out: Drones, Media/Weapons, and the Coming Humanectomy." In *Life in the Age of Drone Warfare*, edited by Lisa Parks and Caren Kaplan, 261–81. Durham, NC: Duke University Press, 2017.

Padrón, Ricardo. *The Spacious Word: Cartography, Literature, and Empire in Early Modern Spain*. Chicago: University of Chicago Press, 2004.

Paglen, Trevor. *Blank Spots on the Map: The Dark Geography of the Pentagon's Secret World*. New York: New American Library, 2009.

Parikka, Jussi. *Insect Media: An Archaeology of Animals and Technology*. Minneapolis: University of Minnesota Press, 2010.

Park, Hyun Ok. "Korean Manchuria: The Racial Politics of Territorial Osmosis." *South Atlantic Quarterly* 99, no. 1 (2000): 193–215.

Partem, Michael Greenfield. "The Buffer System in International Relations." *Journal of Conflict Resolution* 27, no. 1 (March 1983): 3–26.

Paterson, Mark. *How We Became Sensorimotor: Movement, Measurement, Sensation*. Minneapolis: University of Minnesota Press, 2021.

Perec, Georges. *Espèces d'espaces*. Paris: Galilée, 1985.

Perry, Imani. *Vexy Thing: On Gender and Liberation*. Durham, NC: Duke University Press, 2018.

Pew Research Center. "Europeans Divided Over Whether Parts of Neighboring Countries Belong to Them." February 6, 2020. Archived March 25, 2020, at Archive.org. https://web.archive.org/web/20200325173117/https://www.pewresearch.org/global/2020/02/09/nato-seen-favorably-across-member-states/pg_2020-02-09_nato_0-18.

Pickles, John. *A History of Spaces: Cartographic Reason, Mapping and the Geo-coded World*. London: Routledge, 2004.

Pihlaja, Rachael, dir. "The Twins Who Share a Body." *Extraordinary People*. Figure 8 Films, 2007.

Pile, Steve. "Spatialities of Skin: The Chafing of Skin, Ego and Second Skins in T. E. Lawrence's *Seven Pillars of Wisdom*." *Body and Society* 17, no. 4 (2001): 57–81.

Pinet, Simone. *Archipelagoes: Insular Fictions from Chivalric Romance to the Novel*. Minneapolis: University of Minnesota Press, 2011.

Pingree, Alison. "America's 'United Siamese Brothers': Chang and Eng and Nineteenth-Century Ideologies of Democracy and Domesticity." In *Monster Theory: Reading Culture*, edited by Jeffrey Jerome Cohen, 92–114. Minneapolis: University of Minnesota Press, 1996.

Pingree, Allison. "The 'Exceptions That Prove the Rule': Daisy and Violet Hilton, the 'New Woman,' and the Bonds of Marriage." In *Freakery: Cultural Spectacles of the Extraordinary Body*, edited by Rosemary Garland Thomson, 173–84. New York: New York University Press, 1996.

Pisano, Jessica T., and André Simonyi. "Post-Soviet or Eurasian Lands? Rethinking Analytic Categories in the Ukraine-EU and Russia-China Borderlands." In *Eurasian Borderlands: Spatializing Borders in the Aftermath of State Collapse*, edited by Tone Bringa and Hege Toje, 27–57. New York: Palgrave Macmillan, 2016.

Pitts-Taylor, Victoria. *The Brain's Body: Neuroscience and Corporeal Politics*. Durham, NC: Duke University Press, 2016.

Poll, Zoey. "For Decades, Cartographers Have Been Hiding Covert Illustrations Inside of Switzerland's Official Maps." *Eye on Design*, February 24, 2020. https://eyeondesign.aiga.org/for-decades-cartographers-have-been-hiding-covert-illustrations-inside-of-switzerlands-official-maps.

Porteous, J. Douglas. *Landscapes of the Mind: Worlds of Sense and Metaphor*. Toronto: University of Toronto Press, 1990.

Potter, Pitman B. "Theoretical and Conceptual Perspectives on the Periphery in Contemporary China." In *The Chinese State at the Borders*, edited by Diana Lary, 240–70. Vancouver: UBC Press, 2007.

Pratt, Mary Louise. *Imperial Eyes: Travel Writing and Transculturation*. London: Routledge, 2008.

Prescott, John R. V. *Political Frontiers and Boundaries*. London: Allen and Unwin, 1987.

Prince, Todd. "Moscow's Invasion of Ukraine Triggers 'Soul-Searching' at Western Universities as Scholars Rethink Russian Studies." *Radio Free Europe*, January 1, 2023. https://www.rferl.org/a/russia-war-ukraine-western-academia/32201630.html.

Prosser, Jay. "Skin Memories." In *Thinking through the Skin*, edited by Sara Ahmed and Jackie Stacey, 52–68. London: Routledge, 2001.

Pulford, Ed. *Past Progress: Time and Politics at the Borders of China, Russia, and Korea*. Stanford, CA: Stanford University Press, 2024.

Pullan, Wendy. "Spatial Discontinuities: Conflict Infrastructures in Contested Cities." In *Locating Urban Conflicts: Ethnicity, Nationalism and the Everyday*, edited by Wendy Pullan and Britt Baillie, 17–36. Houndmills, UK: Palgrave Macmillan, 2013.

Putz, Orsolya. *Metaphor and National Identity: Alternative Conceptualization of the Treaty of Trianon*. Amsterdam: John Benjamins, 2019.

Qi Xuejun [祁学俊]. *Heihe Shihua* [黑河史话]. Harbin: Heilongjiang Renmin Chubanshe, 2009.

Rael, Ronald. *Borderwall as Architecture: A Manifesto for the U.S.-Mexico Boundary.* Berkeley: University of California Press, 2017.

Ramachandran, Vilayanur S., and Sandra Blakeslee. *Phantoms in the Brain: Probing the Mysteries of the Human Mind.* London: Fourth Estate, 1998.

Ramachandran, Vilayanur S., and William Hirstein. "The Perception of Phantom Limbs." *Brain* 21 (1998): 1603–30.

Ramaswamy, Sumathi. "Conceit of the Globe in Mughal Visual Practice." *Comparative Studies in Society and History* 49, no. 4 (2007): 751–82.

Ramaswamy, Sumathi. *The Lost Land of Lemuria: Fabulous Geographies, Catastrophic Histories.* Berkeley: University of California Press, 2004.

Ramaswamy, Sumathi. "Maps and Mother Goddesses in Modern India." *Imago Mundi* 53 (2001): 97–114.

Ramaswamy, Sumathi. "Maps, Mother/Goddesses, and Martyrdom in Modern India." *Journal of Asian Studies* 67, no. 3 (August 2008), 819–53.

Ramaswamy, Sumathi. "Midnight's Line." In *Lines of Control: Partition as a Productive Space*, edited by Iftikhar Dadi and Hammad Nasar, 27–35. Ithaca, NY: Herbert F. Johnson Museum of Art, 2012.

Rankin, William. *After the Map: Cartography, Navigation, and the Transformation of Territory in the Twentieth Century.* Chicago: University of Chicago Press, 2016.

Reeves, Madeleine. *Border Work: Spatial Lives of the State in Rural Central Asia.* Ithaca, NY: Cornell University Press, 2014.

Reeves, Madeleine. "Fixing the Border: On the Affective Life of the State in Southern Kyrgyzstan." *Environment and Planning D: Society and Space* 29 (2011): 905–23.

Reeves, Madeleine. "Signs of Sovereignty: Mapping and Countermapping at an 'Unwritten' Border." In *The Everyday Lives of Sovereignty: Political Imagination beyond the State*, edited by Rebecca Bryant and Madeleine Reeves, 217–39. Ithaca, NY: Cornell University Press, 2021.

Reeves, Madeleine. "Time and Contingency in the Anthropology of Borders: On Border as Event in Rural Central Asia." In *Eurasian Borderlands: Spatializing Borders in the Aftermath of State Collapse*, edited by Tone Bringa and Hege Toje, 159–83. New York: Palgrave Macmillan, 2016.

Reeves, Madeleine. "#Trumpistan: On the Cunning Familiarity of the Authoritarian Absurd." *Cultural Anthropology: Fieldsights*, April 25, 2018. https://culanth.org /fieldsights/trumpistan-on-the-cunning-familiarity-of-the-authoritarian-absurd.

Richardson, Cliff. "Phantom Limb Pain: Prevalence, Mechanisms and Associated Factors." In *Amputation, Prosthesis Use, and Phantom Limb Pain: An Interdisciplinary Perspective*, edited by Craig Murray. New York: Springer, 2010.

Richardson, Paul B. *At the Edge of the Nation: The Southern Kurils and the Search for Russia's National Identity.* Honolulu: University of Hawai'i Press, 2018.

Ries, Nancy. "Cruel Speech: Russia's Atrocity Rhetoric during Its War on Ukraine." *Ethnologia Polona* 44 (2023): 105–35.

Ripple, William J., Christopher Wolf, Jillian W. Gregg, Johan Rockström, Thomas M. Newsome, Beverly E. Law, Luiz Marques, et al. "The 2023 State of the Climate Report: Entering Uncharted Territory." *BioScience* 73, no. 12 (December 2023): 841–50.

Ritvo, Harriet. *The Platypus and the Mermaid, and Other Figments of the Classifying Imagination*. Cambridge, MA: Harvard University Press, 1997.

Roberts, Brian Russell. *Borderwaters: Amid the Archipelagic States of America*. Durham, NC: Duke University Press, 2021.

Robinson, Arthur H. *The Look of Maps: An Examination of Cartographic Design*. Madison: University of Wisconsin Press, 1986.

Rose, Gillian. *Feminism and Geography: The Limits of Geographical Knowledge*. Cambridge: Polity, 1993.

Rowe, William C. "The Wakhan Corridor: Endgame of the Great Game." In *Borderlines and Borderlands: Political Oddities at the Edge of the Nation-State*, edited by Alexander C. Diener and Joshua Hagen, 53–68. London: Rowman and Littlefield, 2010.

Ryan, Lisa. "Trump's Dick Reportedly Looks Like Toad from Mario Kart." *Cut*, September 18, 2018. https://www.thecut.com/2018/09/donald-trump-stormy-daniels-penis-toad-mario-kart.html.

Ryzhova, Natalia. "Freedoms, the State and Security: Border Exclusion Zones in Post-Soviet Russia." MPhil diss., University of Cambridge, 2014.

Saarinen, Thomas F. "Centering of Mental Maps of the World." Discussion paper. Tucson, AZ: Department of Geography and Regional Development, 1987.

Sacks, Oliver. Foreword to *Phantoms in the Brain: Probing the Mysteries of the Human Mind*, by Vilayanur Ramachandran and Sandra Blakeslee. London: Fourth Estate, 1998.

Sacks, Oliver. *A Leg to Stand On*. 1984. Reprint, London: Picador, 2012.

Sahlins, Peter. *Boundaries: The Making of France and Spain in the Pyrenees*. Berkeley: University of California Press, 1991.

Santner, Eric L. *The Royal Remains: The People's Two Bodies and the Endgames of Sovereignty*. Chicago: University of Chicago Press, 2011.

Sartre, Jean-Paul. *L'être et le néant*. Paris: Gallimard, 1943.

Schaeffer, Felicity Amaya. *Unsettled Borders: The Militarized Science of Surveillance on Sacred Indigenous Land*. Durham, NC: Duke University Press, 2022.

Schilder, Paul. *The Image and Appearance of the Human Body: Studies in the Constructive Energies of the Psyche*. 1935. Reprint, New York: International Universities Press, 1950.

Schmid, Andre. "Looking North toward Manchuria." *South Atlantic Quarterly* 99, no. 1 (Winter 2000): 219–40.

Scott, James C. *Seeing Like A State: How Certain Schemes to Improve the Human Condition Have Failed*. New Haven, CT: Yale University Press, 1998.

Scott, James C. *The Art of Not Being Governed: An Anarchist History of Upland Southeast Asia*. New Haven, CT: Yale University Press, 2009.

Searle, John R. "Metaphor." In *Metaphor and Thought*, edited by Andrew Ortony, 83–111. Cambridge: Cambridge University Press, 1993.

Sedgwick, Eve Kosofsky. *Novel Gazing: Queer Readings in Fiction*. Durham, NC: Duke University Press, 1997.

Sedgwick, Eve Kosofsky. *Touching Feeling: Affect, Pedagogy, Performativity*. Durham, NC: Duke University Press, 2003.

Seegel, Steven. "Any Lessons Learned? Echo Chambers of Staged Geopolitics and Eth-nocentricity in Maps of the Russian-Ukrainian Conflict in February–March 2014." In *Umstrittene Räume in Der Ukraine: Politische Diskurse, literarische Repräsenta-tionen und kartographische Visualisierungen*, edited by Sabine von Löwis, 125–49. Göttingen: Wallstein, 2020.

Serres, Michel. *The Five Senses: A Philosophy of Mingled Bodies (I)*. Translated by Margaret Sankey and Peter Cowley. London: Continuum, 2008.

Shachar, Ayelet. *The Shifting Border: Legal Cartographies of Migration and Mobility. Ayelet Shachar in Dialogue*. Manchester: Manchester University Press, 2020.

Shanghaiist. "Gap Apologizes for T-Shirt Design That Leaves Taiwan Out of Map of China." *Medium*, May 15, 2018. https://medium.com/shanghaiist/gap-apologizes -for-t-shirt-design-that-leaves-taiwan-out-of-map-of-china-cd912b2dd24a.

Sharifian, Farzad, René Dirven, Ning Yu, and Suzanne Niemeier. "Culture and Lan-guage: Looking for the 'Mind' inside the Body." In *Culture, Body, and Language: Conceptualizations of Internal Body Organs across Cultures and Languages*, edited by Farzad Sharifian, René Dirven, Ning Yu, and Suzanne Niemeier, 3–23. Berlin: Mouton De Gruyter, 2008.

Sharma, Aman. "7-Year Jail, RS 100 Crore Fine Soon for Showing PoK, Arunachal as Disputed." *Economic Times*, May 5, 2016. http://economictimes.indiatimes.com /news/politics-and-nation/7-year-jail-rs-100-crore-fine-soon-for-showing-pok -arunachal-as-disputed/articleshow/52117889.cms.

Sharpe, Christina. *In the Wake: On Blackness and Being*. Durham, NC: Duke Univer-sity Press, 2016.

Shaw, Ian G. R. *Predator Empire: Drone Warfare and Full Spectrum Dominance*. Minneapolis: University of Minnesota Press, 2016.

Sheldrake, Merlin. *Entangled Life: How Fungi Make Our Worlds, Change Our Minds, and Shape Our Futures*. New York: Random House, 2020.

Shildrick, Margrit. *Dangerous Discourses of Disability, Subjectivity and Sexuality*. Houndmills: Palgrave Macmillan, 2009.

Shildrick, Margrit. *Embodying the Monster: Encounters with the Vulnerable Self*. London: Sage, 2001.

Shildrick, Margrit. *Visceral Prostheses: Somatechnics and Posthuman Embodiment*. London: Bloomsbury Academic, 2022.

Shildrick, Margrit. "Vulnerable Bodies and Ontological Contamination." In *Conta-gion: Historical and Cultural Studies*, edited by Alison Bashford and Claire Hooker, 153–67. London: Routledge, 2001.

Shildrick, Margrit. "'You Are There, Like My Skin': Reconfiguring Relational Econo-mies." In *Thinking through the Skin*, edited by Sara Ahmed and Jackie Stacey, 160–73. London: Routledge, 2001.

Shoemaker, Nancy. *A Strange Likeness: Becoming Red and White in Eighteenth-Century North America*. Oxford: Oxford University Press, 2004.

Shotter, J., and M. Billig. "A Bakhtinian Psychology: From Out of the Heads of Indi-viduals and into the Dialogue between Them." In *Bakhtin and the Human Sciences: No Last Words*, edited by M. M. Bell and M. Gardiner, 13–29. London: Sage, 1998.

Shteyngart, Gary. *Absurdistan: A Novel*. New York: Random House, 2007.

Shteyngart, Gary. "Out of My Mouth Comes Unimpeachable Manly Truth." *New York Times*, February 18, 2015. https://www.nytimes.com/2015/02/22/magazine/out-of -my-mouth-comes-unimpeachable-manly-truth.html.

Siegert, Bernhard. "The Map *Is* the Territory." *Radical Philosophy*, September/October 2011. https://www.radicalphilosophy.com/article/the-map-is-the-territory.

Simmel, Marianne L. "The Reality of Phantom Sensations." *Social Research* 29, no. 3 (Autumn 1962): 337–56.

Simmons, Beth A. "Rules over Real Estate: Trade, Territorial Conflict, and International Borders as Institution." *Journal of Conflict Resolution* 49 (2005): 823–48.

Simon, Axelle. "Kader Attia, L'art de la mémoire et de la réparation." France 24. Posted on YouTube, November 22, 2016. https://www.youtube.com/watch?v=tUnzhadjo8k.

Simpson, Audra. *Mohawk Interruptus: Political Life across the Borders of Settler States*. Durham, NC: Duke University Press, 2014.

Simpson, Leanne Betasamosake. *As We Have Always Done: Indigenous Freedom through Radical Resistance*. Minneapolis: University of Minnesota Press, 2017.

Sinelschikova, Yekaterina. "How the Bear Became the Symbol of Russia." *Russia Beyond*, June 10, 2019. https://www.rbth.com/history/330484-russian-bear-became-symbol.

Singer, P. W. *Wired for War: The Robotics Revolution and Conflict in the 21st Century*. New York: Penguin, 2009.

Šír, Jan. "Cult of Personality in Monumental Art and Architecture: The Case of Post-Soviet Turkmenistan." *Acta Slavica Iaponica* 25 (2008): 203–20.

Slobodian, Quinn. *Crack-Up Capitalism: Market Radicals and the Dream of a World without Democracy*. New York: Metropolitan, 2023.

Smith, Marquard. "The Uncertainty of Placing: Prosthetic Bodies, Sculptural Design, and Unhomely Dwelling in Marc Quinn, James Gillingham, and Sigmund Freud." *Journal of Neuro-Aesthetics Theory*, no. 4 (2004). https://www.artbrain.org /journal-of-neuroaesthetics/journal-neuroaesthetics-4/the-uncertainty-of-placing-prosthetic-bodies-sculptural-design-and-unhomely-dwelling-in-marc-quinn-james-gillingham-and-sigmu.

Smith, Marquard. "The Vulnerable Articulate: James Gillingham, Aimee Mullins, and Matthew Barney." In *The Prosthetic Impulse: From a Posthuman Present to a Biocultural Future*, 43–72. Cambridge, MA: MIT Press, 2006.

Smith, Marquard, and Joanne Morra. Introduction to *The Prosthetic Impulse: From a Posthuman Present to a Biocultural Future*, 1–14. Cambridge, MA: MIT Press, 2006.

Sobchack, Vivian. *Carnal Thoughts: Embodiment and Moving Image Culture*. Berkeley: University of California Press, 2004.

Sobchack, Vivian. "A Leg to Stand On: Prosthetics, Metaphor, and Materiality." In *The Prosthetic Impulse: From a Posthuman Present to a Biocultural Future*, edited by Marquard Smith and Joanne Morra, 17–41. Cambridge, MA: MIT Press, 2006.

Sobchack, Vivian. "Living a 'Phantom Limb': On the Phenomenology of Bodily Integrity." *Body and Society* 16, no. 3 (2010): 51–67.

Song, Nianshen. *Making Borders in Modern East Asia: The Tumen River Demarcation, 1881–1919*. Cambridge: Cambridge University Press, 2018.

Songster, E. Elena. *Panda Nation: The Construction and Conservation of China's Modern Icon*. Oxford: Oxford University Press, 2018.

Sparke, Matthew. "The Map That Roared and an Original Atlas: Canada, Cartography and the Narration of Nation." *Annals of the Association of American Geographers* 88, no. 3 (1998): 463–95.

Speir, Hans. "Magic Geography." *Social Research* 8 (1941): 310–30.

Spillers, Hortense J. "Mama's Baby, Papa's Maybe: An American Grammar Book." *Diacritics* 17, no. 2 (1987): 64–81.

Squires, Nick. "Welcome to the World's Newest Country—the Kingdom of Enclava." *Telegraph*, May 15, 2015. https://www.telegraph.co.uk/news/worldnews/europe/croatia/11609226/Welcome-to-the-worlds-newest-country-the-Kingdom-of-Enclava.html.

Stallybrass, Peter. "Patriarchal Territories: The Body Enclosed." In *Rewriting the Renaissance: The Discourses of Sexual Difference in Early Modern Europe*, edited by Margaret W. Ferguson, Maureen Quilligan, and Nancy J. Vickers, 123–42. Chicago: University of Chicago Press, 1986.

Stark, Douglas. *When Basketball Was Jewish: Voices of Those Who Played the Game*. Lincoln: Nebraska University Press, 2017.

Stein, Howard F. *Developmental Time, Cultural Space: Studies in Psychogeography*. New York: Library of Social Science, 2012.

Steinberg, Philip E. "Insularity, Sovereignty and Statehood: The Representation of Islands on Portolan Charts and the Construction of the Territorial State." *Geografiska Annaler, Series B, Human Geography* 87, no. 4 (2005): 253–65.

Steinberg, Philip E. *The Social Construction of the Ocean*. Cambridge: Cambridge University Press, 2001.

Steinberg, Philip E., Jeremy Tasch, and Hannes Gerhardt. *Contesting the Arctic: Politics and Imaginaries in the Circumpolar North*. London: I. B. Tauris, 2015.

Stewart, Susan. *On Longing: Narratives of the Miniature, the Gigantic, the Souvenir, the Collection*. Baltimore, MD: Johns Hopkins University Press, 1984.

Stoler, Ann Laura. *Haunted by Empire: Geographies of Intimacy in North American History*. Durham, NC: Duke University Press, 2006.

Stoler, Ann Laura. *Imperial Debris: On Ruins and Ruination*. Durham, NC: Duke University Press, 2013.

St. Onge, Tim. "Null Island Is One of the Most Visited Places on Earth. Too Bad It Doesn't Exist." *Atlas Obscura*, May 9, 2019. https://www.atlasobscura.com/articles/null-island-is-one-of-the-most-visited-places-on-earth-too-bad-it-doesnt-exist.

Storey, David. *Territories: The Claiming of Space*. London: Routledge, 2012.

Strate, Shane. *The Lost Territories: Thailand's History of National Humiliation*. Honolulu: University of Hawai'i Press, 2015.

Stryker, Susan. *When Monsters Speak*, edited by McKenzie Wark. Durham, NC: Duke University Press, 2024.

Svyatenkov, Pavel. "Nyneshnyaya Rossiya—lish 'obrubok' SSSR, ego nepolnotsennyi naslednik." *km.ru* (blog), May 3, 2012. https://www.km.ru/v-rossii/2012/05/03/istoriya-rossiiskoi-federatsii/nyneshnyaya-rossiya-lish-obrubok-sssr-ego-nepolno.

Szmagalska-Follis, Karolina. "Repossession: Notes on Restoration and Redemption in Ukraine's Western Borderland." *Cultural Anthropology* 23, no. 2 (2008): 329–60.

TallBear, Kim. *Native American DNA: Tribal Belonging and the False Promise of Genetic Science*. Minneapolis: University of Minnesota Press, 2013.

Tamanoi, Mariko Asano. *Memory Maps: The State and Manchuria in Postwar Japan*. Honolulu: University of Hawai'i Press, 2009.

Tamminen, Sakari. *Biogenetic Paradoxes of the Nation: Finncattle, Apples, and Other Genetic-Resource Puzzles*. Durham, NC: Duke University Press, 2019.

Taylor, Candacy. *Overground Railroad: The Green Book and the Roots of Black Travel in America*. New York: Abrams, 2020.

Te Punga Somerville, Alice. "The Great Pacific Garbage Patch as Metaphor: The (American) Pacific You Can't See." In *Archipelagic American Studies*, edited by Brian Russell Roberts and Michelle Ann Stephens, 320–38. Durham, NC: Duke University Press, 2017.

Terry, Jennifer. *Attachments to War: Biomedical Logics and Violence in Twenty-First-Century America*. Durham, NC: Duke University Press, 2017.

Thibodeau, P. H., and L. Boroditsky. "Metaphors We Think With: The Role of Metaphor in Reasoning." *PLoS ONE* 6, no. 2 (2011): E16782. https://doi.org/10.1371/journal. pone.0016782.

Thomson, Rosemary Garland. "Introduction: From Wonder to Error—a Genealogy of Freak Discourse in Modernity." In *Freakery: Cultural Spectacles of the Extraordinary Body*, edited by Rosemary Garland Thomson, 1–19. New York: New York University Press, 1996.

Thrift, Nigel. "It's the Little Things." In *Geopolitical Traditions: A Century of Geopolitical Thought*, edited by D. Atkinson and K. Dodds, 380–87. London: Routledge, 2000.

Thrift, Nigel. *Non-representational Theory: Space, Politics, Affect*. London: Routledge, 2008.

Thrower, Norman J. W. *Maps and Civilization: Cartography in Culture and Society*. Chicago: University of Chicago Press, 2008.

Toal, Gerard. *Near Abroad: Putin, the West, and the Contest over Ukraine and the Caucasus*. Oxford: Oxford University Press, 2008.

Tomaini, Thea, and Asa Simon Mittman. *Sea Monsters: Things from the Sea*. Vol. 2. Earth, Milky Way: punctum, 2017.

Traub, Valerie. "Mapping the Global Body." In *Early Modern Visual Culture: Representation, Race, Empire in Renaissance England*, edited by Peter Erickson and Clark Hulse. Philadelphia: University of Pennsylvania Press, 2000.

Tsing, Anna Lowenhaupt. *Friction: An Ethnography of Global Connection*. Princeton, NJ: Princeton University Press, 2005.

Tsing, Anna Lowenhaupt. *The Mushroom at the End of the World: On the Possibility of Life in Capitalist Ruins*. Princeton, NJ: Princeton University Press, 2015.

Tu, Weiming. "Cultural China: The Periphery as the Center." In *The Living Tree: The Changing Meaning of Being Chinese Today*. Stanford, CA: Stanford University Press, 1994.

Turits, Richard Lee. *Foundations of Despotism: Peasants, the Trujillo Regime, and Modernity in Dominican History*. Stanford, CA: Stanford University Press, 2002.

Turk, Cate. "Maps as Foams and the Rheology of Digital Spatial Media: A Conceptual Framework for Considering Mapping Projects as They Change over Time." In *Time for Mapping: Cartographic Temporalities*, edited by Sybille Lammes, Chris Perkins, Alex Gekker, Sam Hind, Clancy Wilmott, and Daniel Evans. Manchester: Manchester University Press, 2018.

Turnbull, David. "Cartography and Science in Early Modern Europe: Mapping the Construction of Knowledge Spaces." *Imago Mundi* 48 (2006): 5–24.

Tyner, Judith A. "Persuasive Cartography." *Journal of Geography* 81, no. 4 (1982): 140–44.

Valeriano, Brandon, and John Van Benthuysen. "When States Die: Geographic and Territorial Pathways to State Death." *Third World Quarterly* 33, no. 7 (2012): 1165–89.

Van Duzer, Chet. *Sea Monsters on Medieval and Renaissance Maps*. London: British Library, 2013.

van Schendel, Willem. "Geographies of Knowing, Geographies of Ignorance: Jumping Scale in Southeast Asia." *Environment and Planning D: Society and Space* 20, no. 6 (2002): 647–68.

Vaughan-Williams, Nick. *Border Politics: The Limits of Sovereign Power*. Edinburgh: Edinburgh University Press, 2009.

Vinokurov, Evgeny. *A Theory of Enclaves*. Lanham, MD: Lexington, 2007.

von Hirschhausen, Béatrice. "De l'intérêt heuristique du concept de fantôme géographique pour penser les régionalisations culturelles." *L'Espace géographique* 46, no. 2 (2017): 106–25.

von Hirschhausen, Béatrice, Hannes Grandits, Claudia Kraft, Dietmar Müller, and Thomas Serrier. *Phantom Grenzen: Räume und Akteure in der Zeit neu denken*. Göttingen: Wallstein, 2015.

von Löwis, Sabine. "Phantom Borders in the Political Geography of East Central Europe: An Introduction." *Erdkunde* 69, no. 2 (2015): 99–106.

Wallach, Yair. "Trapped in Mirror-Images: The Rhetoric of Maps in Israel/Palestine." *Political Geography* 30 (2011): 358–69.

Wark, McKenzie. Introduction to *When Monsters Speak: A Susan Stryker Reader*, by Susan Stryker, edited by McKenzie Wark, 1–19. Durham, NC: Duke University Press, 2024.

Weheliye, Alexander G. *Habeas Viscus: Racializing Assemblages, Biopolitics, and Black Feminist Theories of the Human*. Durham, NC: Duke University Press, 2014.

Weinstock, Jeffrey Andrew. "Freaks in Space: 'Extraterrestrialism' and 'Deep-Space Multiculturalism.'" In *Freakery: Cultural Spectacles of the Extraordinary Body*, edited by Rosemary Garland Thomson, 327–37. New York: New York University Press, 1996.

Weinstock, Jeffrey Andrew. "Introduction: A Genealogy of Monster Theory." In *The Monster Theory Reader*, edited by Jeffrey Andrew Weinstock, 1–36. Minneapolis: University of Minnesota Press, 2020.

Weinstock, Jeffrey Andrew. "Invisible Monsters: Vision, Horror, and Contemporary Culture." In *The Monster Theory Reader*, edited by Jeffrey Andrew Weinstock, 358–73. Minneapolis: University of Minnesota Press, 2020.

Weiss, Gail. *Body Images: Embodiment as Intercorporeality*. New York: Routledge, 1999.

Weizman, Eyal. *Hollow Land: Israel's Architecture of Occupation*. London: Verso, 2007.

White, George W. "Place and Its Role in Serbian Identity." In *Reconstructing the Balkans: A Geography of the New Southeast Europe*, edited by Derek Hall and Darrick Danta. Chichester: John Wiley and Sons, 1996.

Whyte, Brendan R. "'En Territoire Belge et à Quarante Centimètres de la Frontière': An Historical and Documentary Study of the Belgian and Dutch Enclaves of Baarle-Hertog and Baarle-Nassau." Research paper 19. Melbourne: School of Anthropology, Geography and Environmental Studies, University of Melbourne, 2004.

Widdis, Emma. "Russia as Space." In *National Identity in Russian Culture: An Introduction*, edited by Simon Franklin and Emma Widdis, 30–49. Cambridge: Cambridge University Press, 2004.

Wigen, Kären. *A Malleable Map: Geographies of Restoration in Central Japan, 1600–1912*. Berkeley: University of California Press, 2010.

Wigen, Kären. "Orienting the Past in Early Modern Japan." In *Time in Maps: From the Age of Discovery to Our Digital Era*, edited by Kären Wigen and Caroline Winterer, 37–62. Chicago: University of Chicago Press, 2020.

Wigen, Kären, and Caroline Winterer. "Pacific Asia." In *Time in Maps: From the Age of Discovery to Our Digital Era*, edited by Kären Wigen and Caroline Winterer, 35–36. Chicago: University of Chicago Press, 2020.

Wilson, Alice. "Everyday Sovereignty in Exile: People, Territory, and Resources among Sahrawi Refugees." In *The Everyday Lives of Sovereignty: Political Imagination beyond the State*, edited by Rebecca Bryant and Madeleine Reeves, 134–33. Ithaca, NY: Cornell University Press, 2021.

Wilson, Alice. *Sovereignty in Exile: A Saharan Liberation Movement Governs*. Philadelphia: University of Pennsylvania Press, 2016.

Winichakul, Thongchai. *Siam Mapped: A History of the Geo-Body of a Nation*. Honolulu: University of Hawai'i Press, 1994.

Winterer, Caroline, and Kären Wigen. "Introduction: Maps Tell Time." In *Time in Maps: From the Age of Discovery to Our Digital Era*, edited by Kären Wigen and Caroline Winterer, 1–13. Chicago: University of Chicago Press, 2020.

Wishnick, Elizabeth. "Why a 'Strategic Partnership'? The View from China." In *The Future of China-Russia Relations*, edited by James Bellacqua. Lexington: University Press of Kentucky, 2010.

Withnall, Adam. "Norway Refuses to Give Mountain to Finland as Anniversary Present." *Independent*, October 16, 2016. https://www.independent.co.uk/news/world/europe/norway-finland-mount-halti-mountain-centenary-independence-erna-solberg-a7364136.html.

Wittkower, Rudolf. *Allegory and the Migration of Symbols*. New York: Thames and Hudson, 1977.

Wohlleben, Peter. *The Hidden Life of Trees: What They Feel, How They Communicate. Discoveries from a Secret World*. Vancouver: Greystone, 2015.

Wood, Denis. *Rethinking the Power of Maps*. New York: Guilford, 2010.

Woodward, David. *Art and Cartography: Six Historical Essays*. Chicago: University of Chicago Press, 1987.

Woodward, David. "Maps and the Rationalization of Geographic Space." In *Circa 1492: Art in the Age of Exploration*, edited by Jay A. Levenson, 83–87. New Haven, CT: Yale University Press for the National Gallery of Art, 1991.

Woodward, David, and G. Malcolm Lewis. *The History of Cartography: Cartography in the Traditional African, American, Arctic, Australian, and Pacific Societies*, vol. 2, book 3. Chicago: University of Chicago Press, 1998.

Wright, Alexa. "Monstrous Strangers at the Edge of the World: The Monstrous Races." in *The Monster Theory Reader*, edited by Jeffrey Andrew Weinstock, 173–91. Minneapolis: University of Minnesota Press, 2020.

Wynter, Sylvia. "Black Metamorphosis: New Natives in a New World." Unpublished manuscript, n.d.

Yamamuro, Shin'ichi. *Manchuria under Japanese Dominion*. Translated by Joshua A. Fogel. Philadelphia: University of Pennsylvania Press, 2006.

Yavuz, M. Hakan. *Nostalgia for the Empire: The Politics of Neo-Ottomanism*. Oxford: Oxford University Press, 2020.

Yerushalmi, Shalom. "Netanyahu Aims to Fill West Bank with High-Speed Tunnels, in Vision Laid Out by Musk." *Times of Israel*, February 4, 2023. https://www.timesofisrael.com/netanyahu-looks-to-cover-west-bank-with-highway-tunnels-in-vision-laid-out-by-musk.

Yıldırım, Umut. "Space, Loss and Resistance: A Haunted Pool-Map in South-Eastern Turkey." *Anthropological Theory* 19, no. 4 (2019): 440–69.

Yong, Ed. *I Contain Multitudes: The Microbes within Us and a Grander View of Life*. New York: HarperCollins, 2016.

Young, Iris. *Throwing Like a Girl and Other Essays in Feminist Philosophy and Social Theory*. Bloomington: Indiana University Press, 1990.

Young, Louise. *Japan's Total Empire: Manchuria and the Culture of Wartime Imperialism*. Berkeley: University of California Press, 1999.

Yu, Ning. "The Chinese Heart as the Central Faculty of Cognition." In *Culture, Body, and Language: Conceptualizations of Internal Body Organs across Cultures and Languages*, edited by Farzad Sharifian, René Dirven, Ning Yu, and Suzanne Niemeier. Berlin: Mouton De Gruyter, 2008.

Yurchak, Alexei. "Bodies of Lenin: The Hidden Science of Communist Sovereignty." *Representations*, February 2015, 116–57.

Zarkadakis, George. *In Our Own Image: Savior or Destroyer? The History and Future of Artificial Intelligence*. New York: Pegasus, 2015.

Zatsepine, Victor. "The Blagoveshchensk Massacre of 1900: The Sino-Russian War and Global Imperialism." In *Beyond Suffering: Recounting War in Modern China*, edited by J. Flath and N. Smith, 107–29. Vancouver: University of British Columbia Press, 2011.

Zeidler, Miklós. *Ideas on Territorial Revision in Hungary 1920–1945*. Translated by Thomas J. and Helen DeKornfeld. Boulder, CO: Social Science Monographs, 2007.

Zinken, Jörg, and Andreas Musolff. "A Discourse-Centred Perspective on Metaphorical Meaning and Understanding." In *Metaphor and Discourse*, edited by Andreas Musolff and Jörg Zinken. Houndmills: Palgrave Macmillan, 2009.

Žižek, Slavoj. "Neighbors and Other Monsters: A Plea for Ethical Violence." In *The Neighbor: Three Inquiries in Political Theology*, edited by Slavoj Žižek, Eric L. Santner, and Kenneth Reinhard, 134–90. Chicago: University of Chicago Press, 2005.

Index

Page numbers followed by f refer to figures.

maps, 1–3, 7, 12, 16, 30–32, 35–36, 38–45, 47–48, 50, 52–58, 62, 81, 83, 103–4, 107, 127, 163, 194, 219n130, 219n136, 220n141, 223n35, 229n137; anthropomorphic, 10, 58–59, 66, 68, 72, 87–88, 224n36; body, 136; of border areas, 148; in Bosnia-Herzegovina, 231n2; Chinese, 111–12, 115, 178, 207n38, 213n30, 216n87, 234n57, 254n86; Cypriot, 246n86; fictive, 228n126; French, 233n44; geopolitical, 209n80; Google and, 192; imperial, 185, 199; India and, 242n11, 247n6; Inuit, 214n49, 243n20; Israeli, 217n102, 260n33; Japanese, 207n38, 212n27; medieval maps, 23, 40–41, 189; metaphoric role of, 195; modern, 7, 32, 35, 40–41, 205n5, 214n57; national, 46–48, 77; national identity and, 207n40, 217n101; natural features on, 226n92; for navigation, 9, 35, 191; online, 95; Ottoman Empire and, 252n60; Palestinian, 217n102; phantom borders and, 233n47; political, 19, 32, 35, 45, 47, 54, 58, 66, 78, 176, 197; Renaissance maps, 8, 36, 40–41, 213n28; scientific, 8; somatotopic, 144; Soviet, 207n45, 220nn144–45; space and, 218n116; the territorial monstrous and, 182; in Thailand, 214n43; time and, 193; T-O maps, 40, 68, 215n66, 223n35; vernacular, 208n70; weather, 180, 252n66; world, 32, 60, 214n57; zoomorphic, 10, 59, 66, 68, 71–72, 88. *See also* logomap

Martin, Emily, 63, 151, 222n16

Matta-Clark, Gordon, 163, 164f, 172, 175, 247n1

measurement, 7, 12, 35, 58, 200

Melzack, Ronald, 121–22

Mercator, Gerard, 32–33

Mercator projection, 32–34, 54–55, 219n136

metaphors, 10–13, 63, 68, 96–99, 156–57, 210n120, 222n15; of amputation and truncation, 93; bodily, 11, 24, 37, 64, 72–73, 202, 257n115; of bodily loss, 94; botanical, 227n102; cartographic, 31; conceptual, 65, 98, 223n30; corporeal, 11, 24, 63, 66, 75, 78, 85–86, 98–99, 126, 195, 198, 202, 209n86; corporealized, 40; militaristic, 222n16; of the neoliberal state, 25; organic, 10, 13, 66; organicist, 39; for social transformations,

258n134; somatic, 10, 20–21, 23, 77–78, 158, 207n54; somatopolitical, 134; sticky, 15, 208n63; of territorial loss, 120; for time, 212n4

Mexico, 4, 151, 173, 197, 213n40, 238n126; undocumented migrants from, 246n95. *See also* US-Mexico border

Mezzadra, Sandro, 170, 210n110

Miéville, China, 113–14, 180, 234n49

migrants, 5, 86, 114, 197, 234n50, 246n83, 249n32, 259n23; Chinese, 170; illegal, 4; processing of, 177; undocumented, 246n95

Mitchell, S. Weir, 121, 236n80

Mitchell, Timothy, 6, 146

Mongolia, 11, 64, 150, 152, 235n71, 254n86; ethnic authenticity in, 77; independence of, 120; Outer, 111, 119–20, 133; outline of, 253n75

Monmonier, Mark, 35, 52

monster, the, 23, 180, 182–83, 186, 189, 245n58, 253n78, 254n80, 254nn82–83; territorial, 183, 210n115

monsters, 24, 39, 182–83, 188–90, 199, 254n82, 257n112, 258n129; cartographic, 94–95; logomaps and, 59; *mappaemundi* and, 40; maps and, 51; sea, 23, 30, 211n3, 214n57; territorial, 197, 256n105

Moscow, 5, 70, 103–4, 106, 115, 243n23; street maps of, 220n145

mutilation, 106, 157, 226n74; territorial loss as, 10, 21, 59, 77, 125, 145, 231n10

national DNA, 10, 59, 73, 85, 99

nationalism, 7, 13, 20, 37, 86, 99, 136, 151, 202, 217n101, 242n7, 243n16; age of, 36, 47; anticolonial, 8; ethnonationalism, 203; in Europe, 81; modern, 130; rise of, 214n56; Turkish, 57; women and, 87

national territory, 14, 47–48, 81, 216n91; body of citizen and, 8, 215n68; emotional attachment and, 125; map of, 57

nation-state, 4, 37, 46, 64, 77–78, 81, 84, 90, 99, 127, 134, 136, 146, 148, 151, 153; anthropomorphic maps and, 88; border management and, 6; citizen and, 95; corporeal metaphor and, 209n86; emergence of, 35–36, 44, 87, 98, 131; formation of, 149; *homo nationalis* and, 94; hyphen of, 132; imaginary of, 10, 20, 196; imagination of, 125; island as

archetypal, 228n126; logomap and, 8, 86, 164; metageographies and, 199; the monster and, 23; myth of, 13; national airlines and, 217n100; national contour and, 48, 66; organicity and, 66; reproduction of, 142; rise of, 89; space of, 133
NATO, 105–6, 133
natural resources, 14, 167
nature, 20, 81, 84–85, 222n20, 225n67; reserves, 82, 150, 246n95; settler colonialism and, 253n74; women and, 87
Navaro-Yashin, Yael, 6, 114, 117, 156, 226n74, 234n54
near abroad (*blizhnee zarubezh'e*), 106, 175
Neilson, Brett, 170, 210n110
Neocleous, Mark, 10, 63, 76, 208n28, 221n12, 225n60, 226n74, 257n115
Netherlands, 78, 167–70; Spanish, 248n20. *See also* Baarle
Ngai, Sianne, 116, 156
Niyazov, Saparmurat, 60–61, 221n3
no-man's-lands (terra nullius), 150, 171, 173, 180
North Korea, 172, 181, 185–86, 206n35
Northern Ireland, 203, 217n107, 219n134

Ottoman Empire, 57, 68, 128, 226n74, 252n60
outlines, 2–3, 78, 107, 176, 231n2, 243n23, 254n85; border, 126; state, 72, 95, 154, 199, 202, 228n127, 229n150, 248n16

Pakistan, 2–3, 56, 88, 140, 192, 198, 204; conflict with India, 138; Google Maps and, 193f; official map of, 260n33; partition and, 127, 157, 252n63; Siachen Glacier and, 139
Palestine, 9, 64, 127, 178–80, 204, 215n68; Google Maps and, 258n1
partition, 126–27, 131, 169; of Burma, 145, 209n83; of Cyprus, 156; of India, 127, 139, 145, 157; of Korea, 186
Peace of Westphalia, 39, 167, 216n90, 249n21
Penfield homunculus, 141–45, 160
Perry, Imani, 17, 190, 249n25, 255n90
phantom limbs, 39, 120–25, 129, 136, 160, 240–41n167
phantom pains, 10, 21–22, 99, 102–21, 129, 132, 141; territorial, 14, 94, 229n146, 237n106
phantoms, 14, 94, 106, 116–17, 119, 121, 130–32, 197, 238n123; bodily, 188,

236n92; telescoped, 134; territorial, 22, 111, 180, 183, 235n64; trauma and, 237n105
Philippines, 56, 111, 128, 139, 177, 219n136, 241n1
Poland, 68, 106, 108, 208n80, 232n11
Policraticus (John of Salisbury), 73–74
political, the, 22, 63, 66, 73, 78, 84
political cartography, 31, 37, 39, 176
political geography, 8, 15, 24, 76, 166, 174, 185, 187, 197; contemporary, 45, 164; maps and, 2; metaphors and, 63; modern, 171; orthodox, 256n105; premodern, 216n90
politics, 19, 75, 81, 188; of amputation, 238n123; border, 107, 244n56; of contiguousness and tactility, 133; electoral, 196; European, 39; somatopolitics, 73; of vision, 234n51. *See also* geopolitics
power, 11, 15, 17, 71, 90; of atlases, 216n82; bordered, 146; centers of, 253n67; differentials, 170; evocative, 228n127; geography of, 196; imperial, 38, 127; jurisdictional, 107; legislative, 184; of the logomap, 48, 161; of maps, 46, 52–54; metaphors and, 99; military, 150; monarchical, 84, 223n35; of national imaginaries, 114; political, 4, 197; relations of, 124; royal, 41, 43, 215n75; ruler's, 45; soft, 224n39; sovereign, 2, 9, 19, 62, 225n56; of the Soviet Union, 103; state, 3, 197, 205n8, 225n56, 244n38, 246n83; structures, 192; symbolic, 47, 93; white hegemonic, 183
Prescott, John, 80, 113, 128, 226n93
prosthetics, 39, 183, 197, 247n101; territorial, 10, 94
prosthetic territories, 22, 131–32, 136
Putin, Vladimir, 14, 70–71, 73f, 125, 229n144, 231n10

Qing Empire, 111, 119
quantification, 7, 35
Rabelais, François, 75, 183
Ramachandran, Vilayanur, 122–23, 141, 229n136
Ramaswamy, Sumathi, 6, 11, 37, 57–58, 87–88, 107, 190, 208nn69–70, 209n100; on maiming, 226n74
Ratzel, Friedrich, 76, 225n67
refugees, 4, 114, 127, 206n29, 234n50
Reeves, Madeleine, 8–9, 15, 19, 126, 165–66, 185, 196, 201, 215n66